DRY BONES RATTLING

PRINCETON STUDIES IN AMERICAN POLITICS:
HISTORICAL, INTERNATIONAL, AND COMPARATIVE PERSPECTIVES

SERIES EDITORS

Ira Katznelson, Martin Shefter, Theda Skocpol

A list of titles
in this series appears
at the back of
the book

DRY BONES RATTLING

COMMUNITY BUILDING TO
REVITALIZE AMERICAN DEMOCRACY

Mark R. Warren

PRINCETON UNIVERSITY PRESS   PRINCETON AND OXFORD

Library of Congress Cataloging-in-Publication Data

Portions of chapter 6 appeared in "Beyond Tocqueville: Civil
Society and Social Capital in Comparative Perspective," in *American
Behavioral Scientist* 42 (September 1998), edited by Bob Edwards
and Michael W. Foley, copyright © 1998 by Sage Publications, Inc.

Warren, Mark R., 1955–
Dry bones rattling : community building to revitalize
American democracy / Mark R. Warren.
p.   cm. — (Princeton studies in American politics)
Includes index.
ISBN 0-691-07431-3 (alk. paper) —
ISBN 0-691-07432-1 (pbk. : alk. paper)
1. Community organization—Texas. 2. Community development,
Urban—Texas. 3. Community organization—Southwestern States.
4. Community development, Urban—Southwestern States.
5. Industrial Areas Foundation. I. Title. II. Series.
HT176.T4 E37   2001
307'.09764—dc21   00-061147

Photo credits: Figure 1 used with permission,
© San Antonio Express-News. Figures 2–13, Alan Pogue,
Texas Center for Documentary Photography.

This book has been composed in Sabon.

Printed on acid-free paper. ∞

www.pup.princeton.edu

Printed in the United States of America

10 9 8 7 6 5 4 3 2 1

10 9 8 7 6 5 4 3 2
(Pbk.)

To Roberta

WITH LOVE AND APPRECIATION,

and to Folasade and Imoh

WITH HOPE FOR A BETTER FUTURE

Contents _____

AT THE very time that democracy appears to have triumphed on the world stage, it faces a profound crisis at home in America. Many Americans have simply lost faith in the ability of traditional forms of democratic politics to address the most critical questions facing their families and communities. In response to our democratic malaise, Americans across the political spectrum have been looking for ways to revitalize American politics. But gains seem hard to come by. If we could just make it easier to register to vote, some argue, then more people will go to the polls. If our parties would just develop a platform that spoke to the interests of working Americans, others say, then they would gain people's support. If we could just find the right issue, then people would swing into action. But liberalized registration laws, and the constant search for better party platforms and important issues, never seem to result in engaging Americans very broadly, particularly those most often excluded in low-income communities of color.

I started this study out of frustration with our current understanding of how to revive American politics. While volumes have been written about the causes for lack of participation, there were surprisingly few studies of promising new models for democratic action. I decided to study an effort that appeared to be having a significant degree of success. I chose to study the work of the Industrial Areas Foundation (IAF) in Texas and the Southwest because, from what I had heard or read, the network involved indigenous community leaders in a type of political action that appeared to be making a real difference for inner-city communities.

In the IAF I found a group of committed people of faith striving to forge a new way to conduct politics, one that reached deeply into communities to address the heartfelt concerns of families struggling to raise their children. The network has found a way to engage the kind of person so often left out of elite-dominated politics, particularly Hispanic[1] and African American women active in the daily life of their churches and communities. Moreover, the network brought together Hispanic, black, and white residents to cooperate on issues that affect their communities, a relatively rare phenomenon in American politics.

I found that the leaders of IAF organizations were active in a rich array of community building and political activities, forging ties with their neighbors, conducting research, developing their own programmatic initiatives, and leading political battles to launch them. The IAF appeared to engage the energy and commitment of people to improve their communities, an energy that appears to be growing in America even as traditional forms of political involvement decline. Rather than start at the top with the "right" issue or party platform, the IAF was working to reconstruct politics by infusing it with ideas, commitments, and strength at the bottom.

Just as I began my research on the IAF network, Robert Putnam published the results of his study of governance in Italy. Normally, a study of regional government effectiveness in Italy might be thought to hold little bearing on the problems of American democracy. Yet I found in this study an important starting point for understanding the organizing work of the Texas IAF. In his book on Italy, Putnam argues that social capital provided the key to "making democracy work." Social capital refers to "features of social organization such as networks, norms, and social trust that facilitate coordination and cooperation for mutual benefit." Putnam shows that Italian communities rich in trust and cooperative associations have more effective government and even healthier economic development compared to those with low levels of such social capital.[2] Applying the concept to the United States, I began to consider the IAF's strategy as an effort to "make democracy work" by engaging people in politics through their participation in the stable institutions of community life, especially religious congregations.

I became determined to identify the lessons that could be learned from the interfaith network for those who care about revitalizing democracy and rebuilding our most troubled communities. The main lesson to be learned is simple: a key to renewing American politics is to rebuild its foundations in the values and institutions that sustain community. How to do that, in a way that is broadly inclusive and brings effective power to community action, is a more complicated matter. That is what this book is about.

My experiences studying the IAF and writing this book have made me more hopeful about American civic and political life. I see the possibilities and rewards of value-based politics, of multiracial collaboration, of patient relationship building in local communities. But I also see the challenges ahead, if community-building efforts like the IAF are to become a serious national force for political renewal. I hope that this book will take us a step closer to that goal.

In order to write *Dry Bones Rattling*, I have had to draw upon the support and assistance of my community—my family, friends and colleagues. First of all, I would like to thank all of the leaders and organizers of the Southwest Industrial Areas Foundation who agreed to share their life's work with me, and help me to understand it. Ernie Cortes made the project possible in the first place by approving my study of the Texas network and opening doors throughout the state for me. He has taught me a great deal about politics and about human character. Pearl Ceasar and Perry Perkins hosted my more lengthy stays in San Antonio and Fort Worth, while Christine Stephens, Maribeth Larkin, Joe Higgs, Robert Rivera, Mignonne Konecny, and Tim McCluskey welcomed me for shorter visits to other IAF organizations. Frank Pierson, Consuelo Tovar, Joe Rubio, Willie Bennett, Lady Coleman Byrd, Tom Holler, Elizabeth Valdez, Julia Lerma, Carole Patterson and many others spent hours helping me to gain a better understanding of the IAF's organizing.

Meanwhile, scores of IAF leaders agreed to answer my seemingly endless string of questions. Patricia Ozuna, Virginia Ramirez, Andres Sarabia, Homer Bain, Terry Boggs, Gerald Britt, Tony Fleo and many others did more, talking at length with me, keeping tabs on my research over time, and welcoming me to their homes or churches. Carrie Laughlin, Patty Penorio, Steve Jackobs and Del Watson at the Texas network office in Austin helped inform and coordinate my efforts. And several individuals provided crucial assistance by letting me stay in their homes or parishes. These generous hosts include Carole Patterson and Brett Campbell, Father Jim Janish, Steve Jackobs and Betty Weed, Carrie Laughlin, Angela Flounory, Louisa Meacham, Tony Fleo and the brothers of the Society of Mary at St. Mary of the Assumption in Fort Worth. Jack Salvadore, Cliff Borofsky, and other staff at Project QUEST were always happy to provide the latest information on the progress of their job-training program.

In conducting this project, I have been committed to discussing the results of my research and analysis with IAF participants. Ernie Cortes, Frank Pierson, Pearl Ceasar, Christine Stephens, Maribeth Larkin, Perry Perkins, Willie Bennett, Judy Donovan, and Mike Gecan, in particular, made thoughtful comments on earlier drafts of this book. I thank them for their efforts to deepen my understanding of their work, and more broadly, of the problems and prospects for American democracy.

Theda Skocpol provided crucial intellectual and practical support to this study at all stages. Her efforts to pursue scholarship that is socially and politically engaged has served as a model for me. Margaret Weir and John Campbell helped me formulate the research project, challenged my ideas, and offered much needed personal encouragement. Margaret stuck with me through the book-writing stage, making insightful comments on successive drafts and helping me see the light at the end of the tunnel. Robert Putnam has been a generous supporter and an important influence on my work.

I would also like to thank the many people, scholars, activists, and friends, who helped me formulate the ideas in the book or commented on drafts of my work. These include Derek Bok, Mark Chaves, Cathy Cohen, Dayna Cunningham, Tomni Dance, Michael Dawson, Jorge Dominguez, Peter Dreier, Jean Bethke Elshtain, Rudy Fenwick, Janice Fine, Jeanne

Flavin, Marshall Ganz, Mike Gecan, Ranjay Gulati, David Hart, Neil Jamison, James Jennings, Roger Karapin, James Kelly, Robert Kleidman, Cameron MacDonald, Mike Miller, Manuel Pastor, Jr., Robert Pekkanen, Kent Portney, Rudy Rosales, Susan Saegert, Michael Sandel, Heywood Sanders, Dennis Shirley, Carmen Sirianni, Randy Stoecker, J. Phillip Thompson, Roberta Udoh, Jon van Til, Russell Warren, Mary Waters, Robert H. Wilson, Clyde Wilcox, William Julius Wilson, and Richard L. Wood.

I presented parts of this research at meetings of the American Sociological Association, American Political Science Association, Association for the Sociology of Religion, and the Association for the Advancement of Social Work with Groups. I also made presentations at the Sawyer Seminar on the Performance of Democracies, the Program on Non-violent Sanctions and the American Political Development Seminar at Harvard University, as well as seminars at the Woodrow Wilson International Center for Scholars, the Georgetown Public Policy Institute and the Sociology Department's colloquium at Fordham University. I would like to thank participants at all these forums for their helpful comments.

The research for this study was funded in part by grants from the American Academy of Arts and Sciences Project on Social Capital and Public Affairs, the Ford Foundation, the Louisville Institute of the Lilly Endowment, and Fordham University. I received fellowship support from the Sawyer Program on the Performance of Democracies and the Program on Non-violent Sanctions, both at Harvard University's Center for International Affairs, as well as from Fordham University.

I would like to thank the faculty and staff in Fordham University's Sociology Department for friendship and collegial encouragement, and especially Rosemary Cooney and Doyle McCarthy for support as Departmental Chairs, James Dobson for research assistance, and Rosa Giglio and Paula Genova for practical help and warm support. Judith Vichniac, Sue Borges, and other members of the Committee on Degrees in Social Studies at Harvard University provided a friendly and supportive academic home at an earlier point in the study.

My family and friends have been tremendously supportive to me during the writing of this book. I could not have made it without their encouragement and faith in me. I would particularly like to thank my parents Russell and Elena, my sisters Cindy and Nancy and their husbands Michael and Russ, my mum Florence and my brothers David and Adam, and so many of my uncles, aunts, and cousins who have cheered me on. Thanks as well to Ranjay, Anu, Christina, Jerry, Huguette, Tunde, Crystal, Barbara, Gary, Nancy, Marshall, Phil, Dayna, Sylvia, Ricardo, David, Marion, Jeanette, Rhea, Jean, Andy, Melanie, Sandra, Vivien, Emily, Greta,

Jeanne, Mary, Bill, and so many more friends. Finally, I would like to thank Brian Ricci and all my friends at his karate school, especially Jack and Richard.

I was fortunate to go through graduate studies and the struggles of writing a book with Tomni Dance, an experience that has made us lifelong friends. Her uncle, Bernard Duse, graciously offered his home to me so that I could get away from it all for a quiet time of reflection and writing. This book would never have been finished without his support and friendship.

Roberta Udoh has been my intellectual, political, and emotional soulmate through life. Her spirit of intolerance toward poverty and her determination to fight injustice infuse the words in this book. My debt to her is forever. Our daughter Folasade was conceived at just about the same time as this project. Our second daughter Imoh has enriched our lives since then. My children have helped me understand in a much deeper way why so many parents spend their precious time working in the IAF. I hope my research may contribute to making the world a better place for our girls and for all children.

DRY BONES RATTLING

Introduction ─────────────────────────────

Dry Bones Rattling

"Them bones, them bones," Father Al Jost began his prayer.[1] The thirty community leaders present were nervous. These women— school secretaries, homemakers, and nurses—came from poor Mexican-American neighborhoods of San Antonio, Texas. They were nervous because they were about to take the stage to lead the twentieth-anniversary convention of their organization: Communities Organized for Public Service (COPS). Thirty-five hundred supporters waited for them behind placards announcing "Saint Leo's" and "Saint Gabriel," that is, the Catholic parishes of the west and south sides of San Antonio. The leaders were going to face the governor of Texas, the mayor, a majority of San Antonio's city councilors, and the CEOs of the largest local banks. They intended to demand support for COPS' programs in the areas of affordable housing, job training, and school reform.

The leaders formed a circle, gathered hands, and Father Al prayed: "them bones, them bones." He told the story of Ezekiel's prophecy of the valley of the dry bones, a symbol of a community in ruins, physically and spiritually, a community without hope and in despair. Father Al spoke of the bones beginning to rattle, to come together, of sinews forming, and flesh and blood growing. He told of a great army emerging as a symbol of the community coming together to rebuild itself. When Father Al finished, the COPS leaders responded with a resounding "amen" and strode onto the stage to the sounds of a mariachi band. All thirty climbed the steps to the podium, exuding an attitude of confidence and collective determination. The community leaders proved equal to the test. Over the next two hours, Texas Governor Ann Richards pledged $500,000 to COPS' job-training program, and bank executives promised $110 million in housing loans for COPS neighborhoods.

────────────

SCHOLARS AND ACTIVISTS used to looking to the east or west coasts for bellwether progressive initiatives may be surprised to find in Texas a group of deeply committed people of faith at the forefront of efforts to revitalize democracy in America. Many Americans think of Texas as a politically conservative state and view the involvement of religion in politics with deep suspicion. Yet anyone concerned with the future of American democracy cannot afford to ignore the work of the Texas Industrial Areas Foundation (IAF), an interfaith and multiracial network of community organizers. In the twenty-five years since Ernesto Cortes, Jr., founded COPS in San Antonio, the Texas IAF has been rattling bones across the state to find a way to fulfill Ezekiel's prophecy, that is, to rebuild some of our most devastated communities. Over the years the Texas IAF, and its sister organizations in the Southwest IAF network, have figured out a way to combine faith-based community building with nonpartisan political action, a combination that has made the network one of America's premier experiments in reviving democracy.

If these groups were simply religious advocates for the poor, they would not be very remarkable: America is full of advocacy groups, secular and religious. We lack not advocacy groups, but organizations in which people themselves actively participate in democracy. What makes the Texas IAF distinctive is its ability to engage hundreds of community leaders in active political participation and mobilize thousands of supporters to address the needs of their families and communities. Moreover, in contrast to the racial segregation of American community and political life, the network strives to bring together leaders from Mexican American, African American, and Anglo communities of a variety of faiths and economic circumstances to find common ground for action. IAF-style politics is participatory, and it appears to create organizations with staying power that can get results. Leaders from twelve IAF organizations in Texas, and another nine across the Southwest, work with professional organizers to produce the political power necessary to generate resources for ambitious improvements to their communities. While many organizations come and go in poor communities, through the IAF network, COPS has sustained and expanded its efforts over twenty-five years, delivering more than one billion dollars in resources to improve its neighborhoods and the lives of Hispanic families.

This book challenges conventional assumptions that religious intervention in politics can only mean the effort to impose a group's moral teachings on society. To be sure, many IAF participants see their political activity as moral work. Religious commitments to community caring, family well-being, and social justice inspire and sustain political participation in IAF organizations. But the IAF network does not pursue hot button social issues like abortion, gay rights, or prayer in school. Instead, the network engages faith traditions in an effort to construct a politics that addresses the concrete needs of families in low-income communities of color and of working Americans more broadly. IAF organizations work to build housing, improve schools, develop job-training programs, construct parks and libraries, and otherwise strengthen the frayed social fabric of neighborhood life. We will want to consider the kinds of limitations imposed by the religious base of the IAF network. Yet it is important to recognize that faith values can bring essential resources to efforts at democratic revitalization, depending on how those energies are directed.

As the opening to this Introduction suggests, the deep religious faith of people and the support they receive from fellow parishioners help generate the vision and confidence necessary to enter the public arena as leaders of long-neglected communities. But the IAF is a political organization, not a religious one. Although people of faith in the Texas IAF are deeply committed to community caring, the network is anything but a "feel good" community organization. Shrewd and tough political fighters lead the network's organizations, with the explicit goal of building political power. Poor communities in America face tough challenges, and the IAF exudes the kind of no-nonsense, pragmatic approach that makes the long hours of hard work pay off for people's communities.

The IAF's brand of power politics has earned the network its share of critics. Any serious effort to empower the poor and people of color is likely to have its detractors; the IAF is no exception. We will want to examine these criticisms, even as we place them in the larger context of the network's impressive and often unique accomplishments.[2]

Just as democratic activists in the fifties might have been surprised to see the first mass stirrings of the civil rights movement in places like Baton Rouge, Louisiana, and Montgomery, Alabama, many Americans would not normally look to Texas for cutting-edge democratic initiatives. As it turns out, though, Texas presents an excellent setting for studying democratic renewal. Texas has a more varied political tradition than most people realize. The IAF builds upon a rich history of progressive efforts by African Americans, Mexican Americans, and white populists in Texas.[3] The state, moreover, is at the forefront of broad trends in American civic and economic life. Because of its rapidly growing Hispanic population, Texas will become a majority-nonwhite state within the next twenty years.[4] The rest of the United States will follow after another twenty or thirty years. So we might be well served to seek lessons from the efforts of the Texas IAF to increase political participation by African Americans and Hispanics and to foster understanding and collaboration across racial lines. Meanwhile, Texas is an important center for the information technology and telecommunications industries, especially in places like Austin, Houston, and Dallas. Initiatives by the Texas IAF to improve public schools and develop job-training programs place the network at the forefront of the nation's efforts to open up opportunities in the new economy for low-income black and Hispanic families and their children.

Although the work of the IAF in Texas and the Southwest places it within a progressive tradition, the network defies easy categorization into either liberal or conservative camps. IAF organizations are officially nonpartisan. While the network has more often collaborated with Democrats, it does include Republicans within its ranks and has often found common ground with Republican officials. Moreover, the network's membership is quite representative of the diversity of views of mainstream America on a variety of social issues. If progressive democracy requires passing a litmus test on a full range of social issues, the Texas IAF would likely fail. As noted above, the network takes no position and no action on such culturally divisive issues as abortion and teaching about gay lifestyles in schools—although the network's commitment to inclusiveness means it defends the rights of gays to full participation in public life, including its own network. If progressive democracy, rather, means actively cultivating the participation of low-income Hispanic and African Americans and empowering them to address some of the critical issues facing their families and American society more generally, in housing, education, employment, and health care, then the IAF network is very much at the forefront of revitalizing American politics.

The Industrial Areas Foundation and Its Texas Network

The IAF was first established by Saul Alinsky, considered the "father" of American community organizing, through his efforts to organize Chicago's working-class neighborhoods in the 1930s. The IAF gets its old-fashioned name—Industrial Areas Foundation—because Alinsky organized in the areas (neighborhoods) where Chicago's industry was located. Almost moribund at the time of Alinsky's death in the early seventies, the IAF network was rebuilt through the efforts of Alinsky's successor, Edward Chambers, stimulated by the innovations to Alinsky's methods developed by Ernesto Cortes, Jr., in organizing COPS in San Antonio.

Founded by Cortes in 1974, COPS became the flagship chapter for the revitalized IAF and the foundation of the network's efforts in Texas and the Southwest. Over the next twenty-five years, Cortes and his staff built local organizations in Houston, Dallas, Fort Worth, Austin, El Paso, the Beaumont-Port Arthur-Orange area in East Texas, Lubbock-Amarillo-Midland/Odessa in West Texas, Fort Bend County outside of Houston, and in the lower Rio Grande valley and Del Rio-Eagle Pass. In the eighties, the local organizations began to operate as a state network, launching statewide campaigns to reform education and bring water services to *colonias*, America's equivalent of shantytowns along the Mexican border. In 1990, the Texas IAF held its founding convention with 10,000 supporters in attendance. Since the early nineties, the Texas IAF has operated in the context of a growing Southwest IAF network, supervised by Cortes, including affiliates in Phoenix, Tucson, and Tempe, Arizona, Albuquerque, New Mexico, as well as organizations in neighboring Omaha, Nebraska, Des Moines, Iowa, New Orleans and Northern Louisiana. By 1999, the Los Angeles-area IAF organizations had become part of the Southwest IAF as Cortes personally took charge of reorganizing them into a metropolitan-wide affiliate.

The Texas IAF is part of a national IAF network, which includes over sixty local affiliates spread throughout the United States, and is rapidly growing. The national IAF offers training services and professional organizers under contract to local organizations, but does not direct its staff from the national level. Instead, the organizations are grouped together into five semiautonomous regions, with each regional staff directed by a supervisor.[5] The IAF is most heavily concentrated in the Southwest and along both coasts, but it has expanded in the South and Midwest as well.

Network affiliates operate in most of the nation's biggest urban areas, including Houston, Dallas, San Antonio, and Phoenix in the Southwest, New York, Baltimore, Philadelphia, Washington, D.C., and Boston on the east coast, and Los Angeles, the Bay Area, and Seattle on the west coast. The IAF moved its national headquarters to Chicago in 1996 in conjunction with founding a major new affiliate in that metropolitan area and to help expand its operations into the Midwest. The IAF has long worked in cities in Tennessee and has begun to spread to other Southern population centers, including Atlanta and New Orleans. Beyond the U.S., the IAF works with sister networks in Great Britain and South Africa as well.

The reach of the IAF is quite extensive, as each local IAF organization is composed of member institutions, mainly congregations, but also schools, unions, and other community-based organizations. Most IAF organizations have twenty to sixty member institutions. United Power for Action and Justice, the Chicago organization, is the largest with 200 member affiliates. Altogether, the IAF reaches roughly one million families through about 2,000 member congregations, schools, and other institutions.

The work of a number of IAF affiliates has begun to attain national recognition. The Texas network's innovative job-training program, Project QUEST in San Antonio, won an Innovations in American Government Award from Harvard University. Meanwhile, its Alliance Schools education initiative, involving over 100 schools across the state, has drawn the attention of school reformers nationally. The IAF's East Brooklyn Congregations organization has built over 2,200 moderately priced homes in one of New York's poorest communities, and is in the middle of constructing another 700 houses. Drawing upon the Old Testament prophecy from the book of Nehemiah to rebuild the walls of Jerusalem, the Nehemiah

Homes program became the model for legislation of that name passed by Congress. BUILD, the IAF's affiliate in Baltimore, worked with the local AFL-CIO to get the city council to pass a livable wage bill that requires all recipients of city contracts to pay workers enough to support a family. The effort raised the wages of 4,000 workers by 44 percent, totaling $8 million in 1995. The IAF's Metro New York network followed suit and scored a similar victory with New York's City Council, prompting more than forty other "living wage" initiatives around the country. Meanwhile, the IAF's network in California succeeded in passing what it called a "moral minimum wage," substantially raising the pay of California's poorest workers.[6]

The work of the Texas IAF gains added significance because it is at the forefront of a growing trend of religious involvement in progressive community and political organizing efforts in America's inner cities and elsewhere, for which it has often served as a model. In addition to the IAF, three other faith-based community organizing networks work with local organizations around the country. Estimates from a study conducted by Interfaith Funders indicate that the 133 organizations involved (including the IAF groups) incorporate upwards of 4,000 member congregations and other institutions. About 2,700 Americans serve on the governing boards of these groups, 24,000 participate regularly in their activities (e.g., on a working committee), and about 100,000 people attend their public actions. Although white evangelicals are largely absent from this field, Catholics and mainline and black Protestants are well represented. About 2 percent of the congregations are Jewish, and some black evangelical groups are present as well.[7]

Meanwhile, religious institutions serve as the backbone for many independent community development initiatives that have emerged across the country in the last twenty-five years. There are now over 4,000 nonprofit community development corporations active in building affordable housing, in promoting economic development, and in a variety of neighborhood improvement programs. Independent efforts by African American religious leaders and others emerge almost daily to address the problems of crime and drug abuse among inner-city youth.[8]

A wide range of more secular community-building, environmental, and populist organizing efforts has also been inspired by the work of the IAF's original founder, Saul Alinsky, and the achievements of IAF organizations today. Labor unions, for their part, have begun to take an interest in community-oriented approaches, hiring the network to provide consulting services to some of their organizing drives. The Service Employees International Union scored the biggest organizing success since the thirties by using a community-based approach. It signed up 74,000 home-care workers in Los Angeles County, mostly low-wage women of color, by working through their ties to community networks and faith institutions.[9]

Across the U.S. a wide variety of independent community-building efforts have emerged in the nineties as well. These incipient efforts are not connected to the national networks of faith-based organizing, community development corporations, or unions, but they are spreading as well. No systematic study exists of these efforts, but there is much evidence of them. The National Community Building Network has attempted to act as an umbrella for 163 groups involved in combating poverty and promoting comprehensive solutions to economic and social development. In rural areas, Carol Stack has identified the new wave of community-building activities unleashed by African American women who have returned to southern communities, and Richard Couto documents extensive organizing efforts in central Appalachia.[10]

Community building is rapidly emerging as a vital new force for revitalizing democracy at the ground level. It represents a serious effort to reverse what scholars have recently identified as the decline of social capital, that is, the steady deterioration in the social fabric and civic life of American communities.[11] What unites these diverse phenomena is a focus on patient, relationship building at the local level, with efforts directed towards concrete improvements to the communities where families live and work. These efforts are rooted in community institutions that engage the participation of Americans often left out of elite-centered politics, especially women and people of color. These participants draw upon value-based commitments to family and community, and, at their best, to social justice and racial inclusiveness as well.

Because the IAF and other community-building efforts eschew media-centered campaigns and controversial moral agendas in favor of patient base-building work, they have so far remained a fairly quiet, often unnoticed phenomenon on the broader public stage. Placing a priority on local organizing, they have yet to come together to produce a national force for political transformation. Nevertheless, they represent one of the nation's best hopes for reinvigorating our democratic life and reconnecting political institutions to the needs and aspirations of working people and their communities.

Methods of Study

I chose to study the Texas IAF network because it is the essential place to begin to understand this emerging phenomenon of democratic organizing. Texas represents the place where a new model for faith-based community building and political action first emerged through the efforts of Ernesto Cortes and COPS leaders in San Antonio. Moreover, the Texas IAF has built the first community-based effort of its type to reach beyond the limits of local organizing and operate at a statewide level. Although other IAF organizations coordinate staff development and leadership training in other regions, and have recently begun to experiment with state-level initiatives, only in Texas has the IAF forged an active statewide political network and sustained it over a number of years.[12] Strong local organizations combined with state-level action has allowed the Texas network to launch some of the IAF's most ambitious and sophisticated programmatic initiatives, like Project QUEST in San Antonio and the Alliance Schools reform effort in over 100 schools across the state.[13] Studying the Texas network presents an opportunity to assess the IAF's innovative model for community building and political action where it first emerged, where it has reached the farthest, and where it has made the most gains. Moreover, Ernesto Cortes and his staff have consciously sought to elaborate the IAF's strategy and to influence debates about social capital and democratic politics.[14]

Dry Bones Rattling is a work of political ethnography, presenting an examination of the historical development and contemporary experience of the Texas IAF. It identifies the critical contributions to community building and democratic action made by the network, and considers as well the limitations and challenges to its current organizing. By highlighting the broader lessons that can be learned from the interfaith network, I seek to advance our understanding of how to build social capital, forge multiracial cooperation, and revitalize democratic politics in America.

I conducted field work for this study between 1993 and 1999. In order to paint as complete a picture as possible of the Texas IAF, both in its internal operations as well as in its public activity, I collected data from as many sources as possible. First, I made use of whatever printed data existed. Although the news media covers these organizations sporadically at best, I did consult available newspaper accounts. Placing an almost exclusive priority on face-to-face relationships, the Texas IAF publishes remarkably little material. The network distributes no newsletters, and only the very occasional leaflet. I did, however, collect written constitutions, programs distributed at annual conventions, membership lists, and annual reports. I have also examined the several published accounts written by scholars and journalists.

Second, I relied upon interviews to gather most of the historical data on the development of the network. To get the fullest picture from a variety of angles, I conducted in-depth interviews with organizers and leaders in the Texas IAF, elected officials, business people, other community leaders, and observers. Semistructured interviews in each category followed a similar format, with a set of open-ended questions asked consistently of each interviewee. In all, I conducted 80 interviews with IAF leaders, 35 interviews with IAF organizers, and 36 interviews with community/political leaders and observers. Interviews with IAF participants also provided insights into their motivations for participation and upon internal dynamics within the network.

Third, I conducted participant observation of IAF activities on the local, state, and national levels.[15] On the local level, I observed internal organization meetings, large public actions, and private meetings among IAF participants and between IAF participants and other political/community leaders. In all, I observed over 60 activities of local Texas IAF organizations, including annual conventions, "accountability nights," smaller public actions, steering committee meetings, delegates assemblies, leadership training sessions, action committee meetings, one-on-one meetings, and small negotiating sessions with public officials. I observed 5 seminars for Southwest IAF organizers, each of which lasted 2–3 days, and 3 Texas/Southwest meetings of IAF leaders from local organizations. I also attended the IAF's national 10-day training session held in July of 1994 in Los Angeles.

In order to increase the validity of the study, I triangulated among the data sources. In other words, I used each source of data as a method to test and confirm the information provided by the others. For example, if an IAF organizer reported the number of supporters that attended an affiliate's annual convention, I checked that number with media accounts and the recollection of elected officials in attendance. If leaders and organizers described their relationship with each other, I considered those descriptions in light of the interactions I observed at internal meetings.

I have sought to increase the analytic power of the study by making use of a number of different comparisons within the network. For example, at various times and for various purposes, I compare the participation of different kinds of churches, the activities of different local organizations, and the motivations of participants from different racial groups. Moreover, I have worked to place this case in a broader comparative context. In other words, comparing the Texas IAF to other American political organizations and community building efforts, I highlight what makes the Texas IAF different and why.

Overview of the Book

Chapter 1 argues that revitalizing American political life requires connecting it to community-based institutions and the values that sustain them. Since these institutions and the social fabric of many American communities, that is, their social capital, are so weak, democratic renewal requires community building. In other words, the two processes must be linked. The chapter discusses the challenges required to build community and revitalize politics in a way that is racially inclusive and politically effective. It then summarizes the key elements of the approach the IAF has developed to meet these challenges. The following chapters of the book offer a detailed examination of how the IAF developed this approach and attempts to implement it in its contemporary organizing.

Chapter 2 examines the development of the IAF's model for democratic action. It charts the historical process through which professional organizers from the IAF developed a new organizing strategy through their collaboration with community leaders drawn from religious congregations in Texas. The chapter probes the roots of what I call the modern IAF in the work of Saul Alinsky in Chicago during the thirties. It then focuses on the innovations made to traditional Alinsky organizing begun by Ernesto Cortes in San Antonio in the early seventies. By the late eighties, the IAF had developed a "theology of organizing," a strategy that sought to create a powerful connection between faith imperatives and political action.

Chapter 3 shows how the IAF developed statewide issue campaigns in Texas and built a regional network in the Southwest. In the eighties, the Texas IAF became the first community organizing network to move beyond the limitations of local organizing to become a powerful statewide political force. I explore the network's Alliance Schools reform initiative to show how the federated, network model developed by the Texas IAF seeks to create synergy between local and higher-level political action, so that gains at one level can advance the other. I also discuss some of the tensions that occur in efforts to create broader power without losing a focus on local participation. Meanwhile, as the network expanded to other cities in the Southwest, IAF supervisor Cortes built a large and sophisticated organizing staff, with strong connections to the academic and policy worlds. The Southwest IAF's institute for organizers, I argue, proved key to advancing local organizing so that the network could establish multilevel collaborations and more ambitious efforts at institutional reform.

Chapters 4 and 5 focus on the development of multiracial collaboration, what I call bridging social capital. Chapter 4 identifies the elements of the IAF's early multiracial approach through the network's organizing in Fort Worth. It considers the importance of faith traditions, the network's institutional structure, and the role of relational organizing to help leaders find common ground for action across racial lines. As essential as this framework is, however, the chapter ends with a consideration of the limits to multiracial understanding when a largely Hispanic and Anglo network fails to pay explicit attention to questions of racism toward African Americans. Chapter 5 then discusses the emergence of a critical mass of African American leaders and organizers in the Texas IAF. It shows how the network came to promote an understanding of the black experience among participants. That process deepened multiracial understanding in the network and prompted some affiliates to take a more assertive posture towards combating racism.

Chapter 6 analyzes the construction of campaigns for community-based policy initiatives. It focuses on the IAF's political strategy through a case study of Project QUEST, the innovative job-training program developed by the two IAF organizations in San Antonio. In this chapter, I examine how IAF organizations generate effective power by combining confrontation with collaboration. I show how a dynamic between participation and authority in the network creates programs that respond to local needs while incorporating a broader policy perspective. And I explore the set of practices that Texas IAF organizations use to influence candidates to back their proposals and to keep public officials accountable to their agreements. Finally, I consider the contributions and limitations of the IAF's nonpartisan strategy to holding public officials accountable and to creating effective power for local communities.

Chapter 7 returns to the question of the religious foundations for democratic revitalization. It examines and compares the participation of Hispanic Catholic parishes and African American Protestant congregations in the Texas IAF. I show how both religious traditions contain a rich source for grounding political action in community well-being, but that, in some ways, the African American tradition requires more work to direct toward nonpartisan and multiracial political action. Moreover, I consider the institutional structure of these religious communities to show that, contrary to utopian preferences for "horizontality," authority remains important to political action, and can be effective when combined with broad participation.

Chapter 8 extends the discussion of authority and participation by examining leadership development and decision-making processes in participatory democratic organizations. I show how leadership training in the IAF goes beyond narrow skills training, to encompass training in the "arts of politics." IAF leaders experience tremendous personal growth through participation in the network, which serves to sustain their commitment through the hard work of organizing. Moreover, IAF leaders and organizers structure consensual decision-making processes that provide a dynamic alternative to more formal, majority-rule structures—an alternative that contains its own strengths and weaknesses.

In the last chapter, I explore the broader lessons of the IAF experience for democratic renewal. I compare the IAF with the political interventions of the Christian Right to show how faith-based community organizing can result in a broadly progressive politics, one that constructs an organized base of support for public policies that respond to the needs of poor and working families and their communities. At the same time, I consider some of the important limits to the reach of IAF efforts so far. I then discuss the prospects for multiracial organizing in the IAF context to offer a new strategy to unite Americans across racial lines, while confronting the critical conditions faced by many communities of color. Finally, I identify the contributions the IAF makes to our understanding of how to build civic and political participation locally, while generating the broader power necessary to confront the pressures on community life and democracy that lie at higher geographic and governmental levels. Although the network has far to go before it can effect a transformation of our national politics, it shows the possibilities for faith-based efforts to collaborate with more secular initiatives to create a national force for democratic renewal.

This Introduction opened with a vignette, "Dry Bones Rattling," that symbolizes many of the themes of this book. It shows the importance of faith traditions and values to inspire people of modest backgrounds to face powerful elites. It demonstrates the possibilities for multiracial organizing to cross-fertilize communities, so that an Anglo Catholic priest can tell an Old Testament story of deep historic significance to African American Protestants in order to inspire a group of Hispanic lay women. And it illustrates the power that such organizing can generate, as it resulted in pledges of $500,000 from the governor of the state and of $110 million by regional banks.

But many supporters are moved by the human side of the IAF story, the personal growth and empowerment experienced by ordinary people through IAF organizing. Near the end of the convention, Patricio Flores, the Archbishop of San Antonio and a key early backer of the group, presented a check for $10,000 to COPS out of his own personal funds. He recognized COPS' important material achievements for Hispanic communities, but explained his donation with a more spiritual reason. According to Flores, "the greatest achievement of COPS is that through their participation people discovered their self-worth, dignity and greatness." The archbishop then led the assembly in a rousing chant of "¡Con COPS todo. Sin COPS nada!"—with COPS, anything is possible.

One _____

Community Building and Political Renewal

THIS chapter argues that the key to reinvigorating democracy in the United States can be found in efforts to engage people in politics through their participation in the stable institutions of community life. It draws from recent scholarly work on social capital to help us understand why a strong community foundation is necessary for a vibrant political life. Yet I argue that strong communities can often be isolated and politically weak. Or they can be narrowly protectionist, working against the interests of communities different from their own. Therefore, the chapter elaborates a framework for understanding the challenges to be faced in building social capital in a way that promotes multiracial cooperation and generates effective power in the political arena. The chapter then summarizes the key elements of the strategy developed by the IAF to meet these challenges, and ends with a discussion of how the network located alternative resources to generate civic and political participation at a time when other organizations found participation waning.

Social Capital and Democracy

American democracy has suffered during the last half of the twentieth century as our political institutions have become disconnected from strong community-based organizations, which, in turn, have weakened. Robert Putnam has shown that America's stock of social capital, that is, "features of social organization such as networks, norms, and social trust that facilitate coordination and cooperation for mutual benefit," has suffered a dramatic decline in the United States, weakening our democracy.[1] Putnam has emphasized the decline of social capital in almost all forms of associational and group life. But I think we need to be particularly concerned with the decline of the more stable institutions of community life which used to play a particularly important role in sustaining an active democracy through connections to our political system.

Americans participated in politics at much higher levels when political parties served to connect people to government at least in part through community-based organizations. Parties used to compete to get people out to vote through their local branch organizations. A candidate's election depended upon the ability of the party's local branches to mobilize in neighborhoods and through a rich array of social and cultural organizations. This model of political mobilization reached its height in the late-nineteenth-century urban North, where parties fought highly competitive elections. As Michael McGerr has shown, local party organizations interpenetrated with a dense network of social organizations, like fraternal associations, volunteer fire departments, Catholic parishes, and local business associations. Political campaigns typically included marches and local fairs where bands played and people socialized. In the thirties labor unions became another organized institutional base for the expansion of democratic participation to immigrant workers. Through their unions, and through ties maintained by such institutions as churches, fraternal orders, and veteran's associations, workers made a significant impact on the Democratic Party, some of its urban political machines, and on the national political system.[2]

Since the sixties, the connections between electoral politics and community institutions have frayed as elections have become candidate-centered, rather than party-centered, affairs. With the rise of television, candidates have had a means to reach the electorate without going through local party organizations. The expense of television advertising has forced candidates to rely upon fund-raising. To supplement big donors, direct mail technology has provided a means to collect money from citizens, again without going through party organizations.[3] Consequently, while political parties still play an important role in elections as nominating and fundraising vehicles, their local party organizations have atrophied as mobilizing vehicles.[4]

Along with political parties, America used to have a rich network of locally rooted, but nationally federated, organizations that also connected people to government. As Theda Skocpol has shown, organizations like the PTA and the American Legion played important roles in constructing some of America's most successful social policies, but have faced sharp declines recently. These community based institutions structured the engagement of people in political action around a range of issues. They represented a place where people could meet and develop relationships with each other out of which emerged a sense of common purpose and programmatic plans of action. Higher levels of federation allowed local chapters to influence state and federal policy. At the turn of the century, federations of locally rooted women's clubs (including the forerunner to the PTA) initiated and won passage of some of America's first social welfare legislation to protect mothers and their children, even at a time when women did not have the right to vote. The American Legion helped create the GI Bill.[5]

By the early nineties, many Americans reported both that they felt the social fabric of their communities had seriously frayed and that they were alienated from our political system.[6] Scholars of social capital have stressed the connection between these two phenomena. They point out that, historically, the United States has relied upon a rich tradition of civic life to support democracy, a connection first noted by Alexis de Tocqueville in his study of nineteenth-century America. Tocqueville, a French aristocrat, came to the United States in the 1830s to determine why American society supported a democratic form of government while his native France was so easily controlled by a central political authority. The key to democracy in America, according to Tocqueville, could be found in a set of social and political institutions—voluntary associations, town meetings, a free press, churches—that sustained cooperative activity and self-government. Associational life in the small towns that Tocqueville studied accomplished two key things. It developed in citizens a "habit of participation" that spread across social institutions and political life. Moreover, participation in associations developed in people a sense of "self-interest rightly understood," that is, an understanding that an individual's well-being was intimately connected to the health of the whole community. Lacking associational life, people in France pursued their private business, leaving politics in the hands of a central authority. Through civic associations in America, people came to see the importance of working for the public good, and developed a habit of participating in self-government to achieve it.[7]

Robert Putnam makes a strong case that America has suffered a serious erosion in social capital since the fifties. Putnam documents the declining participation of Americans in a broad array of associations and forms of group life. For example, participation in parent-teacher associations (PTAs) has dropped from more than 12 million in 1964 to about 7 million. Membership in the national Federation of Women's Clubs is down by more than half since 1964, while membership in the League of Women Voters is off 42 percent since 1969. Male-dominated fraternal organizations have suffered too, with the Lions off by 12 percent since 1983, Elks down 18 percent since 1979, the Shriners down 27 percent, Masons down 39 percent, and Jaycees off 44 percent. Volunteers for the Boy Scouts are down by 26 percent since 1970, while the Red Cross has lost 61 percent of its volunteers since 1970. Using survey data, Putnam shows that total associational group membership has dropped by roughly one-quarter since 1974. He has also been careful to document the decline in more informal social connectedness as well. For example, between 1974 and 1998 the number of times Americans spent a social evening with a neighbor declined by one-third. Putnam captures America's declining social capital in the metaphor of "bowling alone," observing that league bowling has decreased by 40 percent even though the number of bowlers has increased by 10 percent.[8]

Putnam's thesis has provoked a broad debate about the state of civic America and the causes of changing patterns of civic participation.[9] Little of the debate, however, has focused on the decline in the stable institutions of local community life that Tocqueville recognized were so key to democratic processes. These institutions provide a venue for face-to-face democracy in the context of long-term attachments to fellow citizens. Overlapping patterns of participation in congregations, PTAs, fraternal orders, and community centers create a web of relationships and civic action in support of families and communities. Understanding the importance of these forms of social capital helps to shed light on the debate over Putnam's thesis.

For example, some scholars suggest that America has experienced the rise of new forms of group activity since the sixties. Robert Wuthnow documents the tremendous growth of the small-group movement, suggesting that fully 40 percent of Americans now participate in small groups that provide support or caring. The range of these groups is quite large, including Bible study groups, Alcoholics Anonymous, and hobby clubs. Small groups do offer face-to-face relationships that support the social connectedness so important to social capital. And small groups can encourage broader civic participation: Wuthnow reports that many participants become more interested in social or political issues through these groups. Nevertheless, small groups are, by definition, narrowly constituted. They are seldom rooted in, or concerned about the well-being of any particular community. In other words, this new social capital has not replaced the stable institutions of community life that declined. As Wuthnow concludes, "some small groups merely provide occasions for individuals to focus on themselves in the presence of others. The social contract binding members together asserts only the weakest of obligations. . . . We can imagine that [these small groups] really substitute for families, neighborhoods, and broader community attachments that may demand lifelong commitments, when, in fact, they do not."[10]

While small groups have proliferated below local community institutions, national social movements and advocacy groups have sprouted "above" them. Since the sixties, there has been an explosion of such organizations, including feminist groups like the National Organization for Women (NOW), environmental groups like the Sierra Club, and a wide variety of organizations committed to the concerns of African Americans, Hispanic Americans, gays and lesbians, etc. The American Association of Retired Persons, the largest of these organizations, had 33 million members by 1993. Debra Minkoff argues that such groups make important contributions to democracy. They link people who are isolated in local communities, and they raise the concerns of previously marginalized people so as to broaden the inclusiveness of the public sphere. Nevertheless, there is little evidence that such advocacy groups generate or sustain high levels of participation. Most of their members exist simply on mailing lists. They participate by donating money or perhaps by writing letters. Dominated by staff based in Washington or state capitals, few have active local chapters where large numbers of people work together.[11]

Even if the country has experienced the growth of smaller groups and national networks, we have indeed suffered losses in the stable institutions that structured local communities in which people live and raise their families. In my view, neither small groups nor national social movements, whatever their contributions, have helped to restore the community foundations for democracy. If we want to revitalize democracy in America, then we need to find ways to build social capital at the level of local community institutions.

But building such social capital may not be sufficient, if those community institutions remain detached from our political system. What has been largely overlooked in the debates about social capital is the growing disconnection between politics and what remains of American community life, a still significant resource. The political efficacy of turn-of-the-century political parties and twentieth-century cross-class federations both promoted civic participation and benefited from it.[12] By concentrating exclusively on the decline in social capital, we ignore how our older forms of social capital were effective, in part, because they were coupled to politics and government.

A Framework for Analysis

Revitalizing democracy, then, requires community building, but also something more: creating institutional links between stronger communities and our political system. In the following section, I present a four-part framework that can help specify the necessary components of the process of building social capital to revitalize democracy. I will elaborate the following points: First, the process of building social capital needs to start with the institutional life that still exists in local communities. These institutions structure cooperative relationships and bear traditions and values in which people express their commitment to community. Second, since these institutions and the social fabric of communities are weak, an effective strategy is needed to develop cooperative ties and enhance the leadership capacity of community members. Third, strong local communities can be isolated, inward looking, even antidemocratic. In order to develop broader identities and a commitment to the common good, we need a strategy to bridge social capital across communities, especially those divided by race. Finally, building strong communities with diverse connections may not matter if they lack the power to shape their own development. Effective power requires mediating institutions capable of intervening successfully in politics and government.

Grounding Democratic Revitalization in Community Institutions

A necessary starting point for building social capital lies in the institutions that still exist in local communities. The logic of the concept of social capital itself suggests that it will be difficult to get people to cooperate with each other from scratch. Existing institutions incorporate networks of citizens who share some level of initial trust and cooperative ties. Moreover, institutions embody the traditions and values that can sustain community life. A commitment to community, and the motivation to care for it, rarely exist in the abstract. Communities and their institutions share a history through which people develop particular traditions that bind them together and motivate them to act.

Debates about social capital have often ignored its institutional foundations. Some studies, including Putnam's groundbreaking *Making Democracy Work*, treat social capital as a set of universal cultural phenomena, that is, trust and habits of cooperation that move in and out of various institutional forms through history. Yet, people learn to trust and cooperate with others in particular social arrangements. They cooperate in specific institutional settings, or within less formally organized social settings, for specific purposes. Social capital loses its meaning the further it becomes removed from specific kinds of institutions, like churches, schools, or even unions.[13]

A recognition that social capital forms for specific purposes reveals that all community institutions may not be equal in their potential contribution to democracy. Some, in fact, may be antidemocratic.[14] The Michigan militia represents an obvious case here. Most forms of community institutions are not so inherently contrary to democratic norms; many provide a potential basis for democratic action. But, that does not mean they all contribute as readily, or as much.

In considering the possible institutional bases for democratic action, religious congregations stand out for two reasons. First, congregations represent, by far, the country's largest form of social connectedness. Whether measured by volunteering, philanthropy, or time spent on civic participation, religious participation accounts for roughly half of America's stock of social capital. Despite a significant decline in church attendance since the sixties, about 40 percent of Americans still attend a weekly worship service, while almost 70 percent claim church membership. In many poor communities, churches are often the only social institution left with any degree of vitality. In fact, a recent survey of congregations shows that, as other institutions have collapsed under the weight of inner-city economic decline, poor communities remain as well endowed with religious institutions as more affluent suburbs.[15]

Inner-city churches, like their suburban counterparts, play the largest role in structuring community life. They sponsor an impressive array of group activities, among them schools, religious education and study groups, choirs, self-help programs, support groups for single parents, family counseling, sports teams, fraternal associations, women's groups, benevolent associations, lay and youth ministries, and evangelical societies. Moreover, religious congregations have staying power, so they can engage people in long-term processes of community building and democratic participation. While other types of associations may come and go, churches represent one of the most stable institutional bases for democracy.

Second, religious institutions embody strong traditions through which people can learn and express the value of community, as well as the obligations members have towards each other. Some denominations emphasize individual devotion over social ministry. Others define their community responsibility quite narrowly to their own congregation or denomination. But many take an expansive definition of their obligations to the broader community. Many religious communities are quite involved in the civic life of their locality and the national polity. Many religious institutions sponsor civic organizations that play important roles in community life, like the Young Men's and Women's Christian Associations (YM-WCAs) and the Jewish YM-WHAs, Boy and Girl Scouts, and schools. They play important roles in providing social services through religiously sponsored day care centers, hospitals, and soup kitchens. A religiously inspired concern for community helps motivate churchgoers to participate in community life. In surveys that measure volunteering, 34 percent of all volunteers say that religious structures were responsible for their volunteering. Moreover, 58 percent of adults reporting church membership volunteered, while only 35 percent of nonmembers did so.[16]

Finally, religion can offer a moral vision for political action. If we are particularly concerned with addressing the problems of low-income communities of color, commitments to social justice must inform understandings of community. A vision of social justice can inspire members of oppressed groups to action.[17] And, at least potentially, religious commitments to care for the poor and to welcome the stranger can encourage members of dominant groups to join in concert with them.

As community-based institutions, congregations provide a tremendous resource for the expansion of American democracy through their connections to networks of community caring and action. The people who enter politics through religious congregations are not the disconnected individuals appealed to by our political parties. Rather, they are members embedded in congregations and immersed in community relationships. As such, they can potentially bring a value-based concern for community well-being into our fractured interest-based system.[18]

Although churches offer the potential institutional basis for grounding American politics in community attachments, we need to understand how to unleash that potential in a way that expands democracy. Political religion to most Americans means the Christian Right, which, at best, is a "mixed blessing" for democracy. On the one hand, the Christian Right has demonstrated the potential for mobilizing many Americans into political action through their congregations, expanding the basis for political participation. But, on the other hand, religious teachings define a specific moral agenda for the Christian Right, like prayer in school or opposition to abortion. This approach can be just as divisive as exclusively interest-based politics. Moreover, the Christian Right often opposes the democratic aspirations of other excluded groups, like gays and lesbians.[19]

Rather than root politics in narrow religious teachings on controversial social issues, we need an approach that engages the community networks and religious traditions of congregations to inform an agenda that serves the more concrete needs of families and communities. The starting point for that process is at the local level, not because local action is sufficient, but because it provides the necessary grounding for democracy in the communities in which people live and raise their families. It is at that level that people can enter into the kind of face-to-face interactions that build trust and cooperation around a community-based agenda.

Developing Citizens' Capacity to Cooperate in Local Communities

The foundation for people's development as members of society and as democratic citizens lies in local communities. It is the institutions of local community life, schools, churches, and less formal interactions that integrate people into democratic society. Communitarian theorists have stressed that people are relational beings, not the disconnected individuals or "unencumbered selves" of liberal democratic theory. In fact, as Amitai Etzioni has argued, it is only "when community is properly cultivated, by contrast, [that] the kind of citizen liberals take for granted flourishes." Such an approach does not deny the integrity of the individual, or his or her capacity for independence and creativity. As Etzioni notes, "persons are shaped by and oriented toward their communities even as they are more than the sum of the social influences that inform their behavior, character, and thoughts."[20] But it suggests that full personal development relies upon, and, in turn, enhances healthy communities. It is in community connections that individuals can develop the will to act collectively, that is, to enter democratic political processes.

The importance of local communities has not been well appreciated in discussions about social capital. Debating macro-level trends, that is, on the state of social capital in the country as a whole, can draw our attention away from the quite serious deterioration of social fabric and institutional life in many communities. Moreover, macro-level studies can mask quite significant variation across localities.[21]

If we are going to develop the capacity of people to cooperate as public citizens in the inner city, we must confront the serious deterioration in the quality of urban community life over the past thirty years. Descriptions of urban life in the fifties characterize both white and black neighborhoods as rich and vibrant, with active churches, small businesses and strong community support networks. Despite the pernicious effects of poverty, discrimination and segregation, black community life had great strengths. It was these strengths which served as the basis for the social and political gains African Americans made in the civil rights movement of the fifties and sixties. By the late eighties, however, the streets of poor African American neighborhoods seemed empty and deserted.[22]

The community life of inner-city neighborhoods suffered in the seventies and eighties as poverty became more concentrated, and government cut social provision. As industry disappeared from the inner city, and good-paying jobs became harder to find, poverty intensified. At the same time, many inner-city residents, including many middle-class blacks, took the opportunity to leave for the suburbs, further concentrating the poverty of these areas. As the social diversity and economic resources of the inner city collapsed, the rich array of social institutions that had once characterized American urban neighborhoods came under threat. Small businesses closed and social clubs disbanded. Meanwhile, increased poverty brought with it a host of associated social problems, including crime and drug abuse. With the increase of crime came an even greater fear of crime; people became afraid to come out onto the streets or to attend community events. They became hesitant to intervene with young men who were causing trouble, to help them avoid risking their own futures through criminal behavior and drug abuse. "Old heads," older black men who used to play an important role counseling young men and serving as role models, grew silent and retreated into their households.[23]

Informal social networks of family and friends continue to play an essential role in helping poor people survive on a daily level. Lacking connections to outside resources, however, these survival networks are largely ineffective for helping people overcome poverty. More importantly for our purposes, support networks rarely advance broader community and political action on their own.[24]

The deterioration of the social fabric of urban communities indicates the need for a strategy to build social capital. We can start with existing institutions, but we will have to rebuild them, as well as expand social connectedness and develop public citizenship. Building social capital, however, requires leadership, people with the capacity to bring community residents together and provide direction for their efforts to develop cooperative action. Poverty, community deterioration, and the lack of educational opportunities make leadership development and public action more difficult in the inner city. The demands of survival sap energy, while the prejudices of mainstream America can undermine people's efforts to be public citizens. Local communities represent the first-order places where leadership can emerge and develop, because, here, citizens can gain strength and support from each other as they attempt to rattle the dry bones of their communities and become leaders of American society.

Scholars have taken a fairly narrow approach to understanding the contributions of community institutions to democracy, focusing on an individual's acquisition of skills. In the most important study of this type, Sidney Verba and his associates showed that religious institutions play a key role in equalizing political participation because they are sites where people of color and low-income people have the opportunity to learn skills that can be translated to politics, skills like writing letters, making speeches, and planning and making decisions in meetings.[25] Verba's study is important because it measures precisely the contributions of religious participation. But it takes a quite limited, technical view of leadership development and does not fully consider the importance of collective processes.

Providing leadership to developing cooperative action requires more than having the skills to advocate for a group or issue. Leaders require the capacity to build relationships with and among others, relationships that can lead to a politics of collective action. As Sheldon Wolin argues, politicalness means "our capacity for developing into beings who know and value what it means to participate in and be responsible for the care and improvement of our common and collective life." In this view, democratic participation requires more than taking part in elections or officeholding. It involves originating or initiating cooperative action with others.[26]

This kind of democratic leadership emerges out of community, building upon its traditions, and gaining strength from solidarity. Leaders then enter the public sphere, not as disconnected individuals, but as embedded members of a community. Leadership development that reflects a "stronger" sense of democratic participation can be quite empowering and transformative for the individual, particularly for women. Women in poor communities of color have often been restricted to the private sphere and denied opportunities for personal growth and public action, even though they shoulder the main burden for community caring and participation. Collective processes that emphasize relationship building can build upon the contributions that women have traditionally made to their communities and engage their leadership.[27]

The relentless glorification of the individual by American culture, and the dissolution of the community foundations of our political system, have served to disempower people in low-income communities even more than the rest of American citizens. The affluent have more of the individual resources, like money and education, that can substitute for a decline in social assets. They can, for example, contribute to lobbying groups to advocate for their issues. If their public schools and community centers fail, the affluent can and do send their children to private schools and summer camps. The poor are left defenseless.

Building social capital creates the necessary foundation for the emergence of new democratic leaders in the context of healthier communities. Michael Sandel has articulated the continued importance of community to democratic citizenship in this way: "the global media and markets that shape our lives beckon us to a world beyond boundaries and belonging. But the civic resources we need to master these forces, or at least to contend with them, are still to be found in the places and stories, memories and meanings, incidents and identities, that situate us in the world and give our lives their moral particularity."[28]

Bridging Social Capital

Building strong local communities is a necessary, but not sufficient, strategy for democratic renewal. Fostering such within-community "bonding" social capital provides the foundation for members of those communities to enter democratic life. But local communities can be isolated, inward looking, even antidemocratic. In order to develop broader identities and a commitment to the common good, we need a strategy that brings people together across communities. Bonding social capital strengthens connections among people much like each other. But we need bridging social capital as well, that is, cooperative connections across the lines, particularly those of race and class, that separate communities.[29]

The limitations of any effort that focuses exclusively on strengthening local communities are exacerbated by the fact that community life in

America is so segregated by race and economic class. As whites began to flee urban communities in the fifties and sixties, America's inner cities became increasingly populated by people of color, and increasingly more concentrated in poverty. Although some African Americans and Hispanic Americans have also left the inner city, they tend to live in black or Hispanic suburban neighborhoods. Meanwhile, despite school integration efforts since the fifties, our public schools are nearly as segregated today as they were forty years ago. Congregations are segregated as well, with Sunday morning continuing to represent "the most segregated hour in America." In sum, our metropolitan areas are deeply divided between predominantly poor inner-city communities of color and predominantly white and relatively affluent suburbs. Despite an increasing representation of multiracial America in the media, the large majority of Americans live their lives in racial isolation.[30]

Racial segregation, in fact, developed in part because white communities used their social capital to block the democratic demands of African Americans. Simply put, many strong white ethnic neighborhoods of the urban 1950s refused to let African Americans move in. John McGreevy shows how the parish conception of community combined with racist attitudes to make ethnic Catholic neighborhoods in the urban North fiercely insular. The church helped establish a whole host of social institutions to meet the daily needs of parishioners and to bind them together as a parish community. But the rich social fabric of ethnic neighborhoods, and the political connections they had to city hall, were used to keep African Americans out. White Catholics perceived the entrance of Protestant African Americans as a threat to their whole way of life. Resistance to integration began in the early twentieth century and took many forms. White homeowner associations organized residents to sign restrictive covenants which forbade them to sell to blacks. White real estate agents refused to show property to blacks. If, despite these efforts, some African Americans moved into white neighborhoods, resistance often became fierce and violent, with houses bombed. White Catholics directed their anger against any fellow Catholics who supported African American efforts to integrate. The first time a Catholic nun was ever publicly attacked on the streets of Chicago was at the hands of white Catholics while she marched in a pro-integration demonstration. According to McGreevy, "when she fell, the crowd cheered."[31]

Any effort to build social capital to revitalize democracy will require a strategy to confront this deep history of racism and racial conflict. Such a strategy is all the more important if greater democracy is to lead to concrete improvements in the quality of inner-city life. Poor communities lack the resources to address their needs, no matter how strong they become internally. Bridging social capital is necessary to create the broad understanding of the common good and the public will to address problems of poverty and racism in America.

But the task of creating racial bridges faces yet another challenge. While a black/white paradigm served to capture race relations in most American cities in the past, today the racial composition of our cities is much more complex. Hispanic Americans of different nationalities are rapidly becoming the largest "minority" group, with states like California, Texas, and Florida leading the way. Many cities have large and diverse Asian American communities as well, and some have significant black populations from the Caribbean or Africa. In many cases African American and Hispanic communities have found themselves in competition with each other for jobs and limited public resources. Conflicts between African Americans and Korean Americans have also erupted in many cities. At the same time that we need to "bridge" the suburb with the inner city, we must find a way to bring communities together across a variety of racial lines.[32]

However weak the social fabric and institutional structure within particular communities may be, America appears to be singularly lacking in bridging forms of social capital. We simply do not have very many institutions in which Americans from different racial groups cooperate with each other. The logic of social capital suggests that when people cooperate together, they can find their commonalities and develop a shared sense of the common good. Research in social psychology supports this hypothesis. When people are placed in interdependent situations where they believe that they need each other, they forego initial prejudices and enact cross-ethnic and cross-racial helping, rather than competition. The challenge, then, is to create these interdependent and cooperative forms.[33]

Given America's deep history of racism and interracial conflict, however, starting a cooperative process in the first place will not be easy. Religion could provide an initial basis for cooperation by grounding such action in a set of common values, goals, and commitments to the public good. This is not unprecedented in American history. Since Tocqueville's time, religion has played a central role in some of the most important movements to extend and broaden American democracy. White Northerners inspired by their faith played an important role in the abolition movement of the nineteenth century. At the turn of the century, the settlement houses and women's associations that sponsored early American social welfare policies were often religiously based. And churches, of course, played the key role in the civil rights movement of the fifties and sixties. At its best, religion has provided a moral basis to conceive of our place in a larger human society and inspired people to work for racial equality, social justice, and democracy.[34]

Although religious values may provide an initial basis for multiracial efforts, we still require a strategy for discussing and resolving differences, finding common ground, and building the trust necessary for cooperative political action. Such a strategy does not require complete unity, or lack of differences. Instead, it should foster mutual respect and understanding for diverse traditions, so that people can find, and work to expand, their common commitments to each other.

Effective Power

Building strong communities and bridging ties will not matter if communities lack the effective power necessary to exert some control over their destinies. Revitalizing democracy requires effective connections between well-organized communities and our political system. As political parties have lost their organized base in communities, new forms of mediating institutions are needed that can hold public institutions, and eventually, global corporations, accountable to communities.

The need for such political institutions has not received much attention in debates about social capital. Contemporary theorists of social capital refer to Tocqueville's discussion of the "habits of the heart," and imply that they translate quite naturally and automatically to politics. Yet Tocqueville himself was quite interested in the specific political institution of the town meeting. Even if we accept that the habits of participation in civic life translate to political activity, we still need to identify the specific set of institutional mechanisms that can make that connection.

We must first recognize that a political institution capable of mediating between communities and government will have to be able both to forge consensus and manage conflict. Communitarians and advocates of social capital have rightly noted that contemporary politics are short, not of conflict, but of cooperation. But they have often failed to appreciate that what social capital offers is the necessary complement to conflict, not a replacement for it. For some proponents of social capital, the concept has come to represent an aspiration for complete consensus and unanimity in public life, an "escape from politics" in the words of Michael Foley and Bob Edwards.[35] Politics, by contrast, assumes that conflicts of interests are endemic to society.

Stressing the virtues of social capital and the value of a more communitarian approach does represent a refreshing antidote to a daily politics which strikes many Americans as solely an enterprise of power and naked self-interest. Many Americans feel politics has degenerated into a dirty game where money and power contend for the spoils of office, where no one can be trusted to take care of the common good. Perhaps more dispassionately, many political scientists have come to understand politics as a process in which disconnected individuals calculate their self-interest and act to maximize it, irrespective of its effects on their fellow citizens. Voters elect those who will represent their preferences; while politicians seek to win office in part for the power that it offers and in part to enact their own policy preferences.[36]

Yet strategies to build social capital that ignore the reality of conflict do so at great peril. American society has deeply rooted structures of inequality in its economic, social, and political systems. Efforts to harness social capital, especially for the purpose of bringing effective power to inner-city communities, must confront the reality of oppression and inequality. Whether social capital contributes to democratic outcomes will depend on how community-building efforts negotiate the terrain between conflict and cooperation.

Over the past ten years, a broad set of community-building initiatives has emerged in American cities, but by and large they have remained disconnected from our political system. Community development corporations and a wide variety of church-based efforts seek to involve residents in bettering their neighborhoods. By fostering collaboration, community-building efforts have made important gains in combating crime and drug use, involving youth in constructive group activity, cleaning up neighborhoods, and fostering community pride and spirit. But community building has shied away from politics to such an extent that, by and large, citizens involved in these efforts do not even see them as political. A survey conducted for the Kettering Foundation revealed that a broad range of Americans are deeply involved in efforts to improve their communities, but that the very people who are active in addressing public issues refuse to call their activities political.[37]

Without an adequate strategy for developing political power, the gains of the community-building movement have remained localized and limited. Community development corporations (CDCs) have mobilized community resources and brought in public and private funds to build affordable housing and promote economic development. However, as CDCs become focused on developing and later administering housing programs, few have been able to sustain broad popular participation. Like many of our advocacy groups, community-building efforts become dominated by a few staff or key leaders. Relying solely on building consensus with financial institutions and public officials, few develop an independent base of power capable of demanding broader change when resistance occurs.[38]

Institutional forms are needed through which communities can be organized and power generated over a sustained period of time. Such community-based political institutions will have to be capable of building cooperation as well as handling conflict. In a society structured by profound inequalities along race, class, and many other lines, good faith discussion represents only part of the process necessary to rebuild a conception of the common good. In fact, confrontation is often required to open up institutions and to push groups or individuals to reformulate their conceptions of self-interest.

In order to bring effective power to communities, local institutions will also require the capability to operate at higher levels. Although a local base provides the foundation for participation and power, it is not sufficient to influence the larger institutions that affect the health of communities. Most of the advocacy groups active in American politics concentrate their activity at the top, with lobbying in Washington. They lack firm local, participatory roots. Rebuilding the community foundations for political action may be our main priority. But, eventually, strong local efforts must find a way to combine to influence national, and eventually, global decision making in a way that redounds to the benefit of local organizing.

The IAF Strategy

The IAF has developed some important strategies that begin to meet the challenges identified above for building social capital in a way that revitalizes democracy. These strategies offer a distinct alternative to dominant forms of political organizing in the U.S. This section describes, in brief, the elements of the IAF's organizing strategy. Later chapters of the book analyze these strategies as they were developed and implemented in the work of the network.

Faith-Based, Institutional Organizing

The IAF grounds political action in community through a faith-based, institutional strategy. In other words, while most political organizations are composed of individuals, the IAF builds local organizations composed primarily of religious institutions, that is, congregations. The official members of local IAF affiliates are not individuals, but Catholic parishes, Protestant congregations, and some institutions of other faiths as well. These institutions pay the dues that provide the bulk of the organization's rather spartan finances. Individuals become active in IAF organizations through the institutions of which they are members.

While most political organizations recruit the relatively disconnected activist, the IAF approach engages citizens as they are rooted in relatively stable community networks. The institutional strategy provides the stability to take a long-term approach to community revitalization, to sustain efforts in the face of difficulties and setbacks. The IAF insists upon calling all of its participants "leaders" to emphasize their connections to fellow congregants and neighbors.[39] Drawing upon the lay leadership of congregations encourages women who have historically shouldered the burden for community caring to emerge as leaders. Through participation in IAF organizations, community leaders gain the opportunity to express their religiously derived commitment to the needs of their immediate congregation and neighborhood on the broader public stage.

The IAF recruits clergy and lay leaders by engaging faith traditions that emphasize a commitment to community building and to social justice. Religious values provide a powerful motivation for participation in practical efforts to improve community life. Leaders in the Texas IAF work to build affordable housing, improve local schools, fund libraries and health clinics, repair streets and infrastructure, develop job-training programs, and improve public safety. In this way faith-based political action improves the health of the very communities upon which the faith institutions depend. Community building and democratic action are brought toward a synergistic relationship.[40]

Relational Organizing

While most political organizing can be characterized as issue mobilization, the IAF has developed an alternative strategy to build cooperative action, called relational organizing. As opposed to mobilizing around a set of predetermined issues, the IAF brings residents together first to discuss the needs of their community and to find a common ground for action. Conversation and relationship building lead to the identification of issues around which participants are prepared to act together. Rather than starting from the top with the "most important" issues, IAF organizations build their political capacity over time, through patient base building rooted in the issues as they have meaning in the lives of participants and their families.

The IAF works to develop the leadership ability of its participants through the issue campaigns that emerge from relational organizing. Leadership development includes skills building (like research, public speaking, mobilization of followers) but encompasses the broader arts of political leadership, like relationship building, negotiation, and compromise. The IAF, in fact, places the highest priority on leadership development. Local organizations sign contracts and pay fees to the IAF for training services, including participation in the network's ten-day training program.

The job of the IAF organizer hired by local organizations is not to manage issue campaigns. Following what it calls the iron rule, "never do for others what they can do for themselves," IAF leaders have the main responsibility to pursue all aspects of political action. IAF organizers, ideally at least, are meant to remain focused on recruiting new leaders and training them in relational organizing. While many advocacy and community development groups become dominated by a few key staff and leaders, the IAF has developed an institutional mechanism that works to renew its participatory base and leadership pool.

Broad-Based Organizations

While much of American political organizing caters to particular group interests and identities, the IAF works to create bridging social capital by bringing leaders from different faith communities together in what it calls broad-based organizations. IAF local organizations are supposed to include the diverse array of religious and racial communities that make up the local area in which they operate. As a result, while the member institutions reflect distinct communities themselves, Texas IAF organizations often unite African American, Hispanic, and white communities of various economic levels.[41]

The IAF encourages leaders from these different communities to work to find a common ground for action together. IAF training places a priority on relationship building among the leaders, so that each can get to know the experiences and concerns of other communities. At the same time, the IAF organizers recognize that interests vary across communities, and encourage leaders to become expert at negotiating and compromising to create consensus. IAF organizations create a process where trust and cooperation can develop over time. If consensus cannot be achieved, divisive issues are typically dropped.

However, leaders do not enter into cooperative processes with people of other faiths and races as disconnected individuals. The IAF's institutional strategy means that leaders draw upon the traditions and support shared with fellow congregants, their bonding social capital, as they build new bridging relationships across different communities. The institutional structure devolves an important degree of autonomy and initiative within local organizations to racially and religiously defined institutions. The IAF approach draws upon the strengths of group identity, while working to overcome the weaknesses of isolation and narrow group outlooks.

Independent, Nonpartisan Political Strategy

While many advocacy groups rely upon inner-circle lobbying for political influence, the IAF follows a nonpartisan strategy, which seeks to generate effective power for communities through an independently organized base.[42] Through IAF organizations, community leaders work to command resources for their initiatives, collaborate with allies to reform public institutions like schools, and hold public officials accountable. IAF organizations do not endorse candidates, although they often conduct voter registration and get-out-the-vote drives. The IAF's nonpartisan strategy allows its organizations to be fairly inclusive of community residents, despite their partisan preferences. It also facilitates collaboration with public officials holding different party affiliations.

IAF organizations generate the power to back up community demands through the support of their member institutions and the participation generated by relational organizing in community networks. In developing issue campaigns, IAF leaders hold discussions in church committees, converse with their neighbors, and organize house meetings. IAF organizations regularly mobilize hundreds, sometimes thousands, of supporters from their community networks to "accountability nights," where political candidates and other officials are asked to make commitments to support organizational initiatives. Although the organizations do not formally endorse candidates, they do inform their supporters about the positions candidates take, and sometimes mobilize people to vote. In this way, the interfaith network backs up its demands with an implicit electoral threat. At the same time, following its relational strategy, IAF leaders and organizers seek to foster long-term relationships with public officials, and other potential allies, pragmatically negotiating and compromising to achieve broader objectives.

The IAF strategy prizes the development of strong and independent organizations to advocate for low-income communities. The IAF has a well-known slogan, "no permanent allies, no permanent enemies." Many observers have interpreted that slogan in a limited, tactical sense as reflecting a pragmatic approach to politics. But the slogan has a deeper strategic significance. The IAF's strategy assumes there are no fundamental, irreconcilable conflicts between groups, and that our political institutions are ultimately open and accessible to all. Nevertheless, the IAF recognizes that confrontation is often required to open up institutions and to push groups or individuals to reformulate conceptions of their own self-interest. Constructive solutions can be found that can accommodate all parties, if the political capacity exists. IAF organizations, however, insist upon their independent role in creating that political capacity.

The IAF has developed a federated, network model for statewide action in Texas that has allowed local communities to expand their effective power. While many advocacy groups dictate policy to local affiliates, local organizations in the Texas IAF retain decision-making authority. The network seeks to forge consensus across localities as the basis for concerted action. Statewide leaders meetings, coordinated by the IAF's staff of professional organizers, provide a venue for local participants to develop common agendas to which they can all agree to contribute. Participation in the statewide network offers local organizations the opportunity to bring in outside resources, as well as to attempt the more complex programs of institutional reform that require allies at higher levels. In this way the federated model promises to facilitate synergy between local- and higher-level political action, so that gains at one level can advance the other.

Authority and Participation

The various elements of the IAF approach can be brought together under the umbrella concept of relational organizing. Relational organizing places relationship building at the heart of everything the IAF does. This kind of organizing directly attempts to strengthen the social fabric and institutions of frayed communities, that is, to build bonding social capital. Relationships created across racial lines provide the foundation for bridging social capital. And the relationships embedded in the organizations and networks of the IAF generate political power behind community initiatives.

One of the most critical types of relationships created by the IAF is between professional organizers and community leaders. In fact, the development of the IAF network in Texas and the Southwest can best be understood as a collaboration between leaders drawn from local community institutions and professional organizers on the regional staff. The Southwest IAF has built a staff of sixty organizers, reputedly one of the largest and best-trained corps of professional organizers in the country.[43] Staff organizers meet regularly for two to three days every other month at seminars given by scholars and policy analysts. The meetings also offer the occasion to discuss network business and forge a degree of unity and coherence that helps cement the network's activity.

At the local and state level, organizers operate in conjunction with the IAF leaders they recruit and train. And here we find a dynamic that lies at the heart of IAF organizing. This dynamic involves a particular combination of participation and authority. The authority of organizers, clergy, and experienced leaders offers central direction to help make the network effective and respected. Meanwhile, relational organizing in local institutions generates participation and initiative from the "bottom-up."

Most observers miss this dynamic and end up characterizing the IAF as either entirely "bottom-up" and participatory, or "top-down" and hierarchical. Scholars like Harry Boyte, one of the first to call attention to the accomplishments of the IAF, have written extensive descriptions of the activities of some IAF affiliates and good accounts of the explanations the IAF itself offers for its methods.[44] Boyte emphasizes how IAF institutions serve as free spaces in which citizens can collaborate for common ends. Many analysts like Boyte have been particularly impressed with the IAF's ability to bring poor and working people together to discuss political issues and policy solutions. These scholars often present the history of the public struggles of the IAF organizations, and the personal stories of IAF leaders and organizers. But they have seldom probed the authority structures that infuse the network. Consequently, these accounts suggest a one-sided interpretation of the IAF as a "grass-roots" organization.[45]

Peter Skerry, on the other hand, does probe some of the authoritative mechanisms at work in his comparison of COPS, the Texas IAF's founding organization in San Antonio, with the network's affiliate in East Los Angeles, the United Neighborhood Organization (UNO). Although Skerry acknowledges the existence of decision making at lower levels, that is, the freedom of member churches to pursue specific campaigns, he concludes that "the organizers are unquestionably in charge."[46] In this way his account suggests, somewhat stereotypically, that IAF organizations are composed of uneducated racial minorities controlled by professional organizers and priests.

In my view, the Texas IAF combines authority with participation to create a dynamic form of intervention in democratic politics. The network may not always get that combination exactly right, erring in one direction or the other at times. But a key lesson of its work is the effectiveness that can come from authoritative leadership well grounded in broader participatory organizations.

Most advocates of participatory democracy have become uncomfortable with discussions of authority. But utopian preferences for pure egalitarian relationships are unrealistic for developing effective power for communities. Social relations that are characterized entirely by hierarchy, of course, are oppressive and lend little to democratic action. Yet most communities contain some pattern of authority. Political leadership in collective processes, in fact, requires the development of authority. The question is whether authority is legitimate, inclusive, and accountable to the broader community, an issue that will be explored closely later in this book.[47]

In popular imagination, the IAF today is still associated with the militant, direct action tactics of its founder, Saul Alinsky. Again, there is some truth to this view, as IAF organizations do not shy away from mobilizing members to vociferously demand action by public officials. But there is another, "softer" side to the IAF's work, the side that is willing to discuss, negotiate, and compromise—even with its enemies.[48] Where the IAF has worked best, it has combined both of these strategies to create organizations with the power to be heard and leaders with the necessary flexibility to forge consensus policies.

Either-or characterizations of the IAF turn out not to be very helpful. The dynamism of the IAF lies in its ability to combine confrontation with negotiation, power politics with communitarian political discourse, racially homogeneous religious institutions within multiracial local affiliates, and broad participation with central authority. Rather than focusing on "who's in charge?"—organizers or leaders—it makes more sense to see the Texas IAF network as representing a dynamic collaboration between people of faith and professional organizers.

New "Old-Style" Politics

The new mediating institutions built by the Texas IAF are reminiscent of forms of organization that used to link Americans to the political system, discussed at the beginning of this chapter.[49] Party organizations, and in particular, the urban political machine, worked to connect urban residents and their community institutions, that is, churches, fraternal orders, business associations, and professional clubs, to government.[50] The party boss and his ward heelers organized residents to turn out to vote for the party's candidate in exchange for delivering jobs, contracts, or neighborhood improvements. Although the machine worked on patronage, and largely excluded African Americans, women, and others from any real influence, it did serve to connect many Americans to a political organization that responded, albeit in limited ways, to their needs. With the advent of television and mass marketing, politicians have come to rely on media consultants, pollsters, and fund-raisers, rather than party organizers, in order to reach voters. The urban machine lost its function, and the organized base of political parties withered.[51]

Alongside the party machine, cross-class federations like the PTAs, the American Legion, and fraternal orders also helped connect Americans to politics through their communities. These federations were largely social organizations; but, concerned about community affairs, they intervened in politics as well. With their strong local roots and national scope, they were able to help create such important public policies as the GI bill. Like the urban machine, though, these federations have also declined with the advent of mass marketing and globalization. Mailing list memberships supply the finances for organizations that now advocate for issues in Washington without engaging people directly in cooperation and action in local chapters. Meanwhile, local elites that used to gain career-enhancing prestige from their leadership in the civic life of their communities now work for companies more tied to the global economy than their localities. Elites have turned from civic organizations to participation in national professional associations for career enhancement. They give money to advocacy groups, rather than participate alongside working class members in local chapters of fraternal orders or groups like the PTA. By favoring those who can give money, however, advocacy groups have become even more the province of the middle and upper classes, while lower-income Americans included in the old-style federations have lost an effective voice.[52]

To offer a kind of replacement for the urban machine and the cross-class federation, the IAF has had to find a route around the trends that have undermined the participatory bases of these older institutional forms. In particular, the network has had to find an alternative source of funding for its operations. Parties funded their bosses and ward organizers at the local level through patronage. But parties now concentrate on mass marketing techniques and donations from the affluent to fund media campaigns. The old cross-class federations gained their funds from local chapter membership, while the advocacy groups that have replaced them now rely upon mailing list memberships and large foundation grants.

While the machine and the cross-class federation have declined, new groups that have sought to empower poor people have struggled to gain a source of funding for their efforts. The large private foundations that so heavily influence the civil society sector have been adverse to funding political conflict. In the sixties, the Ford Foundation largely withdrew its funding to African American and other groups politically active in the inner city after it was criticized for supporting radicalism. Other large private organizations followed suit, funding social reform projects rather than political or community organizing efforts that empower poor people to determine their own agendas. Foundations became happy to fund project directors, program administrators, and service providers, but usually not organizers. Meanwhile, government funds became available for service provision as well, encouraging groups that were originally involved in community and political action to shift their efforts to program administration.[53]

Some foundations have helped to foster advocacy for the rights of various excluded groups. But they have not funded organizations that sought to promote the active participation of members of those groups themselves. According to J. Craig Jenkins in a report on foundation giving to social movements from 1955 to 1980, "participatory democracy has not been the central goal of foundations. They have instead taken an indirect approach, funding professional organizations which have removed legal and institutional barriers to minority political participation or operated as advocates for under represented groups."[54] While the more progressive foundations shifted to advocacy, newer conservative foundations emerged and began to work against group empowerment through their efforts to promote personal responsibility and limited government.[55]

Rather than relying upon funds from political parties or government on the one hand, or funds from private, secular foundations on the other, the IAF has developed an alternative strategy. It draws the resources to hire organizers primarily from its member faith institutions. In order to preserve the organization's independence of action, the IAF stipulates that one-third of the budget for local organizations must come from member institutions. On average, churches pay 1 to 2 percent of their yearly budget in dues to local IAF organizations. While the proportion of local budgets derived from institutional dues sometimes falls below one-third, the IAF struggles to maintain that percentage as a way to guarantee its independence and to demonstrate continued support from its base.

Local IAF organizations also draw contributions from a mix of local businesses of various sizes—and from foundations. But these have been primarily religious foundations, first among them, the Catholic Campaign for Human Development (CCHD). The CCHD was founded in 1970 by the Catholic Bishops in response to the urban riots of the sixties and the efforts of many American Catholics to get the church to respond to the social justice concerns sparked by Vatican II. The CCHD has been the single largest funder of Texas IAF organizations, and in fact, probably the single largest funder of poor empowerment groups of all kinds across the country.[56]

More recently, the Texas IAF has received funds from large, secular foundations, like the Ford and Rockefeller Foundations. These funds have proved critical to the ability of Cortes to build an institute to train organizers through its bimonthly seminars.[57] But, formally at least, foundation funds support projects (school reform) and education (organizer seminars), not organizing. The funds do not go to local IAF organizations to hire organizers. Nevertheless, the ability of the IAF to garner these funds has resulted from a more recent recognition by private foundations of the weaknesses of American democracy and the importance of citizen participation, sparked in part by Robert Putnam's work on social capital.[58]

While the old party machine delivered jobs and contracts to its supporters, the IAF works for public goods that will benefit residents more broadly—like improved roads, affordable housing, and better schools. Nevertheless, we should not underestimate the priority the IAF gives to delivering concrete benefits this way, because continued grass-roots support for the network relies upon its effectiveness as an instrument for community development. The IAF's political effectiveness relies upon its ability to influence voters, albeit not in a directly partisan manner. Since IAF organizations follow a nonpartisan strategy, they cannot directly trade votes for jobs. But the IAF does work to educate its supporters and get out the vote, thereby using an implied electoral threat to influence politicians.

Like the old federations, though, people participate in the IAF out of community commitments and attachments, not just for material gains. In the IAF these attachments are often derived from religious tradition. Such a faith context helps the IAF recreate the cross-class partnerships that characterized the old federations. Elites become involved in the IAF, not for career advancement as before, but out of religiously motivated commitments. Meanwhile, the ability of the IAF to draw upon community attachments to encourage and sustain participation means that material benefits do not have to supply all of the grease for the wheel of organizing.

The issue of community attachments brings us, once again, to the role of faith in politics. How did the IAF come to ground its political action in faith communities? More specifically, how did a network founded by the hard-nosed and often coarse agitator, Saul Alinsky, develop a "theology of organizing"? That is the subject to which we now turn.

Two

A Theology of Organizing: From Alinsky to the Modern IAF

ON A winter's day in 1975 George Ozuna's grandmother asked him to accompany her shopping in downtown San Antonio.[1] The high school senior got his shoes and began the long walk from the Hispanic south side of town to Joske's Department Store, the largest retail establishment in the city. When the pair arrived, George immediately realized something was going on. Hundreds of Hispanic grandmothers, housewives, and churchgoers had gathered outside the store. They entered en masse and began trying on clothes. And they didn't stop. They continued to try on clothes all day, grinding store operations to a halt. The protesters were all members of Catholic parishes active in Communities Organized for Public Service (COPS), a new organization fighting to improve conditions in San Antonio's impoverished and long-neglected south and west side neighborhoods. While they disrupted business, COPS leaders and its organizer, Ernesto Cortes, Jr., met with the store's owner. They demanded that he use his influence on San Antonio's city council to pass COPS' $100 million budget proposal for infrastructural improvements and increased services to Mexican American neighborhoods.

The next day COPS supporters disrupted banking operations on a busy Friday afternoon at the central branch of Frost National Bank by continuously exchanging pennies for dollars and vice versa. Upstairs COPS leaders and organizer Cortes met with Tom Frost, Jr., one of the most influential men in San Antonio. The Joske Department Store manager had refused COPS' demand for assistance, and now Frost, although polite, declined to call the mayor as well. Cortes, as the organizer, was supposed to let COPS leaders do the negotiating; but he watched them fold as Frost stalled.

As Cortes later recounted in a speech to farm workers, "My leaders freeze, and they don't do anything. . . . I believe in the iron rule of organizing: never do anything for anybody that they can do for themselves. But they ain't doing for themselves! They're collapsing; they're folding. Our people are downstairs waiting with no instruction, no word and they don't know what to do. I decide I've got to do something, so I move my chair over to Mr. Frost, and he's got a blood vessel that's exposed, and I focus on it and I look at it. I just keep moving, he moves away, and I move closer with the chair. Then finally he says something, and I say, 'Mr. Frost, that's a bunch of balderdash. You're the most arrogant man I've ever met.' And he gets up. We have a priest there and Mr. Frost says, 'Father, you better teach your people some manners and some values.' And finally the priest says, 'Well, Mr. Frost, I don't know about that, but you know, you're apathetic and I think that's much worse.' "[2]

Despite little initial success, COPS continued its protests and the tide began to turn. Prime time television crews started covering the actions, scaring away paying customers. Pressure mounted on business leaders. The head of the Chamber of Commerce came to negotiate with Cortes. But the organizer made him wait until COPS leaders could be rounded up to participate. Through the organizing strategy discussed later in this chapter, COPS eventually won the city's commitment for $100 million worth of desperately needed improvements to its neighborhoods. For the first time, Mexican Americans had flexed their political muscle in San Antonio, and they gained new drainage projects, sidewalks, parks, and libraries for their efforts.

Many Hispanics were surprised to see the Catholic Church become involved in such militant tactics. But according to George Ozuna, his grandmother and her parish friends knew exactly what they were doing. "I'm doing this because we're winning. Your grandfather and I came from Mexico to try to build something. But we were losers. There were things that always worked to keep us down. In Mexico, it was the government taking away our animals and chickens. Here it was poverty again. Grandfather working at Finesilver with no union. All my life I've worked very hard to win, to find something where you're really winning. We've always lost. Now I'm winning. *We're* winning. And we have a say-so in what's going on. And we're going to have more of a say-so."[3]

Militant, direct action tactics geared towards winning put COPS squarely in the tradition started by Saul Alinsky in founding the Industrial Areas Foundation (IAF) in the 1930s. Alinsky codified many of these principles in his books *Rules for Radicals* and *Reveille for Radicals*. After his encounter with Cortes, the banker Tom Frost bought a case of these books and distributed them among the power elite of San Antonio so that they could better prepare to deal with COPS. COPS and the IAF are still known for these militant tactics. The casual observer who sees only these tactics, however, will miss the fundamental changes to Alinsky's way of organizing that Cortes began to make with his work in San Antonio. Twenty years after the tie-up at his bank, Frost, now an influential figure in Texas state politics as well, gave this author his last remaining copy of *Rules for Radicals*, claiming it was no longer relevant. According to Frost, "I told Ernie [Cortes] he's now working out of another book. And I asked him just what is that book? Ernie said he's still writing it."[4]

This chapter is the story of that new book. It starts by examining the organizing efforts of Saul Alinsky in the working class neighborhoods of Chicago in the thirties. Considered the "father of community organizing" Alinsky was the first to attempt to mobilize industrial workers and their families into direct action where they lived, as opposed to where they worked. Although Alinsky's organizing projects scored impressive victories, most were short-lived or failed to maintain the progressive vision and participatory character upon which they were founded. Trained under the IAF in the early seventies, Cortes began organizing COPS using Alinsky's methods. Almost immediately, though, he began to revise Alinsky's approach. This chapter explores those changes, showing how Cortes and his colleagues in the IAF developed a new model of organizing to overcome the limitations of Alinsky's methods. The modern IAF would come to base its local organizations in the institutions and values of faith communities. Its organizers would become a permanent feature of local affiliates using relational organizing to reach beyond pastors to foster the participation of lay leaders. And the IAF would come to link these leaders across racial lines, attempting to build broad-based organizations that would help ensure a commitment to the common good, rather than narrow group interests. While Alinsky took a rather utilitarian view of churches as repositories of money and people to be mobilized, the modern IAF developed a close collaboration with people of faith, fusing religious traditions and power politics into a theology of organizing.

Saul Alinsky and the Origins of the IAF

Saul Alinsky founded his first community organization, the Back of the Yards Neighborhood Council (BYNC), on Chicago's southwest side in 1939.[5] Alinsky formed the organization both to support the union organizing drive of the Congress of Industrial Organizations (CIO) in the nearby stockyards as well as to address the broader needs of the impoverished community. Upton Sinclair had made the Back of the Yards neighborhood famous in *The Jungle*, his expose of filth and degradation in the largely immigrant community surrounding the meat packing industry. Catholic Bishop Bernard J. Sheil played a pivotal role in the creation of the BYNC by helping to convince local pastors to support the CIO unions and the new neighborhood organization. Although the community consisted of a diverse group of white ethnics, 90 percent of them were Catholics. Union leaders, small merchants and local churches worked together in the BYNC, using militant tactics—like sit-downs and boycotts—drawn from the CIO repertoire. Originally seen as a threat by Chicago's Democratic machine, the BYNC early on won many concessions from city hall to improve local services.[6]

After his initial success in Chicago, Alinsky wanted to extend his work to other parts of the country. Through the BYNC project, Alinsky developed a close relationship with Bishop Sheil and the philanthropist Marshall Field III. With their support Alinsky founded the Industrial Areas Foundation (IAF) in 1940 to raise money to assist his efforts to organize in other communities. The Industrial Areas Foundation owes its somewhat anachronistic name to BYNC's roots in the CIO tradition. It was meant to be a foundation that organized in the areas (neighborhoods) surrounding industry.[7]

Alinsky launched several organizing projects in the late forties and fifties. He began hiring and training organizers, setting up projects in Lackawanna, New York, Butte, Montana, and the Chelsea section of Manhattan. Alinsky also worked with Fred Ross to organize Mexican Americans in California through the Community Service Organization, where Cesar Chavez (later the president of the United Farm Workers Union) first trained as an organizer. Catholic pastors invited Alinsky to set up the Organization for the Southwest Council (OSC) to stem racial tensions and violence in southwest Chicago in 1959, and to start another project on the northwest side. Except for the Chelsea project which folded quickly, these organizations all scored significant successes.[8]

Alinsky received widespread public recognition in this period through his work with The Woodlawn Organization (TWO) on the black south side of Chicago. In 1960 a coalition of local ministers asked Alinsky to set up a community organization in Woodlawn, near the University of Chicago. Woodlawn had recently undergone dramatic racial turnover. Within the ten years between 1950 and 1960, Woodlawn's residents changed from being 86 percent white to 86 percent black. TWO represented an important new departure for Alinsky in two ways: Protestant churches supported an Alinsky project for the first time; and Alinsky attempted to organize in a large black community. TWO made use of picketing and boycotts to stop exploitative practices of local landlords and merchants. It also organized to stop plans by the city and the University of Chicago for urban renewal in Woodlawn. Drawing inspiration from the freedom rides in the South, TWO undertook a massive voter registration drive to force the city to give the group representation on a school board and on an antipoverty agency. Through its activities, TWO won improvements in sanitation, public health procedures, and police practices. TWO's victories became well-publicized. The publicity launched Alinsky onto the lecture circuit and generated many requests from local activists for Alinsky to come to their cities and start IAF projects.[9]

After hearing about Alinsky's work in Woodlawn, an interracial group of clergy invited Alinsky to organize in the black community in Rochester, New York. The African American community in Rochester had been largely excluded from employment opportunities at the massive Eastman Kodak plant there, and its neighborhoods were neglected by the city. With Alinsky's help, black clergy formed FIGHT (Freedom, Integration, God, Honor, Today). Alinsky appointed Edward T. Chambers, a white ex-seminarian who got his start with the IAF in Lackawanna, as the head of a staff of black organizers. Reverend Franklyn D. R. Florence, a dynamic black minister fresh from civil rights organizing in the South, became attracted to the potential of the Alinsky model for black power and became FIGHT's president. FIGHT eventually won a pledge from Kodak for a job recruitment and training program for African Americans. When the company reneged on this promise, Alinsky developed a new tactic. He launched a well-publicized campaign that succeeded in gaining control of stock proxies to pressure Eastman Kodak to fulfill its pledge.[10]

In order to expand his efforts, Alinsky set up a national institute to more systematically train organizers and neighborhood leaders. He appointed Ed Chambers who had cut his teeth with FIGHT's work in Rochester, to direct the institute, called by the Industrial Areas Foundation name itself. Moreover, through the Kodak experience Alinsky saw the need to develop allies among the middle classes, and even to organize them directly. In the early seventies he launched his last major initiative, the Citizen Action Program, as a broad metropolitan and multiclass organization to address rising concerns about pollution in Chicago.[11]

Saul Alinsky died in 1972, leaving an organizing legacy that inspired a wide range of populist efforts, from farm worker and welfare organizing to consumer advocacy.[12] Alinsky's legacy derived from the model of organizing he first elaborated in his 1946 book, *Reveille for Radicals*. Alinsky saw community organizations as political institutions with three basic characteristics: indigenous leadership and citizen participation; financial independence; and a commitment to defend local interests while avoiding divisive issues. Alinsky saw conflict as inherent in society, and his community organizations used confrontation as a means to gain recognition and forge compromises with power holders. Alinsky further elaborated his views on organizing in *Rules for Radicals*, published in 1971. In the midst of the highly ideological politics of the antiwar and Black Power movements, Alinsky argued that community organizations must base themselves on the self-interest of individuals and communities in a pragmatic and nonideological manner. These organizations should remain independent from parties and should not endorse candidates. Instead, they should focus on citizen participation through their own independent structures.

Alinsky gained a radical reputation through his efforts to empower the poor and because of his disruptive tactics. But he was not a revolutionary. Alinsky considered the political system, despite its corruption and bias toward the rich, to be open to change if people could organize to demand inclusion. Unfortunately, the only form of inclusion open to many poor communities was through the patronage machine of local bosses, like Mayor Richard Daley in Alinsky's Chicago. Alinsky sought to connect people to politics in a different way, by establishing independent political power. Through IAF organizations citizens could confront the machine and other public and private authorities and negotiate on behalf of their neighborhoods. The establishment of militant, independent organizations in poor communities represented a radical departure in American politics. But Alinsky's acceptance of power politics meant that he did not call for the transformation of the political system itself. He simply wanted to open the system up to a new interest group, that is, political organizations of the poor.

Alinsky insisted that political organizations should be based upon the existing social institutions of a community, like churches, block clubs, and small businesses. These institutions offered the necessary resources to build independent political power. They provided finances for the organization, respected institutional leaders who already had roots in the community, and an organized base of followers who could be mobilized by such leaders to participate in the militant tactics for which Alinsky was so well known. Alinsky's organizations in this period were really coalitions of organizations. Unions, block clubs, and small businesses joined churches to make up the Back of the Yards Neighborhood Council in Chicago, while the black organizations TWO and FIGHT consisted almost entirely of churches. Member institutions sent official representatives to organization meetings and conventions, where they debated formal resolutions and elected officers.[13]

Alinsky was not particularly interested in the culture and belief systems embedded in the churches he recruited. When Reverend John Egan, a Chicago priest who became a long-term supporter of the IAF, advocated more discussion of religious values within IAF organizations, Alinsky responded, "You take care of the religion, Jack, we'll do the organizing."[14] Nor did he often try to reach beyond the established institutional authorities to cultivate and sustain political leadership among the membership of these institutions. The job of Alinsky's organizers was to forge coalitions of institutions, get the projects up and running, and then leave, passing on the responsibility for organizational development to the institutional leaders.

Despite Alinsky's impressive achievements, and the significant legacy he left to American populist organizing, the local organizations he built largely failed to sustain themselves as participatory political institutions. After a string of early successes, Alinsky's first project, the Back of the Yards Neighborhood Council, was gradually taken over by a small group of leaders. The council degenerated in the fifties and sixties into a conservative organization, cooperating closely with Chicago's Mayor Daley. Although Alinsky had taken steps to promote interracial understanding in segregated Chicago, by the fifties the council had come to oppose black demands for racial integration of its neighborhood. In 1968, the council endorsed George Wallace for President, prompting Alinsky to comment, "this is why I've seriously thought of moving back into the area and organizing a new movement to overthrow the one I built twenty-five years ago."[15]

While Alinsky's projects in black communities did not become reactionary, they did lose their grass-roots participatory character. In the sixties, The Woodlawn Organization (TWO) on Chicago's south side became more involved in administering services to the community than in continuing to organize broad participation. TWO set up an innovative job-training program developed with gang leaders as well as an experimental school program. Opposition from the city eventually ended both programs. In the late sixties, TWO launched community development efforts. In a progression common to many activist organizations, as TWO moved toward economic development, it lost its more participatory side as well as its ability to be an independent community advocate.[16] Meanwhile, FIGHT in Rochester also shifted its efforts to economic development programs, taking on administrative responsibilities for these efforts. FIGHT suffered a factional struggle that debilitated the organization, which formally dissolved in the early seventies.[17]

By the early seventies, the IAF could count many individual successes, at least in the short run. But neither the local organizations it formed, nor the IAF itself, had found a way to establish long-lasting institutions that could sustain broad participation and an independent base of power for poor communities. When Alinsky died in 1972, he left a compelling organizing model that served to inspire a new generation of activists. But he also left a weak institution. At the time of Alinsky's death, the IAF had only two professional organizers and a secretary on staff.[18]

Upon Alinsky's death, Ed Chambers took over as director of the IAF, and began to make some significant changes to Alinsky's organizing approach. Chambers had worked for Alinsky in Lackawanna, Chicago, and Rochester, and had been the director of the IAF training institute when it formed in 1969. While Alinsky was the agitator and charismatic orator, Chambers was the classic organization man. To stabilize the IAF's precarious financial situation, Chambers moved to extend contracts with community organizations after the initial two to three year start-up period.

Alinsky, in *Reveille for Radicals*, had argued that the IAF should break its ties with these organizations after four or five years at the most. Chambers wanted to develop long-term relationships with local organizations, both to keep the flow of money into the IAF, and also because he thought community organizations needed the kind of extended training that the IAF could provide. Chambers also systematized the training of organizers themselves and promoted the professionalization of the occupation by upgrading pay. While Alinsky liked to run a one-man show, Chambers set up a cabinet of senior organizers to provide collective supervision to the IAF's efforts. In 1979 Chambers moved the IAF's headquarters to New York, after Cardinal Cody broke the ties between the IAF and the Archdiocese of Chicago that stretched back to the thirties.[19]

When Chambers established long-term contracts to supply organizers to local affiliates, he put the IAF on a new road that held out the possibility of mutual interaction and collaboration between professional organizers on the one hand and community leaders from local organizations on the other. Alinsky had an instrumental interest in the kinds of resources churches and other social institutions could provide to organizing efforts. The ex-seminarian Chambers, with his theological training, began to see religious leaders as more than the instruments for mobilizing resources. He thought their ideas and traditions might provide important values to sustain participatory politics. Although Chambers had the germ of these ideas in his head, the new model of organizing would be initiated in practice through the organizing work of Ernesto Cortes. Shortly after Alinsky's death, Cortes began to organize Communities Organized for Public Service (COPS) in San Antonio. Through that effort, and in coordination with Chambers and IAF efforts in other parts of the country, Cortes began to write the new book on organizing to which the banker Tom Frost alluded.

Communities Organized for Public Service (COPS)

Ernesto Cortes, Jr., arrived back to his hometown of San Antonio in 1973, fresh from his training in Alinsky's Industrial Areas Foundation. His goal was to build an organization to give voice to poor and working Mexican Americans in San Antonio's forgotten west and south sides. Within a few short years he and a group of committed Catholic clergy and lay leaders had built a powerful organization, which broke the Anglo elite's monopoly on political power in San Antonio. In the process, the modern IAF came to base its organizing work almost exclusively in religious congregations and to reach deeply into religious networks to build organizations based upon religious values as much as material interests. By doing so, the IAF began to build organizations meant to last and to maintain participation over time.

While Hispanics made up a majority of San Antonio's nearly one million residents by the early seventies, they were almost entirely excluded from political representation at city hall. The Good Government League (GGL), a small association of wealthy Anglos from the north side, had dominated city politics since the fifties and normally placed only one handpicked Hispanic representative on the city council it controlled. While concentrating on Anglo development on the north side, the city neglected Hispanic neighborhoods on the west and south sides of town. Roads there were often unpaved, sidewalks nonexistent, schools poor, and floods a common and deadly occurrence. Mexican Americans were concentrated in lower paying, mainly service occupations. The city displayed an old-fashioned colonial atmosphere, as the growing Hispanic community, reaching a majority of the city's population by 1970, remained a "sleeping giant."[20]

Cortes, however, thought the sleeping giant might be ready to wake up. Cortes had been involved in several efforts to mobilize San Antonio Hispanics in the sixties. In 1966 he worked to elect the Mexican American Johnny Alaniz to the Bexar County Commissioners Court. If Alaniz had won, a coalition between Hispanics and progressive whites would have become a majority of the court. But the city's elite used overtly racist advertising, picturing a black hand descending over San Antonio, to defeat the coalition.[21] The failures of political mobilization in the sixties led Cortes to seek training with Alinsky to find a more effective way to empower Hispanics. When he returned, the Good Government League was starting to show some cracks in its monolithic hold over the city. Builders and developers wanted to push the fairly passive city government to take aggressive action to support growth. Fed up with the old guard in the League, they backed independent candidates for mayor and city council in the 1973 election. Their candidates for mayor and several council seats won the election, signifying the possibility of new opportunities for Hispanic empowerment.

At first, Cortes followed Alinsky's methods and attempted to recruit to COPS a variety of neighborhood social organizations, including churches, PTAs, and social clubs. About twenty-five Catholic parishes, however, soon emerged as the bedrock of COPS, while the other institutions proved too unstable or unsuited for the ensuing political conflict. The Catholic Church hierarchy provided both funds and encouragement of pastoral support for COPS. Initial funding of $40,000 came from a variety of religious denominations, including Unitarians and Methodists. But the Archdiocese contributed $4,000 itself, with the Catholic Society of Jesus (the Jesuits) giving another $3,000. Meanwhile, the U.S. Catholic Bishops' funding agency for social action, the Campaign for Human Development, provided $15,000, beginning a long and consistent tradition of support for COPS and IAF affiliates in Texas and around the country.[22] As COPS became established, the largest part of its budget came from dues paid by member parishes, the funding principle followed by all IAF affiliates. Meanwhile, San Antonio's Archbishop Furey publicly endorsed the COPS effort and gave his blessing to priests who became active in the organization. Auxiliary Bishop Patricio Flores served on the sponsoring committee for the effort.

Support by the Archdiocese of San Antonio for COPS represented the culmination of several trends both in the larger Catholic Church and in the diocese of San Antonio. Vatican II heralded a greater openness in the church, encouraged lay participation, and pushed the church to address concerns for social justice and the plight of the poor.[23] In many ways the diocese of San Antonio was ahead of these trends. Archbishop Lucey had involved the diocese in social reform during his tenure from 1941 to 1968. Known as the "pink bishop," he lent support to labor strikes and school desegregation, and agitated for federal antipoverty money for San Antonio. Archbishop Furey, and Furey's personal secretary Grahmann (who later became Bishop of Dallas), continued Lucey's activist tradition through their support of COPS.[24]

In addition to the support of San Antonio's bishops, a movement of Hispanic clergy contributed to the development of COPS. Historically, the American Catholic Church served the religious needs of Mexican Americans in the Southwest through missions. Many San Antonio churches began as open-air meeting places. Church buildings and the consolidation of parishes came quite late, for many not until the fifties and sixties.[25] The diocese did not staff many of these parishes in the west and south sides, leaving those duties to religious orders. Several of these order priests would become early COPS leaders. In addition, the diocese ordained very few Mexican American priests, only seven in the 250 years up to the sixties.[26] During the sixties, however, Hispanic priests and seminarians began to organize themselves, forming a group called PADRES.[27] Members of PADRES in San Antonio wanted to initiate a diocesan presence in the west side, and they wanted the church to address the poverty and discrimination faced by Hispanics. Their titular leader was Patricio Flores, appointed Auxiliary Bishop of San Antonio in 1970 and Archbishop in 1977, the first Mexican American bishop in the United States. Supported by Bishops Flores and Furey, young Hispanic priests like David Garcia and Albert Benavides took up posts on the west side and became important leaders of COPS. They joined the Jesuit priest Edmundo Rodriguez, the pastor of Our Lady of Guadalupe Church on the near west side, who was Cortes' first ally when he arrived back in San Antonio.

Tapping the funds, legitimacy, and institutional leaders from the Catholic Church conformed to traditional Alinsky methods. But in organizing COPS, Cortes began to make a profound innovation. He went beyond the priests and the usually male presidents of parish councils and began to reach more deeply into the networks of lay leaders that spread out from the church. Parishes on the south and west sides served as the center for a variety of social activities. Cortes met with over one thousand residents active in some way in the community. He started with priests, got the names of potential supporters from them, and moved through the community. He recruited leaders, now mostly women, from the ranks of parish councils, fund-raising committees, and churchgoers who were active in PTAs and social clubs. Many were members of the Guadalupanas, a Catholic association of Hispanic women. Andres Sarabia, the first COPS president, and its last male president, was head of his parish council at Holy Family. Beatrice Gallego, the second COPS president, was a PTA leader and active in the Council of Catholic Women in St. James parish. These new COPS leaders were also different from the Hispanic activists with whom Cortes had worked in the sixties. They were not individual activists committed to the cause. Instead, they were connected to parishes and rooted in the dense networks of extended families and friends that constituted San Antonio's Hispanic neighborhoods. Rather than activists committed to the cause, COPS leaders cared primarily about the needs of their families and the religion that bound them together.

Reflecting on the early years of COPS, Cortes explains that "we tried to bust the stereotypes . . . to see leaders not necessarily as someone who could speak or persuade a crowd. We wanted to see leaders as people who have networks, relationships with other people." These leaders were often women, and many of them were excited about the opportunities the new organization offered. According to Cortes, "Many of the women leaders were real powerhouses in their private families. They had a lot to say about who does what. But that's not enough. The public side of them didn't get developed because they are invisible outside of the home. They may have gravitated to leadership in our organization because of the need to develop this aspect of their personality. We offered them the opportunity."[28]

Once Cortes found someone whom he thought had potential to be a COPS leader, he could be dogged in pursuit. He first met Beatrice Cortez at a parents meeting about the closing of a neighborhood school.[29] Mrs. Cortez was an office worker at the time, married to an electrician, and active in her church, St. Patrick's. She became angry when she heard that the San Antonio Independent School District planned to close her children's elementary school, as well as two others in the community. The school department planned to take the money saved by the school closing to help fund a new administration building. Mrs. Cortez came to a meeting to discuss the matter along with seventy other parents. Inexperienced in politics, and fearful of speaking out, Mrs. Cortez tried to avoid the organizer Cortes at the parents meeting. "There was a man, Ernie, sitting next to me at the meeting. He encouraged me to push for us to take some action. So I was asked to speak with school officials. But I was afraid because I had never spoken in public before. Ernie met me outside the meeting and pinned me down to agree to speak." The parents were not able to stop the school closing. But they did stop the construction of the new administration building and got the school department to use some of the money saved to reduce class sizes in other neighborhood schools. And Mrs. Cortez was hooked. "I told Ernie to teach me everything. I stopped being a victim. Now you know what's going on because you're making it happen. But the quid pro quo with COPS was that I had to bring my church into the organization." Along with other parishioners who became involved over the school issue, Mrs. Cortez did get St. Patrick's to join COPS. In 1981 Mrs. Cortez became COPS' fourth president.[30]

In COPS the IAF began to develop a strategy different from Alinsky's to recruit lay leaders, a strategy the IAF would come to call relational organizing. Rather than mobilize people around an issue, Cortes engaged people's value commitments to their community. He got community leaders to talk with each other about community needs first, before identifying an issue around which to act. Specific plans for action emerged out of conversations at the bottom, rather than issues identified by activists at the top. Relational organizing worked to bring community leaders together to find a common ground for action and to develop the capacity to act in the interests of the broader community.

By reaching beyond institutional leaders, the IAF unleashed the deeper capacities of the communities within these churches. Once women like Beatrice Cortez began to learn to assert themselves in public leadership, IAF organizations could become more dynamic and expansive. Compared to Alinsky's projects, which often stagnated eventually under the same small pool of institutional leaders, COPS had a method to create broader participation. By continuing to recruit from these networks, the IAF generated a continual stream of new leaders to bring fresh energy and new ideas into local organizations.

To unleash the leadership capabilities of these women, however, the IAF needed to innovate again. The organization could not be led by a coalition of official representatives from member social institutions, as Alinsky's organizations had been run. Room had to be made for the leadership of the lay parishioners Cortes was recruiting, many of whom were women traditionally excluded from official church positions. As a result,

COPS created a hybrid organizational form. Its members were institutions, that is, churches. But the organization was not a coalition, composed of institutional representatives. Its leadership was drawn more broadly from the membership of those institutions, and leaders operated together in a single organization. COPS' structure allowed member parishes and neighborhood leaders to take action for the needs of their own particular neighborhoods at the same time as the organization could also act with a single will, as something more than the sum of its parts.

Despite widespread poverty, San Antonio's Hispanic neighborhoods offered an especially rich social fabric upon which to ground IAF organizing. In part, segregation meant that it was difficult for upwardly mobile Hispanics to move out, so communities remained more intact as well as more diverse socio-economically.[31] Furthermore, San Antonio's Hispanic community drew its population mainly from rural Texas, not Mexico. In 1980 only 12 percent of San Antonio's Mexican Americans were foreign-born.[32] As new residents arrived in San Antonio, they often joined family or friends from the same hometown, people who could help them get established. With a modest amount of new immigration, San Antonio's Hispanic community maintained relatively stable social ties.

Hispanic cultural traditions like *compadre* and *comadre*, literally co-father and comother, also contributed to the strength of neighborhood networks. Parents appointed close friends as *compadre* and *comadre*, their child's godparents. Yet, as the name suggests, the relationship reflects and reinforces the tie between the natural parents and the godparents. The church serves as the nexus of these personal relations, as the godparents are selected for the child's baptism in the local parish church. By rooting COPS in churches, the IAF was able to tap the cultural and social resources of the wider community.

COPS mobilized its strong church base to challenge the power monopoly of the Anglo elite. In these early battles for recognition, COPS acquired a reputation for pursuing militant and confrontational tactics. COPS engaged in large-scale protests at city council meetings over flooding and drainage issues. It organized disruptive actions at local symbols of economic power, like the protests at Joske's Department Store and the Frost Bank described at the beginning of the chapter. Drawing upon the legitimacy of the bishop's blessing and the authority of supportive priests, COPS leaders mobilized church-based networks to these actions. Because COPS leaders were embedded in social relationships, they could consistently provide large turnouts of hundreds of Mexican Americans to these actions, something never accomplished before in San Antonio. The deep roots of COPS provided the power to back up the organization's demand for its $100 million counterbudget for infrastructural improvements and increased services to the neglected west and south sides of San Antonio.

The budget proposal represented an unprecedented demand from a community long excluded from access to power. San Antonio's public officials and business leaders were not accustomed to such an active and aggressive posture by the Hispanic community. But the militant tactics proved successful, and COPS began to win important victories.

While mass mobilization provided one key source of COPS' power, the organization quickly began to see the importance of voter turnout as well. In 1976 it allied with environmentalists to block the construction of a large shopping mall over the Edwards Aquifer, the city's only source of drinking water. By mobilizing their friends and neighbors, COPS leaders provided crucial votes to block the project and quickly became a force to reckon with on important public issues facing the city.[33]

The next year COPS threw its weight behind a revision in the city charter that would serve to help institutionalize its newfound power. Prior to the mid-fifties the Good Government League had been able to control the city council in part because all of the council members were elected citywide. Anglos outvoted Hispanics and African Americans to elect citywide candidates. Faced with a court suit, San Antonio held a referendum on a single member district plan for its city council in 1977. After some initial debate, COPS endorsed the plan and played an important role in turning out voters in the charter election that approved it. With Anglos overwhelmingly voting against the charter change, many observers credit COPS with supplying the margin of victory by mobilizing Hispanic voters.[34] In the first election under the district system in 1977, five Mexican American candidates and one African American won election, so that a majority of the nine member city council was no longer Anglo. With increased voting by Hispanics and sufficient support from Anglos and African Americans, Henry Cisneros won election in 1981 as the first Mexican American mayor of San Antonio since 1842 and the first Hispanic mayor of a large American city. Meanwhile, COPS expanded its role in determining city policy through its influence on the councilors elected from the five districts where it was concentrated.

COPS also enhanced its power through its intervention in the Community Development Block Grant (CDBG) program in San Antonio. The federal government had established this program to help fund city-authorized projects to promote community development. San Antonio had a particularly corrupt CDBG system at the time, in which officials went so far as to propose that federal funds be used for a golf course. COPS represented most of the neighborhoods that qualified for CDBG funds in the city, and it organized its parishes to present proposals for neighborhood improvement. Through extensive research and planning, backed up by mass mobilization to the public hearings mandated by federal regulations, COPS took control of the CDBG process from city planners. By leveraging its electoral base in five city council districts, COPS wielded tremendous influence over the council's final allocations and commanded the lion's share of CDBG benefits for its long-neglected parish neighborhoods. A study published in the early eighties shows that from the program's initiation in 1974 until 1982, $78.2 million, over half of all the CDBG funds allocated to San Antonio, went to projects specifically requested by COPS. The city approved 91 percent of the projects proposed by COPS.[35] A later study found that from 1974 to 1993, 69.9 percent of CDBG funds went to city council districts in which COPS organizes, with the great bulk of those funds going to projects supported by COPS.[36]

Although COPS kept Alinsky's nonpartisan principle, the organization became heavily involved in influencing elected officials through its base of voters. COPS would publicize the stands of candidates in relation to the organization's proposals and encourage people to vote. In votes crucial to organizational initiatives, COPS would register and actively mobilize voters. Success in those cases gave COPS influence over elected officials who feared that the organization's electoral power could be turned against them.

During this period the IAF institutionalized what came to be known as "accountability sessions." Originally these public meetings would be the venues at which candidates for office would be asked to support organizational initiatives. The candidates often had a chance to meet with IAF leaders prior to these meetings for discussion. But at the sessions themselves, officials would generally be limited to yes-or-no answers. As COPS mobilized supporters through its church base, candidates would face audiences of potential voters numbering in the hundreds, and sometimes thousands. After the meeting, COPS informed its supporters about the candidate's stand on the issues, thereby influencing the outcome of the election without a formal endorsement. If COPS had gained a public commitment from a successful candidate at an accountability night, the organization pressured the official to make good on that promise after the election. Once the IAF standardized this routine in COPS' electoral campaigns, it extended the format to all its large public actions in all its affiliates, whether the invited guest was a candidate for office, a current public official or a business leader.

City bonds came to represent another source of public funds for COPS' projects and, eventually, an important venue for building alliances. The state of Texas requires municipalities to hold elections for voters to approve the sale of city bonds. In its first major effort in a bond election, COPS demanded the large majority of the funds for its own projects— not without good cause as it did represent most of the neighborhoods with the greatest need. But COPS lost that 1978 bond election, as Anglos turned out in large numbers to defeat it. COPS learned from that defeat, and for the future, decided to negotiate bond packages that spread out funds more broadly at the same time as meeting COPS' most important needs. As a result, bond elections became a way for COPS to build alliances with development-oriented interests and city officials who wanted the city to fund capital projects. Since middle-class voters in established neighborhoods often resist the tax implications of large bond campaigns, COPS could supply the inner-city votes required to pass bond packages. In return, COPS got its share of these funds, as well as leverage for its other proposals. The 1980 bond election passed with such an alliance providing $21.6 million for drainage projects in COPS and other neighborhoods.[37]

COPS now had an organizing approach that proved powerful in gathering many kinds of resources for its neighborhoods. COPS combined careful research and planning by its leaders with large-scale mobilizations to public actions, and demonstrated its ability to turn out voters too when necessary to win its campaigns. With these methods, COPS secured funds from the county for health clinics, state funds for a community college on the south side, and federal money from the Department of Housing and Urban Development (HUD) for affordable housing programs. Many of these programs were quite extensive. By the mid-nineties COPS' programs had rehabilitated two thousand houses, built one thousand new homes, and assisted two thousand families in purchasing their first homes. By the organization's twentieth-anniversary convention in 1994, COPS had channeled to its neighborhoods close to $1 billion from a wide variety of sources.

Pragmatic and willing to compromise, COPS seldom made proposals beyond its political means, and consequently did not suffer many losses. But its most serious failures came when the organization, concerned that the needs of its constituents were being overlooked, attempted to oppose the plans of powerful developers—without proposing constructive projects of its own. Two defeats stand out. COPS became embroiled in a damaging protest effort against the marketing of San Antonio as a low-wage town by the city's Economic Development Foundation (EDF). The EDF and its business allies waged war on COPS, charging that the group had scared off a Midwestern manufacturing outfit that planned to open a plant in San Antonio. Eventually, the two sides signed a truce, but COPS' growing reputation as a constructive force in the city was damaged.[38] COPS' biggest outright defeat came in 1989 when it opposed the public financing of the Alamodome sports facility advocated by popular Mayor Henry Cisneros. COPS opposed such financing in part because it feared the dome would bring nothing but low-wage jobs to the area. After a contentious campaign, voters approved the dome in a referendum. Lured by its promise of jobs and major league sports teams, a majority of voters in COPS' own neighborhoods voted for the project.[39]

If anything, these defeats solidified COPS' commitment to pragmatic politics and the forging of alliances wherever possible. At the same time, COPS remained committed to its own independence and the development of an agenda to meet the needs of San Antonio's long-neglected Mexican American community. This tension between independence and pragmatic alliances would often prove difficult to handle, requiring greater political sophistication from COPS leaders. To the extent Tom Frost and other local elites had expected COPS to be a "flash in the pan" organization like many other urban protest groups, they underestimated the organization's potential to grow and develop.

The IAF's explicit emphasis on organization building helped COPS move from issue to issue. IAF organizers trained COPS leaders not to think primarily about the cause or the issue, but to consider whether that action would build the power of the organization. In this way, when an issue campaign was over, the organization could build upon the capacity generated in that campaign to begin to initiate another. Although streets and drainage concerns dominated the COPS' agenda in the early days, it was never limited to those issues. Meanwhile, COPS drew upon the shared history and culture of Mexican Americans,[40] but from the beginning, COPS insisted that its purpose was not to advocate for Hispanic causes or to work to elect Hispanics to office. In fact, COPS leaders object that their organization is wrongly perceived as Hispanic, even to this day. COPS co-Chair Virginia Ramirez complains that "other Hispanic organizations approach us to support Hispanic people for positions—like the president of the community college—and we say we support the most qualified. We don't care what color they are. We'll hold *all* accountable [emphasis hers]."[41]

There was yet another way that COPS' approach marked a clear change from at least some of Alinsky's projects and helped to sustain its participatory character. COPS did not administer the programs it campaigned for itself. COPS refused to accept any government money directly. Instead, COPS would allow public agencies to handle the administration, while its leaders carefully watched to make sure the programs went as planned. In the early days, when COPS' initiatives called mainly for the building of streets and libraries, it seemed natural to let other agencies administer the projects. But the principle COPS set early on continued later even when it began to launch much more complex initiatives, like the job-training program, Project QUEST, discussed in chapter 6. In these later cases, COPS maintained influence by sitting on the boards of these agencies, but still did not accept money or jobs for its leaders. When Alinsky's organizations—like TWO in Chicago and FIGHT in Rochester—shifted to economic development issues, they gradually lost their participatory and activist character, a phenomenon that has plagued many community development associations. Rather than administration, COPS organizers and leaders remain focused on organizing.

Although many of the Anglo elite in San Antonio despised COPS in its early days, by the end of the seventies the organization had earned a degree of grudging respect from them. In 1976, the San Antonio *Light* newspaper put COPS on its list of the ten most powerful groups in the city. In 1983, the San Antonio city council proclaimed a "COPS week" to honor the organization at its tenth-anniversary convention that year. The council publicly recognized the democratic contributions of the organization in its proclamation.[42]

Bringing Values and Interests Together

In 1976 Ernesto Cortes left San Antonio to begin an organizing project in the largely Mexican American community of East Los Angeles. He founded the United Neighborhoods Organization (UNO), which became a powerful community organization active in the IAF network to this day.[43] In the past, under Alinsky's direction, the IAF would have left COPS leaders on their own to continue their efforts upon Cortes' departure. But this time, in keeping with the new emphasis placed by IAF director Ed Chambers on continuing a financial relationship between affiliates and the organizing staff, the IAF sent organizer Arnold Graf to San Antonio.

While continuing a contractual relationship between the IAF and its local organizations contributed to keeping the IAF itself financially viable, it had a much deeper significance. It placed local affiliates and IAF organizers in a long-term relationship, where each could be influenced by the other. IAF organizers would now be present to ensure that its local affiliates did not violate the network's broad principles, as the Back of the Yards council did when it opposed efforts by Chicago's African Americans to integrate neighborhoods. Continual influence by an organizer connected to the larger IAF network helped to broaden the outlook of local leaders and expand their capacity for action. Moreover, having organizers who were accountable to a larger authority, the IAF itself, for the development of new leaders, made it less likely that local affiliates could become dominated by a small group of entrenched officials, a problem that also plagued Alinsky's projects.

Through their long-term relationship with people of faith, IAF organizers became interested in religious traditions in a way that Alinsky never did. Alinsky tried to motivate church members to political action solely through their practical self-interest, for example, in getting a school funded or city services provided. In the context of the highly ideological sixties, Alinsky wanted to stress that politics was not about doing good, or being right. A self-interested motivation may have been sufficient for the kind of short-term campaigns that Alinsky's projects pursued. But the IAF wanted to build institutions that would last for the long term, not rise and fall around one issue. To sustain people's participation, something more than self-interest would be necessary. The new IAF approach did not reject self-interest as one critical basis for political action. But the IAF began to see the possibilities for religion to provide a set of value commitments to combine with practical self-interest.

The new women leaders of COPS, like Beatrice Cortez, demonstrated the viability of this new approach to organizing. Mrs. Cortes and her colleagues appeared motivated to participate in COPS by something beyond self-interest. The closing of her child's school may have brought Mrs. Cortez into COPS initially. The power and status that came with her election to its presidency may have given her extra drive. But leaders like Mrs. Cortez talked about their involvement in faith terms, as part of their religious responsibility to the community. Meanwhile, if religion helped motivate leaders to action, that political experience deepened and clarified religious commitment. In discussing her participation in COPS, Mrs. Cortez recounts, "It gave more meaning to my faith. I could now relate scripture to my life. If you really care for your brother, compassion and courage become real. It's not anything you learn in school, church, or CCD [religious education]. So when we went to an action, we looked to the Bible for inspiration. That's the depth we want. We have a theology of housing!"[44]

Contact with the priests in COPS and UNO reignited Ernesto Cortes' earlier interest in theology. Cortes was raised in the Catholic Church and had begun to study theology seriously in graduate school. There he read mostly Protestant theologians, like Reinhold Niebuhr, Paul Tillich, Karl Barth, Dietrich Bonhoeffer and Harvey Cox. Cortes brought these theological concerns with him to IAF training in Chicago. But Ed Chambers was initially skeptical. An ex-seminarian himself, Chambers had been involved with the Catholic Worker movement in New York before allying with Alinsky. But he had adopted Alinsky's tough, secular brand of power politics. Nevertheless, now that he was at the helm of a weak IAF network, Chambers was open to considering Alinsky's limitations and trying new approaches. Chambers himself began to argue that political organizing should emerge from the intertwined values of family and religion.[45]

Back in San Antonio organizing COPS, Cortes developed close relationships with several Catholic priests, including Albert Benavides and the Jesuit Edmundo Rodriguez. Cortes began to study Catholic social teachings to combine with his knowledge of the Protestant social gospel. Cortes describes some of the excitement and tension in these discussions. "When I was organizing COPS, I would have these late-night discussions with Father Albert Benavides. I had read a book by S. G. F. Brandon—*Jesus and the Zealots*. And I'd throw out Brandon, and Benavides would come back at me saying Brandon didn't really know scripture and I didn't know what that meant. So I kept reading. Benavides and Father John Linskins of the Mexican American Cultural Center opened a whole world of scriptural scholarship for me. Toward the end of the COPS experience, I began to pull together some priests for once-a-week sessions to talk about organizing. And we'd talk about the philosophy of it and we'd push each other and talk about the theology of it. One of the priests got up one night and said, 'This is the only time we've ever talked about our own experience of God.' And he was angry with all of the other priests. It created a lot of tension and one of the old guys said, 'Next time, let's talk more organizing and less theologizing.' So we dropped it."[46]

When Cortes moved to East Los Angeles to organize the United Neighborhoods Organization, he continued his effort to ground IAF organizing in religious traditions, and to confront the tensions that arose in combining practical politics with faith ideals. He found many religious traditions that spoke powerfully about the obligations of people of faith to intervene in public life. Expressed in Old and New Testament stories, faith understandings proved powerful in motivating people to take action for community betterment. Father Benavides in San Antonio argued that religious symbols crystallized these traditions, but that IAF organizers could not draw from them in a utilitarian, "outsider" fashion. According to Cortes, "Albert [Benavides] brought home to me how important the symbols were to people, how deep they went. But it had to be their symbols, their stories. As an organizer, I had to be engaged and learning from them at the same time I was trying to teach."[47] In other words, an interpenetration of religion and politics was necessary.

Cortes and UNO priests developed a workshop that drew upon the stories of Pentecost and Sinai to strengthen lay leaders' commitment to the UNO effort. The Old Testament story of the exodus of the Jews from Egypt symbolized the need for hope in the face of despair and the commitment to build a new nation. According to the New Testament story of Pentecost, when Jesus' disciples met 50 days after his death, belief in his resurrection inspired them to build a church, that is, an institution for the community of religious believers. In the UNO context, these central events in people's religious traditions became symbols for the decision to draw from faith to take action to build a community.[48]

Over the course of the next twenty years, retelling stories from a largely Christian tradition and identifying potent symbols of community building became central organizing tools for the IAF. The IAF drew from Paul's letters to the Corinthians to emphasize the broader public role that people of faith should play. The story of Moses became a mainstay in IAF training. IAF trainers began to call Moses the first organizer and asked participants to draw lessons about leadership from his example.[49] As African American ministers became more involved in IAF efforts, they brought some new symbols and stories, like Ezekiel's prophecy of the valley of the dry bones, where a fractured people came together to rebuild a broken community. By the late seventies, the IAF had identified the key theme to which every story led: the need for people of faith to take public action to build community.

Stories drawn from the Bible inspired and directed lay IAF leaders towards political action, but more contemporary sources proved particularly important for attracting religious professionals. In particular, the ferment in Catholic social thought in the seventies motivated many priests and women from religious orders to get involved in the IAF. These women, including Sisters Christine Stephens, Maribeth Larkin, Pearl Ceasar, and others, became key organizers for the expanding Texas network. Catholic social thought emphasized that the root cause of evil lay in unjust economic and social institutions, and stressed the responsibility of the church to work for social justice. Catholic teachings therefore provided a way to link religious responsibility with the self-interest of poor communities, precisely what IAF organizing came to be about.

Maribeth Larkin of the Sisters of Social Service, for example, had been working in Hispanic parishes in East Los Angeles for several years, when Cortes and the IAF arrived. Frustrated with the complacency of many local priests, at the very time that Latin American Catholicism was alive with the energy produced by Liberation Theology, she became attracted to the UNO effort. She soon joined the IAF's staff, convincing her superiors in the religious order that community organizing was well within the Catholic tradition and within the order's mission to provide service for the poor. Larkin later moved to San Antonio to work with COPS and became a key part of the IAF's senior staff of lead organizers in the Southwest.[50]

In 1978 the IAF's national director, Ed Chambers, wrote *Organizing for Family and Congregation* to serve as a training guide for leaders and organizers involved in the IAF. In the pamphlet Chambers argued that religious values and self-interested political action could be combined in the IAF's theology of organizing in a way that enhanced both religion and politics. The document began with a Biblical quote, "God did not give us a spirit of timidity but a spirit of power and love and self-control" (II Timothy 1:7). It then discussed the social and economic pressures that place families under stress. The pamphlet highlighted the values of dignity, self-determination, and justice that can come from a religious tradition and be expressed through political action. Although religious institutions contribute essential values to politics, Chambers closed the document with what the IAF offers congregations in return: "In isolation, families and congregations have no chance. With the citizens' organization [the IAF affiliate] as a context and as an instrument, families and congregations can move with dignity and confidence into the arena of institutional power. Families and congregations can fight for their values. Families and congregations can win."[51]

Relational Organizing and Institution Building

IAF organizing in San Antonio built upon the strong social fabric of Hispanic Catholic communities and the viability of their parish institutions. But in East Los Angeles, the Hispanic communities were newer, more transient, and more fragmented. Lay leaders in UNO did not have the kind of well-established and expansive social networks available to COPS leaders.[52] The IAF could not simply mobilize existing networks, it had to build them as well. But this task was beyond the capacity of IAF organizers alone to accomplish. The IAF staff decided to try, for the first time, to train UNO leaders in relational organizing themselves. In other words, leaders learned how to conduct the individual, relationship-building meetings IAF organizers used to recruit leaders. UNO leaders began holding these meetings with each other, in order to deepen collective bonds, as well as with their fellow parishioners and neighbors, in order to forge broader support for the organization's efforts.[53]

In addition to individual meetings, UNO leaders also began conducting house meetings, which then became a standard part of IAF organizing as well.[54] Cesar Chavez had used house meetings to organize farm workers in California. The IAF realized such meetings could help bring disconnected community residents together to talk about common concerns and develop plans of action. House meetings and individual meetings became ways to strengthen community and undertake political action—and to link the two together for mutual benefit.

While Cortes faced the weakness of community social fabric in Los Angeles, he had to confront the fragility of church institutions upon his return to Texas in 1978. Alinsky's organizing methods were predicated upon the existence of a healthy social fabric as well as strong church institutions, but in Houston, the IAF faced strains in both. Organizing in Houston offered the IAF the opportunity to build a base in Texas' largest city, but would require a strategy to strengthen faith institutions, not just mobilize them.

In the mid-seventies a group of Protestant ministers in Houston, impressed by the success of COPS, invited the IAF to organize in their city. With backing from the Metropolitan Ministries, a mainline Protestant social services agency, the ministers hired former VISTA volunteer Robert Rivera to coordinate the effort. The Catholic diocesan chancellor Joseph Fiorenza also supported the effort, but the project fizzled, in part, under attacks in the press about "outside agitators." Fiorenza supported a renewed organizing project, eventually named The Metropolitan Organization (TMO), after he was appointed bishop of the San Angelo diocese.

Sister Christine Stephens became the chairperson of a reinvigorated sponsoring committee and began to rebuild the effort. A member of the Congregation of Divine Providence, Stephens came from a working-class family in Houston. Like Maribeth Larkin in Los Angeles, Stephens had been working with poor parishioners as a social worker. She had already been inspired by Catholic social thought's emphasis on action for the poor, heading the local office of the Catholic church's funding arm for empowerment groups, the Campaign for Human Development. Within two years Stephens recruited thirty-two churches and raised $200,000. The new TMO sponsoring committee convinced Cortes to return to Texas from East Los Angeles in 1978 to organize in Houston. Stephens soon joined the IAF's organizing staff and became Cortes' top organizer in the Southwest.[55]

In the late seventies Houston was a boomtown. Business dominated the city from its founding. And Houston was still run by a small group of economic elites, the heirs to the "Suite 8F Crowd," a group of powerful businessmen who met in suite 8F of the Lamar Hotel during the thirties. Business was used to getting its way in a city that had no zoning laws, poorly funded public services, and weak public institutions. But while much of Houston boomed in the seventies, a large part of its African American and rapidly growing Hispanic populations lived in poverty.[56]

Organizing in Houston posed a different kind of challenge to the IAF than it had faced in San Antonio. There, COPS operated in a relatively compact geographic area containing a well-established Hispanic community with a common history. But Houston was a huge, sprawling city that lacked many clearly definable neighborhoods with shared histories. Houston's Hispanic community was much newer, dispersed around the city, and quite diverse, as it included many Central Americans as well as Mexican immigrants.

African Americans in Houston's fifth ward did form a historic community. But, unlike the parish priests on the Hispanic west and south sides of San Antonio who were largely uninvolved in politics prior to COPS, black ministers in the fifth ward were deeply intertwined with electoral politics. They regularly endorsed candidates, supplying the votes of their members in exchange for some resources to their community. Although these resources were perhaps rather meager, many ministers feared the loss of any desperately needed funds that might come if they disrupted electoral relationships by joining the nonpartisan IAF effort. In San Antonio and East Los Angeles, the IAF worked to convince religious leaders to take their faith beliefs into political action. Houston's black ministers already did that. The IAF had to convince these ministers to engage their faith traditions in a different kind of politics and in an untested organization. For many African American ministers, the IAF represented a gamble. Moreover, although many admired the IAF's achievements in COPS, they saw the organization as one committed primarily to Hispanics.

In Houston, though, the IAF effort did have one unusual source of strength in its efforts to build a base in the black community. Many African Americans had come to Houston from Louisiana and so were Catholics. With the strong backing of Houston's Bishop John Markovsky, TMO attracted several black Catholic churches along with Hispanic Catholics and Anglo Protestants. TMO made it a point to address concerns in the black community, developing campaigns to improve public safety in the fifth ward, for example. And TMO began to have a number of small, but important victories in fighting high electric bills, improving public transportation, and combating drugs in school. Eventually some black Protestant ministers, like the Methodist Robert McGee, saw the benefits of TMO to the black community and took the first steps toward involvement.[57]

In Houston the IAF faced the problem that many of the individual religious institutions within TMO were weak. They had too few members, insufficient finances, and a small leadership base, which often barely extended beyond the pastor and a few key church officials. In the late seventies and eighties economic restructuring and middle-class exodus served to concentrate poverty and undermine community life in inner-city communities across the country. Although the Texas economy boomed in the seventies, when the oil crisis hit in the early eighties, IAF organizing throughout the state had to confront the rapid deterioration of social institutions. For IAF organizing to succeed, it could not assume the existence of healthy base institutions. Although the IAF had always argued that political action would redound to the benefit of communities, it now had to pay closer attention to institution building within communities.

In response to these conditions, the IAF offered the services of its organizers for "parish development." The term reveals its Catholic roots, but was meant to apply to churches in all denominations. While Alinsky seldom dared to intervene directly in religious affairs, IAF organizers now began to work directly with interested pastors to help build their congregations. The parish development process represented an organizing effort to articulate and unite the congregation around the institution's goals and purposes, strengthen church finances, and bring forth new lay leadership to expand church activities. To accomplish these goals, IAF organizers used the network's relational organizing technique of conversation leading to action. Parish development processes helped to identify new leaders, build a consensus, and forge collective leadership for the church.

The practical demand for parish development squared well with Catholic social teaching. Catholic social thought long stressed the central role of the parish church as a mediating institution to connect families to public life. Church institutions were to play a critical role in protecting the family in the face of state and market forces. Moreover, such institutions linked private and public life. According to Catholic social thinking, people could only achieve their full dignity and humanity through relationships in community, relationships structured by Catholic institutions.[58]

Although the Catholic Church had served as a mediating institution to help incorporate generations of European immigrants into American society and public life, the IAF feared the church was now abandoning that historic mission. IAF organizers and TMO leaders, therefore, began to draw from Catholic social teaching to present a vision of parish development that pointed the church towards a broader public role. In TMO's parish development document, they quoted approvingly from Philip Murnion, executive director of the U.S. Catholic Bishops' Project for Parish Renewal:

> Authentic parish life must "enable people to enter into public life and social questions and must offset temptations to retreat from social responsibility into a privatized, pietistic religion;" it must "provide ways for people to be critical of their common lives and culture;" it must "foster mutual support, a sense of personal responsibility for one another;" and finally, parish development "must be about the development of a people with a sense of common life, shared identity and enduring loyalty." . . . the church has an obligation to encourage and foster social responsibility, to transform the world in the direction of justice and to contribute to the hastening of the kingdom of peace.[59]

Not all Catholics, however, accepted the IAF's challenge to engage the church in political action. The IAF effort in Houston nearly collapsed when a prominent group of wealthy and conservative Catholics opposed the church's involvement in TMO. Led by George Strake, later the chairman of the state Republican Party, the group tried to squash the IAF effort. Bishop Markovsky, however, held firm in his support and the effort continued.[60]

TMO held its founding convention in 1979, giving the IAF its second affiliate in the state of Texas. At its height, TMO had sixty congregations representing about 75,000 families. Despite the gains made from parish development work, TMO struggled with Houston's sprawling size and weak neighborhoods. It simply could not achieve the kind of power and prominence that COPS had attained in San Antonio.

Building Broad-Based Organizations

While the IAF experimented with multiracial and interfaith organizing in Houston, COPS was struggling to break out of the confines of the Hispanic west and south sides of San Antonio. By the late seventies COPS had established itself as a powerful player in San Antonio politics and won many improvements for its neighborhoods. COPS' strength derived from its dense organization in Hispanic neighborhoods, where about half of the city's population lived. By confining itself to the Hispanic west and south sides of the city, however, COPS could not reach the other half of San Antonio's population. That meant that no matter how much political power COPS could generate in its neighborhoods, the organization could never attain a large enough base to influence a majority of city councilors. Moreover, San Antonio's growth centered on the north side, away from COPS' neighborhoods, so that the organization's power base was destined to erode over time.

In the late seventies the IAF began to look beyond the Hispanic west and south sides of San Antonio to build a base among African Americans concentrated on the city's east side. Conditions seemed ripe for organizing among African Americans. The predominantly black east side suffered from high levels of poverty and had, like the Hispanic west and south sides, been long neglected by the city government. Moreover, many black pastors were tremendously impressed by the accomplishments of COPS. In fact, they were jealous of growing Hispanic power. In their eyes, COPS was an organization that really worked to bring power to poor people of color, but it was all going to Mexican Americans.

Perhaps even more so than in Houston, however, African American Protestants in San Antonio were hesitant to become part of an IAF operation they saw as Hispanic and Catholic. African Americans constituted a relatively small share of the city's population, about 8 percent. Since COPS was so big and powerful, many black pastors feared they would be dominated by the Hispanic giant and that their concerns as African Americans would be ignored by the IAF. Many important Baptist ministers, like Reverend Claude Black of the Mt. Zion First Baptist Church, spoke highly of the IAF, cooperated with COPS on occasion, but stayed outside of the organization. Many of these ministers hoped to build their own black church-based network instead.[61]

In order to give the black community more independence and autonomy within the IAF, the network decided to build a separate organization for San Antonio's African Americans, founding the East Side Alliance (ESA) in 1983. Although this tactic helped assuage the most immediate fears of African Americans that they would be dominated by the Hispanic COPS, the fundamental problem remained. As in Houston, the IAF looked to black Catholics for ESA's initial base because they shared a common religion with the Hispanic community. Holy Redeemer, the one black Catholic church in San Antonio, became the bedrock church of the ESA. Other black Protestant churches did join from time to time, but the ESA did not succeed in penetrating the core of black Protestant churches on the east side.

IAF efforts to expand its base to the more affluent north side of San Antonio posed another set of issues, those of class and denomination. In 1980, the IAF formed the Metropolitan Congregational Alliance (MCA) among mainly white, and to a lesser extent Hispanic, congregations on the north side. The IAF's theologically based organizing appealed to many clergy and lay leaders in these congregations, both Anglo as well as Hispanic, Protestant as well as Catholic. The religiously motivated MCA leaders, however, struggled to tap the self-interest of their relatively affluent congregants. Although Anglos constituted a minority of San Antonio's population, they monopolized the higher occupational positions and lived in areas with relatively good infrastructure and city services. As a result, many Anglos, reaping the benefits of development, did not see a reason to participate in the MCA. To them, the IAF was for poor Hispanics.

Despite the obstacles each organization faced, MCA and ESA persisted and won victories on a number of issues.[62] In the late eighties MCA and ESA merged into the Metro Alliance, making one stronger organization. Metro Alliance became a triracial organization, roughly one-third each Anglo, Hispanic, and African American. Composed of Catholic, Methodist, Unitarian, Episcopalian, Lutheran, and Baptist denominations throughout the east side and north side of San Antonio, Metro Alliance covered (albeit sparsely) the five city council districts outside of COPS areas.

In the nineties, the IAF moved to bring COPS and the Metro Alliance closer together by having the two organizations work cooperatively on a number of major campaigns, like the job-training initiative Project QUEST discussed in chapter 6. By 1994, the two organizations cooperated on almost all major campaigns, sharing a lead organizer and office space. Cooperation between COPS and Metro Alliance built upon the strengths of both organizations while mitigating against their weaknesses. It provided a way for COPS to break out of its geographic, religious, and racial constraints in order to amplify its power throughout the city. Without giving up its independence, the Metro Alliance gained the political muscle of COPS to make its efforts more successful.

The weaknesses of organizations formed separately by race and neighborhood in San Antonio, and the subsequent difficulties of uniting them, taught the Texas IAF an important lesson. From now on, the IAF would establish its Texas affiliates as what it called broad-based organizations. All organizations would now be metropolitan-wide and multiracial, more representative of the population as a whole. The IAF had the opportunity to try out this new strategy almost immediately in Fort Worth when a multiracial group of ministers, including for the first time a prominent contingent of African American Protestants, approached the network for help.

In Fort Worth, several African American Baptist ministers had been meeting with white Protestant ministers and priests in the Hispanic community, discussing the possibility of establishing a cooperative political organization. After looking into several different community organizing networks, they decided to invite the IAF to help them begin organizing. The group founded Allied Communities of Tarrant (ACT) in 1982. For its part, the IAF was attracted to the possibilities in Fort Worth because it could begin its organization there with an interfaith group of clergy representing all three main racial groups in the city. The twenty-five or so congregations in ACT included African American Baptists, Hispanic Catholics, and Anglo Lutherans and Disciples of Christ.

Diversity gave IAF affiliates like ACT a source of energy, creativity, and power. But building them sharply posed the question of how to unite people from very different traditions. If IAF affiliates were to be mediating institutions through which people of different social backgrounds could come together, the IAF's relational organizing strategy had to meet the challenge of developing new relationships, bridging social capital, where little or none existed before. With the formation of ACT, however, the Texas IAF had at least established the principle that all its organizations would be broad based and strive to reflect the multiracial character of their localities.

Conclusion: A Synergy of Faith and Politics

By the early eighties Cortes and the IAF had written a good part of that "new book" to which the San Antonio banker Tom Frost referred at the beginning of this chapter. This book revised Alinsky's model of organizing in a number of significant ways, allowing the IAF to build and sustain local organizations with broad participation in a growing number of cities across Texas. The new model served as the framework for the modern IAF's organizing efforts across the country and pushed community organizers in other networks to take faith, values, and relational organizing seriously as well.

Alinsky essentially followed a traditional interest-group model of politics. His genius was to take organizing into poor communities and to play no-holds-barred power politics. His method involved identifying an issue and mobilizing a community's resources to fight hard to win. Successful as he was in winning issues, Alinsky was never able to build organizations that sustained broad participation over time. Instead, a few ministers, civic association presidents, and other institutional representatives eventually came to dominate the organizations, moving them towards program administration, if not in more conservative directions.

In San Antonio, Cortes began to reach beyond institutional leaders into the social fabric of the churches on the west and south sides of the city. He chose not to start with an issue around which to mobilize. Instead, he asked lay leaders to talk among themselves to identify their concerns and find a basis for cooperative action. By doing so, he unleashed the capacity of indigenous leaders, particularly women who were immersed in and often responsible for community life. These women cared about their families, their communities, and their faith as much as about any particular issue. Where Alinsky emphasized self-interest, and saw his base religious institutions solely as repositories of hard resources like money and people, the IAF began to take faith traditions, and the relational strengths of women lay leaders, seriously.

IAF organizers began to talk about two kinds of power, unilateral and relational, a distinction it took from Bernard Loomer.[63] Unilateral power represents "power over" others, the kind of power Alinsky generated in his projects. But the new IAF sought to create relational power as well, that is, the "power to" act collectively together. The Texas IAF organizations were not the simple interest groups Alinsky formed to mobilize resources to win an issue. Instead, they built social capital, that is, cooperative relationships, to create a more expansive form of democratic participation. The IAF has not ignored interests or power politics. Instead, it has added the "soft arts" of relational organizing in order to combine values with interests, community building with political action.

While the faith/politics and values/interest combinations proved powerful in founding and sustaining IAF organizations, they were not without their inherent tensions. Too strong an emphasis on faith and values led to idealism, and the failures experienced even by the COPS powerhouse in San Antonio—against the Alamodome for example. Too much emphasis on interests and pragmatic politics, however, led to alliances with development interests that some found unappealing. Metro Alliance leader

Homer Bain, a United Methodist minister, expresses the tension in religious terms: "there is always a balance of grace and works. If you don't have grace, you'll burn out. A religious background keeps you going, so you're not just dependent on winning and losing. But if you get too preachy, Pearl [IAF organizer Ceasar] will get upset."[64]

Another kind of tension between faith and politics resulted in religious opposition to IAF organizing. Houston would not be the only place where Catholics were divided over the appropriate role for the church. In the eyes of IAF participants, scripture, correctly understood, pointed to a public role for the church through IAF political organizing. But some conservative Catholics took a different view, a subject returned to at the beginning of the next chapter.

Despite the tensions, the IAF was able to build a powerful synergy between faith and politics, and other community organizers around the country began to take notice. The Pacific Institute for Community Organizing (PICO), led by organizers trained in the Chicago Alinsky tradition, had built a number of organizations along the west coast that pursued issue-based and neighborhood organizing. By the early eighties, the PICO network was stalled, plagued by organizational instability and lacking the power to tackle the bigger issues its communities faced. Inspired by the IAF's success with value-based organizing, as well as other examples of progressive religious involvement in political action, PICO transformed itself in the eighties into a faith-based network, along the IAF lines. According to Richard Wood, who has studied the network closely, PICO's transformation led to a dramatic increase in organizational power. In Wood's view, however, PICO's gains did not come through a parasitical relationship with churches, rather through a symbiosis. Wood argues that faith-based approaches create a relationship between religious culture and political organizing which "allows churches to make their ethical and democratic values active in the public realm, without undermining the moral community that sustains those values."[65]

Through its organizing the IAF also began to establish an institutional structure to mitigate against the kind of narrowness that plagued Alinsky's projects, which, at the extreme, led the Back of the Yards Neighborhood Council to degenerate into a racist organization. A foundation of religious caring for the community gave IAF organizations stability, so that they could persist beyond one issue and build their capacity over time. Meanwhile, the IAF organizers, permanently attached to local organizations, served as a counterweight against domination by narrow groups of leaders. In addition, the IAF began to build organizations in Texas that reached beyond one constituency, whether by neighborhood or race. Broad-based organizations required leaders from any one community to broaden their perspectives as they attempted to cooperate with people from other traditions.

Here again, the effort to establish broad-based organizations was not without its problems and tensions. In the early eighties, the Texas IAF had taken its first serious steps to incorporate African Americans and Anglos along with Hispanics, and Protestants along with Catholics. But it was hardly a truly multiracial and interfaith effort. Despite some successes, the IAF struggled to connect its theology of organizing with Protestant African Americans in Houston and San Antonio. Chapters 4 and 5 return to this question and explore how the IAF worked to transform itself into a more fully diverse network with significant African American leadership.

––––––––––

This chapter began with the story of George Ozuna's trip with his grandmother to Joske's Department Store in 1975. The Ozuna experience illustrates the ability of the Texas IAF to create a political institution through which families can sustain a commitment to their community through several generations. COPS proved capable of engaging not just the Ozuna grandmother, but her daughter Patricia who became a COPS co-chair and Patricia's son George himself—the boy who accompanied his grandmother to COPS' first big protest action.

After graduating from high school, George Ozuna went off to college at the University of Texas in Austin. While some of his friends searched for a new life in the suburbs, George returned to the south side of San Antonio. As a result of the work of COPS and others, the community seemed to George to be moving forward. Rather than escape the neighborhood, Ozuna wanted to be part of its growth and development. He began to teach high school. Five years later he ran for the school board—and lost. "Losing was the best thing that could have happened to me. I wanted to change things, but was too stupid to see there were people already doing things and doing them more effectively than I could by myself."[66] After attending a COPS meeting about school reform, George became active in the organization. "It was like a machine that stripped away bullshit. I spent five and a half years in the schools and didn't have a clue about *real* politics [emphasis his]!" George became the head of the south side cluster of the organization's parishes and later led the development of Brighton Park, a model affordable housing project in his parish of Saint Leo's.

George's mother, Patricia, followed her son into COPS. She exhibits the combination of relational skills, religious faith, and a healthy dose of Alinsky's fighting spirit that characterize many COPS leaders today. A school secretary, Mrs. Ozuna spent many years campaigning for Hispanic candidates in the trenches of the south side of San Antonio. Looking for a more effective way to improve her community, and impressed by her son's accomplishments through COPS, she joined the organization and eventually became a COPS co-chair. Ozuna responded both to the IAF's appeal to her faith as well as its brand of hard ball politics. Ozuna reports that two things keep her going, "anger at injustice and that I'm doing the Lord's work. It's my ministry for social justice." She emphasizes, though, a further reason for her continued involvement, declaring, "I like banging heads!"[67]

Three

Beyond Local Organizing: Statewide Power and a Regional Network

The "Pentecost" of the Texas IAF

"¡EPISO no, Christo si!" chanted a group of conservative Catholics outside a meeting of the El Paso Inter-religious Sponsoring Organization (EPISO).[1] *The chant had become the rallying cry of a well-organized effort to oppose the IAF's incipient drive to establish a new affiliate, EPISO, in El Paso, Texas, in the early eighties. Working with El Paso's business and government elite, which saw the emergence of EPISO as a threat to their monopoly on political and economic power, the "¡EPISO no, Christo si!" group tried to crush the new IAF effort before it could take hold among the city's vast Hispanic community.*

Sitting on the border with Mexico, El Paso was the poorest of America's large cities. Nearly 70 percent of its 425,000 residents in 1980 were Mexican American. Like San Antonio before the founding of COPS, the city exhibited an old-style colonial air, with Hispanics unorganized and largely excluded from any meaningful share of political power. With the backing of the Catholic bishop and support among United Methodist and Episcopal clergy, the IAF had been slowly building a base among Mexican American parishes. When the local television station aired a San Antonio broadcast entitled "Is COPS Coming to Your Neighborhood?," El Paso's elite was galvanized into action to crush the incipient effort. Conservative Episcopalians mobilized to join the "¡EPISO no, Christo si!" Catholic group. They demanded a meeting with Episcopalian Bishop Richard Trelease. Trelease found himself isolated within his church and pulled out his backing for the IAF effort, withdrawing a $25,000 pledge. Meanwhile the local press carried out a negative publicity campaign, questioning whether the group consisted of "outside agitators" and communists. Protesters arrived to disrupt EPISO meetings.

Although the IAF had faced opposition before, this time it looked like its organizing effort was going to collapse. Although the Catholic bishop held firm in his support, pastors and lay leaders were scared.

EPISO lost eighteen of its twenty member congregations, and it appeared that EPISO did not have enough strength within El Paso to survive. It occurred to the IAF staff in Texas that, for the first time, they might be able to use the influence of the more established IAF affiliates in other Texas cities to help EPISO survive. The 1982 gubernatorial race provided the opportunity.

As EPISO battled for survival, Mark White and Bill Hobby, the 1982 Democratic candidates for governor and lieutenant governor, faced a close election. Searching for a way to mobilize the Hispanic and black voters that might provide the margin of victory, the candidates appealed for support from the IAF. COPS had proved that it could mobilize up to 50,000 Hispanic voters, enough by itself to spell the difference in a tight state election. And the emerging network had two other affiliates in San Antonio (ESA and MCA), as well as TMO in Houston, a new effort in Fort Worth (ACT), and an organizing project in the lower Rio Grande Valley (Valley Interfaith). But the candidates were used to more traditional interest groups who openly endorsed candidates; they were somewhat suspicious of the nonpartisan IAF. Moreover, Hobby, a moderately conservative Democrat who came from Houston, was not convinced that TMO had much support. But TMO impressed Hobby by turning out one thousand supporters to an accountability night for candidates that he attended.

White and Hobby subsequently asked the IAF to conduct a "get out the vote" drive for them. The IAF's supervisor, Ernesto Cortes, agreed to conduct a drive that informed its supporters about all of the candidates' stands on issues relevant to the IAF, something the network planned to do anyway, but not to endorse the candidates. Such a drive, however, would likely redound to the benefit of White and Hobby who had taken favorable stands on IAF issues. In exchange, the IAF demanded, among other things, that Hobby attend an EPISO rally if the slate won. The candidates agreed and, subsequently, the entire Democratic slate swept to office.

Hobby kept his promise and planned a trip to El Paso. The arrival of the newly elected lieutenant governor in El Paso gave tremendous legitimacy to the besieged IAF effort. The mayor and local elected officials, who had ignored or opposed EPISO, now requested representation at the rally EPISO organized for Hobby. With this new found legitimacy, EPISO mobilized fifteen hundred supporters to the public meeting and the rally was a great success. According to IAF organizer Robert Rivera, who had arrived in El Paso in the midst of the crisis in 1982, "the right-wing was just not given the same credibility after the rally. The press stopped covering the anti-EPISO protesters. The crisis was over. And EPISO at last began to concentrate

on developing leaders, recruiting new churches, and increasing His-
panic voter registration, which in 1983 was only 37 percent of its
potential."[2]

Saving EPISO had an impact far beyond El Paso because it taught
the IAF that the emerging state network had power beyond its locali-
ties. According to IAF organizer Christine Stephens, "for the first
time, we could use our statewide network in a useful way. Without
the network connect, we would have lost EPISO. Ernie [Cortes]
began to realize that we could use the network. Up to that time, we
all were limited to our cities. . . . This was the Pentecost of the Texas
network."[3]

THE IAF had long felt the need for greater political power than could be
amassed by one local organization. Many local problems required greater
resources and more complex programs that could only come from a
higher governmental level. Saul Alinsky was never able to build a network
that was more than a very loose collection of independent local organizing
projects. Similarly, community-based efforts across the country have been
hampered by their restriction to the local level. Advocacy groups often
operate at state and national levels. But they lack the participatory base
that comes from active local chapters, the kind of deeply rooted local
organizations the IAF was building in Texas.

What's missing is a way to link local organizing to pursue united action
at higher levels in a way that redounds to the benefit of local efforts.
During the eighties the Texas IAF began to construct a federated institutional framework for such a symbiotic process. The network drew from
the principle of subsidiarity that it found in Catholic social thought to
help frame the relationship between local- and higher-level authority.
Pope Pius XI first enunciated the principle of subsidiarity in the encyclical
Quadragesimo Anno, no. 79, where he stated, "it is an injustice and at
the same time a grave evil and disturbance of right order to assign to a
greater and higher association what lesser and subordinate organizations
can do. For every social activity ought of its very nature to furnish help
(subsidium) to the members of the body social, and never destroy and
absorb them."[4]

The IAF applies the principle of subsidiarity in a way that gives priority
and ultimate authority to local organizations. In that way it differs from
the Catholic application of the principle within the Church, where the
Pope reserves the authority to dictate to lower levels on many questions.
In fact, the principle of subsidiarity hardly specifies the exact relationship
between lower and higher authority. The proper balance has been hotly
contested in Catholic circles, with the current Pope attempting to extend

his authority into many local and national affairs. He has worked to suppress Liberation Theology in Latin America and to push Catholic-affiliated universities to more strongly emphasize their Catholic identity.

As applied by the Texas IAF, the subsidiarity principle meant that local organizations would undertake the primary organizing work and retain ultimate authority over their affairs. The state network could not dictate to local affiliates. But leaders from these local organizations would meet together to build relationships, that is, social capital that bridged across localities. In the state network, locally rooted leaders could work to find a common ground for concerted action, launching campaigns that, in turn, would support and expand their local initiatives.

State-level organizing, however, required a greater degree of centralization to initiate and coordinate campaigns because participants were a step removed from the possibility of daily face-to-face interaction. To unite the network, Cortes began to build an institute for organizers in Texas and then in the expanding southwest region of the IAF. While IAF organizers under Alinsky operated as "one man shows," Cortes proceeded to forge a collective staff, a large and sophisticated corps of organizers.

This chapter charts the development of the Texas IAF network. The first part of the chapter examines the evolution of IAF campaigns at the state level. The second half concentrates on the IAF's efforts to build an institute for organizers in Texas and to expand the network across the southwest. Much of the discussion of developments within the network relies primarily on interview material, that is, reconstructions of the past drawn from IAF participants, verified independently where possible.

Early Statewide Efforts

The Texas IAF began to face the limits of local organizing in the early eighties when several of its affiliates attempted to launch campaigns around utility rate issues. The ACT affiliate in Fort Worth tried to oppose a 1982 rate increase pursued by the local electric company, Texas Utilities. EPISO in El Paso also sought to intervene in a rate increase that year as well. But utilities were regulated at the state level by an agency with little history of responsiveness to local consumers.

Frustrated by the IAF's impotency at the local level, the network decided to call leaders of all the Texas IAF affiliates together to discuss a statewide strategy for utility reform. Working with the IAF staff, leaders from ACT, EPISO, COPS, and MCA in San Antonio, and TMO in Houston, developed a seven-point proposal for reform. They met with industry experts, utility company executives and public officials to hone their proposal. Its key provision called for an Office of Public Utility Counsel to represent consumer interests.

For the utility campaign, the IAF developed a strategy for political action at the state level that has continued to this day. The IAF strategy involved three parts. Local leaders would lobby their own elected representatives in their home turf. The IAF staff and a smaller number of leaders would travel to Austin to meet and negotiate with key public officials, and to build alliances with other political actors. And the local affiliates would mobilize their supporters for bus trips to the state capital in Austin for large-scale shows of strength to influence votes in the legislature. The fact that the Texas state legislature meets part time, holding a session only once every two years, allowed the network to concentrate its resources for state campaigns into limited time periods. In their first effort of this kind, the nascent Texas network scored a victory when the legislature approved six of the seven points in the IAF utility program, including the creation of a public counsel.[5]

Although the IAF proved victorious on utility reform, the network received little public attention for its efforts because the campaign had been fairly low profile. In 1983, however, the IAF became involved in a very high profile effort to reform education at the state level. Community leaders in IAF affiliates had long expressed great concern about the state of schooling in their communities. Their neighborhood schools were underfunded and struggling. Local efforts to improve schools had come up against the shortage of funds available in poor districts. During 1981 and 1982, several Texas IAF affiliates, including COPS and the emerging organization in the Rio Grande Valley (Valley Interfaith), began to investigate school financing and to call for efforts to equalize educational funding in the state. During the 1982 state elections, they pressed candidates for commitments of support. The Sunday after Governor Mark White's election in November of 1982, he attended the COPS convention as promised. There, under pressure from COPS, he pledged to work for more equalized educational funding.

Pressure for education reform was mounting from many quarters in Texas. In the first legislative session after his election, Governor White appointed a select committee headed by H. Ross Perot to consider a number of proposals, primarily to raise standards and increase funding for poor schools. The IAF network decided to enter the process, hoping to influence the reform package. The IAF had something to offer Perot, as it provided grass-roots support to the elite-dominated process. Although there were other representatives of low-income groups involved, the IAF was the only one with an organized base. The network had spent the past two years educating that base in the intricacies of school finance, starting with house meetings and moving up to statewide meetings. Meanwhile, the IAF had been building relationships with state officials like White, Lieutenant Governor Hobby,[6] and House Speaker Gib Lewis, all of whom would play key roles in the reform process. By the time the legislature opened its special session on school reform in 1984, the Texas IAF had crafted its own proposals, concentrating on the equalization of funding.

Cortes and top IAF leaders met with the Perot committee and agreed on a compromise package, which was submitted as House Bill 72 in a special legislative session. The IAF affiliates worked in their local communities to build support for the bill both in their congregations and among a wider group of civic, political, and business leaders. Moreover, IAF leaders aggressively lobbied state legislators from their districts. IAF leaders came to legislative hearings in Austin to tell their own personal stories of poor educational opportunities. Local IAF affiliates brought thousands of supporters to rallies in the state capital in support of the bill.

The IAF's ability to mobilize its supporters proved crucial to the eventual passage of the package. On Father's Day, the House Public Education Committee rejected the reform package. Immediately after the vote killing the bill, which reform supporters dubbed "the Father's Day massacre," Perot's associate Tom Luce asked Cortes for help. Fortunately, the IAF had prepared to mobilize on short notice. It managed to bring several thousand supporters to a rally at the state capital the very next day. The size of the rally, its timing, and the strong sentiments expressed by its participants, turned the tide in the legislature and resurrected the bill.[7] House Bill 72 was eventually passed, increasing state funding to schools by $2.8 billion through the first tax increase in thirteen years.[8]

The size of the rally, and the IAF's ability to organize it at such short notice, tremendously impressed state politicians and put the IAF network on the map as a key player in state politics. The IAF received widespread recognition as an important force in Texas politics for the first time. Flush with the victory, leaders from the Texas network came to San Antonio to celebrate. Capitalizing on the occasion of COPS' tenth-anniversary convention, the Texas IAF announced itself formally. According to Christine Stephens, "there was a lot of homage paid to COPS," because it was the backbone of the state network.[9] But, for the first time, the IAF asserted an identity that was more than a collection of entirely independent local affiliates.

Becoming a Statewide Political Force

The Indigent Health Care Campaign

While its leaders celebrated in San Antonio, the IAF moved to consolidate its organizing efforts in the lower Rio Grande Valley, in the area of Brownsville and McAllen along the Mexican border. Mexican Americans

constituted a large proportion of the population in the valley, but remained economically exploited and politically excluded. IAF organizing
efforts took off fast, and a powerful organization called Valley Interfaith
quickly emerged, encompassing almost half of all parishes in the area.
With some of the poorest schools in the state, the funding equalization
campaign ignited the interests of many parishioners and helped to build
the incipient effort. But, in one-on-one and house meetings which the
IAF conducted as part of its relational organizing strategy, parishioners
consistently mentioned health care as a top priority. Home to an expanding immigrant population, the lower Rio Grande Valley had some
of the worst health care in the state.

Valley Interfaith brought 6,000 supporters to a rally in June of 1983 to
demand action on health care from Governor Mark White. Impressed by
the tremendous turnout, White appointed a task force on indigent health
care with a narrow mandate to propose pilot projects. The Texas IAF and
health care advocacy groups utilized the task force process to demonstrate
the inadequacy of public health care facilities. As the task force held hearings around the state, IAF affiliates in San Antonio and the valley brought
out residents to tell stories of lack of access to primary health care, especially for pregnant women and children. The IAF worked with a number
of advocacy groups to get a bill introduced into the legislature calling for
the state to provide $125 million to county governments to provide health
care to the indigent. The Texas IAF successfully lobbied Governor White
to support the bill and brought hundreds of leaders from its local affiliates
to Austin to meet with state legislators.

On the last day of the legislative session, with the outcome of the house
vote still in doubt, the IAF mobilized its supporters to the state capital.
As Pat Wong, who has studied the campaign closely, tells the story, ". . .
the bill was filibustered to death, much to the disappointment of most of
the observers. Right at the moment that the legislative session was gaveled
to an end, several things happened. Members of TIAF [the Texas IAF
network] organizations flooded the capitol dome, yelling, chanting, and
effectively blocking the major exits. A group of Hispanic legislators went
to the Governor's Office, accompanied by Ernie Cortes and leaders of
TIAF organizations, to demand an immediate special session—or else the
Hispanic caucus would run its own candidate to oppose White in the
next election. And Senator Farabee [one of the bill's key backers], after
embracing his wife in tears, called the Governor's Office in utter frustration and anger. Under all these pressures, the governor had no choice but
to call a special session to begin the following day, specifically to deal with
indigent health care."[10] The special session went on to pass a $70 million
package of state aid to counties, representing the first time the state of
Texas had made a commitment to provide health services for the poor.

Water Services for the Colonias

Credited with playing a key role both in developing and passing an historic initiative, the Texas IAF expanded its reputation as a growing force
in state politics. Building upon its success, the IAF moved to launch for
the first time its own state initiative, a proposal to provide water and
sewer services for the *colonias. Colonias,* the American equivalent of
shantytowns, sprawled along the border with Mexico, in IAF communities in the lower Rio Grande Valley, El Paso, and the Eagle Pass area
where the IAF was launching yet another organizing project. Hundreds
of thousands of immigrants lived in these subdivided former agricultural
fields. Poor workers bought cheap housing there, but the housing had
no running water or sewers. IAF organizations, like Valley Interfaith,
EPISO, and the new project called The Border Organization in the Del
Rio/Eagle Pass area, had fought local campaigns for such services, but
the cost was too great for the poor communities in the area to bear alone.[11]
The IAF helped bring the attention of state officials to the problem, organizing tours by Governor White, Lieutenant Governor Hobby, and
others over a period of several years. It also called national attention to
the problem by testifying before federal hearings and by sending its
lead organizer in El Paso to appear on NBC's "Today Show."[12] Supportive state agencies had also tried to address the *colonias* situation, but
with little success. According to Robert Wilson and Peter Menzies, who
studied the issue closely, "no governmental jurisdiction had the correct
combination of authority, resources, and will to address the problems of
the *colonias.*"[13]

The IAF's staff and Texas IAF leaders worked on the issue for years,
eventually developing a $100 million bond package with state officials to
fund water and sewer services for the *colonias.* Valley Interfaith, EPISO,
and the Border Organization collected 80,000 signatures in support of
the package. Other Texas IAF organizations joined them in lobbying the
legislature. The Texas IAF held one of its largest state rallies up to this
point on the issue, busing a thousand supporters to Austin.[14] The bill
passed on the last day of the legislative session in 1989. The network then
mobilized for the statewide referendum necessary to approve the bond
package. The package had broad support from state officials and other
religious leaders in Texas as well, and faced no organized opposition. It
passed overwhelmingly on November 7.

For the first time, observers gave the Texas IAF credit as the primary
force behind a major state government initiative. *The Progressive* magazine declared that the Texas IAF had launched itself onto the public political stage.[15] According to Wilson and Menzies, the IAF organizations ". . .

were the principal actors, however, in developing the public will to address this problem and forcing the public sector to act."[16]

The IAF's work did not end with the bill's passage, however. Entrenched local institutions in the control of Anglo elites stalled the implementation of the program, while state governmental bodies had little experience in administration in the border regions. Local IAF affiliates had to continue to organize to hold the designated public authorities accountable to the bill's mandate, and to help them resolve administrative problems and conflicts. Meanwhile, the IAF's continued efforts to draw attention to the problems of *colonias* led to another state bond package and to federal funds for waste water treatment facilities. But it has taken years of follow-up to actually get the services in place.[17]

Flush with the *colonias* victory, the Texas network moved to consolidate itself by organizing its first formal convention in 1990. On October 28, 1990, the Texas IAF network held its founding convention in San Antonio. Ten thousand supporters came from affiliates around the state, which now included Austin Interfaith and new organizing projects in the Beaumont-Port Arthur area of East Texas, in Fort Bend County outside of Houston, and in Dallas.

The convention ratified a four-point program calling for improved opportunities in education, housing, health care, and job training. Several candidates for statewide office in the 1990 elections attended the convention, including gubernatorial candidate Ann Richards, the State Treasurer whom the IAF had worked closely with in the *colonias* campaign. Part of the convention was reserved for IAF leaders to ask candidates for their support of the IAF program and for a pledge to work with the IAF if elected. The day after the convention, hundreds of local leaders remained for intensive training. Four representatives from each of the local IAF organizations formed a statewide steering committee.[18] After the founding convention, the Texas IAF proceeded to set up a state office in Austin where Cortes would now supervise Texas as well as new organizing projects in the Southwest. A small staff, including research and policy development support, helped coordinate the state network.

The founding convention proved a powerful experience for local IAF leaders. For COPS co-chair Virginia Ramirez, the convention capped many years of work to create a common vision among low-income communities across Texas. "When you bring that kind of convention together, they have a vision. My vision was reflected across the state. To get ten thousand people from local communities [means a lot]. So it was powerful, historical. Bringing people together and sharing a common vision. To see people coming from the Valley, singing. They came in buses, a long trip. They were tired and they were singing. They need housing, but we need housing. They care about education just like us. It was a high. A lot of people have conventions, but to have a common vision . . ."[19]

Forging Multilevel Collaborations: The Alliance Schools

A functioning statewide network began to allow the Texas IAF to address more complex issues, requiring greater funding and more complex collaborations to achieve. Moreover, the Texas IAF's experience with *colonias* showed the need for the reform of public institutions that serve poor communities, not just greater funding for them. But institutional reform required a longer term involvement by IAF affiliates and higher-level forms of collaboration. Education reform arose at the cutting edge of this realization, with the initiative taken first by African American ministers in the network's affiliate in Fort Worth, ACT.

African American leaders in ACT had long been concerned with the failure of many black youth in school. Individual meetings with church members and house meetings with groups of neighborhood residents had consistently raised the issue of poor academic performance and high dropout rates among African American youth. In 1985 Reverend Nehemiah Davis began to talk with other African American ministers in ACT, and the IAF's organizer at the time, Sr. Mignonne Konecny, about the possibilities of addressing what many increasingly saw as a crisis in their community. Working with business allies in the city and with a new principal at a local middle school, ACT launched a parental involvement program at Morningside Middle School. In a campaign discussed in detail in the next chapter, the Morningside campaign began to demonstrate immediate success. Parental involvement in the school rose dramatically and student test scores increased as well. In 1990, Morningside received the Texas Governor's Excellence Award.[20]

Inspired by the early successes of the ACT effort, the IAF encouraged other Texas affiliates to experiment with school reform efforts. A campaign to improve schools promised to address a central concern of almost every IAF leader and supporter. Moreover, it offered a potential way for the IAF to broaden its institutional base in Texas communities. Many community residents were not members of churches, and so could not be directly reached by IAF efforts. This was a particular problem in African American communities, where local churches drew members from the broader metropolitan area, retaining shallow roots in their immediate neighborhood. Meanwhile, for African Americans education represented a concern with deep historical roots. A campaign for better schools promised to help the Texas IAF deepen its base in black communities.

The state network had already begun to develop some expertise in educational issues through its work on funding equalization. But the IAF saw greater funding as only one part of a strategy for improving schools. In the IAF's view, the causes of school failure went beyond low funding levels and demanded a program of broader institutional reform that needed to be addressed school by school. Never before, however, had the Texas IAF attempted to reform an institution so deeply entrenched, and so deeply flawed. School reform would require a long-term, sustained effort. Given the resistance of local school administration, the efforts of local affiliates to reform neighborhood schools required significant outside support. Building upon the official founding of the Texas network in 1990, the IAF saw an opportunity for a statewide initiative in which every affiliate could participate and benefit.

Meanwhile, economic and political developments in the late eighties helped create a greater opening for a major state initiative by the IAF. First, the oil crisis of the eighties had sent Texas into a long and deep recession, exacerbated by the savings-and-loan crisis. Although Texas always had pockets of poverty, the poor were easily overlooked during the period of rapid economic growth in the seventies. Many assumed poverty was solely a problem of rural Mexican immigrants. Once the recession set in, however, unemployment and poverty grew. Moreover, large Texas cities began to experience a concentration of poverty in their inner cities that devastated communities.[21] Crime, school failure, and drug abuse emerged as public issues of concern in the state.

With the economic crisis, the hegemony of business elites in the state declined as businesses failed. By the end of the eighties, every single Texas bank had been acquired by out-of-state concerns. Meanwhile, African Americans and Hispanics had begun to vote in much greater numbers (in part, due to IAF efforts) and to elect minority candidates to office.[22] Representatives of color often proved to be more favorable to IAF initiatives. But these officials typically lacked a sustained organizational base of their own in communities of color. In many ways, the IAF was the one political force in the state that represented a well-organized base capable of action, in a context of heightened concern about the growth of poverty and its consequences.

In 1990, Democrat Ann Richards was elected governor of Texas, providing a new opening for IAF organizing at the state level. Richards had already worked closely with the IAF on the *colonias* issue when she was State Treasurer. Since the Democratic Party itself had a weak organizational base in Texas communities, the IAF represented a powerful ally that could support (albeit indirectly) her election and the broader goals of her administration. The IAF had survived under the more conservative Governor Bill Clements from 1986–1990; indeed, it succeeded with its *colonias* campaign during that period. But just as Democratic Governor Mark White opened up possibilities for IAF campaigns in educational equalization and indigent health care, Richards' election provided important new openings for IAF action at the state level. After her election, Richards appointed former COPS co-chair Sonia Hernandez as the director of education policy in her office. And she appointed the reform-minded Lionel "Skip" Meno to head the Texas Education Association (TEA), the state's department of education.

The IAF invited Meno to observe some of its local school reform efforts and convinced him to experiment with supporting the role of community organizations in school improvement. IAF organizers and leaders began meeting with Meno's staff and developed the Alliance Schools program.[23] With support from the TEA, IAF leaders lobbied the legislature to pass the pilot program in 1992. The initial Alliance Schools program provided $10,000 in TEA funding to twenty-one schools involved in local IAF efforts. The funds could be used by principals who joined the effort to support teaching training and curricular development in their schools. The bill also provided for special waivers so that local schools could bypass the state's intricate web of regulations and establish innovative reforms more quickly. For its part, the IAF provided professional organizers to engage parents and the broader community in transforming schools and increasing student achievement.

The Texas IAF proceeded to make an organizational commitment to the Alliance Schools far exceeding anything in its past. Cortes lobbied private foundations for the funds to hire new organizers for the local school efforts. Although the lead organizers for local affiliates were prepared to supervise and train school organizers, the effort could not succeed without the new staff. In 1990, Cortes approached the Rockefeller Foundation to fund the experiment with school-based organizing. Henry Cisneros, the former San Antonio mayor, had just been appointed to the foundation's board and supported the IAF request. Impressed with the network's work at Morningside Middle School and elsewhere, the foundation responded with a project grant to hire education coordinators, as the school-based organizers were called, over a five-year period.

The education coordinators went to work, using the IAF's relational organizing strategy to engage parents and other residents of neighborhoods surrounding the Alliance Schools. The more successful campaigns drew upon the base already established in local churches, that is, experienced IAF leaders from congregations near the local schools helped engage parents and school staff. The IAF built school campaigns not around issues identified a priori by school reform experts, but rather by the concerns and interests of local parents. At the Zavala School in an Hispanic neighborhood in Austin, the first campaign sought to establish a health clinic at the elementary school. Some efforts focused on school safety. Meanwhile, school principals used the funds to help teachers develop innovative curricula or to reform the structure of schooling. In the predominantly black Roosevelt High School in Dallas, for example, the principal implemented a block scheduling program.

While local school organizing gave the effort solid roots, the IAF also worked to develop a multilevel collaborative approach to deepen and expand the reform work. Cortes convened a series of statewide leaders meetings on education. Hundreds of local leaders attended a series of meetings in which they read studies and heard presentations from school reform experts. The network drafted a document entitled "The Texas IAF Vision for Public Schools: Communities of Learners," which framed their emerging work. Although professional staff hired by the Texas IAF helped develop the document, the actual text was written by teams of local leaders. Calling for flexibility and experimentation, the document does not commit the network to one strategy for all schools, but hopes to "inspire a thousand strategies." Nevertheless, the network places itself squarely in the camp of progressive educational innovation, criticizing the mass production model of schooling, and calling instead for schools to be communities of learners. "In our vision, the model of a school shifts from efficiency to effectiveness: from that of students as passive learners to that of a community whose members are committed to learning the skills of problem solving, teaching themselves and others, and collaboration."[24]

As the Alliance School program advanced, the IAF deepened its relationships with national experts on school reform and brought them more and more often to Texas. The IAF network sponsored large statewide conferences involving up to one thousand participants. Parents, teachers, and principals from its local school efforts heard presentations at these meetings by leading scholars and activists like Howard Gardner, Ted Sizer, and James Comer. The IAF sent local organizers and leaders, a group that now included some teachers and principals recruited from Alliance schools, to training programs at Comer's School Development Program at Yale University, and later to Project Zero, the Harvard University program directed by Gardner. These outside resources and connections gave legitimacy to local leaders and school personnel struggling to overcome the resistance of district administrators. It also broadened their perspective on school reform, stimulating new ideas and strengthening programmatic initiatives.

The Alliance Schools program, for example, deepened the reform effort at Morningside Middle School in Fort Worth. ACT organizers, Morningside principal Odessa Ravin, along with teachers and parents, attended seminars with education theorists like Gardner, Comer, and Henry Levin. Ravin drew from the discussions at Alliance School seminars to move instruction towards developing higher-order thinking skills among students.[25] Meanwhile, Friend expanded the involvement of parents into instructional issues in the school.[26]

Dennis Shirley has examined the results of the Alliance School efforts in its first few years. Of the relatively small number of Alliance Schools in existence long enough to assess, the elementary schools demonstrated noticeable gains in standardized test scores, while the middle and high schools demonstrated no clear gains as a group compared to other similar schools.[27] But it may be unrealistic to expect immediate gains to be made through complicated collaborative processes, and test scores hardly provide a holistic measure of cognitive development and community improvement. Moreover, the measurable improvements in educational outcomes appear less impressive than the transformation in the culture and practice of schooling created by the Alliance initiative.

The success of the IAF's relational strategy in involving thousands of parents across the state, coupled with some improvements in test scores at Alliance schools, made the Alliance Schools popular, and the Texas IAF more respected, among state politicians and educators. Meanwhile, the participation of nationally recognized educators strengthened the legitimacy of the reform effort. Each succeeding legislative session approved an expansion of the Alliance Schools program so that by 1996 it covered over 100 schools, providing $50,000 in special funding to each one. In 1999, the legislature approved yet another expansion of the program, increasing funding from $8 to $14 million, and allowing each school to receive up to $100,000 in extra funding.

The Alliance Schools effort brought new resources and energy to local IAF organizations in Texas. TMO in Houston rebuilt its organization largely around school-based organizing, working with twenty-one schools by 1998. Local organizations across the state, meanwhile, branched out from the Alliance effort to work to garner local funds for after-school programs. Some have begun to discuss the need to reorganize adult education. And affiliates in the growing southwest region of the IAF began to undertake similar school-based organizing, especially in Albuquerque, Tucson, Phoenix, and Omaha.[28]

An Institute for Organizers

Building local affiliates across the state of Texas and developing sufficient unity among local leaders to operate state level campaigns required an infrastructure that had been lacking previously in IAF efforts. Statewide action required not just a large number of professional organizers. It also required a level of sophistication and unity among the organizing staff that the IAF had not built before. To solve this problem, Cortes created an institute for organizers in Texas, and eventually in the Southwest, that served as the motor force behind the development of the state network and the glue that could unite far-flung local affiliates.

In the view of IAF supervisors, the most important limitation to the network's efforts has always been the lack of good organizers. Under Alinsky, organizers received sporadic training and were left on their own to sink or swim in local projects. When Ed Chambers took over the national IAF in the early seventies, he moved to systematize the training of organizers. Regional supervisors began to oversee the work of local organizers. Moreover, Chambers increased organizer salaries to something closer to professional levels. By the mid-nineties, a local IAF organizer could earn about $25–30,000, a lead organizer $40–50,000, and senior IAF staff as much as $70,000 or more. Chambers also formed a "cabinet" out of the most experienced IAF organizers, which helped standardize training for organizers and affiliate leaders as well. The cabinet oversees the national training program that all organizers and leaders attend.

Despite these improvements, the IAF was still plagued by insufficient numbers of organizers. There was little money to try out new organizers, since their pay had to come from local affiliates. With average budgets of about $150,000, these affiliates could not afford to test out inexperienced organizers who required extensive on-the-job training. Moreover, despite guidance from regional IAF supervisors, organizers often felt isolated and overwhelmed by the demands placed upon them in their localities. Local affiliates could usually afford to pay only one or two organizers, so there was little collective support in the daily lives of organizers. Despite better salaries, organizers would often suffer from "burnout," making turnover a significant problem.

Isolation was especially a problem in Texas, where large distances separated organizers working in local projects. Working day after day in fairly remote neighborhoods, it became hard for IAF organizers to keep the larger vision of their efforts in focus. It's hard to convey just how spread out Texas organizing is. To give just one example, El Paso is 500 miles from San Antonio, with few population centers in between.

Organizer Seminars

The Texas IAF began to move in a new direction to address these problems. To offer collective support and intellectual stimulation—that sense of a broader vision—Cortes developed a series of seminars. He held the first one in 1987 during the Pope's visit to the U.S. As the Pope arrived in San Antonio, the senior organizers gathered in Corpus Christi, Texas. A voracious reader himself, Cortes distributed about twenty articles he had been reading on political philosophy, theology, and economics to his organizers for discussion. Discussions of broad questions led to attempts to relate the readings to the organizing work of the network. In between sessions, organizers discussed local and state network business. Eventually organizers began inviting some of the more experienced IAF leaders in Texas to attend as well, on an ad hoc basis.

One of those leaders, Barry Jackson, a black minister from Austin, gave Cortes the idea to invite guests to the seminars. During a seminar discussion of *Parting the Waters* by Taylor Branch, Jackson called ministers he knew who had been active in the civil rights movement in Selma. Cortes thought the discussions would be richer if guests were present, so he decided to ask scholars he knew to attend.

By then, Cortes knew a lot of people to ask. While organizing projects across Texas, Cortes had been busy establishing relationships with scholars at the LBJ School of Public Affairs at the University of Texas. In the mid-eighties Cortes expanded his pool of contacts to the national level. In 1984, Cortes received a MacArthur "genius" award for his organizing work. He began to attend meetings of the MacArthur fellows and built relationships with a range of scholars and policy makers, like Howard Gardner, William Julius Wilson, Robert Moses, Peter Brown, and Michael Piore. The Aspen Institute later appointed him to its Domestic Strategy Group where Cortes further expanded his connections. He then invited such scholars to come to Texas to discuss their work with his organizers. According to Cortes, the seminars were meant to expand the vision of his staff. "I thought it was important that we get outside views. I get nervous when we're too insular. Let others come and give us reflection."

But it cost money to fly in scholars, and to pay the travel expenses of IAF organizers as well. So IAF staff wrote a funding proposal to the Ford Foundation. Ford awarded the Texas network special funds to pay for the seminars, and also to hire Steve Jackobs for research support. Jackobs' research work would help develop the state network's vision papers on work and schools. The LBJ School of Public Affairs administered the grant which went to the nonprofit organization the Texas network established, called the Texas Interfaith Education Fund.

With the Ford Foundation funds, the seminars became a regular and central feature of network operations. They continue to this day. On average, the network held the seminars every two months. Each seminar involved one or two guests and lasted two to three days. Many of the seminars discussed issues relevant to the work of the network, although the subjects and discussions have been far ranging.

Over the years, the IAF staff in the Southwest has studied and met with over one hundred prominent writers, scholars, and policy analysts.[29] On economic issues, guests included Barry Bluestone, James Tobin, Ray Marshall, Vernon Briggs, William Greider, Paul Osterman, Richard Freeman, Frank Levy, and many others. On education, seminars featured Terry Moe, Chester Finn, Howard Gardner, James Comer, Robert Moses, Richard Murnane, Henry Levin, and Deborah Meier, among others. Cortes has a particular interest in politics and political philosophy, and invited a number of scholars to discuss democratic politics, including Michael Walzer, Benjamin Barber, Jean Bethke Elshtain, Theda Skocpol, Robert Putnam, Richard Bernstein, and William Sullivan. Theology and religion featured strongly in the seminars as well, with Charles Curran, James Cone, Cornel West, Bryan Hehir, and Delores Williams. Discussions of race included William Julius Wilson, Michael Dawson, Glenn Loury, and Thomas Edsall.

For organizers, the seminars gave them an opportunity to get away from the daily demands of their work and find the intellectual stimulation that might help sustain them for the long run. Moreover, they forged the organizer staff into a collective body. To be an organizer often requires a strong will and the ability to work independently. According to Cortes, the seminars promoted a necessary collegiality: "Seminars gave us the opportunity to build a different kind of relationship among organizers. Organizing used to be a solitary kind of business. This gave organizers a way to be useful to each other without being threatening. In the past, if one organizer helped another, that would be an implicit critique. We've transcended that today. The seminars contributed to a different kind of relationship. Now it's more collegial rather than competitive." Small meetings among organizers would take place in between and after seminar sessions, often continuing long into the night. The mutual support and camaraderie generated through this process has appeared to sustain organizers in their local work, so that IAF organizers in the Southwest began to develop longer tenures.[30]

Expanding the Ranks of Organizers

While the seminars helped retain organizers, they did not deal with the problem of a shortage. By the early nineties, the IAF had great ambitions to develop school-based organizing (through the Alliance Schools initiative) as well as to expand the network to other cities in the Southwest. But the network needed organizers. In particular, the IAF needed the funds to put new recruits on the payroll for a training period. During that time, they could contribute to local organizing while also being tested out. But the income generated from local IAF organizations only allowed for one, or at most two, organizers to be on the payroll. No extra funds were available for trainees.

Cortes decided to turn to private foundations for extra funds to recruit and train organizers. The first break came after Cortes appeared on Bill Moyers' *World of Ideas* public television series. With the connection to Moyers, Cortes was able to secure a $1 million grant from the Florence and John Schumann Foundation specifically to pay trainee expenses over several years, some of which supported IAF organizing in other parts of the country. Then, the Rockefeller Foundation grant to fund education organizers, discussed above, brought more outside resources to the Texas IAF. Education coordinators could do the school-based work, while being trained in IAF organizing. The more successful were hired subsequently as IAF organizers. When the Rockefeller grant expired in 1995, Cortes' growing connections to the worlds of academia and policy making helped him find the contacts necessary to sustain funding to hire education coordinators and for organizer training and development. The Carnegie Endowment, Pew Charitable Trusts, the Ford Foundation, the DeWitt Wallace-Readers Digest Fund, the Charles Stewart Mott Foundation, and Southwestern Bell all contributed to the Texas IAF's education work.[31]

While locally based lead organizers had the primary responsibility for the training of new education coordinators and organizers, the seminars gradually assumed an important role in their development as well. During each seminar teams of organizers explained the IAF's work to the guest scholar. More experienced organizers assisted junior organizers with their presentations and critiqued their ability to articulate the IAF's organizing strategy. In addition to the seminars, Cortes began to hold special retreats for junior organizers. By the early nineties, the Texas IAF had established a systematic regional training system to supplement the on-the-job training new recruits received in local organizing.

The Texas IAF had the money and the training system in place, but it still needed to find promising recruits. The pressing demand to find apprentice organizers led Cortes to another significant revision of Alinsky's legacy: he began to hire IAF leaders as organizers. Alinsky had drawn a clear line of separation between organizer and leader. The traditional Alinskyite organizer was male, came from outside the community, and lived a kind of nomadic existence moving from community to community. Leaders, often female, were rooted in their community and stayed there as organizers left. Cortes had already begun to modify that approach. While Alinsky had believed women incapable of being organizers, Cortes had early on recruited women to his staff, especially members of Catholic religious orders. But in the early nineties he began to recruit leaders from local organizations, leaders who were mostly women of color.

Most IAF leaders were not necessarily interested in joining the organizing profession, but some were excited about the potential opportunity. Julia Lerma, for example, joined the organizing staff in Texas after getting involved in an IAF organization in California. Her experience suggests both the potential gains that came from this new form of recruitment as well as the difficulties faced in incorporating a new kind of organizer into the staff. According to Lerma, "what intrigues me is developing leadership and power—common people organizing to make change and have power. And the IAF gave me an opportunity to grow and develop as a person."[32] But she faced obstacles. As a single mother, she struggled to find the time for the long hours required of organizers. As a result, she had to bring her mother with her to her assignment in San Antonio to help with child care. Another problem arose from the limitations of her educational background. "I experienced racism in schools growing up. I was put into remediation because I was Mexican. I never got a real chance." She found the IAF organizer seminars challenging, but struggled with feelings of being different from the bulk of the IAF professional staff. "I was a shy person and lacked a college degree like most of the other organizers. At one point I almost quit, but Ernie [Cortes] helped me see what was wrong and how to overcome the obstacles I was facing." Lerma subsequently enrolled part-time in college, receiving time off and a raise from the IAF to support her efforts. She persisted as did many other women of color, although some did not successfully make the transition from leader to organizer.

By tapping leaders, the IAF now had a large and fairly stable pool out of which to recruit organizers, something the network never had before. With new funds, and a pool of recruits, the Southwest IAF organizing staff grew rapidly, increasing from about 25 in 1990 to 60 by 1999. In addition, recruiting leaders shifted the composition of the staff so that it gradually became more and more female and much more racially diverse. Of the 60 organizers on staff in 1999, 27 were female and 30 were organizers of color (19 Hispanic, 10 African American, and 1 Asian American). About 20 had been recruited out of the ranks of IAF leaders.[33]

A large organizing staff gave the Texas network the capacity to expand in three ways. First, local organizations had a larger staff, now numbering three or four organizers, with which to expand their organizing into schools and elsewhere. Second, the network had extra resources to carry out the work necessary for campaigns at the state level. Third, the IAF could build new organizations in Texas and the Southwest because it was generating organizers with enough experience to lead new efforts. By the late nineties, the Southwest IAF had established nascent state networks of local organizations in Arizona, New Mexico, and Louisiana.

Why Texas?

In many ways, Texas has offered a particularly conducive environment for IAF organizing, which helps explain the network's particular success there. Faith-based organizing might be expected to work well in a state like Texas, with high rates of religious participation and with perhaps greater receptivity to a public role for religion.[34] Moreover, Catholics make up about one-third of total church adherents in Texas, and the majority of them are Mexican Americans. In San Antonio, Catholics are the majority of churchgoers.[35] Since its founding in San Antonio, the network has received strong support from the Catholic hierarchy across Texas for its organizing among Mexican Americans.[36]

The Texas IAF has also benefited from a largely open field for its organizing, where there is relatively little competition from other community or political groups. Because narrowly based Anglo elites typically dominated Texas cities, political parties did not build organized bases of support in most urban neighborhoods. Meanwhile, the lack of much opportunity to influence city hall discouraged the growth of community organizations.[37] In many places, the IAF quickly emerged as the only game in town.

Clergy in Texas have relatively few ties to the political establishment, a situation which also proves conducive to IAF organizing. Since the IAF follows a nonpartisan political strategy that stresses the independence of its organizations, clergy and lay leaders who are used to working through party and political connections need to break those ties to join an IAF effort. In Texas, those ties are relatively rare. Because of this history of elite-style rule, black electoral politics remained somewhat less developed in Texas as well, certainly in terms of establishing an organized base within communities.[38]

In Texas, the Democratic Party and other liberal interest groups have generally felt they benefited from IAF organizing. Lacking their own base within low-income communities, and facing stiff competition from Republican and conservative groups, Democrats and liberals have typically tried to work with the Texas IAF. They may not always have been happy to share power; many candidates would prefer an endorsement from the

IAF; and some have disliked the IAF's style. Nevertheless, to the extent they could support IAF initiatives, politicians could hope to benefit from IAF voter education and mobilization campaigns. Instead of opposing the development of the interfaith network as a source of competition, they have usually tried to work with IAF organizations.

Republicans, conservatives, and independents have also come to see the benefits to cooperation with IAF organizations in Texas. The strictly nonpartisan character of the network helps make these collaborations possible. But so does the "open field" character of community politics. As the economic crisis hit Texas in the late eighties, elites across the political spectrum feared social turmoil. Searching for community organizations that could provide what they saw as responsible leadership in poor communities of color, elites often turned to Texas IAF organizations.

Finally, a history of elite dominance has meant that, compared to many cities in the East and Midwest at least, the public bureaucracies in Texas cities are less well entrenched. COPS, for example, took advantage of this open ground to dominate the Community Development Block Grant (CDBG) program to an extent that seems inconceivable elsewhere. This is not to say that public administrators have always welcomed IAF intervention in what they see as "their" affairs, or cooperated enthusiastically with local organizations. They have often dragged their feet in response to IAF demands. But, on the other hand, rarely have the city administrations been the center of greatest opposition to IAF efforts. Although the network designed its Alliance Schools program to be viable without a high level of *active* support from local school administrations, it did depend on their acquiescence. Some local school officials have disrupted the program, not necessarily intentionally, by frequent transfers of principals assigned to Alliance Schools. But none have sought to block the effort outright.[39]

IAF organizations appear to go through a similar developmental pattern in their relationship to political and business elites in localities across the state. At first, elites feel threatened by the network's efforts to organize in poor communities of color and attempt to squash nascent IAF organizing. Then, once the IAF survives those early battles, many elites come to a grudging acceptance of the network's role. Finally, in the face of growing discontent in poor communities, and the lack of many other indigenous organizations, elites often develop a more positive attitude to what they might gain from cooperation with the IAF. Seeing beyond the confrontational style to the seriousness and responsible character of IAF organizations, many public and private officials seek to collaborate with the network.[40]

Toward a Regional Network
in the Southwest

Even as the IAF worked to consolidate its state network in Texas, organizers began to be sent out to expand organizing to other cities in the Southwest. In the late eighties organizing began in Phoenix, Arizona. In 1990, Frank Pierson was hired as lead organizer by the new IAF organization in Tucson, Pima County Interfaith Council (PCIC). A former divinity school student, Pierson had worked for the IAF in Chicago and Queens, New York, in the 1970s. Inspired by the IAF's success in COPS and Texas, Pierson returned to organizing and helped PCIC establish itself as a metropolitan-wide organization, eventually recruiting sixty member institutions. Tucson's nonwhite population is only 30 percent, so the IAF built PCIC to be multiracial and cross-class from the beginning. Meanwhile, Peter Frears, an ex-labor union organizer, worked to establish Valley Interfaith Project (VIP) in Phoenix. East Valley Interfaith (EVI) formed in 1996 around Tempe and Mesa in Phoenix's east valley. By 1999, the three local organizations began to cooperate as a state network holding their first major statewide assembly in April of 2000.

Organizing in Arizona demonstrated that the strategy worked out by the IAF in Texas could be applied to other states, even ones like Arizona that offered a quite hostile environment. Conservative Republicans have had a lock-hold on state politics in Arizona, and places like Phoenix have a strong libertarian tradition. Arizona is a right-to-work state. Moreover, the state exerts a much higher degree of authority over local affairs than in Texas, restricting their taxing abilities. The state government has been committed to cutting taxes and fees, and even passed a law banning city authorities from establishing a minimum wage. Historically, cities have fought for more power vis-à-vis the state, and so their relatively weak administrations have sometimes been interested in allying with IAF efforts.[41]

PCIC's first major campaign was built around the notion of a family friendly city. That campaign led the organization to launch a series of initiatives for youth programs (after-school and summer) that eventually included 10,000 students, and an after-school employment program to encourage students from low-income families to stay in school. Called Schools-Plus-Jobs, PCIC got sufficient city and county funding to place 300 students in the program on a yearly basis. Pierson, PCIC's original organizer, and later IAF supervisor for Arizona and New Mexico, describes the rationale behind these early efforts:

In Arizona we translated the IAF universals into an unbelievably hostile terrain. People thought we'd be dead in the water. . . . [The family friendly city] was fertile ground for engaging very conservative people as well as moderates. In a conservative state, that was key. . . . People will understand our work better if you reject the notion of isolated issues and focus on the pressures on families. That ties our work together.[42]

PCIC built upon these early successes to move to develop a job-training program, called JobPath, inspired by the IAF's Project QUEST in San Antonio. By 1998, PCIC won commitments of $335,000 for the program from city and county agencies.[43] Meanwhile, in 1995, the organization launched its most ambitious campaign to date, to establish a living wage ordinance in Tucson. PCIC leaders visited successful living wage campaigns by IAF organizations in Baltimore and San Antonio, and sought to ally with local unions like the United Food and Commercial Workers Union. The organization proved capable of mobilizing 1,000 members to walk the neighborhoods of low-income communities to build support for the campaign. It called an economic summit, inviting prominent business representatives, clergy, and school officials to join the effort. Despite opposition from the local chamber of commerce, in September of 1999, the Tucson city council passed the ordinance, requiring businesses with city service and maintenance contracts to pay workers a minimum of $8.00 per hour with benefits, $9.00 per hour without.[44]

Meanwhile, VIP in Phoenix developed its own version of the family development program, working to reform local schools, establish after-school programs, build affordable housing, and offer citizenship classes for the large number of new immigrants in the city. More recently, VIP has worked to establish an Immigrant Family Association to connect the organization more closely to the city's poorest residents. EVI in Phoenix's east valley has also prioritized work around immigration and citizenship issues, among other campaigns.

In April of 2000, nearly five thousand supporters attended the Arizona Interfaith network's statewide meeting to advance a human and family development agenda in Phoenix. Billed as a Convocation of Arizona Families, 201 member institutions attended, mainly Catholic parishes and Protestant congregations. But the presence of many schools and unions, several Jewish congregations, and representatives from Navajo communities demonstrated the growing diversity of the state network. Catholic bishops from Tucson and Phoenix spoke, as well as the United Methodist bishop, Secretary of State Betsey Bayless, and Attorney General Janet Napolitano. IAF leaders asked political and business leaders to work with Arizona Interfaith on such issues as living wages, school funding and reform, affordable heath care, and the improvement of immigrant communities. And the network announced an ambitious plan to build institutes of public life involving 10,000 Arizona citizens. The institutes would conduct voter education and registration programs around the impact of public policy and budget decisions on families.[45]

While the IAF built a network in Arizona, it also proceeded to establish affiliates in Albuquerque, New Mexico, New Orleans, Northern Louisiana, Des Moines, Iowa, and Omaha, Nebraska. In 1998, the national IAF's director, Ed Chambers, asked Cortes to take over operations in Los Angeles where organizing had failed to thrive. Cortes proceeded to reorganize the IAF's affiliates there into one metropolitan-wide organization and to incorporate it within the growing Southwest IAF network. The Metro IAF organization decided to cease all issue campaigns to concentrate on rebuilding its base. In 1999, ten organizers led by Cortes and Maribeth Larkin conducted one-on-one individual meetings for the entire year, totaling 10,000 encounters with prospective leaders. By the end of 1999, the Southwest IAF had eight organizations outside of Texas and an emerging project in Los Angeles. On November 7, the regional network announced its presence by bringing hundreds of leaders from across the Southwest to join leaders from twelve Texas organizations at a COPS convention to celebrate "25 years of organizing in the Southwest."[46]

Conclusion

In Texas and the Southwest, the IAF found a way for community-based organizations to move beyond the confines of their local areas. For the first time, an IAF network could exert and sustain power at the state level. At the same time, though, the IAF remained committed to the primacy of local organizing. Statewide political action and regional staff development were meant to enhance the capacity for local work. Ideally the IAF sought a symbiotic relationship between these processes, each advancing the other.

But there were tensions here too. At times, the allure of being a powerful player in state politics threatened to pull the IAF away from local work. During the eighties, IAF organizers and leaders spent a good deal of time cultivating relationships with state officials, forming alliances, lobbying legislators, and bringing their supporters to Austin. Such work proved decisive in enhancing the local power of IAF organizations. But it often drained resources away from base building in local communities.

Local organizations contract with the IAF for the services of regional supervisors to oversee and guide the work of lead organizers. As Cortes spent more and more time building and developing a regional staff, and organizers spent several days each month or so away from their localities to attend organizer seminars, less immediate attention could be focused on local supervision. Expanding to new cities meant less time for the supervision of existing organizations. From the larger standpoint, regional staff development did generate more and better trained organizers. But local leaders at times expressed resentment. When ACT in Fort Worth was struggling to strengthen its organization in the mid-nineties, one of its long-term leaders, Reverend Nehemiah Davis, suggested that "there is a tendency to organize more units than the organizer staff can handle. The regional supervisor should run with an organizer. If he can only get there once every two months, that's not often enough. . . . We [the leaders] end up training the organizer."[47]

Despite the complaints sometimes voiced, most local leaders could see the benefits of state and regional work. The state network brought the resources necessary to address local problems, like water and sewer services in *colonias*, resources that simply could not be generated at the local level. It offered the possibility to forge collaborative relationships with state and national policy makers to make possible ambitious efforts at institutional reform. The Alliance Schools program, for example, leveraged initial successes in local school organizing to pursue a collaboration, as a state network, with the Texas Educational Association and to gain support from the Rockefeller Foundation. These institutions provided the resources to expand school-based efforts throughout the state. Meanwhile, collaboration with national education reformers deepened the understanding and capacities of local parents, teachers, and principals to improve their schools.

Rather than counterpose local to state or regional level work, it may be useful to consider the relationship between local and state organizing as a creative tension, analogous to the dynamic between authority and participation discussed in chapter 1. Both are necessary, and at their best, contribute to each other. There is no ready-made formula that stipulates the correct balance between the two. But in Texas, the IAF developed a federated structure, following the principle of subsidiarity, that appears to create an effective framework for the emergence of a positive synergy between local and higher-level organizing.

The Texas IAF charges local organizations with generating the participatory base for political action, and, in turn, allows those organizations to retain ultimate control over their operations. The state network cannot dictate campaigns to local affiliates, although it can strongly encourage certain campaigns. At the same time, local autonomy creates the possibility for innovation, that is, the generation of new campaigns. It also encourages the adaptation of state-level initiatives to local conditions. The Alliance Schools initiative, for example, proved to have widespread appeal among all local organizations. But, within the broad umbrella of the network's "vision for public schools," each affiliate, and each local school campaign, undertook reform efforts of its own design.

While the network worked to keep a priority on local participation, it also sought to generate authoritative direction at the state and regional level. The development of a united regional staff of organizers proved decisive in forging extra-local political action. Locally, leaders can meet regularly, face to face, to build a consensus for action. But at state and regional levels, daily interaction among leaders is simply not possible. Leaders across the region did meet and worked to build consensus over time. But the Southwest IAF's institute for organizers gave the network a degree of centralization necessary for concerted action and rapid expansion. The organizing staff served as the main infrastructure for information about issues and strategies to flow between localities. Cortes stood at the center of this impressive collective, and perhaps held the personal authority that provided the necessary legitimacy to the process. As organizer Maribeth Larkin so aptly put it in a 1986 interview, "we operate out of Ernie's vision."[48]

Four

Bridging Communities across Racial Lines

> My ministry has always been tied to social
> justice. I had experienced a lot of defeats, lost
> battles. Generally you had one group, usually a
> church, dealing with one issue. I was invited to
> go to a meeting on the west side of town. Rever-
> end Davis invited me. I saw a group of pastors
> there and it struck a chord in me. They had what
> was missing before—a diversity, a group of sup-
> port outside of one church. Over time . . . I began
> to think this was the only way in America for
> poor black congregations to have a voice, power
> to change things, without going with hat in hand,
> shuffling feet.
>
> *(Reverend D. L. Ellison, Pastor of Pilgrim Rest
> Missionary Baptist Church and a leader of Allied
> Communities of Tarrant)*[1]

AMERICANS committed to revitalizing our democracy face perhaps no greater challenge than overcoming the racial and class divisions that frag-ment the polity and undermine the nation's commitment to combating poverty and racial oppression. Community building within the inner city empowers residents to achieve a measure of control over their communi-ties, but is insufficient to overcome these divisions. We need to find a way to bring communities together across the lines of race and class. Building such "bridging social capital," as this process was called in chapter 1, can create allies for inner-city efforts to combat poverty. And it can also work to overcome divisions to develop the mutual understanding necessary to forge a broad and inclusive conception of the common good.

Many Americans have come to recognize the need to address racism and build multiracial understanding and cooperation. But we are still searching for effective and meaningful ways to accomplish those goals. Cornel West, in *Race Matters*, argues that "to engage in a serious discus-sion of race in America, we must begin not with the problems of black people but with the flaws of American society—flaws rooted in historical inequalities and longstanding cultural stereotypes." West calls for a conversation across racial lines, a serious effort to develop mutual understanding based not on the problems of black people, but upon shared problems and challenges. To confront racism, "we must focus our attention on the public square—the common good that undergirds our national and global destinies." Based upon that understanding, Americans can undertake social and political action to address our common needs, in education, economic opportunity, and democratic progress.[2]

Although West illuminates the tasks before us, we lack arenas in which Americans have the opportunity to build relationships across racial lines for the purpose of common action. Our social life is segregated, in neighborhoods, schools, and congregations. And political groups have been largely organized along racial lines as well.

Efforts to form coalitions among these separate groups represent our dominant institutional model for multiracial cooperation. Coalitions consist of institutional representatives who identify a shared interest. Coalitions that seek to back candidates for office have played important roles in electing African Americans and others to office, while issue coalitions have proved critical in passing antiracist laws and government programs for social provision.[3] But these top heavy cooperative arrangements lack deep roots in communities and remain limited to the particular issue around which they were formed. Interest based coalitions have proven fragile when people take a narrow interpretation of their self or group interest, and come to oppose the demands of oppressed groups.

Studies of electoral coalitions have shown that common interests are a necessary, but not sufficient, condition for multiracial cooperation. Leadership, relationship building, and ideology also play important roles in forging alliances.[4] Relationship building promotes the trust necessary for cooperation. Ideology encompasses the ideas and traditions that shape how people view their interests. But coalitions limit relationship-building processes to a small group of institutional representatives at the top. Leadership on racial issues seldom flows up from broader community-building processes below.

The notion of bridging social capital suggests an alternative. The purpose of bridging social capital is to bring a much broader range of Americans together so that they can build the kind of mutual understanding upon which cooperation for shared interests and the common good can be sustained. Since bridging forms of social capital rarely exist, they have to be built. But bridging organizations cannot be imposed, fully formed, where mistrust, racism, and ignorance have reigned for so long.

Forging multiracial cooperation therefore requires a *process* that builds trust and mutual understanding over time. A certain degree of trust is necessary to get the process going. But, then, cooperative action offers the context for building greater trust, relationships, and mutual understanding. The concept of bridging social capital incorporates the kind of discourse across racial lines that some Americans have sought to create, including President Bill Clinton's initiative on race. But bridging forms of social capital can offer the advantage that these discussions are not "just talk" among disconnected leaders or citizens. They lead to common action and, in turn, build trust and understanding through such cooperative experience.

IAF organizing in Texas and the Southwest represents a leading example of how to build bridging social capital. In fact, a number of scholars have begun to look to the IAF as a promising model for multiracial collaboration. William Julius Wilson, for example, has argued that the current period offers an important opening for the creation of a "bridge over the racial divide." Rising economic inequality in the midst of an economic boom provides working and middle-class Americans of all races with a common interest in a set of governmental programs that can improve their lot vis-à-vis the wealthy. In calling for the construction of a progressive multiracial political constituency, he points to the Texas IAF network as a model worth exploring both for multiracial and cross-class alliance building.[5]

This chapter, and the next, present a close examination of the efforts of the Texas IAF to create a process for building social capital that bridges across diverse communities. As discussed in chapter 2, by the early eighties the Texas IAF adopted the practice of establishing broad-based organizations that were meant to represent the racial composition of the locality in which each operated. But these efforts occurred in a particular historical context for the network. The building of COPS in San Antonio gave the Texas IAF a strong base in Mexican American communities and an early reputation as an effective advocate for Texas Hispanics. Efforts to organize among African Americans and Anglos in San Antonio were hampered by fears of being dominated by the already organized Hispanic community. In Fort Worth, the IAF had the opportunity to build its first broad-based organization that could include African Americans and Anglos on a fully equal basis with Mexican Americans.

This chapter focuses on the experience of this multiracial organization, the Allied Communities of Tarrant (ACT). It identifies the ingredients that helped encourage community leaders from different races, social classes, and religious denominations to work together in a common effort. And it explores how working together in a common organization helped develop trust and mutual understanding. The chapter ends with a discussion of the important limits to multiracial unity in Fort Worth. In the next chapter, the discussion of bridging social capital continues. It charts the emergence of African American leadership more fully in the Texas IAF network as a whole, a development that built upon the advances made in Fort Worth, yet deepened the basis for multiracial collaboration.

Fort Worth in the Eighties

In 1980, Fort Worth had 385,000 residents, about one-third of the surrounding Tarrant County's population. Although much of the area's growth occurred in suburbs outside of the city limits, by 1990 Fort Worth's population had grown to 448,000, making it the twenty-eighth largest American city. In 1980, African Americans made up 22.8 percent of the population, with Hispanics about 13 percent. By 1990, African Americans remained about 22 percent of the population; but Hispanics had risen to 19.5 percent.[6] While some Mexican Americans had lived in Fort Worth for years, many were recent arrivals.

Fort Worth was, and remains, a segregated city. African Americans are concentrated in several neighborhoods, primarily on the east side and in the central city. In 1980 Fort Worth had a black/white segregation score of 77.9, the eighteenth highest in the U.S. That score indicates that fully 77.9 percent of the city's population would have to move to achieve integrated neighborhoods. By 1990, Fort Worth's score had fallen to 63.6, still high, but indicating a certain amount of middle-class exodus from poor black neighborhoods.[7] Mexican Americans, meanwhile, were concentrated mainly in north-central and south-central neighborhoods.

Originally based in cattle, hence the designation "Cowtown," Fort Worth later became a center for the oil industry and developed a large defense economy during World War II. Average pay in Fort Worth was higher than in cities like San Antonio; but many of the more affluent lived outside the city limits. Consequently, in 1989 Fort Worth had a median household income of $26,547, below the state average.

Poverty remained concentrated among both African American and Hispanic communities in Fort Worth. 28 percent of black families and 23 percent of Hispanic families lived below the poverty line in 1990.[8] Meanwhile 31,000 of Fort Worth's residents lived in concentrated poverty, that is, in neighborhoods where 40 percent or more of families lived below the poverty line.[9] A majority of African American neighborhoods and many Hispanic neighborhoods exhibited this level of concentrated poverty.

Before the seventies Fort Worth politics had been controlled by a small Anglo elite organized into the "Seventh Street Gang." The group had been founded by Amon Carter and included leading members of the wealthy Bass family, as well as John Justin, maker of the famous western boots of that name. The "gang," however, was never as large or as tightly unified as the Good Government League in San Antonio. In the sixties a "Town Hall" reform movement emerged, dedicated to broadening city politics through study committees and neighborhood conferences. With the implementation of single-member districts in the mid-seventies, the group dissolved.[10] Meanwhile, the Bass family continued to play an influential role in Fort Worth civic and political life.

A few African Americans won election to the nonpartisan city council prior to the seventies. With the advent of single member districts, however, two African American candidates and one Hispanic candidate won election in 1978, constituting a share roughly equal to their proportion in the city's population. Black electoral politics became organized around individual families, especially the Webbers and the Bagsbys.[11] Meanwhile, Louis Zapata won election to the city council from the older Hispanic community on the north side and held his position until the early nineties.

The Texas Democratic Party had some of its strongest support in Fort Worth, the home of former Speaker of the House Jim Wright. But the party has not maintained a strong organization in the neighborhoods. Industrial unions, more important in Fort Worth than in other Texas cities, anchored the Democratic Party. Meanwhile, Fort Worth's city manager form of government served to diffuse patronage-style local politics. African American ministers traditionally supported white politicians in exchange for benefits to their communities. But they were not strongly committed to any political organization.

Integration, such as it was, came peacefully to Fort Worth in the fifties and sixties, without violence or a strong civil rights movement.[12] The NAACP filed suit repeatedly in the sixties and seventies to desegregate Fort Worth schools. Although legal segregation ended by 1967, de facto segregation rooted in neighborhood segregation continued to characterize the school system through the seventies.[13] According to IAF lead organizer Perry Perkins, "Fort Worth is a subtly segregated town. It had blacks on the city council and public boards well before Dallas. It presents a picture of openness, but underneath it is segregation. There hasn't been public racial conflict like in Dallas. But it's beginning to surface now."[14]

By the late seventies, when IAF organizing began in the city, Fort Worth had a relatively inactive and unorganized polity. There had been no history of sharp racial conflict. On the other hand, there was no history of strong social or political movements either, and little history of interracial cooperation. Fort Worth's communities remained fairly unorganized. Meanwhile, the NAACP pursued legal cases, while political parties and black and Hispanic politicians concentrated on electoral campaigns.

The Founding of Act: Religion as a Source of Initial Trust

Hearing about the success of COPS in San Antonio, a number of ministers in Fort Worth began talking about the possibility of forming an IAF organization in their city. In the late seventies they formed a sponsoring committee and invited Ernesto Cortes, Jr., the IAF's regional supervisor, to Fort Worth for discussions. The sponsoring committee consisted of black Baptist ministers, white ministers from Lutheran and Disciples of Christ denominations, and both Hispanic and Anglo Catholic priests. These ministers had not worked together prior to this initiative. They had known each other within their denominations, though. For example, two white Lutheran ministers had earlier formed an Urban Ministries group among Anglo Protestant clergy to address social issues in Fort Worth.[15] The black Missionary Baptist ministers were connected through the Baptist Ministerial Alliance. Meanwhile, the Catholic clergy knew each other through the church's diocesan structure.

Each group had come to the point of seeing the limitations of separate efforts and wanted to try to cooperate across racial lines. The African American ministers had been pursuing racially based politics, through electoral efforts and through the NAACP, but came to see these strategies as ineffective for dealing with the quality of life in poor African American communities. Witnessing the rapid growth of the Hispanic community, they wanted to try a strategy that promised cooperation for common ends, rather than endless competition where the power structure could "divide and rule." According to one of ACT's founders and one of the most prominent black ministers in Fort Worth at the time, Reverend Nehemiah Davis, "we wanted the organization to reflect the city and to do that we needed to be multidenominational. We wanted to cover the whole city to prevent the local government from playing one section of the city off against another."[16] Moreover, unlike the case in San Antonio, black ministers had the opportunity to be on the ground floor of an IAF affiliate from the beginning and play a leading role in determining its direction. With the participation of Davis, a nationally known religious educator as well as a leading local pastor, the IAF had the opportunity for the first time to build an organization with support and leadership coming from institutions at the center of a city's African American community.

In order to establish an initial basis for multiracial cooperation, the ministers looked for allies that shared a common religious outlook and who sought to bring that tradition to bear in social and political action. The ministers considered inviting several different professional community organizers to Fort Worth, but settled upon the IAF in large part because of its faith-based perspective. ACT founder and Lutheran minister

Reverend Terry Boggs describes why the ministers chose the IAF: "We liked the IAF's institutional base and church base. We were all ministers who felt the church had a larger role."[17]

The trust inherent in their common Christian religion required further development before the ministers were willing to join forces together in a united political organization. The ecumenical group spent five years meeting with each other before ACT was formally launched in 1982. In part, the ministers had to acquire sufficient resources to found the organization. Since the money would come mainly from the member churches, the discussion process really represented the opportunity for ministers to decide if they would make the commitment, financial and otherwise, to form ACT together. The time involved, five full years, suggests the level of mistrust to be overcome, although the IAF typically spends many years in patient base building before a local organization is formally launched.

During this relationship-building, sponsoring stage, the group struggled to find a common ground for the organization that did not ignore the differences between their communities. Many ministers found it difficult to raise differences, especially those based upon race. Reverend Nehemiah Davis says that IAF director Cortes encouraged group members to get out their views: "Ernie [Cortes] is an excellent organizer. He got the sensitive points on the table, even created tension around it. Get it all out—don't submerge it. One black minister asked if whites were serious. It was debated out. Those who felt enriched by the process stayed on. You still have Anglo pastors uncomfortable with it. And we still have African American pastors in the 'can't trust you' zone."[18]

The ministers faced some important obstacles in their effort to create a multiracial organization, especially from the city's Anglo power elite. Ed Wright, the pastor of Ridgely Christian Church (Disciples of Christ) had been a leading proponent of white participation in the formation of ACT. In response, several prominent wealthy conservatives in his congregation initiated a drive to stop his IAF involvement. Led by a vice president of General Dynamics, one of the biggest local employers, the congregants organized a campaign against Wright that resulted in his dismissal. The highly publicized firing frightened many Anglo west side pastors and kept them from joining ACT.[19]

Other white pastors persisted. Many had to struggle to overcome a deeply rooted tradition of relating to poorer communities by providing charity. ACT represented an opportunity to cooperate with low-income communities of color on the basis of equality and a common interest, not charity. Ministers felt that the charitable approach separated "us" from "them," however sympathetic people may be to the plight of others. To participate in ACT, affluent white church leaders needed to be willing to work side by side with poorer leaders of color.

In the end, ACT recruited white congregations that were moderately affluent and where the pastor was highly committed to the effort, congregations like Terry Boggs' St. Matthew's Lutheran Church. Most of St. Matthew's membership of 170 families came from the lower middle and professional classes, for example, teachers, nurses, technicians, insurance people, and engineers. The congregation contained few truly wealthy people, nor did it draw predominantly from the industrial working class. Through the eighties, St. Matthew's families strove to maintain their standard of living during Texas' economic crisis. In the nineties, they felt their quality of life increasingly threatened by defense cutbacks at the nearby General Dynamics facility. According to Reverend Boggs, "there is a feeling of people wanting to leave; but property values are low and so people can't leave so easily. That leads to people wanting to change things."

Reverend Boggs worked hard to provide leadership that channeled insecurity and desire for change towards cooperative efforts with less affluent communities of color. In discussions with his lay leaders, Boggs tried to get his congregants to see that they shared both common needs with poorer people and a sense of powerlessness about their ability to address them. As Reverend Homer Bain, an Anglo IAF leader in San Antonio, argues, "the affluent don't readily identify with the problems of the inner city, but they have their own feeling of impotence around public policy. We work to have them feel their lack of power. The first step is the do-gooder attitude to 'help the less fortunate.' But our philosophy is partnership—an alliance that can offer each other something. And there are issues that cross economic and racial lines."[20]

With solid support from the Catholic Church, and a reputation for representing Hispanic interests, the IAF had less trouble attracting Hispanic Catholic participation in Fort Worth. Several Catholic parishes provided a bedrock foundation for ACT in the north-central and south-central Hispanic neighborhoods. Meanwhile, Raymond Rodriguez, a member of Immaculate Heart parish and a supervisor for social services in Fort Worth's Catholic Charities office, emerged as a key Hispanic leader of the effort. Rodriguez had been active both in Hispanic and Catholic issues, working on the farm workers' grape boycott in the sixties, and playing an active role in his children's parochial schools. According to Rodriguez, "my family, and what I see at my job, that's what gets me involved [in ACT]. Yes, you need services. But how do you get involved in choosing legislators who decide on services? ACT is the only vehicle for participation."[21] Rodriguez knew of COPS through his contacts among Hispanic Catholics in the state. But the ACT effort was to be multiracial, and that appealed to Rodriguez. In Rodriguez's view, it was easier to form a multiracial organization in Fort Worth because the level of tension between Hispanics and African Americans was relatively low, at least compared to nearby Dallas. Moreover, there was some history of cooperation in service provision at least. But tension between blacks and Hispanics did exist. And Rodriguez experienced pressure from some Hispanic community and political leaders who thought Hispanics should organize amongst themselves. Rodriguez persisted, though, because he wanted an organization that could generate political power from a community-wide base.

In 1982, the ecumenical group officially launched ACT. The new organization carefully chose reform of public utilities as its first action campaign. With utility rates rapidly increasing in the early eighties, the issue affected people of all races across Fort Worth. Working with IAF affiliates in other Texas cities, ACT won seven of the eight changes it sought in the state public utilities legislation enacted in 1983, most notably the establishment of a consumer counsel for the public.[22] The victory helped launch ACT as a political force in the city. But it still needed to begin to address some of the core issues that lay at the heart of community decline in Fort Worth's black and Hispanic neighborhoods. Establishing multiracial unity would require not just working on common issues, but support for the pressing issues facing poor communities of color.

Community Initiatives and Mutual Support:
  Morningside Middle School

If common religious values provided an initial basis of trust for multiracial cooperation, the institutional strategy of the IAF created the conditions for trust to deepen over time. The federated structure of broad-based organizations that comes from the subsidiarity principle respects the integrity of historically defined communities to assert their own needs and take initiative. At the same time, leaders from different communities come together within a single local IAF organization to support each other in their campaigns. In other words, African Americans (and all others as well) who joined ACT did not dissolve their attachments to their congregations when participating in ACT. In fact, congregations, and groups of congregations often clustered by race, were encouraged to develop their own initiatives, lobby for organizational endorsement, and then expect support from other congregations for their efforts. The degree of autonomy that comes from the IAF's federated structure serves to lessen the fears of many African Americans that their particular needs will be overlooked in multiracial organizations. At the same time, support and cooperation with others provides a basis to build trust for united action.

Efforts by African American ministers to address the failures of public education in their neighborhood provided the impetus for community-based initiatives and mutual support to develop in ACT. Members of ACT's black congregations had begun to talk about a growing crisis among their children, marked by poor schooling and high dropout rates. In 1985 Reverend Nehemiah Davis began to talk with other African American ministers in ACT about the possibilities of taking some positive action to stem the educational decline. The black ministers asked ACT's lead organizer at the time, Sr. Mignonne Konecny, to accompany them to meet with business leaders and school officials in the city to see what kind of role ACT might play in revitalizing schools.

Meanwhile, in the summer of 1985 the school district appointed a new principal, Odessa Ravin, to Morningside Middle School. Morningside was a predominantly black inner-city school located in an area from which most of ACT's black churches drew members. Eighty-five percent of Morningside students qualified for free or reduced-price lunches. More than half came from single-parent families. Morningside students were scoring last among all Fort Worth Independent School District middle schools on tests of educational achievement. Half of the students had failed the writing component of the Texas Educational Assessment of Minimum Skills (TEAMS) test.[23]

Ravin had taught at Morningside many years earlier. As its new principal, she was committed to turning the school around. In fact, she had begun visiting churches herself looking for community support for the school.[24] But Ravin faced a daunting challenge trying to rebuild such a dysfunctional school. On the night before the new school year began in the fall of 1985, the school's office was firebombed. Ravin spent her first year at Morningside attending to one crisis after another, with little opportunity to make positive changes.

In 1986 Reverend Davis and organizer Konecny began meeting with principal Ravin. They agreed to collaborate and started to talk with Morningside teachers to win their support for a parental involvement program in the school. Ravin acquired the approval of school district officials for the effort, while Davis secured ACT's support. While black participants in ACT would take the lead in the campaign, ACT's Hispanic and white community leaders made a commitment to work to support the effort too.

The Morningside campaign began without a preset reform agenda. Instead, ACT followed the IAF relational organizing strategy of individual meetings to begin the process of building relationships that could lead to action ACT leaders, along with some Morningside teachers, set out to visit the home of every parent with a child at the school. Through these discussions, ACT leaders sought to determine the needs and concerns of parents, and to identify those most interested in participating. The stated goal was to get every parent involved in the education of their child.

The meetings identified an important obstacle to parental involvement. Many parents reported feeling isolated from each other and impotent in dealing with the school administration. In response, ACT organized a series of meetings involving fifty to one hundred parents during the first school year. According to Davis, the meetings provided an opportunity for parents to discuss their relationship to the school:

> At the meetings, we had facilitators and we trained them. Their role is to keep a dialogue going, not to answer questions. To get parents talking to each other. Teachers and principals sit in to listen. . . . We let people vent anger and frustration. That's necessary for healing to take place. After some time, they calm down on the inside and can be constructive. Then the facilitator lists problems and solutions, all from the parents. . . . At the next meeting, the angry parents are often the conciliators. In between time, we try to get them to visit the school. Most parents don't go to school until they're angry. This time their experience is more positive and, at the next meeting, they're positive.[25]

As parents became more positive and empowered, they began to identify specific needs. ACT responded by developing training programs on such issues as how to help a child with homework. Parental concerns expressed repeatedly about unsupervised children during after-school hours led ACT to help parents establish a free after-school program at Morningside featuring sports, arts, and academic tutoring. As the Morningside campaign grew, Reverend Davis got ACT to agree to hire an additional organizer to work solely on school issues. Acquiring funds for that purpose from local foundations, the organization hired Mattie Crompton, a Fort Worth native with deep roots in the African American community. Crompton spearheaded the development of after-school and parental involvement programs.

While Crompton concentrated on the school-based programs, African American churches in ACT developed their own initiatives to support parents. Black ministers began to recognize publicly the efforts of students and their parents by honoring children for attendance and good grades at Sunday services. Reverend Davis expressed the ministers' perspective: "every parent has something to offer a school. Most parents feel they can't help their children. But all of learning isn't in books. And then, parents can learn and educate themselves. We started a summer reading program and recognized people. We recognized parents or guardians who visited their child's school during the past six weeks. [And we gave] certificates to parents who read to their small children."[26]

The parental involvement program at Morningside began to demonstrate immediate success. Seven hundred parents attended the fall back-to-school open house after ACT's first year of organizing. Only forty or so parents had ever shown up previously. Within two years, student scores on the TEAMS achievement test had risen from last among all middle schools to third place. Morningside received the Texas Governor's Excellence Award in 1990, and was one of four schools in Texas to win the Carnegie Initiative Award from the Texas Education Agency.[27]

As discussed in chapter 3, the success of ACT's initiative prompted the Texas IAF network to experiment with school-based reform efforts in other local organizations. By the late eighties, the network was holding statewide meetings on the steps needed to improve schools as part of advancing its Alliance Schools initiative. ACT leaders and principal Ravin played important roles in these meetings, but also got some new ideas from them for their own efforts.

As a result, ACT began a second round of organizing in 1990 to expand and deepen reform at Morningside. ACT hired Leonora Friend to be its new education organizer. Friend, an African American who had been a Morningside student herself, believed that schools could not be improved without addressing the problems of the surrounding neighborhoods that undermined student achievement. So Friend began to organize parents to address neighborhood issues that affected the school. Parents, for example, had long complained about a store that sold alcohol to underage students. Friend then worked with parents to mount a successful campaign to close the store.

Meanwhile, both Friend and principal Ravin felt that instructional reform was needed to improve educational outcomes further. Ravin admitted that the early gains in test scores had come through an emphasis on drilling and memorization. When the school started administering a more difficult test of achievement, the Texas Assessment of Academic Skills (TAAS) test, the school's scores were once again below the state average. Consequently, Ravin used the new funds available from the Alliance Schools initiative to train teachers in how to develop higher-order thinking and problem-solving skills among students.[28] Meanwhile, Friend organized parents to get more involved in instructional issues in the school to begin to share responsibility with school personnel for the education of their children.[29]

Ravin and ACT organized teams to promote more responsibility and innovation among teachers, students, and their parents, the first step towards site-based management. According to Ravin, "[ACT] does empowerment—me, the parents. As a result, I've relinquished some of my power to teachers. Now, parents and staff run the school through a site-based management team. It's the policy-making group in the school. I'm just one person on it."[30]

Stimulation from the national educators the IAF brought to Texas helped encourage innovation at Morningside. Ravin, along with teachers and parents at Morningside, attended seminars with education theorists like Howard Gardner, James Comer, and Henry Levin. Ravin credits her collaboration with ACT and the IAF for her ability to persevere at Morningside. She attended the IAF's national training program and declared it "some of the best leadership training I've ever had—probably the reason I'm still working [at Morningside]."

With funds provided by the Alliance Schools program, and with a new lead organizer, ACT expanded its school reform efforts beyond Morningside. ACT leaders accepted Cortes' nomination of Perry Perkins to be their new lead organizer in 1988. The new IAF organizer brought a rich background to ACT, one steeped in politics, religion, and antiracism. Perkins grew up in a white Southern Baptist community in Mississippi. But his parents took an early stand against racism. According to Perkins, "politics and race were always issues for my family. They taught me to support the civil rights movement. I worked with a left evangelical group in Washington, D.C., and then I found the IAF."[31] After training as an organizer in Houston, Perkins arrived in Fort Worth with a number of goals. One was to stabilize the organization financially, another was to recruit new churches. Perkins also wanted to expand ACT's education work, and to direct it towards the broader goal of building a political constituency for public schools.

ACT began to organize in the elementary schools that fed into Morningside. ACT also began to establish school-based work in the predominantly Hispanic north side, designating J P Elder Middle School and one of its feeder schools, Manuel Jara Elementary, as Alliance Schools. In 1993, reflecting the broader goals of the Alliance Schools effort, ACT changed the name of its parental involvement program to the parental empowerment program.[32]

The bonds of trust within ACT developed greatly when Anglo and Hispanic leaders from ACT actively supported the Morningside campaign, by helping with home visits to parents and by agreeing to the commitment of significant organizational resources to the effort. ACT articulated a vision that all residents of Fort Worth had a common interest in the education of the city's children. It then backed up its rhetoric with the concrete actions of white and Hispanic leaders willing to support an initiative of particular concern to African Americans. Moreover, the Texas IAF network proved receptive to learning from the initiative, and to expanding and developing school reform into its most important statewide initiative of the 1990s. Through the Alliance Schools, education reform expanded to many Hispanic and African American communities within the IAF and engaged many white teachers and school personnel. With origins in Fort Worth's African American community, it became a common campaign across racial lines.

Negotiated and Common Interests

Relationships between low-income communities are often marked by competition for scarce resources, rather than united efforts for common needs. In the contemporary period, African Americans and Hispanics have often fought each other for limited city resources, destroying the fragile bonds of coalition politics.[33] Building upon the trust and cooperative ties generated early on in the Morningside campaign, ACT encouraged its constituent congregations to support each other in a number of different efforts to rebuild neighborhood communities and to combine those efforts into united campaigns wherever possible.

Bond Elections

ACT developed a way to systematize the building of mutual support and to expand its power in the city through its role in bond elections. Fort Worth, like all Texas cities, must raise money for improvements to the city's infrastructure and for other large capital projects by submitting bond packages to a vote of the electorate. In bond elections prior to 1986, the electorate simply approved the total amount, and city managers decided where to spend the money. The city administration had historically directed funds from these bonds to development in the new and more affluent sections of the city.

In 1986 ACT decided to mobilize its members to participate in the bond campaign that the city government proposed for that year. It sought to ensure that this time some of the funds would go to its inner-city neighborhoods for much needed improvements. Each member church had the chance to name specific projects for its area. Before presenting its proposals, however, ACT leaders had to negotiate among themselves for the limited funds that could realistically be included in the bond package. The long-term nature of IAF organizations became particularly important in this process. IAF strategy emphasizes what it calls "quid pro quo," or a mutual exchange of support. But the concerns of different groups arise at different times. The trust built up through the Morningside School campaign produced a willingness by some ACT leaders to forgo certain bond projects in exchange for the promise of future support in other campaigns. Meanwhile, the IAF's "iron rule," never do for others what they can do for themselves, also helped temper competition over resources. Church leaders would have to do the work of researching community needs and mobilizing support within the neighborhood, or else ACT would not include their projects in the package.

After negotiating a package agreeable to all its members, ACT approached the city council as a group with the organization's proposal. ACT demanded that the city government, rather than propose a lump sum, specifically name the projects in the bond package. ACT mobilized its supporters through its churches to pressure public officials. But it also had something to offer city officials who feared their bond package might fail because of opposition from more affluent parts of the city. The city government had included a prized project in its bond proposal. It wanted to build an equestrian center at the Will Rogers Complex, but feared that affluent taxpayers would balk at the price tag. ACT promised to mobilize voters from its neighborhoods to provide the votes that could prove crucial to pass the package. In return, the city had to agree to include ACT's priority projects as well. The city agreed to the deal and allocated $57 million for specified streets and parks in ACT neighborhoods. ACT registered more than 7,000 new voters and campaigned in favor of the bond package in forty precincts, all of which passed the package. Public officials credited ACT with providing the margin of support to secure passage of the whole bond package. According to local reporter Jeff Guinn, "From that point on, business took ACT seriously."[34]

ACT repeated its success by helping to secure $20 million for streets and drainage projects for its neighborhoods in a 1990 bond package. In exchange, ACT promised to support the city government's main project in the package, the establishment of a cultural district centered on the redevelopment of the auditorium in the Will Rogers Convention Center. The backers of the redevelopment project relied heavily upon ACT, because the project was unpopular among many white working and middle-class voters. These voters thought the cultural district would be mainly for the benefit of the wealthy at a time when Fort Worth was being threatened with the closure of the Carswell Air Force Base and a General Dynamics plant. ACT kept its part of the deal, campaigning actively for the redevelopment project as well as for its own part of the bond package. Voting arrangements allowed separate votes on each part of the package. Twenty-one out of thirty precincts ACT organized passed the plan for the center's redevelopment. But the margin of victory did not prove sufficient to overcome opposition in the rest of the city, where only eight other precincts voted in favor. As a result, the redevelopment project went down to defeat. Meanwhile, the $20 million appropriation for streets in ACT neighborhoods did pass citywide. Although ACT could claim victory, the elite backers of the auditorium plan were disappointed that the organization did not produce a sufficient margin to secure its passage.[35]

Synergy

ACT worked to collect the separate demands of its member congregations together in bond packages, but the group also sought to develop a single campaign of interest to the whole organization. Building upon the trust developed in their schools organizing and in bond campaigns, IAF organizer Perkins and ACT leaders thought they were ready to make a major, citywide initiative. Inspired by the success of Project QUEST, the job-training initiative developed by IAF affiliates in San Antonio, ACT began to discuss the possibility of launching a similar program in Fort Worth. In the early 1990s, workers in the region had been hit hard by the downsizing of local defense industries and the closings of military installations. In 1993 a multiracial group of leaders from several member churches joined an action team that developed a plan for long-term job training originally called the Individual Training Account, but later dubbed Synergy.

The job-training initiative presented a campaign where white, as well as black and Hispanic, ACT leaders could see an immediate self-interest for their communities. Consequently, two white leaders, Francine Pratt and Don Gifford, took leading roles in the new campaign. Gifford had a direct personal interest in the effort because his job at Lockheed was threatened by defense downsizing. In fact, he lost his job during the campaign, on the very day he was to present ACT's funding request to the city council.

As the campaign developed, Reverend Boggs became a key leader too. His congregation lived in predominantly white southwest Fort Worth, close to many defense contractors. According to Boggs, "because downsizing at Lockheed [and other industries] hit the southwest of Fort Worth so strongly, southwest congregations could say that job training was legitimately their issue. Issues like educational reform were altruistic for the southwest side. You can only be altruistic for so long. The jobs issue was the organizing issue for the southwest."[36] Job training also represented an important issue for black and Hispanic communities as well. So black and Hispanic ACT leaders took a keen interest in the new project. Maurice Simpson, a black ACT leader, and Juanita Cisneros from the Hispanic community, joined the job-training action team, making it a fully multiracial group.

The team worked closely together conducting research, planning strategies, and meeting with business leaders and public officials. Meanwhile, all member churches were required to mobilize for large actions in support of the campaign. ACT drew upon the political clout of the Texas network to influence Governor Richards to commit start-up funds for Synergy before she lost her re-election bid to George W. Bush in 1994.

In 1995, Synergy was launched with funding from the state and county governments. After the campaign was won, ACT members continued to serve on the board of directors of Synergy, and ACT member churches also played a role in recruiting and selecting candidates for training slots. Unlike Project QUEST in San Antonio, which maintained a separate incorporated identity, Synergy became administered by the county, a component part of its workforce development program.[37]

Building Understanding and Trust

ACT provides the opportunity for leaders from different racial communities to cooperate with each other at a number of different levels. The federated structure of the organization allows participants to develop their leadership within their own congregations and communities, by participating in church committees and cluster groups of such committees. These committees can initiate their own campaigns, with approval (and therefore support) from the organization as a whole. At the same time, church committees have the responsibility to carry out organization-wide campaigns in their neighborhoods. They have to raise money for the organization. And they have to mobilize their networks for actions of the organization.

ACT leaders from different communities have the opportunity to build bridging ties with each other through working together on action teams and on organization-wide leadership bodies. Action teams work on a variety of campaigns, like job training. Meanwhile, about forty-five leaders, drawn from all member congregations, meet monthly as the organization's central decision-making body. The Strategy Team brings about sixteen leaders from the three racial groups in the organization together to act as the executive committee. Bigger delegate assemblies include participants active in member churches and action teams, where they report to each other about their work and discuss the organization's business. Yearly conventions provide the opportunity for the broader ranks of ACT's supporters to meet in a multiracial gathering. Table 1 describes ACT's organizational structure.

ACT leaders from all three racial groups report that IAF involvement has led them to build new and deeper relationships across racial lines. Rosemary Galdiano, an Hispanic lay leader and chair of ACT's Health Care Action Team, grew up in a predominantly Hispanic neighborhood in Fort Worth. She became more comfortable with whites through her studies with students at the University of Texas at Austin and through

TABLE 1
Organizational Units of the Allied Communities of Tarrant, 1993[38]

Co-Chairs	2 or 3 top leaders, including chair of Strategy Team and of TOC
Strategy Team (executive committee)	16 key leaders, triracial meets bimonthly plans strategy; sets agenda for TOC co-opts its members from TOC
The Organizing Council (TOC) (steering committee)	45 attendees (but varies) usually 2–3 leaders from each member church meets monthly decision-making body
Delegates Assembly	size varies, roughly 30–80 in attendance meets occasionally (usually every 3 months) ratifies important decisions
Annual Convention	all leaders mobilize networks 1–2,000 present depending on year ritual events that endorse agenda, leadership, and conducts business with public officials
Action Teams · Job Training · Bond · Health Care · Parental Empowerment (schools) · Education Reform · Poly (neighborhood) Strategy Project · Utility Reform · Money Campaign (fund-raising)	5–7 members; usually triracial leaders drawn from different churches
Member Church Committees	addresses issues for church/neighborhood implements ACT-wide campaigns in the church

Note: All Texas IAF organizations follow this basic structure, but sometimes use different names for the units.

working with nurses at All Saints Hospital. Before her involvement with ACT, however, fear and misunderstanding shaped her attitudes towards the black community. According to Galdiano,

> Growing up in Fort Worth, my experience with the African American community has been negative. My father is very prejudiced. In high school racial tension was very high. There was a riot in school. I became afraid at school. I saw hate and it frightened me. We never mixed after that. . . . This organization

[ACT] changed my fear and misunderstanding with the black community by working together on a practical level. Working a phone bank, you begin to develop relationships, develop trust and begin to depend on each other. . . . I still have a long way to go. Most of my relationships are not with blacks, except now I have a few.[39]

According to ACT leaders, working together in the organization builds deeper relationships than most people have the opportunity to develop in other settings. Joyce Oliver, an African American lay leader of ACT, works with whites and a few Hispanics at her job. She compares those relationships to the ones she has built in ACT:

But ACT is different. On the job, you just do a job. In ACT, you sit down and learn their values, how they feel. You begin to share, build a bond. Because it's church-based, if you say we're all children of God, it will prove that. It will change the way you look at other races, or else you'll leave. And some do.[40]

ACT makes it a point to vary the location of its meetings around the city. This policy brings leaders from one community into parts of the city they normally do not see. Juanita Cisneros, an Hispanic lay leader of ACT, lives in a predominantly Anglo, middle-class community on the south side of Fort Worth. She joined the Job Training Action Team when she first got involved in ACT out of concern for her two sons' futures:

One of the reasons I stayed with jobs work [the job-training campaign] is that my husband and I grew up in poor families. We put ourselves through school and we have good jobs, feel secure. But I've been disappointed that even though we gave our kids all they wanted, my son didn't go to college. So at 24 he finds himself working at $6 or $6.50 per hour and he has a baby to support. He still lives with us. My younger son is serious at high school, but doesn't take education seriously. If you don't go to college, there is a lack of opportunity for good-paying jobs.[41]

Involvement in ACT required Cisneros to go to parts of town she never visited before:

Job team meetings were in the black part of town. I always went, but I felt uneasy, due to the high crime rate there. I would try to go with someone else. I don't think twice about going to South Hills [in a white middle-class area]. I'm familiar with the north side [a poor Hispanic area] because I used to live there. Others might be afraid to go there. But it wouldn't even occur to me to worry about it. Even now, I still try to go with someone if a meeting is in the black community. Black people, the men especially, I've met in ACT are all gentlemen. I wouldn't hesitate to go anywhere with them. But everyone else isn't a gentleman.[42]

Crossing the lines of residential segregation proves to be a powerful force for constructing a sense of the city as a single community in the minds of IAF leaders. Lutheran minister Terry Boggs reports that ". . . everything changes because of relationships [built in ACT]. I can't write off a part of the city anymore because I know those people and have worked with them."[43]

Religious Values as a Broadly Unifying Force

The largely Christian religious tradition that ACT leaders share appears to provide the glue to cement the ties developed through common work.[44] In a society so fractured along racial lines, people from different racial groups often have difficulty seeing a common interest. A set of common beliefs, a shared identity as people of God, helps people to identify themselves as members of the same community. Relationship building through dialogue and negotiation, and through mutual support and sustained cooperation for common goals, contributes to unity; but it does not appear to be sufficient. In the Texas IAF shared religious traditions help define all members of the organization, indeed all members of the broader Fort Worth community, as "children of God."

According to Maurice Simpson, an African American lay leader in ACT, "religious values help keep racism down. It's key to unity along race lines. At every meeting we talk of our values. Religious values are even more important than the common goal. It helps people see the common goal."[45] As IAF leader Joyce Oliver put it above, "if you say we're all children of God . . . it will change the way you look at other races."

ACT leader Reverend Terry Boggs discusses the importance of a common faith to cooperation as well as the necessity to control the divisive potential of religion. "I know no other forum where I can sit down with blacks and Hispanics with common interests and a trust level. It's due to our common faith. Even if we differ theologically, we are all part of God's family. Some would like the faith commitment to be stronger publicly. But we need to be careful not to exacerbate differences theologically."[46]

The importance of shared religious values can be seen by the attention ACT pays to the use of symbols and rituals to celebrate them. ACT starts all of its meetings with a prayer. Even the smallest meetings start with prayer. Prayers serve to tap the religious sentiment that motivated many leaders to get involved in the IAF. Moreover, they act as symbols to remind participants of their religious commonality. Since these prayers are to serve a unifying function, they typically draw from scriptures that stress the importance of community. Prayers that emphasize the affirmation of particular faiths, or that are associated too strongly with particular denominations, are avoided. Instead, ministers (and lay leaders) say prayers that call people to social action, or that refer to the building of community.

ACT also maintains a tradition of holding ecumenical services every year or so. Many ACT leaders report that they consider this service to be one of the organization's most important public actions. Four hundred and fifty people attended the prayer service in 1992, some of whom do not normally attend ACT events. IAF leaders believe that the service shows the wider community that ACT is a different type of political organization. And it inspires leaders to continue their involvement, while attracting potential new recruits.[47]

A common faith has also played an important role in uniting leaders from ACT with the multiracial group of leaders in the Texas IAF network. Mary Beth Rogers reports the experience of Patricia Ozuna, an Hispanic Catholic leader of COPS, at an early meeting of the network.[48] According to Ozuna, the network's leadership thought sharing Bible verses that inspired IAF leaders to help others in the community would be a good way to come together. The readings included a passage from the First Epistle of John:

> But if a man has enough to live on, and yet when he sees his brother in need shuts up his heart against him, how can it be said that the divine love dwells in him? My children, love must not be a matter of words or talk; it must be genuine and show itself in action. (I John 3:17–18)

Another leader read a verse from Isaiah:

> This, rather, is the fasting that I wish: releasing those bound unjustly, untying the thongs of the yoke; setting free the oppressed, breaking every yoke. (Isaiah 58:6)

A third quoted from Matthew:

> Truly, I say to you, as you did it to one of the least of these, my brethren, you did it to me. (Matthew 25:40)

Ozuna described the impact of the experience on herself:

> Here were people who had a wide difference in income. The voices were different, the religions had their differences, but the words were the same. There was a common message that united them. It still gives me goose bumps.

The Limits of Multiracial Unity in Act

In 1991 a white skinhead shot and killed a black man, Donald Thomas, in Arlington, Texas, a suburban city next to Fort Worth. The jury convicted Christopher William Brosky of the hate-inspired killing in 1993. But the court let him go without a prison term, sentencing him only to probation. The African American community reacted angrily. More than ten thousand people, mostly black, marched in protest through downtown Fort Worth the Sunday after the verdict, an historic event for a city where large public demonstrations are a rarity.[49] Several African American ACT leaders, including Reverend Robert Sample of the Holy Tabernacle Church of God in Christ and Reverend C. M. Singleton of the First Missionary Baptist Church, participated in planning and leading the protest.

The ACT organization itself, however, did not participate in the protest. ACT did not explicitly decide against participation; it simply made no decision at all. Afterwards, there was some resentment expressed by African Americans in ACT that the organization did not join the march. Many Anglo and Hispanic leaders also expressed disappointment that ACT could not respond to an issue that was an outrage not just to the black community, but to nearly everyone of all races in Fort Worth.

ACT leaders cited many reasons for the organization's failure to act. First, although ACT can and does react quickly to new developments in campaigns it has formally adopted, ACT's structure does not easily allow it to respond quickly to new issues. Second, ACT does not see itself as a "protest" organization, so does not normally address this kind of issue. Several ACT leaders described the Brosky protest as a "movement" issue, by which they mean it is a single-issue campaign that does not lead to long-term change. Yet the protest did lead to pressure to raise new charges against Brosky, to consider changes in sentencing guidelines, and to hire more black lawyers in the District Attorney's office.[50] Third, African Americans in ACT did not demand that the organization take part in the protest. The IAF's "iron rule," never do for someone else what they can do for themselves, conditions the organization to react when a community pushes their "self-interest." Nevertheless, ACT often does decide centrally if an issue is of benefit to the organization and will send an organizer out to help generate action in a community. In the Brosky case, Anglo and Hispanic leaders, and the white lead organizer, may not have grasped quickly enough the unique importance of the verdict to the black community; consequently, they did not ensure ACT's participation.[51]

Whatever the immediate causes of ACT's failure to participate in the Brosky protest, the event revealed a significant weakness in the organization's level of multiracial understanding. To their credit, ACT leaders had taken initiatives of central importance to the black community, like their campaign at Morningside School. Moreover, they had developed an ability to find common ground for action in bond elections and job-training campaigns. With Fort Worth's most prominent black pastor, Reverend Nehemiah Davis, as co-chair of the organization, and with white ACT leaders willing to actively support campaigns like Morningside School important to black ACT leaders, ACT had achieved significant interracial accomplishments.

But ACT leaders seldom discussed issues of race or racism directly. Nor did the organization provide a forum through which Hispanic and Anglo leaders could develop an appreciation for the historical experiences of the African American community. In fact, through the eighties, the Texas IAF network rarely discussed issues of racism per se publicly. For example, although the Morningside School campaign addressed the failures of public education to provide schooling equally to African American children, ACT never discussed the issue as one of race, either internally or in public. Although race was always an implicit background to the effort, the organization, and the Texas IAF network generally, did not see an advantage to raising the question publicly. When the Brosky case forced the issue of racism so directly, ACT was not prepared to act.

The IAF's relational organizing strategy was supposed to provide an important vehicle for advancing interracial understanding. By having leaders meet in individual meetings to share their personal experiences, leaders were meant to achieve greater understanding of each other's experiences. Many ACT participants, however, report that leaders in the organization failed to pursue fully the IAF's relational organizing strategy amongst themselves. According to Claudia Camp, a veteran white ACT leader, "we never developed the culture of individual meetings. . . . So we developed an inner core of leaders very well informed and who understood things so well. But there wasn't a culture that created a bond between individuals."[52] ACT also had a talented lead organizer, Perry Perkins, who built strong relationships with ACT leaders, and between ACT and important business and political leaders in Fort Worth. In Camp's view, Perkins' exceptional abilities allowed the organization to achieve victories even though it lacked sufficient relationship building among leaders. "Perry [Perkins] was here longer than the other lead organizers, five years. . . . Perry was relational, but didn't teach being relational. He was the spider in the web."[53]

Instead of forging a united and diverse leadership core, ACT relied upon Perkins and a small set of strong institutional leaders, people like Reverend Davis, Reverend Boggs, and Raymond Rodriguez. Between the three of them, they symbolized the triracial unity of the organization. But ACT never developed a strong culture of individual meetings that could forge a united leadership with a deeper understanding of racial experience. According to Camp, "Reverend Davis made an enormous personal step to invest himself in the organization early on. He has an enormous amount of political wisdom. But he didn't share it with anyone. He was the hand of God on the organizers."

In Reverend Davis' view, the problem stemmed from the IAF's efforts to expand the number of its affiliates in the region too rapidly. Consequently, according to Davis, Ernie Cortes and Christine Stephens lacked the time to adequately supervise the lead organizers assigned to local affiliates. He argued that since 1983 he has been trying to work his way out of leadership. "But some come in and see ACT as Reverend Davis and some other's organization. They're right and they're wrong. It's my and Ray Rodriguez's organization because we continually invest time and energy. Others can be here to stay at the table and keep at it and we're open to it."[54]

Relationship building and systematic mentoring of new leaders by experienced ones had produced a collective leadership in COPS unparalleled in size, unity, and sophistication in the Texas IAF. Since the majority of COPS leaders are Hispanic women, they could, of course, draw upon a deep understanding of their shared experiences and traditions. In ACT the diversity of the organization's leadership made relationship building and systematic mentoring more difficult, but all the more important. Some ACT leaders reported that mentoring by leaders, usually of the same gender and race, was important to their development. But many said they lacked such experience. Moreover, a few women remarked that having to deal with experienced male leaders of a different gender and race was quite difficult and even hindered their early development as leaders.[55] Comparing ACT's experience with the strong leadership core built in COPS, Reverend Davis observed, "It can be done. But we're trying to cover a whole city. We're doing an integrated ethnic and interdenominational thing. That makes the potential greater than COPS, but it's more difficult."[56] Reflecting back on the Brosky events several years later, organizer Perkins asserts, "we didn't formulize the discussion of race, but there was always some discussion of race. But was it as deep as it should have been? No. I'd do it much deeper now."[57]

Conclusion

A number of important lessons can be learned from ACT's experience for how to build bridging social capital. First of all, a set of common beliefs and a shared identity provide an important foundation for bringing diverse communities together. In ACT, religious values provided an initial basis of trust to get the process of collaboration going in the first place. The shared identity as people of God helped provide a glue to keep participants committed to supporting each other. In order for religion to play a unifying role, the IAF must search for the commonalities present across religious traditions, at least across Christian and Jewish faiths. The last chapter of this book considers which religious and secular communities the IAF process fails to include, and the extent to which more secular kinds of community traditions can play a similar unifying role. For now, it is important to recognize that shared values can provide a necessary foundation for multiracial collaboration.

The second lesson that can be learned from ACT's experience is the importance of institutional organizing. The last chapter discussed the importance of federation in relation to the state network, but it applies to the structure of each local organization as well. The IAF's broad-based organizations are federated forms that respect the integrity of community traditions and institutions, while also creating forums for cooperative action. Participants do not have to abandon their racial identities in the organization. In fact, the IAF works to enhance the development of particular communities and their institutions like churches and schools. It allows these communities a degree of autonomy to develop their own initiatives. At the same time, while leaders can draw strength from the shared bonds and traditions of their own community, they can also move beyond their inherent limitations to forge new social connections and a broader sense of community.

Compared to coalitions that limit cooperation to institutional representation at the top, ACT set in motion a broader social capital building process. Commitments to support African American initiatives around education, coupled with mutual support and shared campaigns in Synergy, fostered greater trust and mutual respect amongst grass-roots leaders. Working together on action teams and leadership bodies gave many community leaders their first opportunity to build relationships with people of different racial and socio-economic backgrounds. Through cooperative action, stereotypes get challenged and an appreciation of the common good is developed.

While the shared religious values and federated structure of the IAF's broad-based organizations can provide the necessary conditions for building bridging social capital, they do not appear to be sufficient for creating a deep level of multiracial unity. The IAF's relational organizing strategy is supposed to infuse cooperative relationships with deeper understandings of diverse racial experiences. In ACT, relationship building among leaders failed to fully develop, however, and so the organization was ill-prepared to respond to the Brosky affair. Yet the Brosky incident was not a minor issue. It spoke to the historic concerns of African Americans about racial injustice.

By avoiding open discussion of racism both internally and externally, relationship building is likely to remain fairly superficial. The failure to openly confront racism posed a particular problem for the Texas IAF because the network originated in the Hispanic community of San Antonio and yet sought to incorporate African Americans, as well as Anglos, as fully equal partners. In fact, it was the emergence of a critical mass of African American leaders and organizers in the network that would prompt the Texas IAF to deepen multiracial understanding in the network, the subject of the next chapter.

When Lady Coleman Byrd arrived as the new lead organizer for ACT in Fort Worth, she set out to reorganize the group by recruiting new leaders and fostering deeper relationships among them.[58] Byrd, the Southwest IAF's first African American lead organizer assigned to a local organization, became involved initially in the IAF while serving as a nondenominational minister working with drug users and prostitutes in Port Arthur, Texas. She became a leader in the sponsoring committee for what later became the Triangle Interfaith organization. The IAF subsequently hired her as an organizer and assigned her to the network's Houston affiliate and then to Dallas Interfaith. She was promoted to lead organizer with the assignment to ACT in 1995.[59]

Byrd's arrival as the first African American lead organizer in the Southwest IAF was not mere happenstance. In fact, it came as a result of the network's efforts to deepen and expand its base in the African American community. The participation of more and more African Americans in the network, a process in which ACT itself had played an important part, pushed the IAF to hire black organizers. The network then began to address the particular experiences of African Americans more directly and to raise the issue of racism more explicitly. The next chapter examines this development, what might be considered the second stage in the network's efforts to build a model for multiracial collaboration.

Five

Deepening Multiracial Collaboration

EFFORTS to forge multiracial cooperation for the pursuit of common interests in America have often collapsed in the face of continued patterns of racial discrimination and oppression.[1] Finding common interests on the basis of shared values does provide the necessary foundation for multiracial collaboration, as the IAF's experience in Fort Worth suggests. Moreover, working together in a common organizational form offers a basis for deepening understanding and trust over time. But it does not guarantee that a deep appreciation for the experiences of different groups will develop across racial lines. Such an appreciation, and an effort to address internal problems of ignorance and stereotyping, may well be necessary so that multiracial organizations can publicly address the issues of racial injustice that continue to undermine communities of color.

This chapter examines the process through which the Southwest IAF attempted to expand its reach into African American communities so that it could become a more fully multiracial network—of Hispanics, Anglos, and African Americans. It then discusses how growing African American participation in the network prompted the IAF to educate its organizers and leaders about the African American experience and to confront issues of racism within the network. It shows how the network struggled to balance common interests with attention to the particular concerns of African Americans, and began to develop the capacity to publicly address questions of racism. The chapter concludes that the Southwest IAF network offers an important alternate model for multiracial organizing, one that can make important gains in combating racism.

Achieving a Critical Mass of Black Participation

When Ernesto Cortes organized Mexican Americans in San Antonio into COPS, he gave the Texas IAF network an enduring base among Hispanics. During the eighties, the IAF built several other powerful organizations among Mexican Americans in the Rio Grande Valley (Valley Interfaith and The Border Organization) and El Paso (EPISO), and had extensive Hispanic participation in multiracial affiliates in Houston, Fort Worth, and Austin. Meanwhile, the IAF launched its first campaigns as a state network around issues of central importance to Mexican American immigrants in Texas, organizing for indigent health care and to bring water and sewer services to *colonias*. Directed by a Mexican American native to Texas (Cortes), and with a number of Hispanic organizers on staff, the Texas IAF had a solid reputation as a representative of the Hispanic community.

The situation was different for African Americans. The IAF had long been interested in building support among African Americans, but it had to do so from the context of its already established Hispanic base. In the Texas IAF's early days, organizers and leaders tried to be careful to respect black interests and sought to build relationships of trust with important African American ministers even as they stayed outside of the network. For example, Reverend Claude Black, the most prominent black pastor in San Antonio, declined to join the IAF effort there for many years, hoping to form an all black community-based organization instead. Cortes worked to develop a close relationship with him anyway, inviting Black, for example, to the IAF's national training. Moreover, COPS consulted and collaborated with him on campaigns in San Antonio. The organization worked behind the scenes to dissuade Mexican Americans from running for city council in the historically black east side of San Antonio, even as Hispanics began to surpass African Americans in numbers there.[2] Cortes invited Black to state network events, and the minister was invited to give a speech at the Texas network's founding convention in 1990.

Reverend Black, for his part, collaborated with COPS and the Texas IAF for many years, even as he sought to found an all-black network. He eventually did join the multiracial IAF organization in San Antonio, Metro Alliance, in 1995. According to Black, he signed on in part because he was impressed with its work to improve schools in black communities, and in part because he had given up hope for a separate black network which he saw as increasingly irrelevant anyway. Continued Hispanic migration into the east side made multiracial cooperation necessary even in San Antonio's historic black neighborhoods. According to Black, "integration has changed our community structure. There is no way to improve this community as a black community. It must be improved as a biracial community. The circumstances changed. If you've been riding on a wagon and it's now a river, you better get a boat."[3] Black's affiliation to the IAF represented the culmination of a twenty-year relationship-building process. It also reflected the degree to which African American leadership had emerged as a fundamental part of the multiracial IAF network in the Southwest.

The first step in this process was the establishment of several multiracial organizations with some significant African American participation from their founding, like TMO in Houston, and, even more so, ACT in Fort

Worth. Drawing upon the commonalities of religious faith, built upon a federated structure that encouraged a degree of autonomy for African Americans, and cemented by the commitment of white and Hispanic IAF leaders to actively support initiatives like school reform that emerged from black communities, the IAF proved able to draw in an initial core of African American leaders. Along with ACT, the IAF also built a multiracial organization with significant African American leadership in Austin, founded in 1985. Meanwhile, organizing committees in Dallas and Port Arthur emerged in the late eighties with significant black leadership.

Hiring African American Organizers

If the network was to be truly inclusive, however, it would need black organizers as well as leaders. The Texas IAF had long been interested in recruiting black organizers, and had hired one or two from time to time. None, however, stayed on to attain sufficient training to become a lead organizer. In some sense, however, the lack of African American organizers was not seen as a fundamental problem because, philosophically, the IAF resisted the idea that only black organizers could organize in black communities. According to IAF supervisor Christine Stephens, "in principle, we are against the idea of assigning African American organizers to recruit and work with African American churches. We want to hire the best. We may get a short-run advantage from assigning organizers by race, but in the long run, a good organizer can organize anywhere and do it well. . . . Also, we don't want to restrict black organizers to only organize in the black community. They must have a broad perspective and ability to organize in all communities. They will have to if they want to become a lead organizer."[4]

As more African American leaders emerged in the Southwest network, however, they began to press harder for the IAF to recruit and train black organizers. Some of the leaders themselves expressed an interest in becoming organizers, for example Lady Coleman Byrd from Triangle Interfaith. And the network's growing work in black communities gave them additional contact with an expanding pool of potential recruits. The network's success in school reform, itself an initiative that grew out of ACT's work in Fort Worth's black community, allowed Cortes to secure a five-year grant from the Rockefeller Foundation to hire education coordinators to do parental organizing around schools. Combined with a grant from the Florence and John Schumann Foundation, these funds supported a large-scale recruitment and training program for the network, as the more successful education coordinators could be promoted to the organizer ranks. With pressure from African American leaders and funds from private foundations, Cortes launched an aggressive campaign to recruit black organizers.

In rapid succession in the early nineties, the IAF hired a number of promising black organizers, many of them church ministers and community leaders met through the work of local affiliates. Some resigned early, but many stayed on. By the mid-nineties, several African American organizers had completed enough years of supervised experience to be promoted to the lead organizer position. Lady Coleman Byrd became the first black lead organizer with her assignment to ACT in 1995.

In 1996 Willie Bennett became the network's second black lead organizer, assigned to Austin Interfaith. Bennett was a Baptist preacher. He had been working as the associate pastor of a church in a public housing project in Fort Worth and the director of a Methodist community center, when he first had contact with the IAF. ACT's lead organizer Perry Perkins helped Bennett get a crack house out of the project. Bennett was impressed with the IAF's effectiveness and thought he could learn a lot from organizing for the network. Growing up in a fundamentalist Baptist congregation and trained in a Southern Baptist seminary, Bennett reports he came into the IAF "very strict and tight. So I had to struggle to grasp the concepts. I came to IAF because I thought they could teach me, they could make me tougher. Then I planned to leave."[5] He went to Dallas to train under Christine Stephens, and never did leave the network.

But his early days in the IAF were not smooth. "I came in wanting something out of it, not because I liked the IAF. I had real struggles and fights with Christine. And I'm a quick learner." Bennett had to struggle with the tension between his religious conservatism and the more broadminded theological orientation of the IAF. His political liberalism helped. "Part of my tradition is political liberalism, that does something to our theology. [Baptists] can be homophobic, but not want to pass laws to suppress them. Our passion for justice is the biggest thing of all. It's that understanding of justice that allows me to be in a network that is theologically liberal. The work is political, so I can do it. If it was a Christian organization, I couldn't be here. It [the IAF] allows us to live out our beliefs and challenge others to live out their tradition. . . . We say we're a political organization and will challenge people to live up to their tradition of justice and [concern for] the poor."

In 1997 Leonora Friend became the network's third African American lead organizer, when she took over that position for Fort Bend Interfaith. Friend had been a newspaper and television reporter, and then a private employment consultant prior to being hired as an education coordinator for ACT in Fort Worth. She later worked as an organizer in Dallas, to train under Christine Stephens, before her assignment to the IAF affiliate in Fort Bend County outside of Houston. The racial composition of Fort

Bend County, with a fairly small black population, apparently did not matter to Friend. She saw the position as a great opportunity for herself, since she would be pioneering IAF efforts to organize in rapidly growing urban/suburban edge communities.

The Southwest network's new organizing effort in New Orleans proved to be fertile ground from which to recruit black organizers. Perry Perkins went to New Orleans in 1995 to build the Southwest network's first predominantly black local organization, called The Jeremiah Group. The white organizer Perkins came with five years of experience as lead organizer for ACT in Fort Worth, the affiliate with the Texas network's strongest black participation to date. Although the eventual goal was to build a multiracial organization in New Orleans, the IAF decided to recruit only black congregations at first to ensure that African Americans would see the Jeremiah Group as their organization. The plan, according to Perkins, was to start first in the black community, so "the black churches will invite in the white churches."[6] But Perkins immediately began to recruit trainee organizers out of the effort, including four African Americans in the first year alone: Jacqueline Jones, Alan Jolivette, Bruce Fortner, and Donald Boutte.

Through aggressive recruitment in New Orleans and elsewhere, the IAF rapidly expanded the number of black organizers in the Southwest region to ten by 1997, comprising about one-fifth of its staff. Moreover, by 1997, three of the Southwest region's lead organizers were black, nearly one-quarter of the thirteen lead organizers on staff. By 1999, the network had four black lead organizers and one organizer in an interim lead status, as Bruce Fortner and Van Jones were promoted. For the first time, the network had achieved a critical mass of black organizers.

A critical mass of black leaders emerged in the nineties as well. Each of the network's new affiliates in Dallas, the Beaumont/Port Arthur area, and Omaha, Nebraska, had significant black leadership. As a result, by the mid-nineties the Southwest IAF network had perhaps doubled its black participation from a few years back. The new black leaders from New Orleans and elsewhere played more and more of a prominent role at Southwest network meetings. As they began to co-chair network meetings on a regular basis, these affairs began to take on a much stronger African American character. For example, network meetings opened with prayers from black ministers, and many ministers held forth at these meetings with traditional black preaching styles. While affiliates like ACT had long incorporated significant African American leadership, by the mid-nineties the Southwest network as a whole had achieved that status, both in leadership and in the organizing staff.

Deepening Discussions of Racism

Now that they had achieved a critical mass, many black leaders and organizers began to push for the network to discuss questions of racism more explicitly, and to deepen its understanding of the black experience in America. Reverend Claude Black expresses the sentiment of many African American leaders that the network had to find constructive ways to address questions of racism. "I understand the IAF. If you get into the issue of racism, it's divisive. But I also understand that when they don't deal with it, black organizations question its relevance. Blacks say, 'Is education reform really education reform in my community?'"[7]

In response, Cortes invited a series of prominent black intellectuals and scholars to the seminars he held bi-monthly for his organizers. Early seminars had already included discussions of issues of race, with guests like the sociologist William Julius Wilson, the economist Glenn Loury, and writer Thomas Edsall. During the mid-nineties, however, Cortes invited a broad range of scholars to talk about African American religious, social, and political experience, many of whom advanced a strong antiracist perspective. James Cone discussed his book comparing Malcolm X and Martin Luther King, Jr. Cornel West made a presentation on his book *Race Matters*. Eva Loomis discussed the black Catholic experience, while Michael Dawson discussed black politics. The theologian Delores Williams and economist Ron Ferguson also made seminar presentations. The IAF made special efforts to invite black leaders from local affiliates to attend these seminars.[8]

Taken as a group, the seminars represented an ambitious effort to deepen the network's understanding of the African American experience in America. They also served to provoke discussions among IAF organizers and leaders about issues of race. Leaders and organizers held individual meetings with each other during and after these seminars to continue discussions about the issues raised, and to relate them to their own lives and the work of IAF organizations.

Some of the seminars provoked heated discussions. Black IAF organizer Bruce Fortner found the seminar with James Cone quite agitational. "Its effect was to bring anger to the surface and put it on the table. Even in this organization we tend to be nice to one another. Sometimes we (black people) get caught up in our own rhetoric and become cliché—how bad white people are. . . . It's the same anger and passion James Cone brings to the table. I put it into what I do with the IAF."[9] Expressing anger can be explosive and potentially dangerous. But Fortner believes it also affords the opportunity to challenge stereotypes that exist anyway and that can inhibit collaborative relationships. "I've had two organizers say they were afraid of me because I was black. It was out of their experience. I said how useful can you be to me? They had to deal with their stereotypes. And I had to deal with my stereotypes of them: they were white upper class, country club types. We got at our feelings . . ."

Many African American leaders and organizers looked to the seminars as an opportunity to deepen the understanding of the black experience among the more dominant Hispanic, as well as Anglo, participants in the Texas IAF. Reverend Gerald Britt, one of the co-chairs of the Dallas Interfaith organization, has seen his role, in part, as teaching others about the African American experience:

> My own perspective is that whites and Hispanics can be naive or insensitive in regards to issues of African Americans, and they can be defensive when confronted. . . . There is a tendency to compare African Americans with other groups and say your pain is not so bad. You would never do that to Jews. We have to learn how to respect the pain we've all had to process. Mexican Americans have pain that's part of their history. Blacks have pain. . . . [At the IAF seminar, James] Cone brought up the issue of how African Americans lost their culture. Ernie [Cortes] said something similar happened with Mexican culture. I took exception to it. It was a way of watering down the pain. I said to Ernie at least you can name the language or the tribe that was lost. I can't. In my case it was the intentional obliteration of our culture. I trust Ernie more than I trust most black folks. But there was a lot of tension at that moment. . . . I went to the Holocaust Museum and met a survivor. It would have been completely inappropriate for me to say, "You know, my people have suffered."[10]

The effect of the seminars multiplied, though, when they sparked further discussions of race in individual, relationship-building meetings between leaders in their local organizations. After the seminar with James Cone, organizers and leaders from Dallas Area Interfaith held a retreat on racism. Those present at the seminar with Cone presented a report. According to organizer Fortner, though, "what was good was the individual meetings they did over the retreat. We did the James Cone thing. But the educational aspect, to have an effect, should change people's relationships. That's their importance. . . . As a black organizer coming into an organization that wasn't predominantly black, it was hard to develop relationships outside my race, to see the power in that, to see how they can be useful and teach it to other blacks, to get out of my experience and learn about someone with a completely different experience. It happens in individual meetings. . . . That's the most radical thing this organization teaches."

The commitment to cooperative action on the part of IAF participants in local organizations set an important context for potentially divisive conversations about racism. In Fortner's view, "the Cone seminar brought out that to do anything about racism it must be done in the context of action. I'm tired of rhetoric. . . . The IAF takes two diversely different groups, African Americans and Hispanics, and puts them into action. If we can work together and have tension between us, we can see our commonality."

Dallas Interfaith's white lead organizer, Maribeth Larkin, also found the organization's postseminar retreat on racism useful because it instigated a frank discussion about race that related to the organization's political campaigns. "It was useful because DAI [Dallas Area Interfaith] was right in the middle of a fight to get after-school programs. Our school work has engaged new Hispanic residents in traditionally black communities. So we've challenged black leaders and residents to be more open. For example, [in our work at] Roosevelt High School, we build biracial teams to walk through the neighborhood." These teams knock on the doors of parents and neighborhood residents to engage them in discussions about the school.[11]

IAF supervisor Cortes does not think the seminars in themselves have been that crucial. More important, in his view, has been the time and attention the Southwest IAF paid to developing long-term relationships with a growing number of African American pastors, lay leaders, and school principals. Cortes argues that "the fact that we recruited talented African American organizers made [black] pastors take a look." But, more important in many cases, has been the network's work in education which demonstrated a concrete commitment to the needs of black communities.[12]

Nevertheless, Cortes has been struggling to figure out a productive way to have more open and deeper discussions about race within the network. In Cortes' view, they must be placed squarely within the context of common action and practical politics:

> We don't want to chase our tails [on race]. Those discussions don't seem to go anywhere. However, I'm aware of the need to do that. . . . There has been a lot of that in Dallas. That's why we had Eva Loomis come down, a black nun. We spent three days talking about race. . . . Maybe we feel an open-ended discussion about race is not productive. Dealing with race in relation to power makes sense. There are people who use it to divide people. . . . Dallas people have had conversations with each other about race that have been useful. We do it in a way that avoids the excess of what some blacks and Latinos want to do. I'm trying to figure out how you promote straight, tough, hard, productive talk— in a way that avoids all this postmodern talk. [I want] meaningful talk about education for our kids.[13]

According to Cortes, the network has to constantly strive to balance racial differences with an appreciation of the commonalities of people.

"Through individual stories we get to know group experiences and build trust. But stories only become interesting through action. There's a lot of pain in people's stories that can get obscured if people are seen only in racial terms. We want people to deal with race, up front and honestly. But we also want people to lead with their humanity."[14]

Establishing Multiracial Collaboration in Dallas

The Texas IAF used its developing approach to multiracial collaboration in order to meet one of the network's most difficult challenges to date, building a broad-based organization in the context of Dallas' racially contentious politics. In many ways, Dallas is Texas' capital city and the IAF could never hope to become a central player in state politics as long as it lacked a base in that city. But, according to Texas IAF supervisor Christine Stephens, through the seventies and most of the eighties the network was hesitant to launch a project in Dallas. "Because we had faced so much attack from the right wing in Houston, El Paso, and the Valley, we were afraid to tackle Dallas. Dallas was even more closed politically than Houston, generally a very conservative place. But in the eighties when Texas hit the bust, oil, real estate, and banks all were wiped out. That created an opening."[15]

The IAF stepped into the opening and began to meet with ministers and clergy in Dallas in the late 1980s. In 1990, Christine Stephens moved to Dallas from the lower Rio Grande Valley, where she had been serving as lead organizer for Valley Interfaith and supervisor for the Texas network. The IAF saw the effort as so important to the network, and so difficult to establish, that Stephens relinquished her responsibility for supervising other lead organizers to devote herself full-time to building an IAF organization in Dallas.

Politics and Race in Dallas

Although the economic crisis had created an important opening for the IAF, the network faced important obstacles as well. Dallas had little tradition of popular democracy, and the more recent interventions by communities of color into electoral politics were marred by sharp interracial conflict among African Americans, Hispanics, and whites. Dallas, in fact, had a long tradition of narrow elite rule.[16] The Citizens Council, composed of wealthy white men, had run Dallas politics with a tight fist since the Council's founding by Bill Thornton in 1937. Dominated by bankers and the heads of large Dallas-based corporations, the Council shaped development in Dallas, working behind the scenes to select city councilors, mayors, and the city manager. Elite rule was so narrow that Jim Schutze describes the Dallas of this period as a "well-run predemocratic city-state, ruled by a board of elders who valued wealth and ritual over truth and law."[17]

By the eighties, however, the hold of the Citizens Council on Dallas politics had already begun to unravel. New businesses had emerged whose leaders grew up outside the Council's orbit; and they began to influence political developments. Meanwhile, African Americans began to organize and demand political inclusion. With the 1975 court ruling that eight of the eleven city councilors be elected in single-member districts, rather than citywide, African American and Hispanic candidates began to be elected regularly to the council, albeit in a lower proportion than their population in the city. In 1990, a federal judge ordered that all councilors be elected by single-member districts drawn along racial lines. Consequently, the council that took office in the first election after that ruling consisted of nine whites, four blacks, and two Hispanics.

Although communities of color had gained a significant degree of political representation through single-member districts, the majority of power still rested with white political and business leaders. Moreover, the long history of narrow elite rule meant that elected officials had little experience with an active citizenry. Political power in Dallas had become more fragmented and potentially more open to influence from community groups in the nineties. But many white elected officials were used to groups that came "hat in hand" with their requests, rather than to groups with the more assertive style of the IAF.

In fact, Dallas' business leaders proved more open than the city's political leaders to collaboration with the emerging IAF effort. The recession of the late eighties hit Dallas business hard. The collapse in oil, combined with the savings-and-loan crisis, spurred bank failures. By the end of the decade virtually every Dallas-based bank had been sold. Meanwhile, business development grounded to a halt. By the end of 1987 almost 40 million square feet of office space were vacant in Dallas, more than all of the office space in Boston's central business district.[18]

The changing business climate provoked a transformation of the Citizens Council, now no longer dominant in political affairs. With the election of Trammel Crow corporate chief Don Williams to the chairmanship in 1992, a new generation of leaders took charge of the Council. They hoped to regain an influential position in city affairs once again, in part by collaborating with community-based organizations like Dallas Interfaith. According to Williams, "as you rolled into the eighties there was a sense in Dallas that things took care of themselves—we were successful, prosperous, overly prideful. Then came the unrolling of our very fiber—oil and gas people were going down the drain, the service industry was going down the drain, banks were going down the drain—and that process led to reality therapy. It also began to expose some of the deeper problems in the community that the gloss of success and growth and prosperity hid. The darker side is definitely here, and I think over the last few years we've tried to become more sensitive to those kinds of issues."[19] Citizens Council leader, attorney Tom Luce, went so far as to pledge support for Dallas Interfaith at a public meeting in early 1992.[20] A former Republican candidate for governor, Luce had previously worked closely with the Texas IAF network. As Ross Perot's personal attorney, he collaborated with the network on the mid-eighties effort to reform public education in the state.

Meanwhile, many of the African Americans who ran for political office also continued to publicly protest the city's racism. John Wiley Price became the highest elected black official in Dallas when he won election as a County Commissioner in 1984. But he continued to lead public protest while carrying out his administrative duties. He was arrested on a number of occasions in various protest activities. On New Year's Day in 1993, he led a small demonstration outside the Cotton Bowl, chanting "Welcome to Dallas. This is just like Johannesburg. . . . Dallas is the most racist city in the country."[21]

Racial conflict on the school board was particularly virulent, with black school-board trustees concentrating their attacks on the failure of the school administration to fulfill a court-ordered desegregation plan. Other African American activists charged racism in the police department. In 1992, *Fortune* decided to drop Dallas from its long tenure on the magazine's "top-ten" list of the best cities for doing business, citing poor race relations as the reason.

Continued protests against racism came in the context of some significant gains in public employment for African Americans and Hispanics. Under a court desegregation order, the school district had increased minority employment and promotions. By 1992, 51.3 percent of school-level administrators were African American and 17.9 percent Hispanic, while 36 percent of central staff administrators were African American and 17.5 percent Hispanic. 37.2 percent of its teachers were African American and 8.1 percent Hispanic. Minority gains in the police department were slower, but still significant. Between 1983 and 1992, the percentage of minority officers rose from 13 percent to 28 percent, with one out of five officers now African American. By 1992 minority firms had garnered 26.4 percent of city contracts. Moreover, African Americans had begun to be appointed to high offices, so that blacks held the positions of executive director of the Dallas-Fort Worth International Airport, city manager, interim police chief, and school superintendent. An African American, Ron Kirk, won election as Dallas' first black mayor in 1996.[22]

Despite gains for some people of color in employment and contracting, however, protest against racism continued to be fueled by the persistent poverty in which much of the black and Hispanic community lingered. Many Dallas African Americans continued to suffer from a poverty made worse by its contrast to the growth of affluent, white North Dallas. If African Americans had not shared equally in the boom years of the seventies and early eighties, they faced the worst of it in the downturn of the late eighties and early nineties. Although some African Americans did prosper during this period, and many took the opportunity to move to outlying suburbs, many remained behind facing poverty and deteriorating neighborhoods. By 1990, nearly 350,000 Dallas residents lived in poor neighborhoods, almost all of them black or Hispanic.[23] Per capita income for whites in Dallas was almost three times that of blacks, with Hispanics even farther behind. Meanwhile, white exodus from the school system had reduced the proportion of white students to less than 15 percent by 1992. Seventy-two percent of eighth-grade white students still in the district read at grade level, but only 35 percent of black and 38 percent of Hispanic students did so.[24]

Many African Americans in Dallas worried that their tenuous gains would soon be displaced by the growing influence of Hispanics, who emerged in the early nineties as a new political force. After rapidly growing for two decades, by 1990 the Hispanic community, almost entirely Mexican American, constituted more than 20 percent of Dallas' population. Taking a cue from African Americans, many Hispanics felt it was time they received their fair share of political positions and public jobs. The rise in demand for Hispanic political power in Dallas, however, came at the very moment when the black community finally began to achieve a significant measure of power itself, and when many felt these limited gains needed to be aggressively defended.

As a result, African American and Hispanic elected officials fought openly in Dallas' political institutions, with the racial confrontations particularly severe on the school board. While Hispanics were threatening to reach parity with blacks in the city's population, by the mid-nineties Hispanics had already surpassed blacks in the number of children in the school district.[25] Hispanic politicians and activists began calling for their fair share of jobs and school board positions. And African Americans on the school board began charging the white power structure with manipulating Hispanics to keep blacks down. One anonymous leaflet circulated among black activists and clergy characterized school board policy this way: "If you're white you're right; if you're brown stick around; if you're Black get back!"[26]

Such intense racial competition in the political arena made IAF organizing in Dallas quite difficult. Dallas Interfaith wanted to be the vehicle for the empowerment of African Americans, long resident but historically excluded from participation in political institutions. At the same time, the organization also wanted to be a vehicle for the empowerment of a rapidly growing and fairly new Hispanic community. But these two communities were often at odds, competing for limited resources, and battling it out in the political arena. Dallas Interfaith organizers needed a strategy to empower each community, black and Hispanic, in a way that promoted mutual cooperation between them. Meanwhile, they wanted to engage white Dallas, a community in the process of fleeing the inner city, to support the initiatives of these communities, and to come to see Dallas Interfaith as representing the interests of their community as well.

Organizing in Black Dallas

IAF efforts to build a base in black Dallas required a deep appreciation for the experiences of that community in confronting racism. In race relations Dallas has always been more like the deep South than the West.[27] Racism runs deep in Dallas, with a long history stretching back to the city's founding in the mid-nineteenth century. In 1860 a fire of suspicious origin burned the business district of the young city to the ground. In response, the powerful proslavery white community rounded up every black slave in the county. Three were convicted of arson and lynched. Meanwhile, Anglo elites ordered the whipping of every slave in the county.[28] In the twenties, Dallas was the largest center of Ku Klux Klan activity in the country, with a bigger chapter than any city in the Old South. In the forties and fifties, the Dallas black community faced systematic oppression and intimidation when blacks began to make efforts to move out of the ghetto. Open violence, including beatings and arson attacks against blacks trying to move to South Dallas, was common.

A kind of a truce was reached in the fifties, based upon what Jim Schutze has called "the accommodation."[29] The city continued to be run by a small Anglo elite centered in the Citizens Council. Rather than mobilizing and confronting those Anglos, black pastors became the community's spokesmen and developed individual relationships with white power holders. Although that type of relationship was common in many cities, the extent of accommodation in Dallas was particularly profound. Black minister S. M. Wright held a monopoly of power in the black community from his position as head of the Interdenominational Ministerial Alliance. The grip of the accommodationist pastors proved strong enough to prevent the civil rights movement from establishing a base in Dallas, which experienced no riots either. According to William Farmer, "I remember when SNCC was here to organize blacks. S. M. Wright got up and spoke to them. [He said,] 'Do not cut off your arm to downtown.' He was the arm. If there was a problem, have your pastor talk to Dr. Wright and he'd talk to city hall or the business community and he'd work it out."[30] Young organizers from the Southern Christian Leadership Congress (SCLC) fought a losing battle with Wright and the old-line black leadership to establish the civil rights movement in Dallas. After a few brief successes, the movement quickly petered out.[31]

When the IAF began meeting with black ministers in Dallas in the late eighties, Wright and his allies among the pastors of the most important black churches still held a significant degree of power. The IAF represented a threat to their traditional style of accommodationist representation, and the older pastors stayed out of the effort. But many younger black pastors were frustrated, both with the old-guard ministerial leadership as well as with the politics of race as they were being played out on the city council and school board. Heading churches located in some of the poorest Dallas neighborhoods, these ministers struggled daily with the deterioration of black community life at the ground level.

The IAF found a powerful entree to this group of pastors in Reverend Barry Jackson. Jackson accepted the pastorship of Munger Avenue Baptist Church, at one time the largest black church in Dallas, in June of 1988. He had just spent seven years as a pastor and leader of the IAF organization in Austin. Jackson himself came to the IAF originally from a black power perspective, having been inspired by Malcolm X and Muhammad Ali as a teenager growing up in Bastrop, Texas. He led student strikes at his high school and college, going on to serve in the military and then to seminary. In his early contact with the IAF, Jackson argued with Cortes, whom he thought was downplaying the importance of the civil rights movement. Cortes, for his part, pushed Jackson to consider the limits of black power. Jackson recounts his experience:

> So I began to read about the multiethnic model. When Jesus was born, the first people to come were shepherds, those left out. And the rich came. Christ brought them together. Ernie gave me "The Tent of Presence" a piece by black pastors involved in the IAF on the east coast. It talks about the strengths and weaknesses of different strategies and concludes for the need to address common issues. As long as we work separately, we lose.[32]

Jackson gradually moved towards the IAF's multiracial perspective, in part because he still found room within it to appreciate African American experience and tradition. He continued to recognize the importance of black power, but did not want to be limited to it. According to Jackson, "there was a time for black theology as race based. I don't reject that. Integration hurt us more than helped us. Our businesses were destroyed. We forfeited who we are. It's okay to claim your history and culture. But it's not okay to limit yourself to that. It doesn't understand that our welfare is tied up together." By the time Jackson arrived in Dallas, he had become a senior IAF leader, and eventually served on the board of the Southwest IAF network, the leaders' board of the national IAF, and was a member of the IAF's national black clergy caucus.

Jackson took his arguments for a balance between black power and multiracial organizing to black ministers in Dallas, where he found a positive response among younger pastors of churches in poor communities. Out of that group of ministers, Reverend Gerald Britt, the minister of New Mount Moriah Baptist Church, emerged as the most prominent black leader in Dallas Area Interfaith. One of the few Dallas natives in the organization, Britt became a passionate advocate for a more aggressive community-based politics in the black community, as well as for interracial cooperation. Britt found that many black pastors were impressed with the IAF's attempts to promote triracial cooperation in Dallas. But others did not understand the IAF and continued to be suspicious of the network as a mainly Hispanic organization. To those critics, Britt argued that multiracial organizing should not be counterposed to organizing in the black community:

> We're struggling for a piece of the pie. In the black community, there is still a sense that we need an Afrocentric focus, so we need to build up black organizations. Prejudice and bigotry may also play a part. You don't have to be less black to work with Hispanics and Anglos. If you approach it correctly, your involvement will deepen your appreciation for your own culture and see others as allies for the needs of your own community.[33]

Moreover, Britt argued, participation in the IAF has a positive impact on a pastor's church. "The IAF has a focus on building institutions as well. So participation in the IAF effort can help build your church and community. That's not true of organizations like the NAACP, for example," which Britt suggests mainly draw money and activists from black churches without contributing anything back.

Reflecting the existence of strong black leadership in the organization, Dallas Interfaith proceeded to give organizational priority to addressing issues of central concern to the African American community. The group selected the predominantly black Roosevelt High School as its first Alliance School, and later began organizing in the elementary and middle schools that fed into Roosevelt. Since gains in education would come slowly, Reverend Britt and other black ministers worked to identify a campaign that could demonstrate concrete benefits to the black community as quickly as possible. The black South Dallas cluster in Dallas Interfaith launched a campaign to develop affordable housing in the area. The immediate goal was to build fifty houses over three years in the neighborhood around Britt's church. Dallas Interfaith got Nation's Bank to commit $3.5 million in mortgage funds for the effort. And it lobbied the city for public support for prospective homeowners.

Organizing in Hispanic Dallas

With the support of the Catholic hierarchy, and with the IAF's reputation as a powerful organization among Texas Hispanics, Dallas Interfaith started out well positioned to build a base in Dallas' growing Hispanic Catholic community. In the late eighties Bishop Thomas Chapie sponsored the IAF's initial organizing in Dallas, and a diocesan employee, Tony Mansueto, worked on developing local support for IAF efforts. When Charles Grahmann became Bishop of Dallas, he continued the diocese's strong support for the interfaith group, encouraging parish priests to get involved.

Father Ignacio Cizur, the pastor of Our Lady of Perpetual Help, became a prominent leader in Dallas Interfaith's efforts. The neighborhood surrounding his church had rapidly become almost entirely Hispanic. But Cizur and Dallas Interfaith faced the problem that many of the new immigrants were not citizens, and many Mexican Americans did not speak English. Reverend Cizur was himself a Spanish citizen, and many of his fellow Franciscans who pastor Hispanic congregations are not American citizens either.[34] In order to build Hispanic participation, Dallas Interfaith made a commitment to translate all of its public meetings into Spanish and to develop a citizenship program early on. It began sponsoring citizenship classes. And it assigned its organizers to help build campaigns around core issues in the new Hispanic communities. Dallas Interfaith selected the elementary school in Cizur's parish neighborhood, Obadiah Knight, to be one of the first Alliance Schools in Dallas.

In addition to organizing around Cizur's parish, Dallas Interfaith began to concentrate its efforts in the Oak Cliff section of Dallas. Oak Cliff was rapidly becoming a center for the Hispanic community, with 40,000 Hispanic residents by the mid-nineties. A white area until the fifties, Oak Cliff had become mostly black. But in the eighties, Hispanics began to displace African Americans in certain parts of Oak Cliff, as some of the more prosperous black residents moved out to suburbs. Hispanic parishioners at St. Cecilia's church emerged as the core group for Dallas Interfaith's organizing in Oak Cliff. Individual and house meetings revealed the concerns of parishioners about after-hours clubs contributing to the noise, crime, and violence in the neighborhood. Dallas Interfaith seized upon this issue as providing a potentially winnable campaign to help the new Hispanic community see that it could organize and achieve power in the Dallas political arena.

Working with lay leaders in the parish, Dallas Interfaith developed a campaign to close offensive after-hours clubs. Two lay parishioners at Saint Cecilia's emerged as key leaders in the effort. Saul Lopez, a carpenter at a medical center, and Mary Alvarado, an immigration counselor for Catholic Charities, organized house meetings and pressured the city council into passing restrictions on the private clubs. The new effort won its first victory when the city council passed a zoning ordinance, called the "D-1 overlay," which regulated the location and hours of these clubs. The courts, though, overturned the zoning ordinance, squashing the Dallas Interfaith victory, and demoralizing some local parishioners.[35] Dallas Interfaith and St. Cecilia leaders persisted in their efforts to address community needs, however, and launched efforts to establish after-school programs in Oak Cliff schools. In that campaign Hispanic leaders worked directly in cooperation with African American and Anglo IAF leaders in Dallas.

Organizing in White Dallas

Overwhelmingly white and much more affluent than black South Dallas, North Dallas represents the city known to the rest of the world, the Dallas of wealth and showy consumption. Moreover, North Dallas residents appear comfortable with their insular wealth and conservative politics. When Sr. Maribeth Larkin arrived as the new lead organizer of Dallas Interfaith in 1996, she was amazed by the extent to which a self-contained white elite dominated the city's culture. Larkin was a veteran IAF organizer, first recruited to the network in Los Angeles in the late seventies. Prior to coming to Dallas, she had organized for the IAF in New York, San Antonio, the Rio Grande Valley, and El Paso. Despite her experience in many contentious settings, Larkin was struck by the level of racial and class division in Dallas. "The black/white thing is so highly crafted because there's so much wealth in Dallas, and a meaner defense of it. My impression of Dallas is shallow because I haven't been here long. But my perception is that everyone shops at Niemann-Marcus and those that don't, don't count."[36]

From the beginning of its efforts in Dallas, the IAF sought to build a base in North Dallas, in one of the more unlikely spots for IAF organizing in America. Because of the IAF's strong connection to the Catholic Church in Texas, the network had an initial entree to North Dallas' Catholics. Bishop Grahmann knew the IAF from his days in San Antonio and encouraged pastors to support the Dallas effort. He sent a letter to all

Dallas pastors expressing his personal support for Dallas Interfaith just prior to the organization's first large Organizing Assembly in the fall of 1992.[37] A few priests in North Dallas, most prominently Robert Reh-kemper of All Saints parish, got involved immediately and brought lay leaders with them. Tony Fleo, who ran the family counseling program at All Saints, became one of the most prominent white Catholic leaders from North Dallas. In Fleo's view, the formation of a multiracial organization held tremendous significance from the perspective of the insular North Dallas community.

> When my father would drive me around my hometown in Pennsylvania and say, "see that house, I built that. See that building, I built that." He was a fine craftsman. When I look at my children, I can't drive them around and say I built that. The organization has allowed me to build relationships across race lines. How do you measure an organization that brings people together, African Americans, whites, Hispanics, rich, working class? What would one's life be like without that? What does it mean to my children to see their father call people from all over Dallas and invite them to dinner at their house in North Dallas? What other organization allows that to happen?[38]

Working with African American IAF leaders from South Dallas required white leaders in North Dallas like Fleo to address issues of racism. For their part, they have not been passive in these discussions. Fleo has made the effort to attend many of the organizer seminars on the African American experience at his own expense.

> In the last organizer seminar in January we brought in Professor Cone who wrote *Martin and Malcolm*. He challenged us. We had conversations. We stirred people up around race. . . . You have to know someone has integrity before you'll talk with them. Why would I spend time? You determine integrity through action, once you see them step up to the plate. Once Gerald Britt and I have gone to battle together, it's a lot easier to talk about what it means to be a black man in South Dallas than before. Sean [IAF organizer Howe] and I went around the block on the race issue. I regret it now because we didn't have a relationship first. We worked through it. I took on Sean on some of the things Professor Cone said on victimization. Cone said the white church in America has done nothing and still does nothing for civil rights. How important Malcolm was, for agitation. What angered me was that when my sister married a black man and my father said he'd disown her, it was those white nuns in my elementary school who told me that was wrong. So I went to the wedding. We came back and we talked about what he said, that nobody talked about race. We can do it because we have the basis of trust.

In addition to Catholics, a number of Protestant ministers from North Dallas also joined the effort. This group included the ministers John Lee,

Ray Flockmeyer, John Thornburgh, Gordon Roesch, and Tom Plumbley, constituting probably the largest and most sophisticated core group of white clergy in any Southwest IAF organization. By the founding of the organization, about twenty predominantly white churches had joined the interfaith effort. As in Fort Worth and San Antonio, though, many affluent white members of these congregations had difficulty seeing their self-interest in IAF participation.

The Protestant ministers sought to broaden the organization's base of support within white congregations by developing a program of outreach and education that would stress the interests of their members in IAF participation. Gordon Roesch, a Lutheran pastor in North Dallas, spearheaded the effort. Roesch had been one of the founders of the IAF affiliate in Fort Worth, ACT, when he pastored a black Lutheran church there. He came to Dallas during the formative period of Dallas Interfaith and got involved early on. Roesch believed that his congregants should not limit their sense of community narrowly to themselves. "Frequently, this stuff gets shuffled off to a social ministry committee. No, it's a ministry for the whole church. It is not *a* ministry, it's *our* ministry, to engage the community. I was plain [in speaking to the congregation]. Originally I had no intention of coming here. When I saw their interest, I said we would serve the whole community and they agreed."[39]

Roesch met with eight other North Dallas clergy over the course of three years in a study group. Dallas Interfaith's lead organizer at the time, Christine Stephens, suggested they put a course together to use in their congregations. Stephens wanted the Dallas effort to get beyond the kind of charity orientation that often motivated white congregants to become involved in IAF efforts. Charitable motivation might help more affluent people get involved initially, but it proved incompatible in the long run with the IAF's efforts to promote collaboration based upon mutual respect. Stephens told white congregants, "don't come into [black] South Dallas to 'help the poor people' there. There's enough talent in South Dallas to deal with their problems. But they need the power that comes through allies. Do them the honor of coming to the table with your self-interest and negotiating with them."[40]

With Stephens' support, Roesch wrote a proposal for an outreach-and-education course and divided up the topics between the clergy. The "Cultural Critique Curriculum," as the ministers called it, consisted of eight sessions on such topics as Faith in the Public Square, The Culture of Contentment, Civic Culture, Rights versus Civil Responsibility, and the Transformation of the Economy.[41] The stated purpose of the curriculum was "to agitate for a responsive and responsible people of faith acting in the public arena." During the sessions, the pastors argued that the current culture and practice of American political life was alienating and detrimental to their white and relatively affluent congregants, not just to low-income people of color. As the economic security of the middle class declined and its social life deteriorated, relatively affluent whites had a direct interest in working with communities of color to rebuild the infrastructure of society. Moreover, the pastors asserted that their faith tradition called congregants to public action, action that could best be pursued through Dallas Interfaith.

The study process was meant to lead to practical action. The clergy took the course to four or five member churches each year and led discussions among interested congregants. According to Roesch, "our specific purpose was to help those congregations develop a core group. After the last session, the pastor would challenge people to come to a next meeting and then the organizer would follow up. And that's happened to various degrees of success."[42] Some of the congregants who got involved in Dallas Interfaith through this process found that the group's work on school reform spoke to their immediate interests because they were teachers and administrators in the district's school system.

After a long period of base building work in African American, Hispanic, and white communities, Dallas Interfaith announced itself publicly at a citywide meeting in the Spring of 1992. On March 20, 1994, 2,500 supporters from 60 member churches attended its founding convention. At the convention, the organization endorsed school reform work as one of the organization's top priorities.[43]

School Organizing in Dallas

African American leaders in Dallas Interfaith, like their counterparts in Fort Worth's IAF organization, were particularly concerned about the failures of public schooling in their community. As whites fled the public school district, de facto segregation endured and the quality of the education offered to the majority of black students was quite poor.[44] In addressing this issue, however, Dallas Interfaith tried to avoid the pitched battles swirling around the school board and build a multiracial base for improving public schools.

In 1992 Dallas Interfaith chose the Franklin D. Roosevelt High School in East Oak Cliff to be its first Alliance School and one of its very first organizing efforts. The school district had built Roosevelt High School in the waning days of formal segregation in the early sixties to be a black school. During the seventies and eighties, the East Oak Cliff neighborhood declined, experiencing greater poverty and a myriad of social problems. The school suffered from the neglect of the school district administration, as well as the decline of the neighborhood. By the early nineties,

80 percent of Roosevelt students qualified for free or reduced-price lunches. Some children walked past crack houses to get to school. Meanwhile, Roosevelt ranked near the bottom of Dallas high schools in measures of school effectiveness.[45] During the 1991–92 school year, only 16.7 percent of the school's eleventh graders passed an achievement test required for graduation, compared to the state average of 48.6 percent and the Dallas school district average of 32.5 percent.[46]

The initial opening for Dallas Interfaith efforts at Roosevelt, however, did not come out of the black community, but through a white teacher at Roosevelt who was a member of a Dallas Interfaith affiliated church in North Dallas. Maryann Jenkins, an English teacher, explains what motivated her to pursue a campaign at Roosevelt. "It was a last-ditch effort. We were at the bottom in Texas in Math. Everybody was abandoning ship, teachers, students. We had a murder in the hall . . ."[47] Along with a Math and Computer Science teacher, Charmaine Bentley, Jenkins approached the African American principal of the school, Melvin Traylor, to try a new effort to save the school. Dallas Interfaith organizers soon began meeting with Traylor to discuss becoming part of the Texas IAF's Alliance School initiative. Traylor agreed and proceeded to gain the support of school district officials, and the local school board trustee Yvonne Ewell.[48] Meanwhile, Dallas Interfaith began to mobilize its members for an organizing campaign to turn the school around.

On a warm Saturday at the beginning of the school year in September of 1992, one hundred Dallas Interfaith leaders fanned out through the neighborhood surrounding Roosevelt High School. They knocked on doors in the neighborhood to encourage parents of Roosevelt students to get involved in rebuilding the school. They canvassed parents about their concerns and asked them to attend a September 22nd meeting at the school. According to canvasser Jack McCracken, "the main thing was not to answer all of the questions, but to have a conversation, and let them know something is happening here."[49]

The one hundred canvassers who walked the neighborhood included white, black, and Hispanic leaders from Dallas Interfaith. In fact, most canvassers were white, including many teachers from the school. According to Maryann Jenkins, "at the first walk in 1992, most were white North Dallas. They weren't afraid. They were church people and God was with them. There weren't many [Roosevelt School] parents to start with. By the time of the next walk, there were [many] black parents."[50] The IAF assigned Leonora Friend to build the Roosevelt effort among parents, staff, and the surrounding community. Friend, the African American IAF organizer who had worked with Morningside Middle School in Fort Worth, had been transferred to Dallas to further her training, and she worked with the Roosevelt community for the next several years. As the campaign proceeded, African American parents began to play a much more central role.

When Friend asked parents what initiatives they thought the school should take, the parents, it turned out, wanted after-school programs for themselves as well as their children. So Roosevelt set up free computer, literacy, parenting, and English as a Second Language classes for parents. According to principal Traylor, the Alliance School funds allowed these parental programs to be free, and they significantly increased parental involvement in the school and with their students.[51] Meanwhile, Reverend David Henderson of the Greater Mount Pleasant Baptist Church and Brother Cephus Northcutt of the Cedar Crest Church of Christ urged parents to get involved from their pulpits. Over forty parents began to attend regular weekly meetings to rebuild the school.[52]

Initially, many parents were fearful of getting involved in the school reform effort, in part because their own school experiences had often been negative. According to teacher Maryann Jenkins, "for our parents, school was a place of anger, failure. So it was a big deal to come back to school."[53] Organizer Friend found that parents were most comfortable with their traditional involvement in sports activities. She had to convince them to move beyond that limited role and demand that the school be accountable for real academic improvement on the part of their children. According to Friend, "we did what site-based management is supposed to do, but almost never really does. We created collective ownership between parents, teachers, and community leaders, and that feeling of working together gave people a new sense of confidence."[54] As parents gained more confidence as advocates for their children, they began to participate directly in educational efforts in the school. For example, they worked cooperatively with teachers in special tutoring sessions for students over lunch, after school, and on Saturdays.

Meanwhile, school principal Traylor used the special waivers and funds available to the school through the Alliance Schools program to invest in teacher training and programmatic innovations. At a statewide Alliance Schools conference in the fall of 1992 he learned about the experience of Jefferson Davis High School, an Alliance School in Houston, which had switched to a block schedule. In 1993 he sent a team of students, faculty, parents, and counselors to Houston to investigate the program. They returned convinced that longer class periods would help improve learning at Roosevelt. In the fall of 1993, Roosevelt switched from the traditional seven-period day to a four-period block schedule.[55]

Dallas Interfaith's community organizing, Traylor's block schedule, and the new initiative shown by teachers began to make a difference. For the 1993–94 school year, Roosevelt scored an important achievement: it posted the largest increase in student attendance in the school district, winning a $59,000 award from the district administration.[56] After two years of the new block schedule, tutoring programs, and parental involvement, academic achievement scores began to improve dramatically at Roosevelt as well. The percent passing the state minimum competency test rose from 13 percent to over 30 percent.[57] According to Traylor, tenth grade scores on the statewide TASS tests also showed strong improvement. The proportion passing the test in mathematics rose from below 20 percent in 1993–94 to 69.5 percent in 1995–96, while the proportion passing the reading and writing test rose from 40 percent to 84 percent.[58]

In its work at Roosevelt, Dallas Interfaith faced an early test of its ability to promote multiracial cooperation in a community undergoing transition. Although Roosevelt and its neighborhood had traditionally been composed almost entirely of African Americans, Hispanics had begun to move into East Oak Cliff in larger numbers. By the early nineties, Hispanics were steadily increasing their proportion of the student population of Roosevelt, reaching over 10 percent by the fall of 1996.[59] In the neighborhood walks they conducted, Dallas Interfaith leaders met many Hispanic parents who complained that Spanish translation was not available for them at school functions. Moreover, they wanted the school to offer English as a Second Language classes to parents as well as their children. In response, Dallas Interfaith insisted that the new Hispanic parents be fully included in school functions, and that all meetings be translated into Spanish. Meanwhile, Roosevelt's African American principal, Melvin Traylor, recognized the demographic trends in the neighborhood, and moved to make the in-school environment more open to Hispanic students.

Both Dallas Interfaith and Traylor had to confront resistance on the part of some black students, as well as school personnel, to broadening the culture of the school so that Hispanic parents and students could fully participate. Teacher Charmaine Bentley credits Dallas Interfaith with helping school personnel become more understanding of the needs of Hispanic parents. "Roosevelt had a tradition of being a black school and many were proud of it. But we had to become more understanding of the Hispanic community. [Dallas Interfaith facilitated that.] In class, it was a matter of survival. This is not a large school. There is no room for segregation. Teachers made efforts in classrooms. And Mr. Traylor said that all social clubs and sports will be representative, or not exist." According to Jenkins, "DAI [Dallas Interfaith] wouldn't tolerate us being just black. Exclusivity is out. . . . We were xenophobic before the language issue. Racial tension has decreased tremendously since DAI involvement."[60]

Based upon the gains made at Roosevelt, Dallas Interfaith expanded its Alliance Schools initiative into some of the feeder schools for Roosevelt, as well as to several schools in predominantly Hispanic neighborhoods.

These efforts built upon the base of support in Catholic parishes already established by the group. Father Ignacio Cizur's parish assisted the school campaign at Obadiah Knight elementary school, while school-based organizing helped to rebuild efforts in Oak Cliff stalled by the defeat of the campaign against after-hours club led by Saint Cecilia's parish.

Common Interests in Job Training

Although much of the foundation of Dallas Interfaith work lay in the relatively quiet, neighborhood-based organizing represented by the Roosevelt campaign, the IAF also sought to establish itself as an important player in Dallas politics. The organization wanted to develop larger campaigns that could benefit many of its constituent communities and establish a stronger basis for common interests among them. Public political action, however, would place Dallas Interfaith in contention with Dallas' still powerful white elite, as well as with newer power holders from black and Hispanic communities.

The IAF was well aware of the symbolic power of its multiracial leadership group in a city torn by intense racial conflict. Dallas Interfaith carefully managed the composition of its executive committee so that it would represent the three main racial groups in the organization. At all public events, it presented a multiracial face which it saw as a powerful symbol of the city's potential. For example, Dallas Interfaith chose the oldest black church in Dallas for a major citywide meeting on Alliance Schools in 1997. It brought 600 supporters to the February 13th event. Dallas Interfaith decided to have one of its Hispanic leaders, Cynthia Salinas-Dooley, co-chair the meeting with the black minister Gerald Britt. It asked the white Lutheran minister Gordon Roesch to do the opening prayer. In his prayer remarks, Roesch called all of the children to the front of the church. Half of the children present in the black church were Hispanic. Organizer Maribeth Larkin noted approvingly that "the symbol of that event was powerful" both to the IAF's own supporters and to local politicians.[61]

Inspired by the job-training initiative established by IAF organizations in San Antonio (discussed in chapter 6), Dallas Interfaith leaders decided to pursue a workforce development initiative modeled upon Project QUEST. Dallas Interfaith thought that such a campaign would be especially helpful in building allies among the business leaders in Dallas who were showing interest in community-based efforts. In November of 1992, Dallas Interfaith invited representatives from the business-dominated Citizens Council to visit Project QUEST in San Antonio. Council leaders met with former mayor Henry Cisneros and banker Tom Frost. Frost, a former COPS adversary, was now working closely with the IAF on Project QUEST. The Citizens Council members left impressed with the possibility of collaboration with the new IAF organization in Dallas. According to Council Chairman Don Williams, "in the end we have some common goals of safe and secure neighborhoods, a good educational system, the quality of life, and access to services for everybody in the community."[62] Collaboration with the IAF fit well with the Citizens Council's plans to modernize itself in order to respond to the economic and political changes of Dallas. Consequently, the Council gave active support to Dallas Interfaith's emerging job-training program. In 1993, Dallas Interfaith launched its initiative, which came to be called Workpaths Dallas.

The positive response of business leaders on the Citizen Council to Dallas Interfaith encouraged some elected officials to support the job-training effort. At a public meeting with Dallas Interfaith in 1993, Dallas Mayor Steve Bartlett specifically praised Dallas Interfaith's work with the Citizen Council. He pledged support for Dallas Interfaith initiatives in affordable housing, job training, educational reform, crime reduction, and infrastructural improvements, declaring "DAI is coming of age at the same time that the city is ready to be a partner."[63]

Bartlett's enthusiasm for the interfaith group was not shared by most other white elected officials, who began to oppose the organization's initiatives. Despite the opening up of the political system through single-member districts, Dallas still had little tradition of organized citizen participation in the political process. Meanwhile, the IAF brought a particularly assertive style to its interactions with elected officials, a style that some found abrasive. In one incident, council member Bob Stimson had City Hall security officers escort several Dallas Interfaith members out of the area near his office after he walked out of a meeting with them. According to Stimson, he left because the group's leaders "wouldn't let me get a word in edgewise."[64] City Councilor and Mayor Pro Tem Max Wells declared, "They are aggressive. They are confrontational. They are intimidating."[65] Black and Hispanic elected officials, more sensitive to the needs of low-income communities, often supported Dallas Interfaith initiatives. But they constituted a minority of the city council and school board.

In September of 1995, a majority of the city council rejected Dallas Interfaith's request for $2 million in city money to fund Workpaths Dallas over two years. The council refused to fund the initiative even at the reduced request of about $320,000 proposed by Deputy Mayor Pro Tem Chris Luna. Some councilors explained their opposition by saying they were not convinced about the benefits of the job-training initiative. According to Councilor Bob Stimson, the council rejected the job-training request for two reasons: "It was a combination of the intimidation and confrontation politics [of the IAF], and there were a whole lot of questions that still need to be answered about the program."[66] On the other hand, council members may have wanted to stop the young IAF organizing effort in Dallas before it could establish itself.

Dallas Interfaith proceeded with the job-training initiative anyway, and established Workpaths Dallas without city funds. The Texas IAF network helped the initiative lobby Governor Ann Richards, an early champion of Project QUEST, for start-up funds. Richards awarded Workpaths Dallas $1 million before she left office in 1994. In addition, drawing upon its support on the Dallas Citizens Council, Dallas Interfaith got the business-dominated Private Industry Council, the local agency that distributes federal job-training funds, to agree to match Richards' contribution. These funds proved sufficient to·start the program. Eventually the city provided a token contribution of $20,000.

Public Charges of Racism: After-School Programs

Racial polarization became explicit in Dallas Interfaith's initiative to get after-school programs funded by the city. Many parents in the group's congregations and in the Alliance Schools were concerned that their children were coming home to an empty house after school. They wanted the city to provide after-school programs in part for security reasons, and in part because they thought their children would benefit educationally. Several IAF organizations across the Southwest had been campaigning for after-school programs as part of their educational initiatives. Dallas Interfaith leaders thought that a campaign for such programs would appeal to parents across racial lines, as all were likely to benefit from such assistance. In 1994 Dallas Interfaith succeeded in getting the school board to allocate $200,000 to start a pilot after-school program at eight elementary schools, including the Alliance Schools in which the group was organizing. The city would supplement municipal funds with money it received from the federal government. Two years later, Dallas Interfaith tried to expand the program to seventeen schools, requesting $350,000 from the school board for the next two years. By then, however, white elected officials appeared to be getting nervous about the growing power of the organization. They went on the offensive to stop the interfaith effort.

The white school board trustees went so far as to divide up the task of squashing the group's organizing work. Trustee Lynda McDow began looking into constitutional issues of separation of church and state. Roxan Staff questioned violations of the group's nonprofit status. And board chairman Bill Keever took on the responsibility for attacking the organization publicly. "We've divided this sucker up," Keever told a Dallas *Observer* reporter.[67] In response, Dallas Interfaith leaders publicly criticized Dallas elected officials for being way behind other Texas cities in supporting community-based initiatives. Dallas Interfaith co-chair Reverend Gerald Britt told the Dallas *Observer*, "We should look to San Antonio as a model. . . . We're arguing with the school district about funding after-school programs [for a small amount of money] from the general budget when San Antonio regularly puts in $2 million for these programs. The City of Dallas just agreed to give Workpaths, our job-training and placement program, $20,000. San Antonio gives $2 million annually to Project QUEST."[68]

Dallas Interfaith looked to the Hispanic and African American trustees on the school board to support their after-school program, the demand for which, after all, came out of communities of color. Just as most black and Hispanic city councilors supported Dallas Interfaith's job-training initiative, the nonwhite school board trustees backed the after-school initiative. In fact, Dallas Interfaith and some Hispanic officials saw each other as mutual allies to improve schools. School board trustee Jose Plata spoke highly of Dallas Interfaith efforts: "You want education reform, do what DAI is doing. I have never seen a triethnic group of people working for the same cause, peacefully, programmatically. They are truly about accountability, and it is inclusive."[69]

African American officials, while supporting the specific initiatives of the interfaith organization, expressed more ambivalence about the group as a whole. Black school board trustee Yvonne Ewell saw after-school programs as peripheral to her central concerns, which focused on a continuing NAACP desegregation suit against the school district. Since white flight had decimated the white student population of the district and made racial balance impossible, implementation of the court order had come to concentrate on the hiring of black school staff. Ewell wanted Dallas Interfaith to play a more supportive role in the pursuit of the court order. According to Ewell, "the perception is that it's an Hispanic oriented group, although it has a black chair. They've been dealing with after-school programs, but the needs are broader. I have to be concerned with what happens eight to four and not just four to six P.M."[70] Nevertheless, Ewell supported Dallas Interfaith's after-school initiative.

Throughout 1996, the majority-white school board attempted to block the after-school program by raising a series of objections. Dallas Interfaith worked to respond to each objection in turn. When the board argued that there were no evaluation standards for the program, Dallas Interfaith worked with the school administration to develop a set of credible standards. When the board argued that no other civic group was on board for the effort, Dallas Interfaith organizer Mike Dealy put together an alliance with the League of Women Voters and a network of children's advocates. Finally, the board put the $350,000 proposal to a vote. The board split along racial lines, with all four minority trustees voting for the measure and all five white trustees voting against it.

Dallas Interfaith leaders expressed outrage at the vote and decided to criticize the board for racism. This action would represent the first time an organization in the Texas IAF made public charges of racism. The Texas network has been very cautious about making such criticisms, an approach apparently supported by its African American leaders. The black minister Barry Jackson argued that the network never ruled out charging officials with racism, but wanted to be careful about doing so. "We don't use inflammatory rhetoric, making charges of racism with threats behind them, Farakhan-like. But if something is racist, we call it that. To talk about racism is not inflammatory. It's a fact. [But] everything isn't racism."[71]

To IAF leaders in Dallas the refusal of the white school board members to support the demand for after-school programs appeared to be a clear case of racism. The initiative emerged directly out of discussions in the African American and Hispanic communities. Dallas Interfaith leaders felt they worked long and hard on it, cooperating with the school administration to develop a program it could support. According to the white Lutheran, Reverend Roesch,

> when they said we needed broader support, [IAF organizer] Mike Dealy put together an alliance with the League of Women Voters and the children's network. Then the school board voted it down, five whites outvoted minorities. We said "This is racism." What else can it be? Before we went public with that, [Reverend] Britt came to me and said, "This is nothing but racism." I agreed and we decided to call it what it was. It think that had its effect, helped to bring pressure to bear. What it did in the organization was to raise the issue of racism.[72]

Making public charges of racism seemed to strengthen the organization's resolve. Although these charges did not change the school board vote, the process did help to redouble the organization's effort to establish after-school programs through other means. After the school board defeat, Dallas Interfaith continued to lobby supportive school district officials, prompting them to keep the program alive. The officials found a small amount of federal funds that could be used to continue the programs at three schools.[73] Dallas Interfaith then shifted the focus of its efforts to the city's parks and recreation department, convincing that city agency to expand the after-school program with funds from its budget. The interfaith group garnered $2 million from the parks department, six times more than its failed request at the school board.[74]

Conclusion: Beyond Separatism
   and Integration

Dallas Interfaith proved able to publicly address questions of racism because it had been discussing racism internally for several years. Dallas Interfaith, perhaps more than any other network organization, had aggressively pursued the initiatives begun at the Southwest regional level to advance discussions about issues of race within the network. In fact, Dallas Interfaith leaders like the African American pastor Gerald Britt played important roles in pushing the network to discuss race more openly. According to Britt, "we're now more capable of discussing race than before. People are afraid of it because it's volatile. You don't resolve the race issue. What you do is you get better and learn how to operate in substantive relationships. If you become less racist and learn about other cultures, then you're getting what you want out of it."[75]

Historically, the Texas network had been quite hesitant to openly confront racism, either in internal discussions or in public pronouncements. But, as African American participation grew during the 1980s, black leaders and organizers began to push discussions of race to the fore in the network. Cortes responded by holding organizer seminars geared to deepening the network's understanding of the African American experience. The seminars, in turn, prompted discussions of racial insensitivity and racism in the relationships among participants. Dallas Interfaith was at the forefront of this process, and proved able to forge a much deeper level of unity across racial lines than had been established in earlier organizations like ACT in Fort Worth. As a result, for the first time an affiliate of the network initiated discussions of racism in the public arena.

It is too early to fully assess this development. Certainly other organizations in the Southwest IAF have not rushed into launching their own public discussions of racism. It is unclear whether other local organizations will develop the capacity to raise the issue and when they will feel it is appropriate to do so. Moreover, there is too little practice to evaluate in order to assess the effectiveness of raising public charges of racism. Nevertheless, internal discussions about race appear set to continue. Many African American participants in the network are committed to the process, and so is Cortes and a number of other Hispanic and Anglo leaders as well.

The Southwest IAF's accomplishments in combating racism refutes the argument that cross-racial organizing cannot address issues of race.[76] Certainly, some organizations that focus on common interests across racial lines may subsume issues of race in favor of issues that can unite everyone.

From this point of view, cross-racial organizations are subject to the kind of criticism Black Power advocates leveled against integrationism: by appearing to treat everyone as equal, the particular history and traditions of African Americans, and their particular concerns, are denied. Instead, separate black organizations are required to ensure that racial oppression will be addressed.[77]

But the multiracial organizations formed by the IAF are not integrationist. In fact, the institutional organizing approach is meant to respect the traditions of each racial community, allowing these communities a degree of autonomy and initiative, while at the same time promoting common efforts. Institutions are the members of IAF organizations, not detached individuals. Individuals become involved through their institutions, rooted in particular histories and traditions. Participation in the IAF does not require African American participants to submerge their history and deny racial differences in favor of a homogenous whole. The purpose of building broad-based organizations is to bring communities with different traditions and interests together, not so they become the same, but so that they learn to support each other and to find a common ground for action.

While the unusual institutional structure of broad-based organizations sets a foundation for multiracial collaboration, whether these organizations actually develop understanding of different racial traditions and an ability to tackle racism in sophisticated public action is another question. The Texas IAF experience shows that when conscious attention is paid to educating members about each other's traditions and promoting open discussion of race among participants, cross-racial organizing can address racism. Sharing of personal stories in the context of relationship building plays a key role here. But broader educational efforts, like the Texas IAF's organizer seminars, can help push these forums to a deeper level. Moreover, multiracial cooperation is likely to achieve a more direct confrontation with issues of racism when all racial groups have significant representation in leadership. It was only when African Americans achieved a critical mass within the Texas IAF that the network moved to take more conscious action against racism.

The Southwest IAF holds an important advantage over other forums in which issues of racism are discussed in American society, because the network's discussions are set in the context of a commitment to joint action. Most forums are media-centered affairs where Americans remain passive spectators. And these discussions usually lack a context of shared commitment where conversations result in more than "just talk." Coalitions bring leaders together across racial lines with some shared commitment to act together to support a candidate or an issue. But since these forums are restricted to institutional representatives, they fail to engage community residents very broadly.

The Southwest IAF draws a much broader base of community leaders into discussions about race that can lead to action. The network develops the new breed of leaders that Cornel West argues will be necessary to find new solutions to combating racism. In *Race Matters*, West says we need to "look beyond the same elites and voices that recycle the older frameworks. . . . This new leadership must be grounded in grass-roots organizing that highlights democratic accountability. Whoever our leaders will be as we approach the twenty-first century, their challenge will be to help Americans determine whether a genuine multiracial democracy can be created and sustained in an era of global economy and a moment of xenophobic frenzy."[78]

There is a constant tension within IAF organizations between the emphasis on commonality and difference. IAF leaders and organizers appear aware that this tension cannot be resolved in one way, for all time, especially in an organization with few resources. The balance will shift depending on the demands of the time. Reverend Gerald Britt, Dallas Interfaith's African American co-chair, expresses the tension inherent in the IAF's multiracial approach. "Dallas Area Interfaith is not colorblind. We want to be color conscious by realizing and valuing what we bring to the table from our own experiences, while there is a larger agenda that addresses the needs of blacks, Hispanics and whites all together. But we also need to address particular community needs and it's difficult. We want an organizational mesh, not mush!"[79]

Multiracial cooperation in the Southwest IAF represents an ongoing experiment, which, in many ways, is still at an early stage of development. Dallas Interfaith has only begun to create the conditions under which sharp racial conflicts on the school board can give way to practical efforts to improve the education of the city's children. Perhaps the IAF's biggest accomplishment is the building of a multiracial network itself, a rare feat in American political life. With such a network, groups long divided and often in competition can enter a process to combat racism and achieve cooperative action for the benefit of their families and communities. The network's faith basis plays no small part in keeping a diverse community of leaders committed to continuing to work together.

Reverend Britt captures the ongoing nature of discussion and struggle that is necessary to build bridging social capital:

> Working together is a necessary step. We can't address racial baggage first. We'll never deal with all of that. That will take to Jesus gets back. We need to start

working together and build some trust first. But the other side of the coin is to believe that because we go to city hall together that we have dealt with the blight of racism in our nation. . . . I will commend Ernie [Cortes] and Christine [Stephens]. They are trying to find the forum to discuss these things. It's the last thing we haven't done. . . . It's kind of like a marriage. The question is not whether there'll be tension and conflict, but whether you'll stay through it.[80]

Fig. 1. Father Albert Benavides speaks to a COPS rally during the organization's early efforts to improve conditions in Mexican American communities on the south and west sides of San Antonio.

Fig. 2. COPS co-chair Virginia Ramirez speaks to other leaders of the organization just before they take the stage for their twentieth anniversary convention in 1994.

Fig. 3. Leaders from Industrial Areas Foundation organizations in Texas gather on the stage at the state network's founding convention in San Antonio, 1990.

Fig. 4. Ten thousand supporters attend the Texas Industrial Areas Foundation network founding convention in San Antonio, 1990.

Fig. 5. Network leaders from across the Southwest join hands in prayer at a regional meeting in Houston, 1998.

Fig. 6. Southwest Industrial Areas Foundation regional director, Ernesto Cortes, Jr., conducts a training session for network leaders in Houston, 1998.

Fig. 7. Texas Industrial Areas Foundation supervisor, Sister Christine Stephens, talks with Valley Interfaith leaders at a regional meeting in Houston, 1998.

Fig. 8. Reverend Gerald Britt of Dallas Area Interfaith speaks to a group of parents, teachers and community leaders at a rally for increased funding to the Alliance Schools initiative in front of the state capitol in Austin, 1999.

Fig. 9. A delegation from Valley Interfaith in South Texas marches in support of the Alliance Schools, 1999.

Fig. 10. Participants in the Alliance Schools initiative in Houston rally for increased funding for the program.

Fig. 11. A delegation from Arizona Interfaith caucuses at a Southwest IAF regional network meeting in Houston, 1998.

Fig. 12. Texas Governor Ann Richards (right) pledges a half million dollars in state funds to Project QUEST in response to a request by COPS co-chair Patricia Ozuna (left) at the organization's twentieth anniversary convention in 1994.

Fig. 13. Archbishop Patricio Flores congratulates the Industrial Areas Foundation on twenty-five years of organizing in the Southwest at COPS' twenty-fifth anniversary convention in San Antonio, November 7, 1999.

Six

Effective Power: Campaigning for Community-Based Policy Initiatives

"Invest in Us! Invest in Us!" chanted the six-hundred community residents as they marched out of buses arriving from Catholic and Protestant churches across San Antonio. Inside, at the heated city council meeting, the leaders of the IAF organizations COPS and Metro Alliance lobbied San Antonio's mayor and city councilors for the funds to support their job-training initiative, Project QUEST. After long negotiations with city officials through the summer, and after assembling $4 million dollars from a variety of federal job-training funds, the organizations still lacked the critical funds for day care and other support services from the city budget. When the indoor meeting ended in stalemate, COPS and Metro Alliance leaders invited the mayor and councilors outside to meet their supporters. COPS leader Patricia Ozuna recounts what happened next. "Once we were outside, I turned to the mayor and asked him publicly to support QUEST with $2 million, including a specific pledge to find $1.6 million in the city budget. He looked at our people and agreed on the spot. We had a big placard with a pledge for $2 million written on it. Mayor Wolff and six councilors, a majority of the city council, signed the pledge." [1]

THE challenge of generating effective power for community-based efforts has proved difficult for American community builders and political activists to meet. Issue advocacy groups, on the one hand, excel at insider lobbying centered around state capitals and in Washington, but most lack deep roots in low-income communities.[2] Community building and community development efforts, on the other hand, grow out of grassroots efforts to address the problems of poor communities. Many have deep roots and genuine support from their residents. Few, however, have been able to generate and sustain active participation from their base. And most have shunned direct political action, relying instead upon political endorsements or goodwill collaborations at the top to gain support and funding for their projects. Consequently, they have been criticized for failing to generate an independent base of power for low-income communities.[3]

The IAF offers an alternative strategy, one that seeks to combine community building with explicit attention to the generation of power in the political arena. IAF organizations draw upon their deep roots in local communities and the values their residents maintain in work and family life to generate an independent base of power from which to negotiate with powerful private and public agencies. But, contrary to old stereotypes of the IAF as a confrontational protest organization, the network pursues a nuanced political strategy that combines cooperation and negotiation with the assertion of its political clout. Using a nonpartisan strategy, it demands resources and works collaboratively to reshape institutions for the benefit of its constituent communities.

The first purpose of this chapter is to explore this political strategy, that is, to examine how the IAF combines community building with political action. The chapter presents a case study of Project QUEST, the award-winning job-training program developed by IAF organizations in San Antonio. The chapter examines the process through which the IAF developed Project QUEST, campaigned for the funds to launch the program, and worked to implement the training system.

The second purpose of the chapter, however, is to illustrate the kinds of benefits that can be gained through community-based policy development. Policies for low-income communities have traditionally been developed "at the top," that is, by public officials and experts disconnected from the community residents who will have to live with the programs. Many have failed to meet the real needs of community residents—the dysfunctional high-rise public housing projects that dot our inner cities are perhaps the most grievous case. There is a growing interest in the importance of community participation in the development of policies that can work better. Residents at the ground level bring their intimate knowledge of community needs, offer creative ideas, and can help generate popular support for new initiatives.[4] Nevertheless, many efforts to generate community participation in policy planning and development also lack a perspective on political power. If residents of poor communities are truly empowered, they may well demand greater funds and the reform of public institutions. This chapter, then, will explore how the IAF attempts to handle this tension, to develop policies that are politically viable and redound to the benefit of community building.

The job-training initiative Project QUEST represents an important case to study because here the IAF has tackled an issue crucial to the development of inner-city neighborhoods. Our inner-cities have been devastated by the loss of good-paying jobs for low-skilled workers. Yet the public school system has largely failed to educate residents so that they can attain better-paying jobs that require college degrees.[5] As a result, the millions of workers who earn wages in the $5.50-to-$7.00 dollar range cannot support their families above the poverty line. There is a desperate need for training programs through which workers can gain the skills to advance to better-paying jobs.

Yet for many years, the main federal government job-training program has been largely ineffective. Job training funded by the Job Training Partnership Act (JTPA) provides short-term training for jobs that are often unavailable, while providing no support services.[6] As a result, many people cannot afford to undertake training; and of those who do, many leave still lacking skills for a significant job upgrade.

In contrast, Project QUEST was developed to provide training for up to two years, a sufficient time to substantially improve skills, and to provide living stipends and day care services for trainees. Project QUEST has worked closely with the business community to design appropriate training for jobs that are available and that will pay a "living wage." The program received a highly favorable review from M.I.T.'s Sloan School of Management, which documented substantial wage gains among participants.[7] The Ford Foundation and the John F. Kennedy School of Government awarded QUEST an Innovations in American Government Award in 1995.[8]

QUEST's innovative approach comes directly from its ties to the IAF organizations in San Antonio, COPS and Metro Alliance. These organizations could draw upon the political capacity built up through a long history of organizing and accomplishments to launch this complex initiative. Moreover, they could also draw upon their membership in a state network with national connections to generate the power and expertise necessary for more ambitious and sophisticated initiatives. Project QUEST, in this sense, represents a case study of IAF organizing at its best. Examining the IAF's efforts in the project—its methods, accomplishments, and its limitations—can therefore offer important lessons for those concerned about the potential of the network's political strategy to lead to improved work opportunities and healthier communities.

Early Efforts to Address Low Wages

> As an inner-city priest, it's tiring to be just handing out food, helping people with food and domestic problems. Jobs are key.
> *(Reverend Will Wauters, Pastor of Sante Fe Episcopal Church and an IAF leader)*[9]

COPS had long been concerned about the low wages earned by many of the organization's Mexican American constituents. In its early days, COPS had great success in channeling city and federal resources to capital improvements in its neighborhoods in the west and south sides of San Antonio. It directed millions of dollars in city bond issues for drainage projects, streets, and parks in those neighborhoods. By the late eighties, COPS could claim credit for directing to its neighborhoods close to $750 million of public money for physical projects like drainage systems, streets and sidewalks, parks, libraries, affordable housing units, and community health centers. While the physical health of the west and south sides improved dramatically as a result of COPS' activity, the wages of its residents did not. COPS leaders began to discuss the need to increase the educational and skill level of their communities. But tackling these human capital issues required more complex initiatives than simply commanding funds for physical projects.

Early in the organization's life, the Hispanic community's anger over low pay erupted when a copy of the "Fantus Report" was leaked to COPS in 1976. The city's Economic Development Foundation (EDF) had commissioned the Fantus Company, a corporate consulting firm, to study the city's economy and promote the area to industries seeking to relocate. A section of the report highlighted the city's low wages as one of its attractive features. COPS publicly denounced the report and demanded that any industry that moved to San Antonio pay a minimum salary of $15,000 per year.[10]

In response, a group of business leaders led by General McDermitt, head of one of the city's largest employers and chair of the EDF, attacked COPS. They blamed the organization for preventing the relocation to San Antonio of a large midwestern manufacturing company eager to avoid labor trouble.[11] A public war of words ensued that many business, government, and community leaders outside of COPS and the EDF considered damaging to the city's economic prospects. Under public pressure, COPS and the EDF called a truce, resulting in a joint declaration on May 30, 1978.[12]

COPS had flexed its muscle in the Fantus affair, but it did not win anything. In fact, some observers considered it a net loss for COPS. Unlike the IAF's usual approach to an issue, COPS had no positive solution to offer to the problem of low wages. Instead, it took an uncharacteristically oppositional, protestlike stand. The same pattern occurred in 1989 when COPS opposed public financing for a domed sports stadium project in San Antonio, in part because it thought the Alamodome project would provide no more than low-wage jobs for Hispanics. Voters, even in COPS' own neighborhoods, rebuffed the organization and approved the dome.[13]

While the IAF struggled for a positive program to raise wages, the economic prospects for Hispanic workers actually worsened during the eighties. A study of San Antonio's economy by the Urban Institute in 1993, aptly entitled *Growth without Prosperity*, documents a trend that many COPS leaders sensed. Between 1980 and 1990, San Antonio experienced a 27.4% growth in employment, one of the highest rates among big cities. This job growth, however, was concentrated at both the high and low ends of the wage scale, in the growing health services field and in the booming tourist industry. Middle-range jobs declined, while most Mexican Americans could only find lower-wage substitutes. Working poverty increased. Consequently, San Antonio's poverty rate increased from 21 percent to 23 percent during the eighties, a big-city rate surpassed only by Detroit. Almost 20 percent of San Antonio families in poverty had a household member working full-time in 1980, one of the highest rates in the country. Fully 26.9 percent of San Antonio's labor market participants failed to earn enough to lift their families out of poverty.[14]

In January of 1990, the Levi Strauss plant on the south side of San Antonio announced it would shut its doors within two months. The plant employed over one thousand workers, mostly Mexican Americans, paying them between eight and ten dollars per hour, a decent wage in an area with a low cost of living. Many of these workers lived in the neighborhoods of COPS' parishes. The plant closing dramatically symbolized the loss of good-paying jobs and spurred COPS to take action.

COPS' response to the plant closing contrasts sharply with the response of the Workers Defense Coalition. The Coalition consisted of labor lawyers and progressive Democratic Party activists formed in 1989 to generate community support for workers involved in labor conflicts. The Coalition helped Levi workers form an organization called *Fuerza Unida* to oppose the plant closing. Coalition activists tried to build a broad community alliance to pressure the company to support a proposed buyout by a cooperative of workers.[15] The effort never really got off the ground. *Fuerza Unida* and the Coalition failed to keep the plant open, although in the end they helped negotiate severance pay awards to the laid-off workers.

COPS took a more pragmatic approach. Father Al Jost, a south side parish priest and a key COPS leader in the QUEST campaign, explained COPS' response. "Our strategy was different. This [the plant closing] is a reflection of a bigger problem in the community. We can't reverse the trend. But we can help prepare people to make the transition."[16] In other words, COPS realized it did not have sufficient power to stop the Levi plant from closing. Instead, it began to explore a longer term solution to attaining livable wages for San Antonio workers.

Developing Project Quest

> QUEST works because it wasn't a result of bureau-
> crats in Washington, D.C. It came from the pain
> and suffering of our people.
>   *(Patricia Ozuna, co-chair of COPS)*[17]

Although the impetus for action came from the concerns of IAF leaders at the local level, the idea of considering job training as a strategy came from discussions that the IAF's regional supervisor Ernesto Cortes and his staff had been having about human capital approaches to economic development. The Texas IAF staff had been meeting with labor econo-mists at the network's organizer seminars, examining recent economic trends and discussing human capital strategies as a way to improve the job prospects and wages of workers. The idea was that, if a community increases the educational and skill level of the workforce, it can attract industries that pay higher wages. The Texas IAF was already beginning to experiment with efforts to improve public education and access to college through its local school reform efforts, which would develop into the Alliance Schools program. School reform offered to improve the eco-nomic prospects of the children of IAF members, but did little to address the low-wage status of the adult parents. Job-training programs, however, could serve to significantly improve their skill level, making it possible for them to escape the low-wage economy.

Through discussions among Cortes, the IAF lead organizer assigned to COPS, Tom Holler, and local IAF leaders, COPS decided to seize the opportunity presented by the Levi plant closing and explore the develop-ment of a job-training program. Drawing upon the community leadership it had built up over the years, COPS established a committee to pursue the issue, with veteran COPS leader Patricia Ozuna, a school secretary, as chair. Holler played a key role in convincing COPS leaders to initiate a campaign. He later worked to generate and hone the concepts that shaped the campaign, both by contributing his own ideas as well as through funneling ideas between local leaders and regional IAF staff.

Consistent with its relational organizing strategy, the committee did not develop a job-training program immediately. Instead, it first held a series of house meetings. In the summer of 1990 COPS asked its net-work of church leaders to invite friends and neighbors to small group meetings in their homes to discuss their experiences with work and job training. Through these meetings, COPS learned that many community residents had graduated from federally funded job-training programs in

debt and holding a worthless certificate.[18] According to COPS leader
Patricia Ozuna:

> People were being told they had to go to agencies, get tested, then go home and
> wait, and then were sent to another agency, tested again. They were being used
> as pawns. People would tell us stories and we got angrier. They were sent to
> school. But it had very few books and hundreds of students, no day care, non-
> English speakers all thrown together. No one is learning. . . . We heard how
> proprietary schools worked with the PIC [Private Industry Council]. To become
> a welder will cost $4,000. PIC doesn't pay it. PIC only pays for eight weeks or
> so. Since the proprietary schools were on the PIC, the PIC would send people
> to schools for eight weeks or so. Then, when they were ready to leave, the
> school says you don't have the degree yet, so take a loan and pay later. So people
> would do it. But then they find out that the qualification is worthless [because
> the instructor was not certified]. But they still had to pay the loan back.[19]

The IAF expects house meetings to accomplish more than simply gathering information and ideas. More broadly, the purpose of house meetings
was to engage community residents in conversations to find a basis for
action on the problem. A number of studies were available that documented the widely known problems with federally funded job-training
programs.[20] But house meetings provided the human stories to motivate
community residents to take action. Moreover, at house meetings participants were asked about the kind of job training they thought might realistically meet their needs. In response, according to Ozuna, "people mentioned the GI bill as a training program that worked because it gave
education funds to people to choose their own school."[21] Out of the energy generated by house meetings, IAF organizers recruited some new
participants to help build the campaign.

At this point, the IAF sought to include the other IAF organization in
San Antonio, Metro Alliance, in the emerging effort. Effective job training
promised to appeal both to low-income communities in Metro Alliance
as well as to the organization's more affluent workers threatened by the
changing economy. Meanwhile, the campaign could draw upon a metropolitan-wide and multiracial base of power. The two IAF organizations
established a joint committee to lead the campaign, which included ap-
proximately forty participants over the next two years.

COPS and Metro Alliance leaders on the joint committee began to research the employment and job-training situation in San Antonio. As a
first step, they met with a number of local employers. Business representatives told the IAF leaders that San Antonio experienced shortages for
certain well-paid jobs, like nurses and medical technicians. In fact,
many employers actively recruited from outside the area to fill those positions. Moreover, the business officials the IAF met with agreed that ex-

isting job-training efforts were not very successful, or, at least, did not meet their needs.

Like house meetings, research meetings were meant to accomplish more than information gathering. They represented the first step towards identifying potential allies for the emerging campaign. The IAF wanted to understand the interests of potential allies, so that it could develop a program that had sufficient broad appeal while also meeting basic community demands. As part of this research stage, IAF leaders met with representatives of the community college system, which they thought might offer training services. They also talked with local and state experts on workforce development. And COPS began meeting with public officials, like its close ally on the city council Frank Wing. In addition, Cortes stepped up meetings at the state IAF level, inviting local leaders to meet with such economists as Vernon Briggs, Ray Marshall, Barry Bluestone, and James Tobin. National experts could inform the local project as well as provide high-level endorsements to lend credibility to the effort.

Out of the multilevel discussion, the IAF developed the basic outlines of its job-training initiative. IAF leaders and organizers served as the central players in this process, integrating the "bottom-up" input from house meetings with the "top-down" perspectives from experts, business, and public officials. The result was a program they hoped would meet the needs of their community while proving both cutting-edge in policy terms and politically viable in San Antonio. By the spring of 1991, COPS and Metro Alliance had settled upon the basic elements of the job-training program. It would provide long-term training for viable skills; train for jobs that existed and that paid wages sufficient to support a family; provide living stipends, support services, and counseling to trainees; and link funds and training to the needs of the trainee, not the training provider.

The IAF developed a two-part strategy to gain the five million dollars in public funds it estimated would be needed to launch the initiative for its first two years. First, the IAF built up its own internal resources for the drive. COPS, now joined by the Metro Alliance, held another series of house meetings in the summer of 1991 to attract supporters to the emerging campaign. Unlike the first round of house meetings where IAF leaders stressed research and program development by collecting stories from their neighbors, this round emphasized education and mobilization. At these meetings IAF leaders explained their developing plans for QUEST in order to solidify a political constituency that could be mobilized for the fight to win funding for the program. Eventually, COPS and Metro Alliance held a total of over three hundred house meetings, between the two rounds. Meanwhile, COPS lead organizer Tom Holler began to work virtually full-time on the job-training campaign. Holler subsequently devoted the next nine months to launching Project QUEST.

Second, the IAF worked to assemble allies from the business and government community who thought that federal job-training (JTPA) funds were being ill-spent by the local Private Industry Council, controlled by the very proprietary schools which received its grants. The local banker Tom Frost, an earlier opponent of COPS who had become more receptive to the organization through its education work, became a strong ally of the effort. So did officials of the city's Department of Employment and Economic Development and state officials in Governor Ann Richards' office. Frost called a meeting of forty major employers in July of 1991 so that COPS and Metro Alliance could make their pitch.[22] In exchange for tailoring the program to meet employer work requirements, the IAF demanded that businesses provide job commitments. After some resistance, employers committed 650 jobs to QUEST graduates.

Funding Project Quest: Confrontation and Negotiation

The IAF needed a winnable strategy for funding the job-training program. It ruled out federal JTPA funds as the primary source because proprietary schools had a lock on those funds through their control of the Private Industry Council (PIC). Patricia Ozuna recounts, "We knew the PIC will attack us, see us as a threat. We knew we couldn't fix it. They were too entrenched. We needed a new way. We wanted to hook up with some of their money without rattling their boat too much yet. We were too weak."[23] Consequently, they decided to campaign for a mix of funds for the program, at the state and city levels.

An end-run strategy around the PIC had greater prospects for success in San Antonio because the program had recently received press criticism for corruption. PICs in many localities are dominated by business and are often seen as ineffective. But the San Antonio PIC had been charged with outright corruption. As a result, many business and public officials were unusually receptive to supporting job-training initiatives that were not tainted by a connection to the area's PIC.

COPS had already begun to lay a groundwork for its funding campaign by gaining the support of government agencies and the local media for the principles of Project QUEST. In January COPS had packed council chambers and got the city council to unanimously pass a resolution endorsing a new kind of job-training program based on the principles developed through its research and house meetings.[24] Meanwhile, COPS also submitted the plan to a wide variety of agencies, including a blue-ribbon committee set up by the city council to assess JTPA operations, the state legislature, and even the local PIC, all of whom endorsed the plan. Kevin Moriarty, of the city's Department of Employment and Economic Development, had meanwhile begun to discuss the training initiative with the state's Employment and Training division and the U.S. Department of Labor.[25]

In March of 1991, COPS and Metro Alliance specified a dollar amount for the program and began to lobby public officials for $5 million from the city budget. In order to pressure city officials to allocate so much money from the relatively small city budget, the IAF sought to demonstrate a significant amount of public support from its congregations. COPS and Metro Alliance sponsored a series of "accountability nights" for candidates in the spring elections for mayor and city council. Accountability nights comprise an important part of the IAF's standard repertoire of nonpartisan politics because it is here that the organizations demonstrate their strength to public officials.

COPS and the Metro Alliance mobilized constituents through their church networks to the accountability sessions. Leaders announced the sessions at religious services, handed out leaflets outside churches, and publicized the sessions in church bulletins. They asked pastors to speak from the pulpit to encourage their congregants to attend the meetings. IAF leaders recruited their friends, neighbors, and family members to come to the accountability night meetings.

The IAF organizes these mobilizations systematically and carefully. The IAF conveners for each church must propose a turnout quota for the meeting. Leaders often compete to mobilize the most supporters. At the accountability sessions, IAF organizers take headcounts and hold leaders accountable for meeting their quotas. Through this mobilization process, leaders from COPS and Metro Alliance proved able to bring hundreds of supporters to each of the sessions devoted to city council candidates throughout the spring. They mobilized two thousand supporters to a citywide session for the mayoral candidates on April 14.[26]

IAF accountability sessions are run with a set format. Candidates or other officials are limited to responding to IAF demands with yes-or-no answers, given a few minutes at most to explain themselves. If they equivocate, IAF leaders try hard to pin them down. When the session is over, leaders escort the officials out the door, with little opportunity for candidates to engage in gladhanding the audience. Although the IAF does not endorse candidates, it presents hundreds, sometimes thousands, of potential voters directly in front of candidates and officials at these sessions. In this way, an implied electoral threat constitutes an essential part of the IAF's strategy for power.

Some observers have questioned the democratic nature of such a limited dialogue. And some officials themselves express resentment that they do not have the opportunity for lengthy exchanges of views at these meetings.[27] For the IAF, however, accountability sessions are public dramas, rather staged events to be well planned and organized. These events play only one part in building ongoing relationships with elected officials. The IAF holds conversations and lobbies officials mainly in more private meetings. The accountability night offers the opportunity to demonstrate broad public support for IAF initiatives and to acquire a public commitment from an official to back these initiatives. Observers who see only the confrontational quality of accountability nights, whether they are correct or not in questioning their democratic content, often do not recognize the careful attention IAF leaders and organizers pay to negotiation and compromise in private meetings.[28]

At the accountability sessions in the spring of 1991, COPS and Metro Alliance demanded that city council and mayoral candidates commit themselves to voting for $5 million for Project QUEST. But, as a result of private discussions with candidates prior to the sessions, the IAF determined that candidates were not ready yet to make a firm commitment for $5 million, a large sum for San Antonio's relatively modest city budget.[29] So the IAF settled for a commitment to work with COPS and Metro Alliance to search for a way to find the $5 million. The IAF expected that such a public commitment would provide the basis to continue to lobby the candidates, once elected. If any candidate was so opposed to Project QUEST to refuse to make even that commitment, COPS and Metro Alliance would so inform their constituents during the run-up to election day.

In the end, almost all candidates for city council pledged support for the job-training initiative and committed themselves to work with COPS and Metro Alliance to find $5 million in city funds for the project.[30] Four of the five mayoral candidates pledged their support at the April 14th citywide accountability session attended by two thousand COPS and Metro Alliance supporters. However, the candidates varied in how firmly they committed themselves to finding the money, with the eventual mayoral winner Nelson Wolff expressing uncertainty that sufficient funds existed for the project.[31] COPS and Metro Alliance held another mayoral accountability session on May 13 for the two finalists, Wolff and Maria Berriozabal. Berriozabal pledged unequivocal support for the training plan, while Wolff again raised questions about finding the money.[32]

After the election, which Wolff won, IAF leaders began to meet with first-term councilors less familiar with the program and demanded commitments from them at IAF meetings held on other issues. For example, Metro Alliance invited newly elected council member Frank Pierce to a meeting of two hundred Metro Alliance supporters to discuss neighborhood improvements on the east side. Metro Alliance used the occasion to ask him to support a city allocation of $5 million to QUEST. He pledged support to the idea but balked at the price tag.[33]

In a series of private discussions held after the elections with newly elected Mayor Wolff, City Manager Alex Briseno, and city council member Frank Wing, the IAF realized that it was unlikely to get the $5 million from the city's limited general revenues. Since the mood of the city's residents restricted officials from raising taxes, such a large demand for QUEST funds would require cuts in other programs, generating political opposition. So COPS and Metro Alliance turned to the state government for some of the funds, using the power of the Texas IAF network to influence state officials.

In the fall of 1990, the Texas IAF network had brought ten thousand supporters to its founding convention in San Antonio, where it asked gubernatorial candidate Ann Richards to support Project QUEST. At the meeting, Richards pledged her willingness to work to make the program a reality. Richards subsequently won the election with strong support among low-income Mexican American and African Americans. After the election, the new governor instructed Commerce Department staff members Kathy Bonner and Barbara Siganero to work with IAF staff to develop QUEST and find the money to fund it.[34]

As the need for significant state funding became increasingly apparent to the IAF, it began to send delegations of leaders from San Antonio and its organizations in other Texas cities to lobby the newly elected governor for a concrete commitment of funds. Even with the governor's support, arranging to get the state money required IAF leaders and staff to hold a long series of meetings with a variety of public officials. IAF leaders repeatedly traveled to Austin to meet with the Texas Employment Commission, which distributed the state's portion of federal job-training funds, the Commerce Department, which oversaw JTPA programs in the state, the governor's policy council, and the state job-training coordinator.[35] Finally, in the summer of 1991, Richards, privately agreed to commit the entire $2.5 million in her discretionary Wagner-Peyser job-training account that year to Project QUEST. She made the public announcement much later, at a rally of 1,500 IAF supporters in San Antonio in November of that year.[36]

The $2.5 million in state funding still left a shortfall in the projected $6.5 million QUEST budget. The IAF decided to turn to local JTPA funds for a source of additional money. Originally, COPS and Metro Alliance had planned an end run around the local Private Industry Council (PIC) that controlled local JTPA funds. But in early 1991 the simmering corruption scandal in the PIC exploded. A blue-ribbon report documented waste and conflict of interest in the PIC's handling of JTPA funds.[37] As a result, the city set up a new agency to control JTPA funds, called San Antonio Works. The IAF met with city officials behind the scenes to encourage the appointment of business leaders favorable to QUEST to the new board.

Although it still seemed impossible to tap funds committed to proprietary schools, there was now an opening to the agency's $2.3 million in "bonus funds," that is, new funds that could be used in a discretionary fashion. COPS and Metro Alliance appealed to city officials, only too happy to find a source of funds outside of general revenue, and to the new members of the Works board whose mandate was to bring change to the system. On September 3, 1991, the Works board passed a $2.3 million allocation for QUEST.[38]

Neither the state nor local JTPA funds, however, could be used for support services like child care and living stipends for trainees. Yet COPS and Metro Alliance had set such support as a basic requirement of the program, so that heads of families could afford to undertake training. Father Jost argued, "the core group for us was young couples who would be locked into the poverty cycle if they didn't learn skills. That's why a support system was so crucial, especially child care."[39] In fact, child care has turned out to be Project QUEST's largest single expense.[40] The IAF needed $2 million in city funds to cover support services, much less than its original demand for $5 million from the city. But city officials, already facing a $9 million shortfall in the upcoming budget year and an electorate vocal in its opposition to new taxes, were still balking even at the reduced price tag.

IAF leaders met privately with key public officials like Mayor Wolff and city council member Frank Wing to negotiate the necessary city funding.[41] This round of private negotiation built upon the discussions going on since 1990 when COPS leaders informed then Mayor Cockrell and Councilor Wing about their initial plans for QUEST. COPS had even brought constituents from house meetings to tell their stories of job-training failure to the mayor.[42] During negotiations in the summer of 1991, COPS and Metro Alliance offered a further concession to reduce the amount that needed to come from city general revenues. They suggested taking $400,000 out of the Community Development Block Grant (CDBG) funds which were to be allocated to other projects the organizations had proposed to pay part of the city's share.

In exchange for giving up $400,000 of "their" CDBG funds, COPS and Metro Alliance even more vociferously demanded city support for QUEST to cover the remaining $1.6 million. To step up the pressure, IAF leaders met with local media editorial boards and gained a public endorsement of the program from the San Antonio *Light* newspaper.[43] But private negotiations failed to get a firm commitment. Hence the "Invest in Us!" public rally held at the September 3rd city council meeting described in the opening to this chapter. In front of 600 IAF supporters at the rally, Mayor Wolff and six councilors, a majority of the city council, finally pledged their support for QUEST.[44]

As a result of that commitment, the city council unanimously passed the CDBG allocation of $400,000 on September 12, 1991.[45] However, the council still did not vote the $1.6 million in funds for support services. To keep up pressure on the mayor, COPS invited him to the November 17th rally of 1,500 COPS and Metro Alliance supporters at Sacred Heart Parish Hall. At that meeting Governor Richards publicly announced the state's $2.5 million allocation to QUEST, and the banker Tom Frost announced business commitments for 650 jobs.[46] Nevertheless, it still took until March of 1992, after yet another IAF rally, to get the city council and mayor to vote the $1.6 million in city funds to QUEST.[47] Eventually, Councilor Wing proposed taking the money from a capital reserve account funded by the sale of the local cable television franchise. The money never did come out of general tax revenue.[48]

Community Participation in Policy Implementation

With funding acquired, the IAF organizations had to decide their future role. Most community organizations follow one of two routes. They either withdraw from the process and let another agency run a newly won program; or they attempt to administer it directly themselves. Direct administration was so demanding, in the IAF view, that it led too many organizations to withdraw from their organizing work to focus more and more on administrative tasks. Moreover, taking jobs and money from government often corrupted democratic processes, as leaders gained an incentive to scramble for jobs. In the past, therefore, Texas IAF had simply withdrawn from the process once funding was won, except perhaps to monitor progress and hold officials accountable for implementation.

With QUEST, however, the Texas IAF began to chart new ground, a third way between the two extremes. Project QUEST was set up as an independent entity charged with establishing and administering the program, so that the IAF could continue to focus on organizing. But, in order to exert ongoing influence in shaping the program, COPS and Metro Alliance maintained a key role through all phases of project implementation: project design; establishment of a board of directors; staff hiring; and recruitment and screening of candidates. Although leaders of the organizations took no jobs, and accepted no monies, they remained active players in shaping QUEST, guided by IAF organizer Pearl Ceasar.

COPS and Metro Alliance established a committee on which they would participate with business representatives and city officials to oversee the conceptual design and establishment of the QUEST agency. They commissioned Bob McPherson, an employment and training expert at the University of Texas, to write the design specifications for Project QUEST.

Rather than work in isolation in his office in Austin, however, McPherson had to come to San Antonio so that IAF leaders could have daily input into his efforts. McPherson wrote during the day and met with IAF leaders late into the night to go over his work in detail. Together McPherson and IAF leaders developed five key design specifications: the training would be long-term, up to two years if necessary; the training slots would be job driven in that people would be trained for occupations for which there was a demand; QUEST would provide "one-stop shopping," so that trainees would receive assessment, counseling, training referrals, and coordination of support services from one central place; funds would be attached to the trainee, who would also be eligible for financial aid stipends and child care; COPS and Metro Alliance would do outreach in the community, evaluate applicants, and monitor the progress of trainees.[49]

With the conceptual design in place, COPS and Metro Alliance played a key role in establishing QUEST's board of directors. The IAF wanted the board to represent a partnership between the stakeholders in the program, including the IAF organizations, the business community, and public officials. The IAF reserved one-third of the seats on the QUEST board of directors for its leaders. They were joined by the mayor, a vice president of the giant USAA insurance company, a vice president of HEB Foods (one of the largest supermarket chains in the area), the commander of Brooks Air Force Base, and the bankers Charles Cheever and Tom Frost. Frost served as chairperson. The IAF wanted to make sure it had a presence on the board to keep the program in line with the organizations' priorities. For example, when QUEST staff later suggested taking commitments for jobs that paid below the $7.50 minimum pay, IAF board members forced a retraction.[50]

The QUEST board hired an executive director as its first official action in May of 1992. Candidates were subjected to interviews not just by the board, but by a broader group of IAF leaders as well.[51] The IAF leaders subsequently made their recommendation to the board. The board, with the approval of IAF leaders, hired Jack Salvadore, a retired Air Force general who had commanded the service's recruiting division. Salvadore proceeded to assemble a small staff over the summer of 1992. No IAF leaders took any paid positions with the new agency.

In order to ensure that program benefits accrued to its neighborhoods, COPS and Metro Alliance ran the recruitment process for trainees. Many businesses strongly supported this arrangement. Employers felt that with such a system applicants would likely feel more responsible to their communities, and therefore be more responsible workers. The decision to undertake recruitment through its churches, however, required a major community mobilization effort on the part of the IAF. COPS and Metro Alliance kicked off the outreach campaign with a rally on September 27,

1992, where three thousand supporters celebrated QUEST's launching with Governor Ann Richards.[52]

Publicity for Project QUEST outreach went out through IAF church networks. COPS and Metro Alliance announced training opportunities at church services and in church bulletins. They distributed leaflets through church and neighborhood organizations. From there, news of the program spread through personal networks of church members. QUEST publicized the training opportunities itself, directing prospective candidates to IAF churches for applications.

Volunteers conducted interviews at IAF member churches to recruit candidates. The IAF organizations, along with Project QUEST staff, provided training in outreach to these leaders. A group of three leaders interviewed each candidate for twenty minutes. In all, 140 IAF volunteers conducted outreach sessions two or three times a week from October 1992 to March 1993, some continuing on until mid-May.[53] By January of 1994 outreach teams had processed over 3,000 applicants, eventually resulting in 650 QUEST enrollees.

While IAF leaders did screen applicants for program eligibility, their main goal was to identify potentially successful candidates. Eligibility criteria included income level, employment history, and size of family. However, paid counselors on the staff of Project QUEST conducted an official review later for these qualifications. IAF leaders wanted to take the opportunity to explain to the applicants that QUEST was a long-term training program. They looked for candidates who had what some Mexican Americans called "the ganas," rather crude slang for the desire and the will, to work hard and succeed. Sister Gabrielle Lohan, who conducted interviews at Holy Redeemer, explained that "the key thing we were looking for was ambition and commitment. . . . We told people the expectation was that they would succeed and contribute to the community in the future by helping others. . . . We stressed it was a community program, rooted in the community."[54] Genevieve Flores reports she told applicants that "the [IAF] organizations have worked hard for this opportunity, so you got to want it."[55] Pasquale Segovia, an outreach volunteer at St. Joseph's on the south side, stressed that their method was different from the typical government program: "We don't peg it for low-income people. It's for people who want to better themselves. That was one of the interview questions. That was the main thing."[56]

Since the IAF had so much at stake in the success of Project QUEST, it took care to recruit a set of applicants likely to do well. For IAF leaders, the key qualities were determination and responsibility, which reflected the values of the IAF organizations themselves. Outreach interviewers did not discourage people who had a past that would normally indicate less chance of success, like arrest records or drug addiction.[57] In fact, such factors met QUEST eligibility criteria. COPS and Metro Alliance leaders cared more about personal drive and commitment, whatever the candidate's background. The business community had been attracted to the program, in part, precisely because it promised this kind of community screening for responsible workers.

The insistence by IAF leaders for a solid commitment on the part of applicants led many of those interviewed at church outreach centers to decline to pursue their application. Those looking for immediate jobs or short-term training went elsewhere. Between one-third to one-half of those interviewed did not proceed to the evaluation process at Project QUEST itself.[58] Meanwhile, the assessments of IAF leaders accompanied the applications of candidates who pursued a place in QUEST. QUEST staff counselors were instructed to take into account those assessments when screening applicants and counseling them.[59]

The initial pool of Project QUEST participants reflects closely the base of IAF organizations in San Antonio. Five hundred and seventy-three people enrolled in QUEST in May of 1994. At over 70 percent, Hispanics made up the large majority of participants, reflecting their concentration among the economically disadvantaged and their connection to the IAF. With an average age of almost thirty, participants were somewhat older than typical JTPA trainees. Almost two-thirds were women, many of whom were single parents. Age and gender characteristics derived in part from recruitment through the IAF's community base as well. African Americans were overrepresented compared to their share of the population, reflecting both their relative economic need as well as careful IAF efforts to do outreach in the black community.[60]

The two IAF organizations made sure to publicize the stories of neighborhood residents offered training in Project QUEST, so that their followers could see the tangible results of IAF organizing. Metro Alliance leader Reverend Will Wauters argues, "with the Education Partnership, it was COPS and Metro Alliance responsible. But [Mayor Henry] Cisneros got all the recognition. So we learned from that and we wanted the recognition from the community. So when they get the job, we want them to know who got them the job."[61] The IAF ensured that QUEST participants were visible at organizational events. At the COPS Twentieth Anniversary Convention in May 1994, John Acosta, a member of St. Leo's parish in COPS, told his story to the more than three thousand COPS supporters present. Mr. Acosta, who said he heard about QUEST through his mother, who heard about it from other women at church "when they talk," spoke highly of his new opportunity.[62]

While the program disproportionately benefits COPS and Metro Alliance neighborhoods in the inner city, QUEST is open to anyone who qualifies. Reverend Will Wauters argues, "Our interest was that our people get in first. But we didn't exclude anybody."[63] Of the 437 QUEST enrollees in July of 1993, every city council district had a share, the smallest being nine trainees.[64] As a result, QUEST received remarkably little opposition from more affluent communities, at least in its early days.[65]

Meanwhile, many COPS and Metro Alliance leaders made it a point to maintain contact with trainees after they enrolled in QUEST. Genevieve Flores kept a record of all the applicants she interviewed and checked on how each fared in the QUEST screening process.[66] Close friends or relatives of a few leaders got into QUEST, and they are particularly watched over. One leader's son had been skipping meetings of his QUEST weekly counseling group. She got the church's pastor to talk to him about it.[67]

Gabriela Guerra and Mary Rivas, from St. Leo's parish on the south side, report following up with specific applicants. Gabriela Guerra explained her role. "I'm proud of one young man who had been in prison and was working part time. He got in [QUEST] to be an RN. He gets all As and Bs—only one C. I call him once in a while to give him encouragement. He's spoken at some of our meetings. When he becomes an RN, I'll be the first one there."[68]

The follow-up conducted does seem to give important support to many trainees and remind them of their responsibility to their community as well. Unlike the well-structured recruitment and screening process, however, follow-up is left to the individual initiative of IAF leaders. Some leaders reported that they have not followed up with any QUEST applicants. By 1995, however, Project QUEST staff began to contact IAF leaders to ask them for help with trainees who were having problems with schooling, or in finding jobs. The leaders then try to contact the student to encourage them to try harder, or to determine the cause of problems and help them find support.[69]

Keeping QUEST on Track

The IAF's independent political base proved crucial to QUEST's ability to meet two key challenges in its early period, funds and jobs. Prior to the establishment of the Project QUEST agency, the IAF had been the sole organized force backing the job-training effort. Once established, however, the agency maintained a direct interest in its own success. And its board provided avenues for support in the business and government community. Nevertheless, the independent organizational capacities of the IAF proved essential to maintaining funding for the program and to keeping the agency true to the organization's priorities.

By the beginning of 1994, the key question facing QUEST was acquiring an ongoing source of funds. QUEST admitted the program was expensive, costing about $6.5 million per year to train 600 people, or about $10,000 per trainee. For the investment, though, the program promised a highly qualified employee who could earn sufficient wages to support a family. For QUEST to survive, the city would have to continue to contribute at least $1 million to pay for support services which could not come out of any JTPA-related funds, whether state or local. Meanwhile, the state could not be expected to continue to allocate its entire Wagner Peyser budget to San Antonio, especially since the IAF wanted to use those same funds for seed money for new QUEST-like programs in other parts of the state. The IAF reasoned the bulk of the money, therefore, would have to come from local JTPA funds, controlled by the San Antonio Works board. COPS and Metro Alliance developed a coordinated campaign with the QUEST board to acquire $0.5 million from the state, $1 million from the city's general revenues, and $5 million from the Works board.

In the Spring of 1994, however, opponents of Project QUEST orchestrated a series of attacks on the program in various mass media. The San Antonio *Business Journal*, a local TV station, and Rush Limbaugh all ran pieces that criticized QUEST for spending millions while graduating only a few trainees.[70] QUEST supporters, of course, explained that the program offered long-term training so that the vast majority of trainees could not possibly have graduated yet. But the media campaign served to unnerve public officials and threatened continued funding for the program.

Despite the controversial media coverage, the IAF was able to convince the state government to continue to support Project QUEST. Governor Richards announced an allocation of $500,000 to QUEST at the COPS Twentieth Anniversary Convention in May of 1994.[71] The IAF also convinced the city to commit further funding. But the effort to garner local JTPA funds proved unsuccessful, despite a more favorable climate than before. The IAF had friends like Mike de la Garza from HEB Foods on the board of the new PIC, San Antonio Works. In addition, the Works board had already begun to restructure JTPA funding and eliminate competitors to QUEST, for example by reducing the number of JTPA contractors from twenty-six to nine in 1992.[72] However, the city's JTPA allocation had been cut from $25 million to $15 million in 1994, creating greater competition for the limited funds. The traditional proprietary schools lobbied fiercely to maintain their programs. The Works board eventually voted to allocate the scarce funds to traditional PIC providers, not to Project QUEST.[73]

The QUEST staff and IAF leaders then turned to private foundations to save the program. Based upon the project's favorable reviews and growing reputation among employers, SBC Foundation and NationsBank gave $525,000 to the effort. Since then, QUEST has cut its staff to save money and slightly reduced the number of trainees it supports. Using the

Texas IAF's national connections to private foundations, QUEST has been able to continue by combining public revenues with a variety of private sources of funds.[74]

QUEST faced a second challenge in fulfilling the job-guarantee provision of the program. Since making their initial commitments in 1991 for 650 jobs, several employers changed their hiring plans and reneged on their promises. For the IAF, the guarantee of a job at the end of training comprised a crucial component of QUEST, important because so many participants in traditional job-training programs had found themselves jobless and holding worthless degrees after graduation. The IAF, the QUEST board, and its staff worked hard to find alternatives to replace the company-specific job guarantees. In the end, they arranged for companies to pool their job commitments so that industry groups made new commitments to replace the outdated company-specific ones. Meanwhile, QUEST staff sought new occupations, such as diesel mechanic, for the program.

In their constant search for new job commitments, however, QUEST staff began to advocate accepting some commitments from companies that did not pay the program minimum of $7.50 per hour. Disputes broke out on the QUEST board between IAF leaders, on the one hand, and QUEST staff and business representatives, on the other, about the inclusion of such job commitments. The IAF held firm on the $7.50 minimum because it felt that the program had to pay a "family wage." In the view of IAF leaders, accepting lower pay would be a slippery slope that might lead to gutting the family-wage principle entirely. Nevertheless, IAF leaders demonstrated a certain degree of flexibility by agreeing to include one or two companies that promised rapid advancement to higher-paying jobs for trainees initially hired below the minimum pay level.[75]

The Southwest IAF's "Vision for Work"

While IAF leaders and organizers were busy campaigning for Project QUEST in San Antonio, their work influenced, and, in turn, was informed by an ambitious series of discussions at the level of the Southwest IAF network. The network had already been hosting a series of organizer seminars with labor economists to discuss the changing economy in the late eighties. During this process, the IAF opened these meetings up to a broader process including IAF leaders from across Texas and the Southwest region. During this process, leaders from local organizations gathered every three or four months to read economic studies and policy proposals, and hear presentations from such economists as Vernon Briggs, Ray Marshall, Barry Bluestone and James Tobin. Each meeting had fifty-to-one hundred participants, with costs shared by the local affiliates and private foundations, which funded the organizer seminars. Reports on the effort to develop Project QUEST helped give the meetings a practical focus.

The process intensified in 1993 as the network began to write a document entitled "Southwest IAF Vision for Work." The Texas network had already written a vision paper on education which served to build a consensus among the local organizations for the Alliance Schools initiative. Since the low-wage economy also posed an issue relevant to all of the region's organizations, network leaders thought a similar process on economic issues would help spur efforts to expand upon QUEST. To deepen the network's understanding of economic and job issues, Texas IAF staff researcher Steve Jackobs wrote a series of background discussion papers for the network. His first paper documented the stagnation of family incomes over the past twenty years, while the other two explored the growing polarization in skill requirements for jobs and the failure of current job-training programs.[76] Jackobs then provided staff assistance to the network in writing the vision paper, but most of the actual writing was done by teams of IAF leaders. IAF leaders discussed the drafts at a series of regional meetings, and then revised them to reflect the growing consensus.

The last revised version of the vision paper starts by discussing "the theology of work," a section added at the initiative of leaders at a regional meeting in Dallas on June 5, 1993.[77] The document declares that "work is much more than income. As our families face the turmoil and challenges of today's economy, we draw on our faith traditions for guidance and strength." The leaders draw from the book of Genesis, as well as from the writings of Maimonides, whom they describe as a leader to the Egyptian Jewish community and a physician to the Muslim Sultan Saladin of Cairo. They declare that "our faiths teach us that work is the means by which we human beings share in creation," and that "as stewards of creation, we enter moral relationships as we take up our work." Drawing from Presbyterian and Methodist traditions, but especially from Catholic social thought, the document asserts that "a fundamental obligation of the work relationship is a living wage which allows families to live in dignity and security. . . . Catholic leaders following him [Leo XIII] have insisted that work provide a 'family wage' adequate for one worker to support a spouse, children, and a home in dignity."

The vision paper then goes on to present a sophisticated discussion of the construction of a social pact for labor after World War II, on the basis of union organization and mass production industry. The document declares that "our families approach work seeking the opportunity to enjoy the rewards and obligations of the American Dream." At the insistence of African American and other leaders at the June 5th Dallas meeting, the document recognizes that systematic discrimination denied the reality of that dream to many Americans, but still declares that "this American Dream is an important wellspring of hope, even for those of us who have been discriminated against and disadvantaged." The document charts the collapse of the postwar social pact, the decline of the mass production economy, and the new world of insecurity and declining wages for the average worker. The vision paper discusses Project QUEST as one promising strategy "to create new paths into good jobs by forging new linkages among the institutions of the labor market—families, employers, and training institutions." The document ends with a broader list of possible arenas for action, for improved job training, expansion of the Earned Income Tax Credit, increased employment through public investment in the infrastructure, and improved education and school-to-work transitional programs. The document concludes with a call for a new social compact based upon investment in the social capital of communities and new arrangements with economic, public, and other institutions in the new world economy. The vision paper cites Arthur Okun approvingly, that "the market needs a place, and needs to be kept in its place."[78]

Evaluating the Effects of Project Quest

Project QUEST appears to be working better than traditional JTPA approaches. In an evaluation of the program conducted by the Massachusetts Institute of Technology's Sloan School of Management and funded by the Ford Foundation, Paul Osterman found that QUEST, during its first several years of operation, had an unusually high success rate in several areas. First, over 70% of participants successfully completed the program. The average increase in earnings for all participants was between $1.36 and $2.42 per hour, and between $4,923 and $7,457 per year. By comparison, JTPA participants across the nation increase their annual earnings by only $900, and average wages in the San Antonio area rose only 8% during the same period. The average post-QUEST wage of participants was $7.82, just above the program's minimum target wage of $7.50. Moreover, according to the study, the program had other substantial benefits for families: it reduced the use of welfare and food stamps and increased the likelihood of family members pursuing education. Although the cost per trainee was high at about $10,000, Osterman concluded that, given the very high earnings gains, benefits far exceeded these costs.[79] By the end of 1998, QUEST had enrolled 1,598 people; 919 had graduated, with 385 enrollees left in training. The average placement wage for graduates increased to $9.63 by 1998 with 90% of these jobs providing benefits.[80]

Besides its direct benefits to trainees and their families, the IAF has sought to spur broader institutional change by establishing a forum to bring low-income community organizations, businesses, and training providers together to discuss employment needs and design training programs. The new collaborative institution represented by the QUEST board has influenced each of these stakeholders in different ways.

The community college system, which provides virtually all of the actual training that QUEST offers, has changed most as a result of Project QUEST. Paul Osterman goes so far as to say QUEST has "transformed" the community colleges in San Antonio.[81] Since so many of QUEST participants needed remediation, the community colleges developed a new and more flexible "Basic Skills Academy," which they later extended to all of their students. QUEST also worked with the colleges to develop more flexible scheduling and curriculum materials to meet the needs of adults. Moreover, the colleges established new training programs to meet employment needs, including financial customer services and diesel mechanic training. Prior to QUEST, the colleges were not particularly attuned to local employment needs. Through QUEST, community college representatives began to meet regularly with the San Antonio Manufacturing Association and the Contractors Association to discuss training needs and the role of the colleges.

Businesses have changed their practices to some degree through QUEST. Some employers report they never before had a forum to discuss employment needs and to contribute to the design of appropriate training systems. Project QUEST offered them free training, of course, which was a sizable inducement to participate. In exchange, they had to pledge jobs to QUEST graduates. In practice, fulfilling these pledges turned on current business demand at the time. But business officials did not take the act of making public pledges lightly. As the program proceeded to graduate what businesses saw as good employees, Project QUEST became the single most important factor in enhancing the reputation of the IAF among San Antonio's business community.[82]

The most significant impact that the QUEST campaign had on COPS and Metro Alliance was to bring them much closer together. Although the two organizations had cooperated before on specific campaigns, they had remained fairly distinct during the eighties, keeping separate offices and organizers. During the QUEST campaign, the IAF in San Antonio began to operate for the first time as one multiracial network. Close ties and trust were forged between the Hispanic COPS organization and the African American, white, and Hispanic Metro Alliance leaders through the long effort to establish QUEST, recruit participants, and oversee operations in an ongoing way. As a result, COPS and Metro Alliance agreed in 1992 to share a lead organizer, Pearl Ceasar. By 1994 the two organizations were sharing the same office space. After QUEST, COPS, and Metro Alliance came to cooperate on almost every major programmatic initiative. Although each organization still kept a separate identity and set of staff organizers, they began more and more to operate as a single entity.

Limitations of the Workforce Development Strategy

Despite its strengths, Project QUEST faces some important limitations in addressing the economic problems of urban areas. First, QUEST does not address the employment prospects of people with very low levels of schooling. QUEST accepts only those with a high school diploma or a GED. It does refer applicants without such qualifications to GED programs; but it cannot directly help these candidates. QUEST also cannot help those so overwhelmed with familial responsibilities or other constraints such that they cannot make a long-term commitment to training. In fact, financial and personal problems remain the number one reasons given by participants who withdraw from QUEST training without finishing. It is true that QUEST participants are economically disadvantaged and face many obstacles to better jobs. Ninety percent have required remedial education before they were able to undertake their training.[83] Nevertheless, the IAF has not yet found a strategy to address the employment prospects of the most severely disadvantaged.

Second, the IAF strategy does not address the overall structure of job availability in the area. It seeks to provide training for jobs that exist, a practical approach that has proven quite popular and successful. But the IAF does nothing directly to create new jobs. QUEST faces a particular problem as a result. It is quite dependent on jobs in the health care industry, in part because they exist, and in part because residents can be trained for these jobs within a couple of years. In fact, it is precisely those QUEST graduates who enter that field that receive the highest wages. If we exclude medical jobs, the average pay of QUEST graduates is $6.84 per hour, below the target minimum.[84]

Of the 604 job commitments held by QUEST in June of 1993, 432 were made by 12 hospitals for 13 health care occupations.[85] Most QUEST trainees were enrolled in medical training for such jobs as nurses and technicians. In 1991, the health care industry expected to grow. By 1994, however, cost containment and health care reforms began to lead area providers to reduce their hiring plans. QUEST has struggled since then to maintain training slots with career tracks. The restructuring of the health care industry has threatened the long-term viability of QUEST's particular job strategy, and points to the broader weakness in the approach.

It may, of course, be unfair to expect local organizations to affect large-scale economic processes and structures alone, or even with the support of a state and regional network. Moreover, human capital strategies, whether pursued locally or nationally, are premised upon the idea that developing a more highly skilled workforce will lead employers to create industries and jobs that take advantage of that workforce. Nevertheless, as long as good-paying jobs are available in San Antonio, QUEST works. But, to the extent that they disappear, or come to require skills beyond what can be learned in a two-year vocational program, the IAF lacks a viable strategy.

New Directions in Workforce Development

The IAF organizations in San Antonio have been working to address some of the limitations of Project QUEST.[86] To secure more stable funding for the job-training effort, the organizations have launched a campaign to get San Antonio to establish a Human Development Fund. The fund would provide city monies to a variety of human capital initiatives that the IAF is sponsoring. These include QUEST, as well as the San Antonio Education Partnership, which offers college scholarships to inner-city youth, and the After School Challenge, affiliated to the network's Alliance Schools initiative as pursued in San Antonio. The fund would raise revenues from a half-percent economic development sales tax.

Meanwhile, the organizations are in the preliminary stages of developing what they consider to be a new version of the old union hiring halls. With employment instability in the health care industry, some QUEST graduates lost their newfound jobs. COPS and Metro Alliance are seeking to develop a permanent institution that can help people stabilize their employment experience and manage their careers in an increasingly unstable economic environment. The institution could provide counseling, information, and referrals to training, links to job networks, and advocacy to improve wages and working conditions.

Finally, COPS and Metro Alliance succeeded in getting the city council to pass a "living wage" requirement to the city's tax abatement policy. The ordinance requires a firm receiving an abatement from the city to pay 70 percent of its workers at least $10.13 an hour in manufacturing and $9.27 in all other jobs. The policy is expected to increase the wages of at least 500 new workers to be hired by an ITT Sheraton convention hotel being built in San Antonio. This living wage campaign is one of the first and strongest of such abatement policies in the nation.

Workforce Development in Texas and the Southwest

Based upon the success of Project QUEST, the IAF attempted to spread the model through its other affiliates in Texas and the Southwest. Although the regional-level network does not set policy for local affiliates, IAF staff did encourage local leaders to consider undertaking similar campaigns, using the regional leaders meetings "on work" as a forum for discussion. Indeed, the IAF asked leaders and organizers from COPS and Metro Alliance to explain their initiative at these meetings and offer advice to the other organizations. Local leaders were interested because the lack of good-paying jobs was a growing problem facing all of their communities. Eventually, Austin Interfaith launched the Capital Idea, Dallas Interfaith initiated Workpaths Dallas, ACT created Synergy, Valley Interfaith formed VIDA, and EPISO also fielded a job-training project similar to QUEST. But each campaign varied, as local leaders attempted to tailor the basic principles to local conditions. The state network proved capable of delivering commitments for start-up funds from Governor Ann Richards as well as her successor, George W. Bush, for these local efforts. Valley Interfaith has expanded its efforts to encompass tax strategies and other "living wage campaigns" similar to IAF efforts in San Antonio. The IAF organization in Tucson developed the JobPath training initiative, a school-to-work transition program, and a successful living wage campaign. It has joined forces with the Phoenix IAF organization to develop a statewide plan for workforce development in Arizona.

The IAF worked with Texas Governor Richards to broaden the impact of Project QUEST on public workforce development programs beyond the specific IAF organizing campaigns. Richards reorganized job-training programs on the state level to encourage more QUEST-like programs. She appointed a commission headed by banker Tom Frost, the original chairperson of the QUEST board of directors, to spearhead these efforts. Meanwhile, Richards also lobbied the Clinton administration to apply some of the features of Project QUEST to its plans to reorganize federal job-training programs.[87]

Meanwhile the Southwest IAF used its growing connections to policy experts and Department of Labor staffers to tout QUEST as a new model for workforce development. IAF leaders and QUEST personnel traveled to Washington to meet with Labor Department staff, with QUEST's first graduate, Cynthia Scott, participating on a panel with President Clinton and Secretary of Labor Robert Reich at one forum. The effort had an impact. Several of the features of QUEST's approach, represented as well by some other community-based training initiatives, were incorporated into the Workforce Investment Act passed in 1998 that reorganized federal job-training programs. The act requires one-stop shopping centers where trainees receive assessment and counseling. And it offers vouchers for training to the trainee, who can then choose among approved training providers.

Conclusion

Project QUEST has won critical acclaim as an innovative model for job training in urban communities. The Ford Foundation and the John F. Kennedy School of Government at Harvard University selected the program as a 1995 winner of the Innovations in American Government Award. The program highlights creative collaborations between communities and government. The judges chose QUEST as one of fifteen winners out of 1,500 applicants that year.[88] Meanwhile, a variety of employment-training experts came to study QUEST, identifying it as an important new model for community-based economic development.[89]

What is particularly unique about QUEST is that the community component of the workforce development collaboration is independently organized at the local level, but operates with a broader vision and set of connections. There is a widespread interest in the idea of communities partnering and networking with public agencies and businesses. But low-income communities are rarely able to do so from an organized position of strength. Many Community Development Corporations (CDC) have tried to develop innovative alternatives to federally funded JTPA programs in their localities. But, lacking the organized social capital and political clout of the Texas IAF, and isolated in localities, they have struggled to be heard. One review of CDC efforts found that, with only a few exceptions, business-dominated Private Industry Councils that disbursed JTPA funds locally simply did not take CDC efforts seriously and refused to fund them.[90]

A key factor in the IAF's success is its multilevel approach, that is, the ability to combine strong local organizing and participation with resources and expertise at the regional level. At the local level, the IAF drew from its base in community institutions and the values shared by their members. It combined mass mobilizations to accountability nights and public rallies with flexible negotiations with business and public officials to forge a strong local alliance for QUEST. But it was the state network's ability to bring in experts to lend credibility to the effort, and then to deliver funds from the state government that proved crucial to the effort. Project QUEST has continued to depend on the IAF's influence on private foundations and public agencies for funds. And the IAF's organizations have relied on their independent organizing base to keep Project QUEST committed to the needs of their communities, while investigating new approaches to workforce development as well.

With the IAF network, local community leaders did not have to limit their understanding or vision to the immediate environment. They did hold hundreds of house meeting discussions with their neighbors. But they also met repeatedly over several years at the state level with labor economists and policy experts. IAF staff provided direction for writing the network's "Vision for Work" paper, but it was a collaborative project with extensive contributions by local leaders. The Vision process provided a strong moral grounding to the efforts of local leaders as well as an extensive education in economic policy. It gave local IAF participants the depth of understanding to collaborate as equals with business and government officials.

In spreading its workforce development strategy through the region, the network's federated structure also proved effective. The network could not dictate that every affiliate adopt a job-training campaign. On the other hand, local organizations did not operate in isolation, starting each campaign from scratch. Organizations could learn from each other to implement campaigns that met local conditions and the interests of local participants. The dynamic between local initiative and regional direction, between what I have elsewhere called participation and authority, gave the IAF the effective power necessary to launch a wide range of successful local programs as well as broader influence in the region.

The existence of IAF organizations as mediating institutions, their ability to implement community development policy without losing their participatory character, lies at the heart of Project QUEST's success. In that role, IAF organizations have an effect both on the social capital of communities and on the politics and policies of the urban environment. By turning community building towards politics, the IAF creates effective power for local communities, so they generate the capacity to implement their visions. By providing job training, and then good-paying jobs, to residents, QUEST in turn helps strengthen the social fabric of IAF neighborhoods. By mobilizing extended church networks, and then distributing benefits through them, IAF activity strengthens these institutions. In this way, the IAF strategy puts community building and political power in a symbiotic relationship.

When COPS began in 1974, it fought to get drainage systems built in its neighborhoods. Although a difficult fight to win at the time, drainage systems could be implemented easily and with obvious results. With QUEST, the IAF entered the much more complex terrain of workforce development, where program implementation is complicated and where the results take time to become apparent. Like school reform, effective job training is absolutely critical to improving the conditions of families in poor communities. Yet these initiatives represent long-term, complex projects. To former COPS co-chair Father Rosendo Urrabazo, campaigns like QUEST and school reform raise a challenge: "In more sophisticated campaigns, you need a 'vision of the grandmother,' that is, of a generation. Can we work hard if we won't see results for twenty years? If our country will advance, we must do it."[91]

Seven

Congregational Bases for Political Action

THE ULTIMATE foundation for the IAF's political power rests in its member institutions most of which are religious. Congregations pay the dues that supply the independent financial base for local IAF organizations, to pay to hire organizers for example. They supply the pool of clergy and lay leaders out of which IAF organizers recruit and train leaders. The IAF's ability to train hundreds of indigenous community leaders to develop issue campaigns—to hold house meetings, conduct research, develop policy, lobby public officials, and negotiate with business representatives—rests in those congregations. And congregations provide a stable base for the mobilization of broader support for organizational initiatives. Because of its base in religious communities, the network's leaders can mobilize hundreds of supporters—potential voters—to neighborhood accountability sessions with candidates and public officials on a regular basis. IAF organizations regularly turn out thousands to citywide accountability nights and public actions, and the Texas network brought 10,000 supporters to its founding convention in 1990.

All faith communities involved in the Texas IAF contribute similar social capital resources for political power. Faith communities contain preexisting networks of clergy and lay leaders, who are further connected to broader networks of friends and neighbors. These networks contain a degree of trust and legitimate authority that can help initiate cooperative action. The pastor's endorsement of the IAF effort opens the door to church members who may be initially suspicious of "outsiders." Meanwhile, religious beliefs and commitments play important roles in encouraging participation. Religious traditions can motivate ministers and lay leaders to engage in political action and to sustain their participation through victories and defeats. They provide a moral foundation that can deepen and sustain interest-based political action.[1]

Religious institutions enter a collaboration with the IAF that offers important gains to both, and that has led to a certain transformation of both parties. The IAF does not simply mobilize existing networks around a predetermined agenda, but works to develop lay leaders and strengthen the social fabric of communities. These lay congregants, in turn, become leaders of IAF affiliates and shape issue campaigns.

In chapter 2, I argued that religion and politics have become fused in the IAF into a theology of organizing. Supervisor Frank Pierson suggests how IAF organizers see that process: "The expansion of democratic action follows from a right understanding of religious teachings. Most of scripture is about the relationship of the community to the poor. So, if you probe religious teachings deeply, they lead you to a democratic life."[2] In their view religious traditions themselves teach democratic action. But IAF organizers still need to work to shape and focus these traditions in order to direct them specifically towards IAF-style political action.

It turns out that how social capital is organized within congregations matters for their potential to collaborate with the IAF. Denominations vary in the faith traditions and institutional structures through which trust and cooperation are developed. Comparing the IAF's experience with diverse denominations offers an excellent opportunity to explore the contributions that religiously based social capital can make to democratic renewal, and to understand the way that different institutional structures and unifying beliefs affect that contribution.

Religious Communities in the Texas IAF Network

The Texas IAF has been able to engage many types of religious communities in its local organizations. But some denominations are more likely to be involved than others are. About half of the churches active in the Texas IAF are Hispanic Catholic parishes. The other half is made up in roughly equal proportions between African American and Anglo churches, both of which are largely Protestant.[3] Although white and black Catholics, and a few Jewish synagogues, have played important roles from time to time, these three clusters represent the large majority of IAF member institutions in Texas.

The preponderance of Hispanic Catholic parishes can be attributed, in part, to the fact that the rapidly growing Hispanic population makes up almost 25 percent of the state's total. And Hispanics are heavily concentrated in low-income communities. African Americans, meanwhile, constitute about 13 percent of the state's population. Moreover, the origins of the IAF in the Mexican American communities of San Antonio gave the network an initial grounding and reputation among Texas' Hispanics. In addition to COPS, the Texas IAF has three local affiliates in areas where low-income Mexican Americans make up the large majority of the entire population: Valley Interfaith in the lower Rio Grande Valley, EPISO in El Paso, and The Border Organization in the Del Rio/Eagle Pass area. IAF organizers have worked hard to involve African American Protestants in their efforts in Texas, and they have met with growing success. Part of the difficulty lies in the different institutional structure and religious tradition of black Protestants, as will be discussed below.

In addition to their availability for recruitment as members of IAF affiliates, denominations vary in their ability to provide a broader base of supporters. This difference can be seen quite clearly if we compare the ability of churches in different denominations to mobilize supporters to the IAF's large public actions. Based on an analysis of data collected on turnout figures to large actions in 1992 and 1993, most COPS parishes and most Catholic parishes in other IAF affiliates like Metro Alliance and ACT in Fort Worth can turn out 75–100 parishioners to large actions. The strongest can reach 200. Protestant churches in Metro Alliance and ACT, by contrast, turn out 25–50, with the strongest reaching 100.

COPS reaches 50,000 families through 27 parishes. It attracted 3,400 members from 27 parishes to its twentieth-anniversary convention, an average of almost 125 per parish.[4] Meanwhile, the mainly Protestant ACT reaches 25,000 families through 22 congregations. It drew 1,500 members from the 22 congregations to its tenth-anniversary convention, an average of about 75 per church. Observations and reports from other network organizations show a similar pattern.[5]

In absolute numbers, Catholic parishes can mobilize almost twice as many followers on average as Protestant congregations to IAF actions. Per capita figures, however, show a less marked difference, with Catholic parishes mobilizing roughly 25 percent more followers. The overall greater capacity of Catholic parishes for IAF mobilization, compared to Protestant congregations, therefore, rests both upon their larger average size and upon their ability to mobilize a greater proportion of parishioners and neighborhood residents.

The Texas IAF grounds its work primarily in Mexican American and African American communities. Exploring more deeply the theological traditions and institutional structures of Hispanic Catholic and African American Protestant churches can help clarify the contributions that religiously based social capital can make to expanding democratic participation. Comparing the two types of churches will make clear why differences in beliefs and structures matter for efforts, like the IAF's, to engage people in political action through their religious communities.

Hispanic Catholic Communities

Theological Tradition: Catholic Social Thought

Hispanic Catholics and their priests bring a rich faith tradition to their participation in the IAF. That tradition finds its roots in the social teaching of the Catholic Church that began with Pope Leo XIII's encyclical *Rerum Novarum* in 1891. In that papal encyclical, Pope Leo defended the rights of workers in the face of powerful economic and political institutions. The Second Vatican Council (Vatican II) reactivated this tradition for the modern era. Held between 1962 and 1965, the Vatican II meetings served to strengthen the church's commitment to social and economic justice and to inspire action by Catholics throughout the world. In 1982, the American Bishops published their letter on the economy, which called for the church to take action for economic justice. Although Pope John Paul II has taken conservative stands on certain social issues, he has continued to articulate a strong role for the church in defending the rights of the poor.[6]

The IAF's organizing efforts among Hispanics also drew energy from the theological and social ferment stimulated by liberation theology developed in Latin America. In 1968 the bishops of Latin America issued a manifesto from Medellin, Colombia, that called for the participation of the poor in their own liberation and salvation. In many Latin American countries, Catholic priests and lay activists began to oppose ruling elites and military dictatorships. They organized small Christian "base communities" that took political action for social and economic justice. Although Catholics in the IAF took some inspiration from liberation theology, they never followed the base-community strategy, which seemed, to many of them, more appropriate to Latin American conditions. Instead, IAF Catholics sought to participate within mainstream church structures, seeking to engage parishes in political action for community needs.[7]

More important to the IAF's effort to counter the individualism and atomization of contemporary American social and political life, Catholic social thought articulates a strong communitarian conception of human beings. In *Gaudium et Spes*, the church asserts that it is only "through [man's] dealings with others, through reciprocal duties, and through fraternal dialogue he develops all his gifts and is able to rise to his destiny."[8] IAF training sessions regularly draw from this tradition, emphasizing that "this conception imagines human beings as 'persons,' not as 'individuals.' They are mothers, fathers, brothers, daughters, workers, employers, pastors, governors, and so on, not isolated, self-directed singularities."[9]

The large majority of IAF-affiliated priests and lay leaders explain their involvement in the IAF in terms of a Catholic concern for community and a responsibility to take action for social and economic justice. Participation in the IAF offers the opportunity to make the social commitments of their faith real. Moreover, since Hispanic parishioners live in low-income communities themselves, there is a tight connection between the demands of their religious faith and the immediate interests and needs of their communities. Father Mike Haney of St. Leonard's parish explains why he joined COPS:

COPS is a way of implementing the Gospel's call to justice that it imposes on us. This happens in a couple of ways: dealing with issues themselves; and COPS calls us to work as a collective, to find strength in community, and that's a Gospel call itself.[10]

The IAF does have to convince socially committed priests that political action is a legitimate way to pursue community building. But the nonpartisan character of IAF organizations makes these affiliates an attractive venue for priests with a variety of political affiliations, except the most conservative.

Institutional Structure: The Parish Hierarchy

The institutional structure of the Catholic Church has proven quite conducive to IAF organizing. The Catholic Church has historically placed a stress on authority, and continues to be more hierarchically organized than most Protestant denominations. Since Vatican II, though, the church has worked to increase lay participation in its parishes and in the broader life of the church. Exactly how to balance authority with participation is a matter of contention within the church, with Pope John Paul struggling to assert papal authority over many doctrinal matters at the same time as he reiterates the church's commitment to the poor. Catholic women, meanwhile, have worked to assert their leadership in the church in the face of the Pope's defense of the traditional monopoly of men in positions of power. Nevertheless, Catholic dioceses in the United States have been encouraging the development of lay leaders, including women, and giving them much more responsibility for pastoral duties, especially as the shortage of priests has become increasingly more pronounced. Consequently, IAF organizers have a much larger pool of lay leaders from which to draw than they would have had prior to the seventies.[11]

A combination of authority with participation benefits political participation in the IAF in several important ways.[12] The hierarchical structure of the Catholic Church encourages many priests to join the IAF because Texas bishops have fairly consistently supported the Texas IAF organizations. San Antonio's Archbishop Patricio Flores, the nation's first Hispanic bishop, played a key role in supporting COPS early on, and regularly encourages priests to involve their parishes in the effort. Flores has also used his influence to encourage other Texas bishops to support local IAF affiliates. They have seldom been hesitant to do so. Consequently, priests who do get involved in local IAF affiliates can expect recognition from their bishops. In San Antonio, several priests active in COPS have been appointed to important posts in the church, including David Garcia as secretary to the Archbishop and Rosendo Urrabazo as director of the Mexican American Cultural Center. While there appears to be no evidence of retribution against priests who decline to support IAF initiatives, diocesan support makes many priests more likely to get involved.[13]

Within individual parishes the Catholic priest commands authority as well. The pastor's support for IAF efforts carries great weight in encouraging participation by the parish's lay leaders. According to former COPS co-chair Reverend Urrabazo, "participation can be charted according to the pastors. When the clergy is on-board, the parish takes off. When the clergy is not with COPS, participation falls off."[14]

For its part, the Catholic Church in Texas has much to gain from participating in the IAF. Hispanics constitute, by far, the most rapidly growing Catholic community. The allegiance of Hispanics to the church is vital to its survival. The Texas church would like to avoid the kind of defection by Hispanics to Pentecostal churches that has occurred elsewhere in the country.[15] Moreover, because the Catholic Church has a parish structure, the vitality of parish churches depends on the health of the neighborhoods in which they are located. The IAF works directly to help these communities survive and grow, so its work contributes to the long-term health of the Catholic Church itself.

Finally, the IAF can offer direct assistance in developing lay leadership for the church. As the number of priests and nuns has dropped precipitously, the church has become dependent on lay ministries. Because of a long tradition where priests monopolized these responsibilities, the church must train lay parishioners to become ministerial leaders. Many dioceses have set up parish development offices for precisely this purpose. But IAF organizers are experts in leadership development. In the late seventies, IAF director Cortes and his staff established their own parish development program to offer to priests and ministers.[16] In San Antonio, the IAF and the Catholic Church work so closely on these matters, that the diocese hired former COPS President Carmen Badillo to head up its parish development office.

Parish development and IAF involvement is not conflict-free. Once lay leaders take on more responsibility, they have a greater opportunity to challenge parish priests on issues facing the church. In some cases, it has been lay leaders who get the priest to join the IAF effort, not the other way around.[17] In many cases, when an originally supportive pastor moves on, to be replaced by a less supportive one, it is the lay leadership of the church that continues its IAF involvement. Over time, parishes go through cycles of involvement in this way. If a priest is hostile to the IAF, though, participation normally ends.

In a surprising way, the authority of the parish priest often makes lay leadership in IAF efforts more likely. Catholic priests derive their authority from the church; that is, they are appointed by bishops, not elected by parishioners. Since their position in the parish is relatively secure, and their authority does not come from their talent as a community leader, they often let lay parishioners become the IAF leaders in their parish. In COPS, Metro Alliance, and ACT, only several pastors out of the forty or so member Catholic parishes are highly active.[18] Catholic pastors often find it relatively easy to commit their parish to join the IAF, because membership does not necessarily mean extra work for them. As we will see below, African American Protestant ministers face a sharply different institutional structure, and consequently find that they must play a direct leadership role in their church's IAF work.

Institutional Structure: The Neighborhood-Based Parish

The geographically based parish structure of the Catholic Church contributes to the ability of the IAF to build an extensive base of support within low-income Hispanic neighborhoods. Catholic parishes tend to be large in membership, and they incorporate all Catholics in the parish neighborhood. Since the residents of COPS neighborhoods are almost entirely Mexican American and at least nominally Catholic, each member church provides the IAF with access to a large proportion of neighborhood residents. The twenty-seven parishes in COPS represent 70 percent of the Catholic parishes in the south, west, and central sections of San Antonio. Thus, by recruiting only twenty-seven churches, COPS has direct access to 70 percent of churchgoing Hispanics, a total of about 50,000 families. Moreover, lay leaders and church members can reach beyond churchgoers to their families, friends, and neighbors, mostly concentrated in a local community surrounding the parish.

Hispanic Catholic IAF leaders, therefore, are tied particularly closely to neighborhood networks since they normally live in the neighborhoods of their parish. Although working- and middle-class Hispanics appear to be more likely than the very poor to serve as church and neighborhood leaders, they share an Hispanic identity and live with the poor in one neighborhood. Consequently, there is a tight connection between their own self-interest, the needs of the broader community, and a religious commitment to social ministry. In other words, fixing the street in front of her house meets the personal self-interest of an IAF leader, helps the larger neighborhood, and fulfills a commitment to social ministry as well.

Metro Alliance leader Pauline Cabello discusses why she seized the leadership opportunities offered by IAF participation. Cabello lives in San Antonio's near north side, a working-class community becoming predominantly Hispanic, and is a member of St. Mary Magdalene's parish.

My grandmother lives in the deep west side. When it rained, her street was a river of mud. My grandmother always said it was the will of God. A young priest at St. Timothy's changed their lives—Father Benavides [an early COPS leader]. . . . When Father Benavides came to St. Mary Magdalene's, he set up ministries and leaders developed [including me]. It gave me a sense of ownership. That I'm important and I don't have to be a tamale or taco maker. I can have a voice and a vision for me and my family. . . .

What we do comes from our gut—being mothers, we have a sense of community. In the last two to three years we [Linda Froebane and myself] got more involved in Metro because they hit on our area of interest, education. That hit us: it's *our* kids, the children of the community. We buried two or three; we don't want to do that anymore.[19]

Other Hispanic IAF leaders stress the connection between the effective power offered by IAF participation and their religious beliefs. Veteran COPS leader Patricia Ozuna takes pleasure from tough meetings with public officials where she advocates for the community in which she lives. She participates in COPS as a social ministry, and because she likes "banging heads," or "using my skills to accomplish something—knowing you moved an issue forward. . . . With COPS you see the changes—streets, sidewalks. We have the power to do things for the community."[20] In fact, many Hispanic IAF leaders report that involvement in the IAF has strengthened their religious commitment. For Beatrice Cortez, COPS' fourth president, IAF involvement helps her relate scripture to her life: "Faith is a matter of developing, creating the right situation for people. If you don't make a choice, your faith won't mean anything."[21]

The extensive access to neighborhood networks offered by the parish structure, combined with the direct interest of the residents of low-income Hispanic communities in the work of the IAF, helps explain why Catholic parishes stand out in their consistent ability to engage large numbers of neighborhood residents in supporting IAF campaigns. The authority of a supportive priest who encourages participation from the pulpit provides an important incentive for support as well. Meanwhile, the parish and neighborhood stand to gain from their IAF participation. The IAF works to strengthen the community's social fabric and to bring the necessary resources for community revitalization. Moreover, through participation in the IAF, the parish can draw the neighborhood more closely around the parish, enhancing the allegiance of Hispanic Catholics and attracting new parishioners as well.

Hispanic Catholic communities, therefore, contain a nexus of characteristics that have a close affinity to IAF organizing. The tradition of Catholic social thought directs clergy and parishioners toward action for the benefit of their own community. The church's institutional structure combines authority and lay participation in a way that encourages priests to join and lay leaders to emerge. Finally, its parish base provides the IAF with broad and dense access to neighborhood-based social networks, which can be more easily drawn into action with the support of a priest that carries the authority of the church behind him. Meanwhile, the church itself benefits from IAF participation. Clergy and lay leaders find a way to activate their faith and to pursue their social ministry through the IAF. Meanwhile, IAF organizers help develop the lay leadership upon which the future of the church depends. Finally, IAF organizing strengthens the economic and social health of the communities upon which Catholic parishes both serve and depend. Through this process of mutual interaction and benefit, the IAF and Hispanic Catholic communities have developed a very close collaboration.

African American Protestant Congregations

Theological Tradition: Racial Justice and Liberation

Theologically, the themes of deliverance and freedom lie at the heart of black Christian spirituality.[22] Freedom suggests deliverance both into God's kingdom as well as from slavery and racial oppression in the real world. The African American worldview relies deeply upon its religious theology, and its practice draws heavily from the church's cultural styles of worship, such as call and response.[23] The theological tradition of the black church, then, offers a rich resource for efforts to sustain the African American community and work for its liberation.

African American churches have a long tradition of engagement with social and political issues in the black community. As Aldon Morris has shown, during the era of legal segregation, black churches became *the* center of black community life in the urban South.[24] Excluded from mainstream civic and political institutions, African Americans concentrated their community and political leadership in their independent churches. In the fifties and sixties, these churches provided a crucial foundation for the civil rights movement through their preexisting networks of leaders and followers under the influence of their pastors. In order to engage black churches and their pastors, religious leaders like Martin Luther King, Jr., refocused religious beliefs to direct them towards active engagement in the struggle for racial justice and equality. Some ministers declined to participate because they thought the church should concentrate on personal salvation, not political action. But a large number of ministers did play central roles in local civil rights movement organizations.

After the decline of the civil rights movement, many ministers continued to participate in African American social and political efforts. Although King had tried to broaden the movement's perspective to deal
with poverty and economic problems facing Americans across racial lines,
the primary direction of these efforts remained racially based. Black ministers played key roles in civil rights organizations like the NAACP and
in efforts to empower African Americans through the election of black
candidates to office.[25]

This rich African American religious tradition has not been as readily
available for IAF organizing as the tradition of Catholic social thought in
the Hispanic community because the black tradition has been focused
primarily towards racial justice. The IAF has a different emphasis,
avoiding race-based organizing in favor of community organizing in a
multiracial context. Participation in the IAF does not require a rejec-
tion of theological concern for liberation or for the needs of the black
community. But it does require a shift and reemphasis in social and political theology.

For its part, the IAF had long seen its purpose as providing a vehicle
for the inclusion of marginalized and oppressed communities. And, once
African Americans started participating in the Texas IAF and in local IAF
organizations in other parts of the country, the network proved open to
their theological influence.[26] One of the central themes in the IAF's "theology of organizing" became the inclusion of the stranger. IAF organizers
began to stress the origins of that theme in Exodus, a central symbol in
black religious traditions. Cortes explains the IAF's view: "The black tradition is important because it cannot escape Exodus. At Exodus the narrative is about the formation of peoplehood. So that's real rich [for our
organizing]."[27] But, rather than emphasize the theme of liberation found
in Exodus, the IAF has stressed the themes of inclusion and community
building that are also present there.

This shift away from racial justice and towards a broader multiracial
and community-building approach in the IAF proved difficult for some
black ministers to make because they were personally involved in advocacy groups with a specifically racial mission (like the NAACP) or in current electoral arrangements. Many important black ministers in Texas
cities themselves held elective office, particularly at the local level. Or,
they had relationships with elected officials that committed them to support those officials in exchange for favors or resources to their neighborhoods. Seeing the continued effect of racism on their communities, many
ministers felt committed to independent black organizations.[28] Participation in the IAF required not only a theological shift, but also the breaking
of relationships and the development of a nonpartisan style of political
activity. The IAF challenged Hispanic priests who were mostly uninvolved

politically to take their faith commitments into the political arena. Many African American ministers already did that. The IAF had to challenge them, instead, to direct those political commitments in a different way.

While some African American ministers resisted this shift in political direction, others were looking precisely for such an opportunity. Seeing their communities crumble while black candidates ran for office, and while the NAACP pursued legal strategies, many black ministers saw the IAF as an opportunity to create effective power and make real improvement in their communities. Reverend Barry Jackson, an African American leader of Dallas Area Interfaith, is a good example. Barry recognized the importance of black power, but did not want to be limited to it. When he accepted the pastorship of Munger Avenue Baptist Church, he inherited a church with a rich tradition in efforts to address racial justice, but one located in a rapidly deteriorating inner-city neighborhood. Despite his earlier attraction to black power, Jackson felt it was no longer adequate to the tasks at hand. In his words, "I talked to black ministers. I said we can't continue to engage on racial issues. We need to address issues of families, neighborhoods, and if we build multiracial alliances, we can win."[29]

There are still some black congregations which emphasize personal salvation so exclusively that they reject political participation of any kind. That is why the more mainstream black denominations constitute the majority of black church participation in the Texas IAF. Nevertheless, the IAF has drawn in some significant amount of participation from evangelical congregations that are generally fairly apolitical. In particular, a number of churches belonging to the Church of God in Christ (COGIC), a fast-growing evangelical denomination, participate in local IAF affiliates. Often counting among their congregants the poorest African Americans, their ministers tend to emphasize social ministry as much as evangelism.[30]

Institutional Structure: The Independent Congregation

The Protestant congregational structure contrasts sharply with the Catholic ecclesiastic hierarchy and parish base. In Baptist denominations, congregations are fiercely independent.[31] There is no equivalent to an Archbishop Flores to encourage black ministers to join IAF efforts. At the same time, Baptists do form associations, and black ministers often create ministerial alliances in their cities. Pastor networks have proven crucial to IAF organizing. Many pastors joined the IAF organization ACT when encouraged to do so by Reverend Nehemiah Davis and others in the Baptist Ministerial Alliance in Fort Worth. The influence of Baptist minister

Barry Jackson, who had been involved with the IAF in Austin before his move to Dallas, proved crucial to the IAF's success in recruiting a core group of black Baptist churches to its effort in Dallas.[32]

The congregation is typically understood as a more horizontal structure than the parish because the independence of congregations places power in the hands of lay leaders. Black Baptist congregations hire their pastors. Their leadership boards, not the priest or his bishop, hold ultimate authority. Sidney Verba and his associates argue that this structure holds out an advantage to political participation.[33] According to Verba, Protestant lay leaders have more of an opportunity than in the Catholic Church, especially prior to Vatican II, to learn civic skills because they appear to participate more in church life. But this understanding misses a crucial aspect of black congregational dynamics.

It turns out that, despite the fact that ultimate authority rests with the congregation's governing board, many black ministers have developed a reputation for authoritarian leadership styles. Authoritarianism has deep roots in theocratic and patriarchal traditions in the black church.[34] But another reason for this apparent paradox lies in the way that black pastors have to operate to keep their job. Because the authority, and ultimately the job security, of the black Baptist minister does not rest with a bishop, the African American pastor must constantly work to maintain the allegiance of congregants. The pastor acquires this support through demonstrating leadership as well as through charismatic speaking. Given the particular history of black churches as centers for community life, pastors are expected to be community and political leaders as part of their ministerial responsibilities. The tremendous demands on pastors for broad leadership, coupled with the need to maintain constant support, has contributed to an authoritarian style among many black ministers.

The responsibility of the African American pastor to be the political leader of his or her congregation presents, perhaps paradoxically, an obstacle to the recruitment of black churches into the IAF. Since the Catholic hierarchy assigns priests to parishes, the pastor does not have to be the parish's political leader, although some may desire that role. A Catholic priest may therefore sign his parish up with the IAF and then step back to let lay parishioners do the actual work required for participation. Black ministers do not do that. Apparently, if a black minister wants to maintain his or her leadership position in the congregation, the pastor must take an active role personally in the IAF when the church joins. An examination of clergy participation in Texas IAF organizations supports this conclusion. As noted above, only a few pastors of the forty or so Catholic parishes in COPS, Metro Alliance, and ACT are engaged in the organizations on a regular basis. Some associate pastors and nuns also play prominent roles. Whereas, all pastors of the ten African American

Protestant churches in ACT and the Metro Alliance are actively engaged in the IAF organizations.[35]

The participation of black ministers, of course, often contributes important leadership to IAF organizations. The problem lies in recruitment. For a black pastor to commit his or her church to the IAF, the pastor must be willing to put in the time and effort required of IAF leaders. Many pastors may be supportive of the IAF, but unwilling to commit their own time. Consequently, they will not join the IAF effort, whereas similar passive support by a Catholic priest will often be sufficient for the church to join and IAF organizing in that parish to begin.[36]

If the black minister is committed enough to join, the IAF can usually count on his active participation. And that minister can gain from the IAF's assistance in "parish development." Many black congregations are institutionally very weak. They suffer from inadequate income and are housed in old buildings in need of repair. Many cannot pay a salary sufficient to support a minister full-time. Although black congregations do provide the opportunity for greater lay involvement, often their lay leaders are inexperienced and untrained. The IAF helps interested ministers build a leadership team to strengthen the church's finances and programs. But the minister has to be open to a new style of leadership, that is, of collaboration with lay members. According to African American minister and Dallas Area Interfaith co-chair Gerald Britt, the black ministers who come to embrace the IAF are those who can see the compatibility of the work with their religious mission and can see the advantages of shared leadership. "It's a different day and time. . . . The idea of shared leadership within the congregation and within the [IAF] organization—that's a new model of leadership. But when you've been raised in a hierarchy, where you're the final authority. . . ."[37] Barry Jackson argues that the IAF's approach meets the needs of a new era for black churches, declaring, "It's time out for the 'big daddy'!"[38]

Institutional Structure: Pan-neighborhood Congregations

The congregational structure of the black church provides strengths and weaknesses as well in the way it provides IAF organizing with access to neighborhood-based social networks. African American congregations typically provide access to a comparatively smaller number of neighborhood-based social networks than Catholic parishes. First of all, black churches tend to be smaller in size than Catholic parishes. In San Antonio and Fort Worth, the average Catholic parish in the IAF includes about two thousand families. By contrast, the average black Protestant church includes about five hundred families, and several are quite small.[39] IAF organizers, therefore, would have to recruit four black pastors to have access to the same number of potential lay leaders and their networks provided by one Catholic parish.

Moreover, being congregationally based, black churches draw their membership from across the city, not just in their neighborhood. In fact, many inner-city black congregations have more members from outside the neighborhood in which the church stands than inside. A large number of these commuters grew up in the neighborhood of the church. As the more affluent left for the suburbs, many continue to return to their old church on Sunday morning. Many of these more middle-class congregants dominate in church leadership and often in IAF participation as well. In one way, that is a great strength and contribution of black churches: they often help overcome the isolation of poor communities by bringing the more affluent together with the poor within one congregation. On the other hand, the IAF's ability to tap the networks of the church's neighborhood is weakened. The smaller size and less dense access to neighborhood networks helps explain why black churches mobilize, on average, fewer supporters than Hispanic Catholic parishes to the large public actions that provide the foundation for the political power of IAF affiliates.

Although IAF campaigns speak to the immediate interests of inner-city black neighborhoods, for housing, education, public safety, etc., many of the leaders that emerge from African American churches in the IAF do not live in those neighborhoods. Mexican American Catholic leaders have a strong material self-interest in IAF participation that combines with their religious commitments. The involvement of African American leaders from outside the church's neighborhood has to rely more strongly upon a religiously derived concern for the broader black community. Maurice Simpson, an African American leader in ACT, got involved ". . . because I believe in the Great Commission—Matthew 19 and 20. You reach out and teach. If you teach a person to read and write, then they can be a good Christian. It's part of my ministry. Being from the black community, you learn to share resources and help your neighbor. It took those things to survive."[40]

For their part, African American ministers see some important gains from their participation in the IAF for their own institutions. Taking action for community improvement through the IAF helps root the church in its neighborhood. IAF organizing engages neighborhood residents, draws them around the church, and connects them to suburban members within the congregation. Unlike parishes, congregations can move. But many black ministers are committed to their neighborhoods and its residents. Many IAF ministers pastor historic black churches in the inner city, churches with a rich heritage. But, in many cases, these inner-city communities suffer from extreme distress. Participation in the IAF can directly help to improve these communities, and therefore sustain the church as a community institution. According to Barry Jackson, he participates in the IAF because "the church's very survival is at stake."[41]

Anglo Religious Communities

Most of the Anglo congregations active in the Texas IAF are mainline Protestant denominations, like Methodists, Episcopalians, and Lutherans, although some are Catholic and one or two are Jewish.[42] The Anglo Protestant congregations share with the African American congregations the characteristics of dispersed membership and weaker neighborhood base, and therefore offer similar turnout figures to network actions.[43] On the other hand, the faith traditions of mainline Protestant denominations have proven easier to engage in multiracial political action. Although the IAF had its strongest ties to the Catholic Church in Alinsky's days, the network always maintained a significant degree of support from mainline Protestant denominations. Protestant ministers in the sixties worked to develop a theological statement that based their support for the IAF upon their mission to the powerless, poor and racially segregated people.[44]

Many white ministers in the contemporary Texas IAF have roots in the social gospel tradition, and find in the IAF an important vehicle for expressing social action commitments. The social gospel emerged out of liberal Protestantism in the late nineteenth century as a response to the massive changes brought about by industrialization, urbanization, and large-scale immigration. The social gospel urged Protestants not just to save the world, but to change it. Advocates of the social gospel opened settlement houses, led the Women's Christian Temperance Union, and participated in a wide range of reform efforts during the Progressive Era. Some supported the early work of the NAACP. Protestant IAF leaders look to the writings of social gospel theologians like Walter Rauschenbusch to help them understand their organizing work. These Anglo ministers, unlike many black pastors, tend not to be wedded to partisan politics, and so remain more open to IAF recruitment.[45]

One of the biggest challenges for Anglo churches in more affluent communities, however, is to connect with the self-interest of their broader congregations and neighborhoods. They may be able to build a core group of IAF leaders, but the engagement with the rest of the community is often weaker. Several ministers signed their churches up to the network only to withdraw them later because they failed to build enough broad support in the congregation. Reverend Bill Bruggeman committed his Lutheran congregation on the affluent north side of San Antonio to the Metro Alliance's forerunner, the MCA, in the early eighties. But he could not get a group of members to participate and withdrew within a couple of years. His congregation saw the IAF as an inner-city organization. According to Bruggeman, "I have trouble with the self-interest concept. You should do things for others. But if you're going to take self-interest seriously, you need to take it more seriously. Metro [Alliance] needs to come work out here."[46] In principle, the IAF commits itself to do base-building work in the immediate interests of all member congregations. But with limited resources, local IAF organizations tend to devote their organizing time to immediate issues in low-income communities and to citywide issues of potential concern to all.

The network has had success in expanding its base within Anglo congregations when it does devote time and energy to developing campaigns that meet the direct interests of congregants. Colonial Hills United Methodist Church in the affluent north side of San Antonio, has been one of the strongest Anglo Protestant churches in the network. With one thousand member families, the large congregation has an active core of twenty or so and can turn out seventy-five to one hundred supporters to the biggest Metro Alliance actions. Colonial Hills is a socially and theologically moderate congregation made up of middle-class professionals and located in a conservative neighborhood. The pastor, Bill Easum, along with two other ordained ministers affiliated with the congregation, Homer Bain and David Semrad, provide a solid core from which to build a base for Metro Alliance membership. Through participation in Metro Alliance early on, Colonial Hills got the street fixed in front of their church—an issue of immediate concern, if admittedly a small one. But members of the church have gone on to spearhead work on education. They supplied key leadership to the San Antonio Education Partnership, which provides scholarships and job opportunities to high school graduates. Education has remained the most popular Metro Alliance program at Colonial Hills because the church has many members who are teachers in inner-city schools.[47]

Jewish Congregations

Jewish participants in the IAF have a rich tradition from which to draw in participating in social and political action through the IAF. The Old Testament, the Talmud, and Rabbinical commentary all contain prominent themes of liberation and social justice. In the U.S., Jews played important roles in the early labor movement and were strong supporters of the civil rights movement. Reform Judaism has long stood for the promotion of social justice.

Nevertheless, there is also a strong strain of Judaism that pulls Jews in a more insular direction. Given the history of anti-Semitism in the U.S., as well as the experience of so many American Jews who fled or survived Nazism, many Jews resist efforts at cooperation with Christians. In Texas, the Jewish population is relatively small across the state, although Jewish communities carry significant influence in business and political circles in several of the main urban centers like Dallas. And Jews have good reason to be skeptical of Christians in the Bible Belt, where evangelists are aggressive.[48]

The Texas IAF, of course, makes it clear that Jewish leaders join the network to collaborate as equals and with respect—not to be evangelized. Nevertheless, these Jewish participants must enter a network that is overwhelmingly Christian in membership. Granted, the Texas IAF has always emphasized that it reflected traditions that derive from Jewish as well as Christian faiths. If anything, IAF organizers spend more time studying Jewish traditions than the small numbers of Jewish participants would suggest. Old Testament stories, like Exodus, are a mainstay of IAF training. And IAF organizers work hard to create a more comfortable environment for Jewish leaders. Christian ministers, for example, are encouraged to eliminate specific references to Jesus during prayers at IAF events, at least those that include Jewish participants.

Yet the network has to deal with challenges other than religious differences in recruiting Jewish congregations as well. The experience of Rabbi Ken Roseman of Temple Shalom in North Dallas exemplifies some of the problems the IAF faces in working with Jewish communities. Roseman got his synagogue to join the Dallas Interfaith project early on. Roseman had come to North Dallas in 1985 from Madison, Wisconsin, to lead the temple's community of 900 families, most of whom were headed by professionals and business people. His father was a student of Saul Alinsky, the IAF's founder. The rabbi himself was committed to the IAF's philosophy, but struggled to engage his congregation in the organization. In his view, the theological differences were not much of an obstacle. More important was the different institutional structure of Jewish congregations. While a Protestant congregation has a social action and community outreach budget that it controls, Roseman's temple sends its social contributions to the Jewish Fund of Greater Dallas. In recent years, that fund has concentrated on resettling Russian Jews in Dallas, and Roseman has been unsuccessful in efforts to use part of those funds to support Dallas Interfaith. Instead, Roseman has tapped his discretionary funds to cover the synagogue's dues to the organization, which amount to $2,000 yearly. To sustain participation in Dallas Interfaith, Roseman needs more of the congregation to join him in active support. And here, Roseman has not been successful. Roseman criticizes the IAF for not placing enough of a priority on organizing around issues of immediate concern to his community: "When the IAF targets Roosevelt High School, they [his members] want to know what it's doing for them specifically. . . . I bet we don't have twelve kids in the Dallas Independent School District."[49]

Situated on the city limits of North Dallas, Temple Shalom draws from the growing Jewish community north of the city, where more and more middle-class families are moving. In Roseman's view, many of the synagogue's members are fleeing the city, moving ever northward in search of better schools and a greater distance from the problems of Dallas' poor communities of color. He criticizes the IAF for not taking up an aggressive program to address the problems that these members do have, like adequate health care and the widening of the LBJ freeway.

In the late nineties the IAF network began to deepen its relationships with the Jewish community. Despite limited resources, and the organization's commitment to low-income communities, the Dallas IAF organization started working to develop some campaigns to address specific North Dallas issues. The IAF hired Jennifer Barrash to organize in Dallas, and she has stimulated the network to deal more consciously with Jewish concerns. Barrash is more committed to Judaism than other Jewish IAF organizers in the past have been. And she has played an active role both in Dallas and at the region's organizer seminars.

The institutional structure of Jewish synagogues makes it more difficult to recruit them, but in Barrash's view that is not the central problem. According to Barrash, synagogues can find the money for IAF dues if there is the will to join the interfaith effort. And this may require a process of deepening mutual understanding. Barrash may prove central to that process. According to Barrash, her participation in the IAF "comes out of my faith. I've learned much about what it means to be a Jew from this work. This is exactly where I should be as a Jew. By understanding other religions, it breaks down my stereotypes of Christians. We study scripture a lot, Exodus. What it means to be a Hebrew and Israelite. I feel respected here and that I'm adding. There is a real give and take. And since people are trying to know me as a person, an organizer, and a Jew, I've had to articulate my faith."[50]

As a result of concerted efforts, more Jewish congregations are beginning to join the Southwest IAF, in places like Austin and Dallas in Texas, as well as in Arizona and Louisiana. Several organizers are Jewish, and they are talking much more about what it means to be a Jew in interfaith organizing. Meanwhile, the Southwest IAF recently established a Jewish caucus which discusses the relationship of Jewish faith and traditions to IAF organizing as a way to support and increase Jewish participation. Nevertheless, the Jewish community has not yet become a central player in the network.

Conclusion: Participation and Authority

While many types of churches have joined the Texas IAF, some do appear to have a greater affinity than others to the network's organizing strategy. The faith traditions of Hispanic Catholic communities correspond well to the IAF's theology of organizing. While African American religious commitments to racial justice can be turned towards multiracial community-building efforts, doing so requires more work. Religious beliefs do not completely determine a political agenda, as religion has often proven quite malleable in the political arena. But beliefs do shape commitments and influence the direction of political action. With limited resources to perform that organizing work, it has taken the Texas IAF network a long time to develop African American participation.

Even more than faith traditions, however, institutional structure has a profound influence on the ability of religious communities to generate effective power, at least through the IAF's strategy. Catholic parishes in Hispanic communities provide lay leaders to IAF organizations that are well rooted in parish neighborhoods and can mobilize the largest number of supporters to public actions. Parishes provide dense access to neighborhood-based social networks which share an immediate interest in IAF organizing. Neither black nor white congregations have the same complex of characteristics as Hispanic parishes. The combination of authority and participation within the parish seems to be quite conducive to effective political action.

Scholars have not well appreciated the importance of authority for democratic processes. In his early work on social capital in Italy, Robert Putnam emphasized the importance of horizontal relations in social life.[51] Putnam argued that it was the horizontal relations of voluntary associations in north central Italy that made democracy work in that region; meanwhile, Italy's South remained mired in vertical forms of clientelism embedded in the Catholic Church and personalistic politics. If a church, or any other institution, is organized entirely along vertical lines, with no opportunity for participation at all, then it probably will not contribute much to democratic politics. Putnam's Catholic Church in southern Italy may well exhibit such a vertical monopoly. But in Texas, and most everywhere in the United States, the post-Vatican II Catholic Church combines authority and participation in a way quite powerful for expanding democratic participation, at least through the IAF. The authority of pastors and bishops provides legitimacy and encouragement for lay participation and support. Meanwhile, the lay leaders who play an increasingly important role in the church provide a pool of potential recruits well rooted in parish neighborhoods.

Sidney Verba and his associates, meanwhile, have argued that more horizontally organized black Protestant congregations generate greater political participation than more vertically organized Hispanic Catholic parishes. Overall, Verba found that religious institutions play a particularly important role in equalizing political participation because they are sites where people of color and low-income people have the opportunity to learn skills that can be translated to politics, skills like letter writing, speech making, and planning and making decisions in meetings.[52] But Verba argues that church membership increases political participation by African American Protestants more than Hispanic Catholics. In his view, Protestant congregations provide greater opportunities to lay members for skill development, in committees, ministries, and governing boards, than the more hierarchically organized Catholic parishes. Verba, of course, is examining skill development in individuals on a national basis. He is not looking at processes of political engagement and mobilization within church communities. Yet if we are concerned about expanding democratic participation beyond its current level, we need to look precisely at these community dynamics.[53]

Political participation in collective action involves more than skill acquisition, however important that is. Leaders must be motivated and they must be able to command a following. Faith traditions and pastoral direction play key roles in generating collective action, in motivating lay leaders and mobilizing supporters. Yet these are both forms of authority, that is, the appeal to the authority of the faith and of the pastor or recognized lay leader. Combining authority and participation proves to be an effective way to generate power in the public arena.

A pervasive bias against any form of authority has blinded many analysts to considering the essential role that authoritative leadership plays in democratic institutions. In fact, all social and political institutions contain some combination of authority and participation. Otherwise, there can be no real leadership. Political leadership, of course, must be accountable if it is to be democratic. The real challenge for democratic renewal, then, is to develop forms of accountable, authoritative leadership that encourage broad participation and collective responsibility. The next chapter explores how the IAF attempts to meet this challenge through leadership development and decision-making processes in its network.

Eight

Leadership Development: Participation and Authority in Consensual Democracies

> The heart of our organizing is the finding of
> talented potential leaders, the inviting of those
> leaders into training and relationship, and the
> enabling of people to decide whether they want
> to develop, and where, and when, and how fast.
> Creating the context for leadership development
> is in the core of our work.
> *(IAF 50 Years: Organizing for Change)*[1]

AMERICANS have become suspicious of authority, a term which now has negative connotations for most citizens.[2] Instead, an ultrademocratic ideal pervades, where each member of an organization is supposed to contribute equally and hold an equal share of power. Participatory democratic forms seek to provide an antidote to the unresponsive or biased authority of government officials and corporate elites. Perhaps as a consequence, many such organizations are uncomfortable with internal discussions of authority within their own ranks. Scholars, for their part, have rarely studied leadership and decision making within participatory democratic organizations, and less often theorized these processes. In fact, we lack an appreciation for the role of authority in democratic organizations.

Studies have shown, however, that completely decentralized organizations, those that deny the existence of leadership and provide no official role for leaders, often end up dominated in practice by small cliques. These cliques hold the power to make or shape decisions, but remain less accountable because they have no official status. By denying the existence of authority, organizations abdicate any ability to hold it accountable. Meanwhile, such organizations often suffer from ineffectiveness, making them less attractive to join, especially to people in low-income communities struggling for daily survival.[3]

Many community development and advocacy group efforts do emphasize leadership, but often conceive of it in rather technical or procedural terms: the ability to chair a meeting, conduct research, produce a leaflet. Technical skills are important. But, to the extent politics requires collective action, attention must be paid to the substance of leadership offered to organizations and communities. Leadership in democratic organizations requires the ability to help others come to political judgment, that is, to weigh alternatives and decide a course of action together. Leadership then requires the capacity to guide those collective efforts in the political arena.

Authority in the IAF network involves this sort of political leadership. The IAF describes its primary task, its raison d'être, to be the development of leadership. It seeks to teach the skills, knowledge, and abilities necessary to conduct what it calls the "arts of politics." Technical skills are included here. But the emphasis is more on teaching participants to weigh alternatives, negotiate differences, analyze power dynamics, and strategize. Although the IAF sponsors dedicated training sessions, most training of leaders occurs "on the ground," that is, as they participate in developing and conducting issue campaigns.

The IAF reverses the order in which the processes of issue campaigning and leadership development are normally understood. Advocacy groups and community based organizations typically recruit participants and train leaders in order to win issue campaigns or implement programs. By contrast, the interfaith network pursues issue campaigns as a venue to train leaders. In practice, in the heat of a major issue campaign, training may take a back seat for a while. In the long run, though, IAF organizers struggle to keep their priority on leadership training. The idea is that leaders will undertake the responsibility to improve their communities through the enhanced capacity to provide political leadership developed in IAF organizations.

Grasping the priority the IAF places upon leadership development requires a certain paradigm shift in thinking, and has often not been well understood by the network's observers. It turns out, though, that how democracy works in the network, that is, how leaders are selected and held accountable, and how decisions are made, rests fundamentally on the IAF's conception of leadership development. The very idea of leadership itself suggests that all do not participate equally. Moreover, leadership *development* implies that there is an authoritative agency with the skills and knowledge lacking in others who need such training. Local organizations contract with the IAF to receive training services from the network's organizers. In other words, local leaders see the IAF and its organizers as that authoritative agency.[4]

Authority, however, does not rest solely in the hands of organizers. The most experienced leaders in local IAF affiliates share the prerogative to train new leaders with organizers. Moreover, in consultation with organizers, leaders ultimately make key organizational decisions. Although it does not use the term hierarchy, the IAF is quite explicit about the role of different levels of leadership in decision-making processes. Authority in the Texas IAF, then, works through a hierarchy of grass-roots leadership and the network's institute for organizers. Moreover, while the IAF often emphasizes its grass-roots character in public, within the network, the IAF is not at all shy about the importance of authority.

More important, though, is the combination, or more precisely, the dynamic between authority and participation which provides the driving force behind IAF organizing. IAF organizations do exhibit a broad and deep participatory character. The Texas network is full of the kind of "salt of the earth" community leaders that seem so missing from most forms of American political life. But there is another, more hierarchical, side to the IAF, one that emphasizes the importance of authority. At their best, each should enable the other. The authoritative roles of the organizers and of the network's experienced leadership help cultivate broad participation within the network by recruiting and training new leaders. On the other hand, the initiatives of "salt of the earth" community leaders ground the organization's work, generate the power behind its actions, and spark innovation in the network.

This chapter begins by examining the roles of leaders and organizers in the IAF network. It explores what motivates leaders, and then how they are trained. The second part of the chapter concentrates on leadership selection and decision making. IAF organizations rely on consensual processes to select leaders and make decisions, a method that proves highly compatible with the network's approach to leadership. It turns out that the IAF's concept of leadership development provides a unifying thread to the form of democracy practiced internally in the network.

The Institutional Roles of Leaders and Organizers

The role of leaders in IAF organizations reflects both the network's relational organizing strategy and an open recognition of the hierarchical relationships implied by the concept of leadership development. In *Organizing for Family and Congregation*, IAF national director Ed Chambers defines a leader, with his characteristic bluntness, as someone capable of delivering a following. More subtly, he argues that a leader must be willing to be taught how to train other leaders in a collective context:

> By leaders, we mean men and women who have a following and who can consistently deliver that following. Most so-called leaders are isolated individuals, either self-appointed, or fronts promoted by politicians, the media, or outside economic interests. Responsible elected leadership maintains its quality and reliability through a disciplined system of mutual accountability. The system is

simple: If you can't deliver either people or dollars to the organization, you are not a leader of that organization. If you are not committed to an internal training process in which the central value is to teach primary leaders how to find and in turn teach other leaders, you don't belong. These leaders recognize that leadership is not by nature a form of individual aggrandizement, but rather a means continually to expand the number of their fellow-leaders in the interest of collective power.[5]

While defining a leader as someone with a following seems, upon first glance, as common sense, such an approach is seldom followed consistently in most organizations. Charisma, commitment, and hard work often substitute for the ability to develop relationships with a group of supporters and bring them into the organization's field of action. By contrast, IAF affiliates do take care to hold leaders personally accountable for delivering a following. Leaders have to make commitments in advance for a certain number of people to bring to accountability nights or to other large public actions. Organizers count heads at the meetings and hold leaders accountable for meeting their quotas. When affiliates decide to hold house meetings, leaders, again, must commit to organizing a certain number of them, not just getting other people to do so.

Although the IAF follows the practice of calling all participants in its organizations leaders, the network does not consider these leaders to hold equal status. The IAF explicitly recognizes three levels of leadership within its affiliates: primary, secondary, and tertiary. Although this hierarchy is not written down in any manual, IAF organizers teach this approach at the network's national training, as well as in local training.[6]

The bottom level of tertiary leadership corresponds to what would otherwise be called members of an organization. The formal members of IAF affiliates, however, are technically the institutions like churches which pay dues. Tertiary leaders, therefore, are the ground-level participants who get involved in the local organizations out of the institutions to which they belong. These adherents attend large public actions like conventions and accountability nights, sometimes bringing their friends or neighbors along. Tertiary leaders meet in organization-wide conventions, which ratify the action agendas of affiliates and endorse slates for leadership bodies. The IAF's appellation of leader to these people reflects, in part, an aspiration for their potential role, as well as a recognition that many of these participants do influence their friends and neighbors.

The next level up is what the IAF calls the secondary leader. These participants are the leaders of member institutions, like pastors or influential parishioners, and/or are active in one of the issue campaigns of the IAF affiliate. While primarily concerned with one issue or the needs of their own institution, these secondary leaders do discuss organization-wide concerns. These discussions occur in what most IAF organizations call their delegates assembly, which typically meets every three months. These assemblies draw fifty to one hundred leaders on average, depending on the size of the organization and its level of activity at the time. Delegates assemblies have the responsibility to ratify decisions taken by an organization's executive committee.[7]

The executive committee consists of the top leaders of the organization, its primary leaders. In the IAF's view, primary leaders are meant to take responsibility for the organization as a whole. These leaders hold the authority to make organizational decisions, to adopt campaigns, allocate resources, and hire organizers—subject to ratification by delegates assemblies or conventions. Meanwhile, as the most experienced leaders, they are also expected to play a more active role in recruiting and training new leaders. They help select promising candidates and, in many cases, mentor them. Most local organizations establish a set of co-chairs, usually numbering three to five, out of the executive committee.

The IAF requires the leaders of local organizations to do more than deliver a following. As Chambers specifies above, they must also commit themselves to the IAF training process. This requirement points to the central role of the IAF organizer as trainer. The primary job of the IAF organizer is to recruit and train leaders.

The distinction between organizer and leader in the IAF is premised upon what the IAF calls its iron rule, that is, "never do for people what they can do for themselves."[8] The organizer is supposed to train leaders in how to conduct an issue campaign, not do it him- or herself. The network admits that this rule may often be broken because there is sometimes a tension between teaching and winning. For example, organizers often face the dilemma of whether to hold a crucial meeting with public officials themselves, or to give a new leader the chance to grow, while risking costly mistakes for the organization. Organizers, from my observation, do constantly get involved in the practical work necessary to undertake an issue campaign, or to raise money. In particular, they often play central roles in developing relationships with key public and private officials, especially in newer affiliates that lack highly experienced leadership. But, as I have also observed, IAF regional supervisors do hold local organizers accountable for recruitment and training as their primary task. To the extent that the organizer remains focused on recruitment and training, the network is able to build and sustain broad participation over time.

The IAF's defined institutional role for the organizer is deceptively simple, but profoundly different to the role of professional staff in most political or community-based organizations. Professional staff in most participatory organizations spend their time fighting for issues and administering the organization or its programs. Elected officials do the same.

Most organizations contain no official responsible to ensure that new blood constantly refreshes the organizations, and that new leaders have the opportunity to cultivate their capacity to lead the organization. As a result, over time, most community and political groups become dominated by a few key leaders, while their participatory base withers.[9] IAF organizations are not immune to this tendency, particularly when the organizer overstays an assignment and begins to consider the group his or her "baby."[10]

The IAF organizer, then, is supposed to remain focused on the recruitment and training of new leaders. But why do leaders join and remain involved over time? An examination of the motivations of IAF leaders reveals that several factors combine to explain their participation. But the opportunity for leadership development is a critical inducement to participate in the IAF.

What Motivates IAF Leaders?

An analysis of the composition of executive committees of IAF affiliates in Texas reveals that about one-third of the primary leaders of IAF affiliates are clergy. The remaining two-thirds consist of lay leaders who are predominantly middle-aged women. Some are from more affluent middle-class congregations, but most come from congregations in poor and working-class communities of color. Although most have been involved in community activity in their churches or neighborhoods, few report much previous political experience.[11]

Lay leaders appear motivated to join the IAF network, and to sustain their participation, for three interrelated reasons: self-interest in the material gains to be had through IAF organizing, a religiously inspired caring for community, and the opportunity for personal development and power. The balance between these motivations varies somewhat, however, across participants from different racial groups within the network, and even for the same participant over time. Significantly, the motivation to sustain participation and advance in leadership appears to rest squarely with acquiring a "self-interest" in personal growth and empowerment.[12]

Interviews conducted with Mexican American Catholic women active in Texas IAF organizations show that material self-interest often leads to their initial participation. For example, COPS co-chair Rachel Salazar got involved initially through her friendship with Elisa Aguilar in her church. After her divorce, she moved back into her old neighborhood, taking care of her mother who had Parkinson's disease. The neighborhood was in desperate need of decent housing. Salazar became active in a COPS campaign led by her church to build affordable housing in her neighborhood.

Her parents purchased one of these homes. Through their participation in IAF organizations, many leaders have gotten the street in front of their house fixed, a police substation located in their neighborhood, or a job-training slot in Project QUEST for their daughter.[13] However, if their motivation remains narrowly self-interest oriented, many of these leaders drop away when they get what they want.

Those who stay involved and become top leaders already have—or develop—a concern for the community and an anger at the injustice that its people suffer. Leaders typically communicate this concern in religious terms. COPS co-chair Patricia Ozuna has said that the two things that keep her going are anger at injustice and that she's doing the Lord's work. To Ozuna, COPS represents her ministry for social justice.[14] For many, in fact, involvement in the IAF has strengthened their religious commitment.

Those leaders who become and remain primary leaders in the organization, however, speak of their participation in the IAF and its leadership development process as a transformative experience. They stay involved because they develop a "self-interest" in personal growth and their newly won power.[15] The experience of COPS co-Chair Virginia Ramirez typifies the kinds of transformation that IAF leaders, especially women from low-income communities of color, undergo. Ramirez first became involved with COPS in 1983, when she was a full-time homemaker and mother.[16]

> I got involved in housing. I live in some of the oldest housing. I had been helping a little old lady. She died [of pneumonia] because her house was so cold. Her house was old and in bad shape. I was so angry. I started looking at housing in the community and saw that we're all in the same boat. They [COPS] told me we don't do for others what they can do for themselves. . . .
>
> There was a COPS organization at my church at the time. But my father had always said "don't make waves." He was trying to protect us. COPS was a new idea and I stayed away from it [at first]. My mother was a strong woman. It took me ten years to become a co-chair.

Ramirez grew tremendously through her involvement with the IAF. She went from working on affordable housing in her parish to lobbying for community development block grant (CDBG) funds for neighborhood projects. Later, she registered and mobilized voters, and organized to get Bexar County to open health clinics in Southwest San Antonio. She became a COPS vice president and then co-chair. Ramirez came to enjoy her new-found power as a public leader in the city.

> I enjoy working on the money campaign [fund-raising]. We meet with business leaders in the community and see what they think of COPS. And I would tell them we're not for sale. We've turned money back!

Ramirez gained confidence through her IAF involvement, and then decided to go to college. These new directions in her life disrupted the traditional relationships in her family.

> My husband wasn't supportive at first because I wasn't there for my family all the time. I was becoming a new person and my husband was insecure. But I was teaching him too. He felt threatened and so did my parents [because I had cared for them]. So I had to learn how to make my brothers and sisters take more care for my parents. Now my husband is my major supporter. It's made our marriage stronger. He was a laborer for the Yellow Cab Company. So when I went to school [community college], it was a challenge for him. . . .
>
> I learned that we could make changes. I developed my inspiration and desire. Then I went back to school and got my [associates] degree. Back ten years ago, I never dreamed I'd work for a major university.

By the mid-nineties, Ramirez had graduated from college and secured a job working for the University of Texas Health Sciences Center. She worked in a pilot program that utilized community volunteers to encourage Hispanic women to get breast and cervical cancer screening and nutritional counseling.

Ramirez explains the particular attraction of the IAF for Hispanic women who have had little other opportunity for empowerment:

> More women are leaders because it's a new opportunity for us and we grab it. We've become movers and shakers. Before, there was little opportunity for Hispanic women; so we move fast. And many men must work many hours to support their families. . . . Middle-aged women have already raised their family. We love the organization, that is, we love our people.

Personal empowerment appears to be fostered through the support of collective leadership in IAF organizations. Fairly soon after joining ACT in Fort Worth, Josie Duran was asked to chair the accountability night at her church with 150 supporters in attendance. She reports that she would never have done it without the encouragement of other leaders. The experience had a dramatic impact on her.

> It was the first meeting I ever chaired. I give credit to God. I used to be a shy person. [But this time] I felt powerful and in control of the meeting. I didn't care if a candidate liked me. I've never felt that way before. I used to be a people pleaser. . . . I felt powerful because of the support from other people.[17]

Compared to Hispanic Catholic women, African American leaders in the IAF tend to be a more mixed group socio-economically. Many are middle class and live outside of the neighborhood surrounding their congregation, but return to attend church. Personal growth emerges for African American leaders as well, however, in explaining their motivation for

advancing in leadership. Even black professionals, who have had opportunities for growth through higher education and careers, report the transformative experience of IAF training. School principal Pamela Walls, an
African American leader in Metro Alliance, describes how becoming a
political leader provided a different kind of opportunity for personal empowerment:

> I've changed a lot [through Metro Alliance involvement]. I entered arenas I
> never dreamed of. I talk to the city council on crime and code compliance. I've
> become a leader. . . . It's been a dream. I feel very blessed. I never thought I'd
> help in this fashion, to help people in a meaningful way. . . . I get to do things,
> like speak to the governor, you don't usually do. I'll never be the same. They've
> empowered me. I've become a public figure.[18]

African American ministers are, in this way, like the other black professionals drawn to the IAF. Their participation is also sustained by opportunities for personal growth through the IAF. Reverend D. L. Ellison of ACT
in Fort Worth reports:

> I've grown in my ability to operate publicly as well as in my church. Training
> in leadership building is invaluable. I'm a better person. Doing the stick figure
> at national training helped me prioritize myself. My tradition is to put God
> first. That's right. But the first thing God wants you to do is be a strong family
> man, a good father. The black preacher is always on the move for others and
> neglects his own family. . . . That first year with ACT and national training
> really helped me. I'll be a better public person, because I'm a stronger private
> person. I got my values straight.[19]

Personal growth and empowerment emerge as a critical motivation for
Anglo middle-class participants to stay involved in IAF organizations and
advance in leadership as well. The comments of Claudia Camp, a professor and leader of the ACT organization in Fort Worth, are indicative of
the perspective of many white IAF leaders:

> I became an ACT addict, partly because it's a constant challenge. I'm introverted
> in a big way. The challenge of ACT is to be out there—relational. I need and
> enjoy that. . . . In the last couple of years, especially in the last six months, I
> have gotten a greater sense of self-confidence, a sense of personal power. I
> have, in fact, become more relational. . . . When I started as a thirty-year-old
> white sheltered person, I couldn't challenge other ACT leaders or organizers.
> Now I can.[20]

Some leaders of IAF affiliates have become so "addicted" to the IAF's
opportunities for development that they have sought paid positions as
organizers for the network. As a result, at least in the Southwest IAF
network, there appears to be a growing convergence between the social

backgrounds and motivations of leaders and organizers, although their institutional roles remain distinct. Many new organizers, whether ex-leaders or not, report that the opportunity for personal development has been a central reason for applying for their positions and sustaining their work. For Joe Rubio, a junior organizer assigned to COPS, the IAF has given him the equivalent of a college education:

> The best thing about the IAF is education. It's my college for me—my university experience. . . . We [organizers] help people to think. We start with ourselves and figure out how to do it with leaders—in an action/evaluation context. It works for me. That's why I stay.[21]

A steady diet of personal development can be difficult to sustain on a full-time, permanent basis. The organizers who stick with the IAF and become lead organizers appear to love being "movers and shakers" as well. In other words, they relish the power that comes with their position. Lead organizers hold quite a bit of power within IAF organizations because they claim the highest authority to develop leaders. And, to the extent the network projects power in the public arena, lead organizers are movers and shakers in their cities and the state of Texas.

Leadership Development

Leadership development rests centrally in the IAF's relational style of organizing, specifically in the relationship between the professional organizer and the leader. The organizer develops a relationship with each leader individually, to teach them the "arts of politics" in the course of their participation in its practice, that is, in the issue campaigns of IAF affiliates. National IAF director Chambers suggests that "the organizer's job is like a tutor's—to share insights, to teach methods of analysis and to provide tools of research, to challenge citizens to sharpen their public skills, to develop their ability to reflect and to act."[22]

Organizers identify potential leaders by holding one-on-one individual meetings with contacts referred by other leaders. According to Southwest IAF supervisor Ernesto Cortes, the key qualities he looks for in a potential leader during these meetings are a clear sense of self-interest in getting involved, a willingness to act, and a type of anger at injustice that can be controlled, what the IAF calls "cold anger." Cortes lists a number of other qualities he looks for in potential leaders as well, including imagination, maturity, responsibility, risk-taking, aggressiveness, integrity, sense of humor, and a healthy ego.[23]

Beyond recruitment, the individual meeting constitutes the key form through which organizers train leaders, to enhance these qualities and expand the participant's leadership capacity. Organizers regularly conduct individual meetings, each lasting about 30 minutes, with leaders in which they discuss the leader's work in the organization. Training connected to the work of an organization is not unique to the IAF approach, but the IAF does it consciously, systematically, and with an emphasis on learning through reflection.

Reflection constitutes a central aspect of participation in the IAF. After every action, the organizer must conduct an evaluation. According to national IAF director Chambers, actions have no place if they do not lead to the growth of leaders through reflection.

> Action has a two-fold significance for a citizens' organization. On the most simple level, the action is the focusing of organizational energy to effect certain results—police attention to neglected drug traffic, favorable insurance rates, building a branch bank in a neighborhood that needs and wants it. More importantly, action fuels the organizing process. Action is to organization what oxygen is to our bodies. Without the action, the process is reduced to a sociology class or navel-gazing. Action is the womb of discovery—discovery of self, of values, of power. In the actions new sides of current leaders emerge. New leaders come to the fore; talkers evaporate. And actions create reactions from opponents which require flexible and factual decision-making by the collective leadership. Action enables the organization to grow, to deal with increasingly complex issues, to win more substantial victories, and thereby again increase its growth.[24]

According to supervisor Cortes, the IAF aims to create not action alone, but *praxis*, that is, a more theoretically informed practice which, in turn, is consciously reflected upon.

> In *praxis* the most important part of the action is the reflection and evaluation afterward. Our organizations plan "actions"—public dramas, where masses of ordinary people collaboratively and collectively move on a particular issue with a particular focus—which sometimes produce a reaction that is unanticipated. This reaction then produces the grist for the real teaching of politics and interpretation—how to appreciate the negotiations, the challenge, the argument, and the political conversation.[25]

Postaction reflection takes place collectively with other leaders. But organizers cannot be as completely frank in their "critiques" of individual leaders in group situations as they think is necessary for leadership development. So the individual meeting remains the key form for relationship building and leadership development. In these one-on-one meetings, harmony and friendship do not always prevail. Organizers are taught to agitate leaders, to challenge them to grow and develop. The organizer aims to help the leader determine obstacles to growth and develop a plan for overcoming them.[26]

While intimacy and friendship between organizers and leaders often result from their relationship, so does tension between them. Carmen Badillo, COPS' third president describes this dynamic in her experience:

> The organizers helped us sort through our lives, see what's positive. . . . I built a good relationship with Tom Semway [the organizer]. When I became president, I had to deal again with the question of why being Hispanic is important to me. Tom Semway pushed me on it: did I choose to be Hispanic just for the security? The issue was not being Hispanic; it was being poor and powerless. These issues affect other races. That you're Hispanic is fine and you should get in touch with that.[27]

The Content of Training: IAF Organizing Principles

What is the content of the training that organizers conduct? National IAF director Chambers specifies the skills organizers seek to cultivate in leaders in the following way:

> . . . how to make clear to yourself your self-interest; how to be an initiator rather than a reactor; how to listen to and affirm other people; how to distinguish between leaders and followers; how to identify and proposition current and potential leaders; how to run a meeting; how to hold members of your own networks accountable; how to hold other leaders accountable; how to raise money; how to analyze institutions (both your own and those you're up against); how to negotiate with other decision-makers; how to run an action; how to run an evaluation of an action; how to pick issues so that you're not running into the biggest issues at the start; how to plan issue campaigns; how to develop realistic schedules; how to view and accept tension; how to live and grow with a *process* of dealing with issues rather than with the particular issue or task; and how to invite in new institutions and develop allies.[28]

This long list begins to convey the idea that training in the IAF is not a narrow, technical affair. Many of these "skills" can only be acquired through learning political judgment from experience. However difficult to specify, the concept of developing political judgment serves to clarify what leadership training in the IAF is about. Moreover, in the IAF's view, the "arts of politics" can only be learned by someone who has acquired the ability for critical self-examination and personal growth.

The IAF teaches what it considers its most important fundamentals of organizing at its ten-day national training sessions for leaders and organizers. One hundred or so participants from IAF organizations across the country attend the training program together at a central location. The IAF's national staff conducts this training, which it offers three times per year.[29] Most leaders attend national training relatively early in their involvement in IAF organizations, although veterans sometimes come back for a refresher course. Attendance at the training conference requires a serious commitment from participants because they must arrange time away from work and family, and because most pay at least part of the cost of travel and tuition themselves.

An analysis of the content of national training sessions confirms that IAF training is not at all technically focused.[30] The IAF devotes a majority of sessions to teaching the IAF's organizing principles and its broader philosophy of politics. The first session asks participants to role play the Athenian conquest of the Melians as chronicled in Thucydides' *History of the Peloponnesian War*. The IAF believes that many people who get involved in social justice politics are too righteous and fail to understand that politics is about practical power. In the story, the Melians heroically defend their liberty, refuse to give in to the Athenians, and are eventually slaughtered. The point of the exercise is to show that negotiation and compromise over interests, not the assertion of principles, constitute the essence of politics, and consequently the basis for IAF political activity.[31]

Other sessions present the principles of IAF organizing: they situate IAF organizing in relation to social movements and civic associations; discuss the IAF view of leadership and relational organizing; and elaborate a distinction between public and private relationships. Some sessions are devoted to more technical matters like fund-raising, how to develop an issue campaign, and how to conduct a public action. But even here, the emphasis is on the IAF organizing principles involved, not skills training narrowly conceived. At every national training, the participants also attend and evaluate a public action organized by a local IAF organization. Surprising to the outside observer, but quite consistent with the IAF's relational organizing approach, there is no discussion of any particular political position or policy.

While IAF trainers frequently refer to the experiences of Moses and other Biblical stories to draw lessons about organizing, IAF national training includes no discussion of the religious or value base of IAF organizing. Presumably, that can be taken for granted. If anything, as the example of the Athenian role-playing suggests, IAF trainees attempt to stress the pragmatic side of politics. Nevertheless, the emotional high point of the national training I attended came at an ecumenical religious service on the penultimate day. Several clergy participants had organized this event on their own, without encouragement from the IAF organizer staff. The service included prayers, sermons, and hymns from Catholic and Protestant traditions, and created a feeling of comraderie and fellowship in the diverse group of participants.

In addition to the focus on IAF principles described above, IAF national training places great emphasis on personal development. The IAF devotes an entire day to the analysis of a person's "self-interest," which the network defines broadly. IAF trainers stress that the Latin root of the word interest is *interesse*, which means "to be among or between." The IAF suggests participants should take a relational, not individual, understanding of self-interest, since a person's interests develop in the context of their relationships with others.[32] Furthermore, IAF trainers want participants to expand their notion of self-interest beyond material concerns: "A person's self-interest incorporates all of their concerns, values, and desires, including the need for self-preservation, creativity, self-definition, power, money, love, and meaning in life."[33] Personal history shapes a person's conception of his or her self-interest, an understanding that can change over time. IAF trainers teach session participants to analyze self-interest by constructing a stick diagram, first of themselves and then of other people.

When national training turns to the subject of individual meetings, once again self-analysis is emphasized. Participants pair up and practice one-on-one meetings with each other in front of the group. Organizers instruct participants to elicit from each other their personal "story," that is, the important experiences that have shaped their life. The precondition for success in that endeavor lies in understanding your own story and being willing to share it with others.

Individual meetings conducted between leaders in front of workshop participants at the IAF's national training sessions provide many dramatic examples of connections made through story sharing. Many leaders recount powerful personal stories of injustice which, in turn, move other leaders. At the session I attended, an African American woman from Los Angeles told a moving story of being shot as a teenager in a movie theater. Recently, a gang shooting in her neighborhood, where she is trying to safely raise her young son, reignited her anger. She concluded her story by declaring, "I'm in it [the IAF] for my son's life."[34] A middle-aged Hispanic woman from Phoenix recounted her experience raising her family twenty years ago. She had to stay home while her husband worked and went to political meetings with his male friends. She declared that nobody cared what mothers thought, what she thought, about anything. Starting to cry, she recounted, "I've always let people take care of me. I can't do that anymore. . . . Now that my children are older, I'm doing this [the IAF] for me."[35]

IAF supervisor Christine Stephens suggests stories can be deeply unifying, if they are directed towards action. "We're looking for political anger, not just grief and sorrow. Leaders who fight together get to know these stories and that's why they can trust each other."[36]

The process of connecting through stories, though, can sometimes be problematic, especially when race is involved. In one encounter, a white man from Portland, Oregon, recounted an incident when he saw black kids attack a white woman. He tried to stop the kids. But no one else did, and that made him angry. There was a definite air of tension in the room, as the thirty or so participants were quite racially mixed. Apparently to defuse the situation, Cortes, who was leading the workshop, replied that "young males, whether they are black, white, or anything, will act up. What's not normal is for adults to refuse to do anything about it." He asked the Portland man if he was interested in building a relationship with one of the African American women in the network, and if he will go beyond stereotypes to do so. Later in the session, Cortes admitted that anger can be destructive and divisive, so it must be controlled and channeled. "We're looking for people whose anger at their own personal experience of injustice makes them connect with other people's injustice.[37]

The IAF structures its national training around teaching what the IAF claims is the "correct" way to organize. Participants come to learn, not to discuss as equals. In that sense, training is quite an appropriate term for the educational sessions. IAF training is not a "sharing experience," as it can often be in other community-building or participatory democratic settings. IAF organizers at national training are not seeking to elicit the contributions of participants to reach a deeper level of shared understanding. That is not to say that no conversations occur. IAF organizers use the Socratic method in teaching, so that there is constant interaction between and among participants. But the educational process is more akin to taking a college course with a professor who uses interactive methods of teaching, than it is to a study group among equals.

Organizers may sometimes overstep their authoritative role. Some training participants appear to resent what they see as arrogance among IAF trainers.[38] But the vast majority of IAF participants accept the IAF's authority to teach. Otherwise, they would not be attending the sessions, and the local organizations to which they belong would not pay for these services.

Most participants, in fact, report a high degree of satisfaction with national training. Indeed, attendance at national training appears to constitute a quite important experience in their lives. IAF leaders report the significance of the event less in terms of the specific IAF principles or practical skills learned, which, after all, are repeated in local training sessions as well. Instead, they cite two things. First, many comment on the deeper level of self-understanding they gained through stick diagrams and individual meetings. ACT leader Joyce Oliver's reflection captures the view expressed by many leaders: "It was a challenge, and different from any other training I'd done. It was like a mirror reflecting your inner parts: it made you realize what was there but you never realized. It taught me how to build relationships even with people I don't like."[39]

Second, national training offers leaders the "big picture" and cements their allegiance to the IAF. It exposes leaders to the breadth and diversity of the IAF network nationally. It brings this diverse group together for ten days in a secluded setting. Through such an intense experience, national training achieves a symbolic importance beyond the specifics of its sessions. Veteran ACT leader Claudia Camp reports that the national training she attended in 1984 gave her a different kind of vision of what politics can be. By having the opportunity to meet with people from around the country, she got a sense of something bigger than her own local organization. "National training is so intense it serves to break down your old picture and get a new one as a whole. It's hard to do that piecemeal, from one meeting or training every few months."[40] ACT leader Josie Duran was impressed with the hundreds of people committed to their communities and the sincerity of the trainers at the national training she attended in 1993. "It was like falling in love with the soul of a person right away."[41]

Consensual Democracy in the IAF

Leadership is exercised in the IAF network through consensus-building processes. In fact, decision making, leadership selection, and accountability within the network all rest upon consensual processes. In other words, IAF organizations tend to shun majority-rule voting, instead working to create a consensus for action. As such, the IAF represents a consensual democratic institution, an unusual type of organization, and one that has been seldom analyzed.

It will be useful to start a consideration of democracy within the IAF by recalling the distinction that Jane Mansbridge makes between adversary and unitary democracies.[42] Mansbridge studied participatory democratic institutions, a town meeting in Vermont and a small, egalitarian workplace that emerged out of the New Left of the sixties. She called these institutions unitary democracies because they were premised upon the assumption that members shared predominantly common interests.

They represented the "democracy of face-to-face relations," rooted in an older understanding of democracy that could be traced, in the Western tradition, back to classical Greece. In unitary democracy, people do not vote. They reason together and build a consensus for action.

By contrast, adversary democracy, the kind that has become hegemonic in the modern world, assumes members predominantly have conflicting interests. Here, leadership in these institutions is chosen by competitive elections to representative bodies. Each member has one vote, and decisions are taken by majority rule. In pure adversarial democracy, there is no common good, only the arithmetic total of individual interests. Although minorities are represented, the majority rules, whether as a permanent bloc or on an issue-by-issue basis.[43]

The IAF is more like Mansbridge's unitary democracy than her adversarial form, but the term "consensual democracy" is more accurate for the following reason. The IAF does not assume members have common interests. In fact, IAF organizations are premised upon the understanding that people have different interests. The IAF intentionally seeks to build broad-based organizations, that is, affiliates made up of institutions that have diverse traditions and interests. Unlike adversary democracy, though, the IAF quite explicitly rejects the notion that these interests are in permanent conflict. Instead, it seeks to structure a process in which a diverse group of participants can find a commonality of interests and an understanding of the common good. To do so, the IAF utilizes the consensual processes of reasoned discussion, negotiation, and compromise—rather than majority rule voting.[44]

Relational organizing, that is, building relationships among IAF leaders, is meant to provide a partial foundation for internal consensus building. When leaders share their personal stories in individual meetings with each other, they glean a deeper understanding upon which to build trust for cooperative action. Mansbridge argues that unitary democracy "makes formal and extends to the level of a polity the social relations of friendship" (p. 8). In the IAF, some participants are already friends within their church or neighborhood. But the organization then works consciously to build a degree of friendship among leaders from diverse communities through these relational meetings.

However, there are limits to friendship within the IAF's broad-based organizations, since they are more diverse than Mansbridge's unitary democracy. Negotiation and compromise over differences plays an important role as well. The IAF makes a distinction between what is appropriate in the public and private realms. According to IAF supervisor Christine Stephens,

In the world as it should be, we should all be one big happy family. But in the real world, we're not. There is nothing wrong with tension as long as the relationship endures. . . . Leaders should be able to tell each other what they think. The worst thing is for someone to break the tension, that is, to paper over difference and make everyone feel better.[45]

The IAF cautions leaders, therefore, to respect the limits of friendship, otherwise their leadership bodies will become cliques. Decision-making processes within the organization need to reflect the diverse interests included. In practice, then, the IAF combines relationship-building processes, where leaders get to know each other privately, with more public processes of negotiation and compromise over interests. Both appear necessary to build a community capable of cooperative action, if that community is going to be more than a small, homogeneous group.

Leadership Selection

IAF organizations do not elect their leaders in contested elections. Executive committees co-opt new members onto the body at the initiative of the lead organizer and several top leaders, usually the co-chairs. Informal consultation among executive committee members leads to a consensus for co-optation decisions. Similarly, co-chair positions are decided among top leaders and the lead organizer through informal discussions, as are the selections of the chairs for various action teams. Meetings of delegates assemblies or organization-wide conventions formally ratify executive committee member and co-chair slates. These ratifications, however, typically take place without discussion and are made by acclamation. Opposing slates do not run.[46]

IAF participants accept this selection process as legitimate because differences are aired and resolved during the informal discussion and negotiation stage. If a consensus is not reached, or differences are not properly handled to the satisfaction of participants, they can raise their concerns during the formal ratification stage at delegates assemblies and conventions. Although opposition could theoretically be expressed in such a forum, it seldom is. The IAF works hard to ensure that any significant disagreement is raised, and consensus built, early on.

Why does it appear fairly easy for the IAF to incorporate all of those who are interested in leadership positions? Suffering from a permanent shortage of leaders, IAF affiliates are continually looking for people willing to lead. Top positions require a lot of time and work, with no monetary reward. They do, of course, bring a degree of power and other personal rewards, like the opportunity for personal development, to the holder of the post. But, in general, the IAF promotes a model of leadership that is collective, constraining the power of one individual and mitigating against individual incentives to hold office. As a result, while there may be some competition for the few top co-chair positions, the executive committee is relatively open to anyone who wants to serve—*and* is approved by the organizer and other top leaders.

COPS, like some of the older IAF affiliates, did originally elect its leaders in contested elections. It held competitive elections for president, vice president, and several other top positions. By all accounts, candidates ran lively campaigns, culminating in elections at biannual conventions. Since anyone who attended the convention had one vote, candidates made sure to mobilize their supporters. Presidents were limited to two years in office. Candidates, however, did not present rival platforms, stressing instead their superior leadership skills.[47]

In the mid-eighties, COPS abolished the system of electing officials in contested elections and changed to a more collective leadership body of co-chairs. No other Texas IAF since then has elected its leaders through contested elections. IAF leaders and organizers favor the new system for several reasons. In the past, after two years in office COPS presidents had to step down and could not find a role for themselves in the organization, except as "elder statesmen." With the present system, co-chairs can maintain leadership roles for longer periods, and no one gets excluded by defeat in an election. COPS leaders argue that the change to the co-chair system promoted more collective leadership and expanded the capacity of the organization.[48]

Leadership selection appears, then, to have proven more compatible with efforts to be more inclusive and to forge a stronger group identity— and therefore a wider field of action. This method, however, devolves a significant degree of power into the hands of organizers and top leaders to shape selection decisions. If leaders do not run in open elections, do not offer platforms on issues or directions for the organization, upon what basis are they selected? Leadership ability has become the number one criteria. Candidates must demonstrate the ability to carry out the responsibilities of primary leadership described above: concern for the organization as a whole; ability to deliver a following; and success in carrying out IAF political strategy and tactics (issue development, negotiation and compromise, running a public meeting). Since a leader develops this ability through training conducted by the organizer and other top leaders, these officials become the judge of an emerging leader's success. Consequently, new executive committee members are selected by top leaders and the organizer, with ratification, not election, by other participants. IAF affiliates do take care to ensure that leadership bodies are balanced, particularly by race, but also by representation from all the diverse constituencies in their membership. But the primary criteria for selection of a candidate from within any racial, denominational, geographic, or other group, is their leadership ability, as determined by the lead organizer and top leaders of the affiliate.

Decision Making in IAF Organizations

Like leadership selection processes, top leaders and organizers structure all decision making within affiliates through informal, but highly systematic, consensual processes. The IAF teaches leaders to carefully prepare all meetings through prior discussion with key leaders. Before any meeting, leaders develop an action plan or proposal and consult with other relevant leaders to revise the plan and reach agreement. Meetings primarily ratify plans which have already been developed and then discuss implementation. The IAF justifies this approach as the most democratic and effective, suggesting, as organizer Christine Stephens put it, that "people operate, and ought to operate, through leadership."[49]

Informal consultation, that is, discussions outside of formal meetings, are key to the process. Leaders sound out consensus prior to meetings and take the views of others into account. They do not propose controversial courses of action for open discussion at meetings. If substantial opposition exists to a course of action, and these differences cannot be resolved through negotiation and compromise, leaders will not submit a proposal to a final vote. The organization will simply not take the action.[50]

For example, in the run-up to the final adoption of a fall 1993 issue agenda by ACT, the IAF's Fort Worth organization, top leaders, and lead organizer Perry Perkins spent two months hammering out a consensus on the organization's priorities. On each issue, Perkins first consulted with a three-person strategy team. The team informally consulted with key ACT leaders who had special interests in each issue. The executive committee, consisting of all the group's top leaders, then reached consensus on a three-point program. The committee proposed three campaigns to the delegates assembly: on job training, the city bond election, and school reform. Plans for ACT's education work had been particularly controversial, with some leaders advocating concentration on parental involvement, while others favored broader school reform. Eventually, the issue was resolved *before* the delegate's assembly by a compromise that moved the organization closer to a school reform proposal. At the delegates assembly where the action agenda was formally adopted, there were a number of votes taken on procedural questions or minor details of proposals. But the issue agenda was adopted by acclamation. Perkins and top leaders then spent most of the meeting holding a training session to prepare the leaders present on how to carry out these campaigns.[51]

While this process might appear to be highly controlled at the top, it is actually more dynamic in practice. IAF affiliates, as voluntary organizations, depend upon the hard work and commitment of large numbers of leaders, who, in turn, must be able to mobilize large numbers of supporters. Organizers are trained to look for people with energy and interest in participating. Initiatives do emerge regularly from the bottom-up and become adopted by top leaders, as the Morningside school campaign in Fort Worth demonstrates. Meanwhile, decision-making processes do, by and large, build consensus and genuine (often enthusiastic) agreement within the network, or else the IAF would have no capacity to undertake its issue campaigns.

On major initiatives of an organization, the influence of top leaders, organizers, and regional IAF supervisors is that much greater. But even here, decisions rest with the organization and may go contrary to staff advice. COPS undertook a major campaign, and one of the few it has lost, to oppose public financing of the Alamodome in a 1989 referendum because its top leaders, reflecting the consensus of the organization, pushed for the campaign. Cortes and the IAF staff were reluctant. But COPS leaders decided to adopt the campaign, put a tremendous amount of organizational resources into it, and lost.

Accountability in the IAF

Since top leaders and organizers select new leaders and structure decision-making processes, they have a tremendous degree of power within IAF organizations. It is therefore important to consider the mechanisms that exist to hold that leadership accountable. As we've seen, the constitutions of IAF organizations grant delegate assemblies and annual meetings the final authority to adopt action programs and elect leadership. In practice, this authority is seldom exercised. Informal consensus building preempts votes at larger meetings. Meanwhile, the authority vested in organizers and top leaders, as holders of the legitimate claim to the best understanding of how to organize, often obviates the need for formal ratification by annual conventions in the eyes of supporters. At COPS twentieth annual convention in May of 1994, for example, the meeting did not even bother to ratify by acclamation the new set of co-chairs selected by the lead organizer and top leaders.[52]

The IAF is not unaware that any organization faces pressure on leaders to abuse power or to seek their own narrow interests rather than the broader interests of the organization. The network has institutionalized several important practices to prevent the co-optation of local leaders, that is, to limit the power and advantages that come from office. First, leaders of IAF organizations cannot run for political office. In order to do so, they must leave the organization, and very likely break some of the most important relationships in their lives. When COPS ex-president Helen Ayala took a job with a big developer and ran for city council, for example, she became an object of scorn among her former friends in COPS. Second, IAF affiliates do not administer programs themselves, accepting no public funds. As a result, leaders do not control very much money, with annual budgets for most affiliates less than $200,000. Moreover, leaders cannot even take administrative positions within programs like Project QUEST that their organizations develop and spin off. This rule helps keep leaders focused on political organizing, rather than job seeking. Finally, the IAF strongly discourages leaders from accepting positions on government boards or commissions, although they do serve on boards of IAF-initiated projects. Local observers sometimes criticize the IAF for this practice, suggesting it restricts the development of leadership from communities of color.[53] But the IAF believes these positions are too time consuming. Once again, the practice serves to limit the status and broader power of leaders, while concentrating their energies on collective organizing within the IAF organization. When COPS ex-president Sonia Hernandez became an aide to Governor Richards, for example, she had to give up her position in COPS. Although the IAF considers her a friend and ally, COPS underlined her separation from the organization when it excluded her from the group of past presidents seated prominently on the stage at its twentieth-anniversary convention.

In addition to top leaders, IAF organizers retain great authority within the network. Their primary source of power lies in their role as trainer to leaders. As teacher, the organizer has great influence on the selection of leadership, although other top leaders also participate in the decision. While top leaders often mentor some new leaders, the organizer develops a relationship to virtually all leaders through carrying out individual meetings. Through that relationship comes a certain degree of power over every leader an organizer has "trained." As COPS' third president, Carmen Badillo, explains:

> Organizers always have had power in COPS, very much so. It's teaching power, the ability to help us grow and develop and that's a lot of power over a person. Challenging us. We got into arguments too. But the organizers always understood their role—Ernie [Cortes] could have run for office. It's about the same today. Except with the expansion of other sister organizations, the organizers interact more. That gives them power through networking. They have common interests and projects in the network. . . . IAF training shakes you up, makes

you think. I surprised myself that I had more in myself than I knew. That's the power of organizers to search in you and draw you out.[54]

The IAF maintains a set of institutional rules that serve to mitigate the power of organizers and ensure the ultimate control of leaders over their organizations. First, executive committees do make formal organizational decisions, and only leaders can speak publicly for IAF organizations. Although organizers do play important roles behind the scenes, organizational leaders must be willing to formally adopt campaigns and speak for them in public, or else they will not be pursued. Second, lead organizers are rotated every three to five years, so they cannot build permanent dynasties.[55] Finally, as mentioned above, the executive committees of local organizations hire lead organizers and can fire them.

It is difficult to fully assess the relative power of organizers and leaders by examining formal institutional rules because so much of the real decision making occurs in more informal consensus-building conversations. For example, to my knowledge no executive committee has ever fired a lead organizer in the Texas IAF. On the other hand, if a consensus by leaders emerges against an organizer, they will likely be transferred by the IAF.

In practice, the relative power of top leaders appears to vary across local organizations. In new and weaker local organizations, the organizers exert more direction and control. On the other hand, the more sophisticated and united the leadership, the less power the organizer retains. One of the striking characteristics of COPS is the strong relationships COPS women leaders have built amongst themselves. COPS leaders, more than those of any organization, mentor new emerging leaders. A large number of COPS leaders interviewed for this study volunteered that mentoring by other leaders played a central role in their development as a leader. COPS co-chair Rachel Salazar reports that other leaders, not organizers, have had the most to do with her development: "It's just like growing up, our mothers were our role models and teachers."[56]

Strong mentoring, in addition to fostering the rapid development of new leaders, produces a different balance of power between leaders and organizers. When COPS co-chair Virginia Ramirez needs advice, she says she calls co-chair Pat Ozuna as well as ex-presidents and executive committee members Beatrice Cortez and Andres Sarabia. She says that organizers and leaders train each other in COPS.

It's a two-way street: we train each other. If we just take from them [organizers], they become leaders. They're here to help us set an agenda, not tell us what it should be. We have to make the choice. I'm not dependent on an organizer; I'm dependent on other leaders. My role is to teach new leaders to draw on others. . . . Leaders must have the passion to own the organization. We want our organizers to have it too. So people think we're tough on organizers. By the time they [organizers] leave here, they can organize anywhere—because we train them well![57]

Ramirez's comments are not mere boastfulness. Several junior organizers volunteered the opinion that they want to organize in San Antonio precisely in order to learn from COPS leaders.

Except for perhaps the very newest organizations, however, organizers and leaders share power. Joint direction of local organizations by organizers and top leaders is confirmed by the assessment of local elites across several organizations with varying degrees of strength. I asked public officials, top business representatives, and important observers in San Antonio and Fort Worth whom they think of when they think of COPS, Metro Alliance, or ACT—or whom they would call to contact those organizations. Respondents invariably listed the lead organizer and a couple of top leaders. Occasionally, respondents would omit the organizer; but no respondent failed to mention at least one leader.

Assessing the IAF's Consensual Approach

The IAF's approach emphasizes consensus building to resolve differences, rather than the majority-rule voting of the more typical adversarial democratic model. Despite what one might expect in more informal consensual processes, the IAF very explicitly encourages participants to recognize differences of interest and opinion—and then to work hard to negotiate and reach a consensus, or compromise, to resolve them.[58] When differences cannot be resolved, the IAF tables the issue. Essentially, such an approach gives the minority on an issue a veto power within the organization.

There are advantages and limitations to this veto power. The veto within IAF consensual processes does allow minorities a degree of power they lack in majority-rule systems. In the case of racial minorities, or other enduring group affiliations, the veto provides a kind of ultimate guarantee that majorities cannot be insensitive to their concerns. On the other hand, the power of the veto can allow a minority to be obstructionist on an issue that might be quite critical to the organization's future. A small group of leaders, whether they share some enduring identity or simply represent an ad hoc coalition on one issue, can refuse to be persuaded through informal processes, if they are determined enough. Consensual processes in the IAF can work to keep it from addressing some issues that may be critical to community well-being, when it cannot forge a consensus.

Since the IAF prizes informal processes rather than formal votes, there is the danger of intimidation that results in a false consensus.[59] In decision making, however, false consensus on issues appears to be less of a problem in the IAF. Since attention is paid to differences, with each participant constantly encouraged to identify their self-interest, most find the opportunity to raise their voice on any particular issue. They can certainly be pressured into changing their minds despite their heartfelt opinions. But, to any close observer of internal processes in the Texas IAF, there appears to be no shortage of discussions and negotiations over issues.

The problem of intimidation can exist, though, in leadership selection processes connected to the IAF's conception of training. If a participant wants to become a more powerful leader in an IAF organization, he or she must accept the IAF's organizing principles. These principles include: nonpartisanship; action by consensus; broad-based organizing rather than racially based organizing; tactics combining confrontation with negotiation; and the teaching role of the organizer.[60] While issues are always negotiable in the IAF, the network's principles of organizing are not. IAF participants do not discuss these principles; they are trained in them. Unity on these principles is inherent in the IAF's notion of leadership development. Development means learning these principles, which are simply considered the correct way to do organizing. These principles are skills to be learned, not political alternatives to be debated. The principles are *taught*; they are not *discussed*.

The IAF defends this approach by arguing that every organization has some unifying principles that need to be beyond dispute. Organizations cannot continually renegotiate their founding principles. In fact, people join the IAF, and local community institutions agree to sign contracts for training services with the IAF, precisely to learn these principles and develop the ability to apply them.

Since participants cannot raise their voice to dispute these principles, a leader who takes a different view on one or more of them will not be promoted. Organizers and top leaders who are highly committed to these principles control promotion to higher levels of leadership. The criteria of a candidate's advancement is precisely the leader's grasp of these principles and ability to implement them, as judged by those already at the top. Clearly there is room for abuse in this system, or for personality conflicts or other prejudicial attitudes to intervene.

The IAF has internal mechanisms to guard against such discrimination. Top leaders meet collectively to select new leaders, so that no one leader is likely to dominate the process. Meanwhile, organizers are accountable to that leadership collective as well as to their regional supervisor, providing avenues for recourse against abuse. But what if the organizer, supervisor, and leadership collective all agree, as they do on the IAF's organizing principles?

In the end, those who disagree in an important enough way with the organizing principles are likely to leave local organizations because no legitimate space for dissent on these principles exists within the IAF. Since they do so relatively early on in their involvement, they are often hard to identify. However, at the IAF national training I attended, several participants who had disagreements with some organizing principles, particularly the role of organizers in leadership development, privately expressed frustration. They felt there was no space in which to raise their concerns; and they felt insecure that the lead organizer from their organization might judge them unfavorably and penalize them for their opinion. They suggested that they might leave their local IAF organization.[61]

The threat of participants leaving the IAF supplies a degree of accountability, though, in an organization that relies upon mobilization and action for its existence. If certain key leaders in a city leave, or threaten to leave, the resulting fallout could result in their voices being heard. However, some participants can always exit with low cost to the IAF, because the network continually invests resources in recruiting new leaders.

While the IAF has elaborated a set of institutional rules that help guard against abuse of power at the local level, it has yet to fully elaborate formal mechanisms at the state and regional level. For example, the network has not put the necessary resources into operating a formal leadership body at these higher levels that can serve to balance the power of organizers in the way that local executive committees do. Officially, the Texas IAF network formed a statewide steering committee of leaders at its founding convention in 1990. But the committee only met a few times and lapsed into inactivity.

Instead, the IAF has chosen to rely on informal mechanisms of leadership and accountability at state and regional levels. The network regularly convenes regional meetings of leaders, at a great cost of time and money. Here, leaders from localities spread across great distances do build relationships over time and shape network policy collectively. Nevertheless, face-to-face relationship building is more difficult to accomplish at regional levels; it works best in smaller settings at the local level.[62]

Given the distances involved, the IAF has come to rely heavily on the tremendous personal authority of its regional supervisor Cortes to help unite the disparate organizations. Cortes makes sure to spend time in every locality to build and sustain personal relationships with key leaders. Cortes then relies upon the authority of the local organizers he trains and unites in regular regional meetings to serve as an infrastructure for higher-level consensus building.

The dangers of informality loom larger at the regional level in part because consensus must rely more upon Cortes, his organizers, and a smaller number of leaders with weaker collective ties. Local participants do not at all appear worried about this situation, in part because their key leaders seem to be well respected. Moreover, leaders trust "Ernie" to do the right thing. The question, of course, is not the personal trustworthiness of Cortes. Instead, the network has yet to build upon its current strength to elaborate institutional processes of accountability for when Cortes is no longer there. The Southwest IAF has a group of senior organizers who may be well qualified to take Cortes's place in terms of their organizing ability; but none has his level of personal authority.

Conclusion

The processes of leadership development and consensual decision making in the Texas IAF offer several lessons for participatory democracy and effective community building. First, the IAF experience suggests the gains to be had from leadership training that is geared to developing political leadership broadly conceived. So much of the training people receive in community building and development is limited to learning technical skills. Moreover, our understanding of civic education itself is often quite narrow in its focus on individual skill acquisition. In one of the most important studies of civic participation, conducted by Sidney Verba and his associates, relevant skills for participation included the ability to write letters, run meetings, and speak in public.[63] Granted, these are necessary skills, and information about them was available to the researchers for a nationally representative sample of the population. The requirements of political leadership, however, include the ability to exercise political judgement and cultivate collective, not just individual, action.

This kind of leadership development is required for community residents to become leaders in the public arena. Women of color in low-income communities often have few other venues for personal development of this sort. Yet IAF leaders of all genders, races, and economic circumstances report the tremendous transformation in their lives that has come through their IAF participation. Political action in the IAF reflects a more classical view of politics as an essential means for people to reach their highest human potential as active, moral agents. If we are satisfied with the kind of citizen participation that collects money for the school PTA, however important that is, then narrow skills training may be sufficient. But if we are concerned with revitalizing American democracy, then the citizens who currently provide the day-to-day support for their communities, in churches, schools, and neighborhoods, must develop the capacity for participation at the highest levels of public life in their cities, states— and, eventually, nation.

While the appeal of the IAF to many observers lies in its ability to engage these "salt of the earth" leaders, its effectiveness comes no less from hierarchical structures of authority within the network. Another lesson we can learn from the IAF is the importance of authority to democratic processes, a subject to which scholars have paid little attention. We must overcome an ultrademocratic prejudice and begin to investigate the kinds of authority that can contribute to democratic action and community building. Many residents of low-income communities, frustrated with ineffective and unprofessional efforts to address neighborhood needs, are attracted to the IAF precisely because it can generate effective leadership—because it works.[64]

We need to expand our understanding of the forms of legitimate authority available to participatory democratic organizations. Contested elections and majority-rule voting on issues are not the *sine qua non* of democracy. The IAF experience suggests that consensual processes offer an important alternative to adversarial forms of democracy, especially for organizations committed to community mobilization and building common ground for action. Each type of democratic process has its own strengths and weaknesses. But an uncritical prejudice for the norms of adversarial democracy precludes undertaking an investigation of the weaknesses of that form as well as the strengths of more consensual systems.

Consensual processes require leadership. And local mediating institutions need this kind of authoritative leadership in order to represent and negotiate with power holders for the benefit of their members. Moreover, if we want participatory democratic institutions to be able to operate beyond the local level, trusted and authoritative leadership becomes even more important. State, regional, and eventually national networks can involve fewer leaders in less frequent face-to-face meetings. Those leaders must bring with them the authority to build consensus and take action, an authority that can only come from strong local processes of leadership development.

Veteran Metro Alliance leader Homer Bain captures quite well the dynamic between leadership and participation that the IAF, at its best, strives to achieve:

> The IAF is the optimal blend of central leadership with grass-roots, the representative and the participatory. It's a rhythm. Paid professional staff is key. Everything can't be done by town meeting, but the town meeting has the final say. Ernie [Cortes] can have the vision, but they have to sell it to us and they take our ideas in and change their views. [I call it] looking for the fire and blowing it together.[65]

Nine

Conclusion: Restoring Faith in Politics

SIX THOUSAND supporters packed San Antonio's municipal auditorium on November 7, 1999, to observe COPS' twenty-fifth anniversary. Billed also as an occasion to celebrate "25 Years of Organizing in the Southwest," IAF organizations from across the region sent large delegations to the convention. The network took the occasion to unveil its human development program, a new initiative that attempts to place a unifying umbrella over the impressive range of issues the IAF was now addressing across the region: job training, living wage ordinances, school reform and after-school programs, citizenship classes and voter registration, health care and neighborhood safety. Once again, COPS and its San Antonio sister organization, Metro Alliance, took the lead, proposing a $250 million human development fund to finance job training, after-school enrichment classes, and college scholarships for low-income students. Paid for out of a one-eighth percent increase in the city's sales tax, the fund would secure long-term financing for the IAF's projects in these areas, and be the first municipal endowment of its kind in the nation.[1]

To gain backing for the ambitious initiative, IAF leaders spent a good part of the meeting asking for commitments of support from the impressive collection of public officials and business leaders assembled at the convention, including Texas Senator Kay Bailey Hutchinson, two U.S. Congressmen from San Antonio and several more from across the state, and Mayor Howard Peak. All lent their support to the human development fund. The range of officials present also served to demonstrate the growing political clout of the network. In fact, the congressional delegation presented a resolution passed by the U.S. Congress congratulating the IAF on twenty-five years of organizing in the Southwest.

The twenty-fifth anniversary convention demonstrated some of the fruits of concentrated efforts made by the IAF in the last ten years. First of all, it was clear that the IAF had now firmly established a regional network beyond Texas. IAF organizations sent large delegations from across the state and from Arizona, New Mexico, Louisiana, Nebraska, Iowa, and southern California as well. The IAF made sure that leaders from across the Southwest introduced their organizations, so that the COPS convention was transformed into the coming out party for the Southwest IAF region.

The assembly demonstrated the growing diversity of the IAF in the Southwest. While Hispanic Catholics were well represented, and Catholic bishops from across the state spoke, African American and Anglo Protestants also attended in large numbers. Reverend Curtis Lucas, a black minister from the Fort Bend county suburb of Houston joined veteran COPS leader Patricia Ozuna to call the meeting to order. And a gospel choir closed the affair. The network also made an effort to show the presence of its growing number of Jewish participants. The opening prayer, at what was ostensibly a largely Catholic COPS convention, was offered by Rabbi David Kline from the Northern Louisiana Sponsoring Committee in Monroe.

Finally, the convention illustrated newer efforts by the IAF to broaden the base of the network beyond faith congregations to include schools, unions, and other institutions. The Alliance Schools program brought a large number of principals, teachers, and parents to the convention. Now firmly committed to forging more diverse metropolitan-wide organizations at the local level, the IAF has begun to incorporate unions, especially in Los Angeles but in other localities as well. Linda Chavez Thompson, executive vice president of the AFL-CIO spoke to the assembly, marking the growing collaboration between the IAF and unions across the country.

Nevertheless, the faith basis of the network remains its bedrock. At the close of the meeting, a large group of clergy gathered on the stage. The composition of the group reflected the network's multiracial diversity. And the prayers chosen demonstrated the IAF's commitment to an interfaith collaboration. A white Catholic priest, Fr. Richard Beck, offered the following words:

> What will fuel our efforts for the next twenty-five years? The same thing that has fueled the last twenty-five. Faith in God and faithfulness to God's demand for justice. . . . We cannot stand idly by and watch our cities and our children crumble.

Reverend Terry White, a black minister, added:

> As we leave this place may the power of God's Holy Spirit be the fire that burns within us and fuels us in our efforts to do God's justice.

Finally, the interfaith group on stage asked all delegates to hold hands. Drawing upon a Jewish tradition, the delegates declared:

> We stand together as citizens. We work within our communities. Our feet may be tired. But our souls are rested. Our faith will give us strength to mend our world. Tikun olam. Let us mend our world. Tikun olam. Tikun olam!

The Southwest IAF's twenty-fifth anniversary convention demonstrates the network's accomplishments in building an organized base for a public agenda focused on the needs and aspirations of poor and working families and their communities. The network's achievements in this area are of no small significance because an organized constituency for that agenda is sorely lacking in American politics. President Clinton's health care reform effort, for example, went down to defeat in the early nineties at the hands of conservative Republicans not because the American public opposed the plan. In fact, polls showed that the majority of Americans supported its basic provisions. But the well-financed conservative forces won the day in a public relations battle because advocates for health reform could not organize supporters and bring that kind of power to bear on the effort. Political activists need to rebuild the "missing middle" in American politics, as Theda Skocpol calls it, in order to make possible the creation of broadly progressive social policy.[2]

The main conclusion of this study is that IAF organizing offers a compelling model for rebuilding this "missing middle." The network offers our best strategy for creating participatory organizations that work for public policies responsive to the needs of poor and working families. The network accomplishes this goal because it grounds democratic participation in the institutions and values that sustain community life, first among them, those of religious faith. But the network goes farther: it offers a new model for multiracial collaboration that creates broad-based alliances for progressive social policy by linking together diverse communities. And, drawing upon patient base building in these local communities, it builds federated networks that generate the power necessary to shape a public agenda on their behalf.

This chapter explores the lessons that can be learned from the work of the Southwest IAF. In other words, it examines the possibilities for a faith- and values-based politics that is broadly progressive, multiracial, and capable of generating public policies for poor and working families. It will also consider some of the limitations to the IAF's work so far, exploring the challenges still to be met in building the kind of broad and national effort that will be necessary to transform our nation's politics.

Faith in Politics

The closing prayers at the twenty-fifth anniversary convention illustrate the powerful contributions that faith makes to politics, providing energy, passion, and vision to democratic action. Faith commitments to community well-being and to social justice brought 6,000 people, mostly from low-income communities of color, to the Southwest IAF convention. Faith institutions served as organizational vehicles to mobilize supporters and to develop leadership. Indigenous leaders, drawing upon faith traditions embedded in community-based institutions, helped shape an emerging agenda to sustain families and pursue human development.

As our politics have become centered around Washington-based advocacy groups that lobby for separate issues, the participatory underpinnings of American democracy have withered, especially in poor and working class communities. The IAF's innovation is to reground politics in community institutions and their values as a way to reinvigorate political participation and public leadership.[3] The network's experience shows that faith institutions and values provide a particularly powerful foundation for democratic action. Parishes and congregations remain a key source of connection to people in low-income communities.[4] And, more importantly, faith traditions offer a rich source of inspiration for public action on behalf of community well-being and social justice.

Yet the power of faith frightens many Americans. With the Christian Right in full public view, many conclude it would be better to keep religion out of politics, to consign it to the private realm. We do so to the detriment of our democracy. To the extent that we isolate our public life from the values that sustain so many Americans, we exclude many citizens from meaningful participation. As a result, a secular elite directs narrow interest-based politics at the top, while large numbers of Americans remain alienated at the bottom.

Moreover, we simply cannot keep religion out of politics. People of faith will continually turn to their religious traditions for inspiration to remake their world, for faith is a constituent part of who they are and what binds their community. Within the faith traditions of our dominant religions, there is a powerful strain that calls people to do God's justice in the world. This voice emerges not just in the IAF, but in a myriad of faith-based community organizing, community development, and social justice efforts across the country.

The question for Americans concerned about revitalizing American democracy, then, should not be whether faith enters politics, but how and to what political ends. This is where the work of the Southwest IAF becomes so important. The IAF offers a way for faith to shape a broadly progressive politics. The IAF, and what has come to be known as faith-based community organizing more generally,[5] pose a dramatic contrast to the Christian Right. The way faith connects to politics in each effort, and the political goals they pursue, are quite different. Contrasting the two phenomena will help demonstrate the alternative paths they present and clarify the contributions that faith can make to democratic renewal.

First, people of faith involved in the IAF draw upon different faith traditions than those involved in the Christian Right. As we have seen, the large majority of participants in the IAF look to three strains in the broader Christian tradition. Many Catholics ground their public work in Catholic social thought, as invigorated by the contemporary developments in Vatican II, liberation theology, and the efforts of the Catholic bishops to speak to issues of economic justice. Black Protestants draw upon the themes of liberation and justice embedded in African American Christianity, and the civil rights movement tradition in particular. Meanwhile, Anglo Protestants root an understanding of their work in the social gospel tradition of American Protestantism. All of these traditions call Christians of various faiths to be active agents in the public world, to work for the poor and in the service of justice.

The Christian Right grows out of the branch of evangelical Protestantism that explicitly rejected the social gospel's call for public responsibility.[6] From the 1930s to the 1970s, fundamentalists largely retreated into their own world, which they saw as morally pure in the face of a corrupt modern world. Through the efforts in the 1970s of evangelical leaders like Jerry Falwell, head of the Moral Majority, many fundamentalists became convinced that a private retreat was no longer sufficient. To counter the cultural liberalism of the sixties, Protestants took on the duty to fight for fundamentalist morality through political means.[7]

The goals of politics, then, differ substantially between the IAF's faith-based community organizing and the Christian Right. The Christian Right attempts to pursue its particular moral agenda and make it the morality of the whole society, as the name Moral Majority suggests. Key issues for the Christian Right include opposition to abortion, bans on pornography, support for prayer in public schools, and restrictions on the rights of gays and lesbians. The Christian Right pursues the goal of legislating fundamentalist morality.

IAF participants see their political work as deeply moral, but draw upon those values to inform an agenda of economic and social justice. Key issues for faith-based organizing include the improvement of public education, job training, housing, and health care. The goal of these efforts is to train leaders to legislate programs of social and economic development, not morality.[8]

While the goals differ between these two kinds of faith-oriented politics, so does the way each intervenes in the public arena. America's public sphere is quite diverse, inhabited both by people of various faiths and by secular Americans as well. The Christian Right steps into this contested domain and makes public claims on the basis of its particular religious beliefs.[9] According to the Christian Right, for example, abortion should be outlawed because God condemns it as the taking of human life.

The IAF certainly draws upon the particular faith beliefs of adherents to inform its political agenda. But in the public sphere, the IAF argues for its campaigns on a wider basis of shared values and interests. For example, IAF organizations develop job-training programs for unskilled workers, in part because their faith directs them to work for the poor and to help sustain their own families and communities. In public, however, IAF leaders advocate for job training on the basis of more widely shared values of fairness as well as the public interest that can benefit from a better educated workforce and economically healthier communities, not because God requires it.

Admittedly, the line drawn here between internal motivation and external organizing is not absolute. To the extent that IAF organizations advocate their causes on the basis of fairness and justice (and they most certainly do), then faith-based values enter the public realm too. But, here again, IAF organizations seek to appeal to the values Americans share broadly, whatever particular roots they have. These roots can be religious. Or they can be secular, as the democratic tradition shared by Americans incorporates values of fairness and justice.[10] In the view of IAF participants, their own faith traditions lead them to seek common ground with others to sustain families and communities, to mend the world, not to impose their own particular beliefs. How values are to be translated into concrete programs is subject to discussion, negotiation, and compromise; they are not to be imposed.

In fact, it is the IAF's absolute insistence that politics is about negotiation and compromise over interests that keeps faith beliefs in balance with public discourse. In every training session and during the pursuit of every issue campaign, IAF organizers instruct emerging leaders to analyze the self-interest of potential allies and opponents, not their morality. The IAF insists that leaders be pragmatic and willing to compromise, not seek to impose a morally correct standpoint on others.

The Christian Right attempts to recruit the true believer to its cause. It builds organizations that are largely homogeneous, composed of white evangelical Protestants, especially Baptists. By contrast, the IAF explicitly seeks to build broad-based organizations that bring more diverse constituencies together across faiths, racial groups, and economic means. Obviously, people of faith and others attracted to the IAF share a broadly similar outlook, as all organizations require a certain degree of unity. Nevertheless, the closer an IAF organization gets to the status of a group of true believers, the more it is seen to have failed. IAF organizers work hard to make affiliates as diverse as possible, and to insist that leaders enter the organization with that commitment.[11]

To some extent the Christian Right has sought to bring evangelicals together across denominations and occasionally produced joint local action with Catholics on such issues as opposition to abortion. In 1997, the Christian Coalition launched its Samaritan Project to reach out to the black community and to address inner-city needs.[12] But these were largely efforts to find supporters of the Christian Right's particular moral agenda within the Catholic and African American communities. In that sense, the effort did not seek to diversify the movement by creating a forum in which people could find common ground together. Perhaps because the Christian Coalition followed such an hegemonic strategy, its efforts to broaden the movement to include African Americans and Catholics largely failed.

The Christian Right has expanded much more rapidly than the IAF and other faith-based community organizing networks. It became a national force relatively quickly. Not surprisingly, it has proved easier to mobilize a homogeneous group of true believers behind moral causes, rather than attempt to build more diverse organizations committed to the needs of poor communities. But the strategic choices of each effort matter too. The Christian Right chose to focus on influencing national politics, raising large sums of money from televangelists and corporate sponsors. It prioritized electoral work for Republicans committed to its moral agenda.[13] Only later did the movement turn to local organizing and work to elect supporters to school boards and to city and state positions. The IAF, by contrast, emphasized patient base building at the local level, pursuing issue campaigns through a nonpartisan strategy, rather than electoral work. It chose to raise money primarily from its local institutional members, recruiting congregations one by one. That strategy has given the IAF and faith-based organizing firm local roots, but less national reach as yet.

While the Christian Right's strategy of intensive mobilization of a minority of true believers scored early electoral victories, scholars largely consider the movement ineffective in achieving its policy goals. The movement lacks an effective strategy for building a broader consensus among Americans. The IAF, on the other hand, through local base building and state-level work, has been fairly effective in achieving its policy goals. Always pragmatic, IAF organizations rarely demand more than they have a realistic possibility of achieving. By insisting that faith values be placed in tension with practical interests, the IAF offers a model for connecting faith to politics that tempers the potentially divisive role of strongly held group beliefs.

Since this model of values-based politics seems so promising, it is important to consider some of the limitations to its current application in the work of the Southwest IAF. I have argued that the network has been able to engage people of various faiths in its interfaith organizing efforts. Indeed, the Southwest IAF can claim remarkable success among Hispanic Catholics, black Protestants, and members of a variety of Anglo Protestant denominations. But the network has so far failed to include some significant faith traditions.

Southern Baptists remain almost entirely outside the network. Admittedly, including this largely white fundamentalist group poses a difficult challenge. Southern Baptists resist cooperation with faith communities outside of their own denomination, and so would be hesitant to join an interfaith effort. Racial division and animosity also play a role. The center of gravity for the IAF network lies in communities of color, while Southern Baptists have a historic legacy of racism reflected in their opposition to the civil rights movement.[14] In addition, the Christian Right has succeeded in directing the political efforts of many Southern Baptists towards the pursuit of a moral agenda. Although Texas does not provide the strongest base of support for the Christian Right, Southern Baptists have remained outside the IAF.[15]

If the goal is to build broad-based organizations that are as diverse as Texas communities, however, Southern Baptists cannot remain outside indefinitely. That denomination constitutes fully one-third of total church adherents in the state.[16] White working-class Texans are often to be found in Southern Baptist churches. Any fully multiracial and cross-class alliance must begin to incorporate the group.

The Texas IAF has made efforts to engage Southern Baptists. IAF staff retain relationships with some progressive Baptist officials and have collaborated with them on a few campaigns. In Los Angeles, the Metro IAF has attempted to work with the group around Robert C. Linthicum, a white evangelical who advocates Christian responsibility to the poor and has written extensively on community organizing.[17] In the spring of 2000, Wilshire Baptist Church joined the Dallas Interfaith organization, marking the first time any Southern Baptist congregation has joined an IAF group. Wilshire Baptist is part of the more moderate wing of Southern Baptists, which has significant strength in Texas. IAF organizers are hoping to expand upon this opening, but whether they will be successful in recruiting other Southern Baptists remains to be seen.

With limited resources, the IAF has understandably decided to concentrate on cultivating more fertile fields for recruitment, although the rewards of serious engagement with Southern Baptists, if successful, could be as great as the present obstacles. An alliance of Hispanic Catholics, black Protestants, and white evangelicals, supported by mainline Protestants, could potentially transform politics in the state in a way the network has yet to achieve.

The Texas IAF has still to firmly engage faith institutions outside of the Christian context. As this work has documented, serious efforts have been made to recruit Jewish congregations and Jewish organizers. In this effort, the network has the advantage that it has long looked to the Old Testament as a central part of the faith tradition that grounds its work. To date, about seven or eight Jewish congregations have become active in the

Southwest IAF network, with several more involved in the new effort to reorganize the IAF in Los Angeles. To its credit, the IAF has been aggressive in placing those participants up-front at internal meetings and public actions, so that Christian members have to learn to work together with the more recent Jewish additions. As a result, some Christian ministers have begun omitting references to Jesus, and otherwise toning down the specifically Christian references in their prayers at IAF events, at least the ones where Jewish leaders are present.

In contrast to the promising efforts to engage Jewish communities, not much work has been done with religious communities outside the Judeo-Christian tradition or with Asian Americans. These communities are relatively small in Texas, although the population of Asian Americans has grown significantly in places like Houston. Nationally, millions of Americans belong to Hindu, Buddhist, Muslim, and a variety of new age faiths. There are fully one million Muslims in the United States, for example, with large concentrations among African Americans in low-income communities.[18] The IAF has begun to incorporate several Muslim immigrant communities in places like Los Angeles and Chicago. But the amount of work it takes to connect to Muslim, Hindu, and Confucian traditions makes the effort to incorporate Jews pale by comparison. So, in sum, the extent to which the IAF can engage people of non-Christian faiths is still unproven.[19]

Despite some of these limitations in the breadth of its base, the IAF network has begun to lay the foundation for a political revival for America's working families and low-income communities. Rooting politics firmly in faith, a development begun in San Antonio in 1974, proved the critical innovation that established the network on a firm foundation and shaped its growth for the next twenty-five years. How well the network meets the challenges to broaden that foundation to other faiths and to other institutions will likely be the key to determining the future of IAF organizing in the next twenty-five years.

A New Model for Multiracial Collaboration

The work of the Southwest IAF offers a compelling new model for creating multiracial collaboration in the political arena. It shows that multiracial organizations can bring black, white, and Hispanic people together around a common agenda that works for the needs of poor and working families. Drawing upon an initial basis of common values, trust and cooperation are built over time as participants develop policy initiatives and work together to pursue them. The network's relational organizing strategy offers people from different racial backgrounds an opportunity to develop a deeper mutual understanding of the needs and aspirations of their respective communities so that common action rests on a firm foundation.

The Southwest IAF's experience does more than show that people can forge a common agenda across racial lines. The network offers an approach that unites Americans broadly without sacrificing attention to the particular needs of communities of color, a weakness that often plagues multiracial efforts. The IAF's strategy can accomplish this balance because its multiracial organizations are themselves composed of institutions which represent different community traditions and interests. For example, African Americans do not participate in IAF organizations as isolated individuals, but through their membership in institutions like churches that have historically defined their community. Member institutions can advocate for the needs of their own communities within IAF organizations while searching for common ground across racial lines. Multiracial collaboration in this model does not deny difference or unique needs. Diversity instead develops out of respect for traditions particular to each community and a willingness to act on their behalf.

The IAF's multiracial strategy offers an innovative way to restore the "missing middle" to American politics, that is, to unite Americans across racial lines for the pursuit of public policies for poor and working families, without losing sight of the need for racial equality and justice. As such, it represents an alternative that avoids either-or positions on the question. Debates over the creation of multiracial alliances in America have traditionally been polarized between strategies that emphasize multiracial organizations and agendas on the one hand and those that stress the need for independent black organizations on the other. The IAF strategy combines the strengths of both, although the overall framework is firmly multiracial.

Advocates for multiracial organizing, including the IAF, point out that the problems facing people of color, like low incomes, poor schooling, and lack of adequate housing and affordable heath care, face large numbers of white Americans as well. All would benefit from a common effort to address these issues, to create that "missing middle" in American politics. William Julius Wilson argues that the current period is particularly conducive to the formation of multiracial alliances because the wealthy are taking the lion's share of the benefits of economic prosperity, while the majority of working Americans of all races are struggling with living standards that are stagnating. The economic boom provides the funds for government to aggressively address the problems Americans face. So white and black Americans share a common interest in forging multiracial alliances to campaign for governmental programs that can improve their lot vis-à-vis the wealthy.[20]

Yet critics of multiracial organizing argue that all Americans do not suffer equally in the face of economic transformations. Historic patterns of racial inequality persist, as communities of color receive poorer education, lower levels of income and wealth, poorer health care, and worse housing than whites. Moreover, communities of color experience particular issues of racial injustice, like oppressive policing and discrimination in the criminal justice system. Efforts that seek to improve the conditions of working families generally have often failed to adequately address racism and the greater poverty faced by communities of color. Some critics, like Phillip Thompson, point out that efforts ostensibly committed to addressing the needs of all working Americans have ended up sacrificing the particular needs of the black community on the altar of unity.[21]

Contemporary criticisms of multiracial organizing have their roots in the critique of integrationist strategies developed by Black Power advocates in the sixties. Stokely Carmichael and Charles Hamilton, in their classic work on Black Power, argued that oppressed groups must first close ranks before they enter the broader society. Integrationism, as the liberal idea of free and equal individuals, failed to appreciate the importance of the strengths the black community forged through years of oppression. For Black Power advocates, African Americans need to come to an understanding and appreciation of their history, culture, traditions, and identity in order to achieve equality and respect from whites.[22]

But Black Power has its limits. Advocates for racial justice that don't seek to connect with the broader interests of Americans can end up isolated. Black Power advocates recognized those limits and advocated forging coalitions with sympathetic white Americans. But coalitions simply negotiate about interests; they do not constitute a forum for Americans to learn about people different from them, find common ground, and forge a deeper conception of the common good. At best, coalitions provide an opportunity for representatives of organizations to build relationships, while the rest of the membership of these organizations remain separated.

The IAF's strategy for combining bonding and bridging social capital does offer a promising alternative. Community leaders participate in IAF organizations not as individuals, but through their membership in community institutions like churches. The bonding social capital represented by their families, congregations, even schools, nurtures participants and binds them to each other. Such bonding social capital provides the foundation for people to enter the public realm as members and leaders of historically defined communities, not alone. It gives participants collective support and encouragement, the more necessary for citizens who lack high levels of education and income. The strength of bonding social capital helps ensure that oppressed groups can voice their concerns and exert a measure of power, a key concern of Black Power advocates.

Bridging social capital as represented by IAF organizations is built upon the foundation of bonding social capital but expands its reach. The network creates links across communities so that Americans can forge a conception of the common good as something more than a collection of different community needs. An IAF affiliate is not a coalition of institutions where only a few institutional leaders ever meet to negotiate. Rather the larger ranks of indigenous leaders from member institutions become involved in the search for a consensus with people different from themselves.

The IAF clearly favors multiracial organizing, but is not blind to the realty of racism and the importance of black community institutions. Most IAF leaders and organizers recognize that racism plagues American society and oppresses communities of color. The network encourages African American leaders to meet together, as well as in multiracial settings. Many local IAF organizations sponsor cluster meetings, where congregations typically of one predominant racial group in one part of a city can meet together. Black IAF pastors have also met from time to time on the national level as a caucus.

The IAF encourages black organization and initiative to take place within a multiracial framework because such an alliance provides the firmest foundation and broadest basis of power from which to address the pressing issues confronting poor communities of color. As a result, the IAF constantly has to balance a conception of the common needs of American families with the specific needs of the most distressed communities in its organizations. With limited resources, that balance is often difficult to achieve. Nevertheless, the innovation in the IAF approach is to attempt to combine the two forms of social capital (bonding and bridging) in one multiracial political organization.

Echoing the earlier critics of multiracial organizations, some scholars and activists have argued that the IAF's approach still does not sufficiently tackle the issue of race. For example, James Jennings has argued that "although Alinsky's theoretical and practical work was very important, his model at times has been implemented in ways that have maintained a racial hierarchy, despite the objective of change based on community agendas."[23] More recently, Gary Delgado has argued that "with the exception of independent organizations in communities of color, racial issues have been subsumed by issues of class solidarity in most community organizations."[24] This criticism packs an historical bite because Alinsky's first community organization, the Back of the Yards Neighborhood Council, degenerated into a white protectionist group, which actively opposed efforts by African Americans to integrate Chicago's neighborhoods. The critics fail to mention, though, that Black Power advocates of the sixties admired Alinsky. Black leaders hired him to help them build power organizations in African American communities like the Woodlawn section of Chicago and in Rochester.

Despite the critics' assertions that issues of race are being ignored, a careful examination of the record of the Texas IAF shows its work is largely centered in black and Hispanic communities. Virtually every one of the 100 Alliance Schools in which the IAF works across the state of Texas, for example, is located in a low-income community of color. If anything, IAF organizations in Texas have ignored the particular needs of its white middle-class constituents in favor of concentrating its work in low-income communities of color. Most local IAF organizations are just beginning to develop campaigns targeted at the specific needs of its more affluent Anglo constituents. Of course, the network's school reform work does appeal to the interests of white teachers; and its job-training program also speaks to the needs of Anglos who have lost their jobs through industrial restructuring. But there is no question that the IAF places a clear priority on the needs of low-income communities of color.

Contrary to the critics, the IAF actually excels in addressing issues that any race-conscious activist would agree represent institutionalized racism. The network builds affordable housing, works to improve schools and establish after-school programs, develops job-training programs and living wage campaigns, lobbies for water and sewer services to border area *colonias*, and improves city services to minority neighborhoods. In fact, the IAF has often been more successful in addressing these community concerns than organizations with a racial agenda like the NAACP, which have concentrated on legal strategies.

What the Texas IAF has so far largely failed to do, however, is address issues that concern racial injustice per se, like police brutality towards African Americans or the Brosky hate killing discussed in chapter 4. This failure is the more tragic because IAF organizations often represent the only multiracial political institution in many localities that could cultivate broad public support for creating initiatives in these areas. The IAF, however, does not view these issues as "political," by which participants mean actionable. IAF organizers and leaders see them as legal or protest issues around which they cannot build and sustain organizations. But why police brutality is a less political issue than school failure, for example, is not readily apparent to the outside observer. Certainly, IAF organizations could work to make these issues "political" in the IAF sense. For example, the IAF could organize residents to work collaboratively with police to transform the culture and methods of law enforcement in the same way it organizes parents in schools to transform the educational system.

Transforming the culture of policing might prove harder than school reform work. But IAF organizations already work around issues of public safety, trying to increase and improve policing in its neighborhoods. Through those campaigns they have created better relationships between African American (and Hispanic) communities and police departments, with the understanding that closer relationships will reduce police abuse as well as provide more effective public safety. Yet the network has not been willing to mount a direct campaign against police brutality, or more broadly, the kind of racial injustice represented by the Brosky incident in Fort Worth.

Issues of racial injustice have tremendous symbolic as well as practical importance for African Americans. William Julius Wilson, while advocating multiracial alliances like those created by the Texas IAF, argues that affirmative action is one such acid test for African Americans at the national level. In Wilson's view, no multiracial coalition will fully engage the black community unless it speaks to that issue. Wilson advocates reformulating affirmative action, which is typically seen as an issue of racial preference, into what he calls "affirmative opportunity." Such a shift moves the discussion away from race towards the values Americans can broadly share, and hopefully broadens its appeal to whites. The IAF typically takes such an approach when the network argues for improved education, not as a "race issue" per se, but as what all Americans deserve. It could certainly experiment with analogous approaches to issues of racial justice. Such experiments may be crucial to convincing African Americans still suspicious of the network that multiracial organizing can respond to all of their deeply felt concerns.

Tackling issues of racial justice will require the Southwest IAF to overcome its historic reluctance to talk explicitly about issues of race and racism. The network, as we have seen, has been quite cautious about making public charges of racism against societal institutions. This reluctance is based upon the fear that talk about racism can divide people who have yet to establish sufficient trust and commitment to stay together through these conversations.[25]

The network has, however, been sponsoring internal educational seminars on race and the African American experience for quite some time now. And here we can find another important lesson from the work of the Southwest IAF. Conscious attention to education and open discussion about race deepens multiracial understanding. If the network's experience is any indication, this will more likely occur when African Americans achieve a critical mass in the multiracial context. When done well, education and relationship building around race can lead to a greater capacity to address the issue of racism in the public sphere. Dallas Interfaith publicly identified decisions by political authorities to reject their proposals for greater resources and improved services to minority communities as racist. Although most affiliates have not managed as public a discussion of racism yet, these recent trends might well point toward the future of the network.

The IAF's multiracial political organizations show the gains that can be made when discussions of racism take place within the context of a commitment for cooperative action. Trust is built over time through personal relationship building as people work together. In this way the potential divisiveness that comes from frank discussions about racism can be tempered with the binding force of mutual obligations. At its best, the IAF combines education about the historical experiences of different racial groups, learning about group experiences through personal relationships, and analysis of the racial character of public decisions, all within the context of collaborative action. Through this multifaceted approach the Southwest IAF network has broken new ground in advancing a multiracial strategy that works to construct the "missing middle" in American politics, while addressing the particular needs of communities of color.

Local Organizing and Effective Power

By rooting politics in patient base building in local communities and then networking local organizations together into federated networks, the IAF offers an effective strategy to create the organized power that will be necessary to orient public policies toward the needs of poor and working families. The Southwest IAF has found a way to foster participation locally while leveraging power at higher governmental levels. There are important lessons here. Many well-grounded community groups remain weak and isolated in their localities. Most advocacy groups, on the other hand, are top-heavy, lobbying in Washington without an organized base. The IAF has found a way to balance the two sides, placing a relentless concentration on local organizing while leveraging power at higher levels.

The Southwest IAF's experience demonstrates the gains that can be made when political action is grounded in patient, base-building efforts in local communities. Here is where the values and issues people care deeply about will emerge in a way that can foster their participation. So much of the quality of life for Americans still rests in local communities, where they raise their children, house their families, and strive for a safe and healthy environment. Local communities provide the primary place where citizens can engage in the personal relationship building so crucial to community coherence and to the formation of a collective political will. The greater national linkages made through advances in telecommunications can expand upon face-to-face connections, but not easily replace them.

It is quite easy to dismiss this local organizing in the face of the globalizing economy. Many analysts jump immediately to an effort to figure out the correct policy, the right issue, to solve local problems. Activists rush to influence the highest levels of power. To do so is a serious mistake. Political and policy elites have much to offer to our understanding of public policy, but they can't operate alone. Grand schemes launched by Washington-based advocacy groups often lack the organized backing to be adopted in the political arena. They are not necessarily the most effective policies anyway. Local knowledge, a close understanding of the needs and aspirations of Americans at the ground level, must inform social policy if it is to be effective.[26]

The IAF experience demonstrates that communities can make important strides in tackling national and global issues at the local level. Project QUEST, the innovative job-training program initiated by IAF organizations in San Antonio, brought immediate gains to low-income workers in that city and also promises to affect broader trends by encouraging high-skill, high-wage economic development. This kind of development strategy has local as well as national applicability. BUILD, the IAF's local organization in Baltimore, initiated the nation's first living wage campaign. The city ordinance requires public contractors to pay wages significantly higher than the minimum wage and to offer benefits. IAF organizations and other coalitions then spread this local initiative across the country. Meanwhile, the Texas IAF's Alliance Schools project works school by school to turn around persistent patterns of educational failure and low achievement in communities of color. The IAF has worked hard to disseminate the lessons from its efforts to inform the national level discourse on education reform.

Despite the critical, and largely underappreciated, role of local organizing, higher-level power is still required and can create openings for local work. The IAF recognizes that fact and makes good use of federally created opportunities. Project QUEST drew upon federal job-training funds, even as it contributed to the government's effort to restructure the training program. IAF organizations use the requirements of the Community Reinvestment Act, passed by Congress, to force banks to serve inner-city neighborhoods.

The IAF has taken the first steps to expand its power beyond the local level by forging a state network in Texas, a development closely examined in chapter 3. Beyond Texas, the Southwest IAF has worked to coordinate a regional strategy on issues that affect the whole region, including immigration, the conditions of border communities, schools, and employment training. As the anniversary convention suggests, the IAF is creating a human development strategy as an umbrella for these efforts. Although there is no regional political authority, public officials do meet regionally, and some corporate institutions have regional divisions. The idea is to bring together power holders (like members of the Congressional delegation) around the human development strategy and develop the capacity to address issues on a regional basis. Statewide campaigns and regional coordination among local IAF organizations are growing across the country as well.[27]

What's significant about the Southwest IAF's strategy is that it works to build participation locally at the same time as exerting power at the state level. Local leaders come together regionally to build consensus so they can generate higher-level resources, multilevel collaborations, and more complex programmatic initiatives like the Alliance Schools. The network structure seeks to ensure that state and regional work does not occur at the expense of local base building. The state network cannot impose campaigns on local organizations, which retain ultimate control over their own affairs. Instead the IAF networks build up from the local level while exerting power statewide. Higher-level initiatives bring resources and alliances back down to expand the work of local organizing. The IAF's network follows the structure of American government, allowing the IAF to intervene in political authorities at the relevant local, state, and regional levels.[28]

The network structure attempts to balance the development of authoritative leadership by IAF leaders and organizers at higher levels with local participation. As we have seen, a certain degree of tension between the two can arise when a network with such limited means attempts to accomplish both tasks. In fact, the IAF has devoted a significant amount of its resources to build networks capable of concerted action. Leaders have to spend their time attending regional meetings, and the network must use precious resources paying for travel. Without such attention, though, the network would remain a collection of separate projects capable only of cooperating from time to time around certain issues. Instead, the IAF seeks to build united and authoritative leadership at the state and regional levels. And this requires opportunity for relationship building, discussion, and reflection among leaders drawn from the localities. Yet face-to-face relationships are more difficult to develop and strengthen across large distances. The Southwest IAF network has drawn upon the personal authority of its regional director, Ernesto Cortes, to help provide united leadership and direction for the network.[29]

The IAF and faith-based organizing are on the rise in America, spreading throughout the country by sinking roots into more and more of our nation's communities. The IAF has over sixty local affiliates, with three other faith-based networks adding another seventy. The number of organizations within the field has more than doubled in the last ten years. For the first time achieving national significance and power lies within the reach of these efforts. To meet the challenge of national action, however, will require a significant transformation of the IAF network.

The need for national action is clear. Without denying the gains made by the IAF at local, state, and regional levels, it is important to recognize that many of the key processes affecting poor and working families occur at the national level. Economic developments and corporate decisions at the national (and increasingly, the global) level affect wages and environmental conditions across the country. Federal policy shapes access to health care, job training, affordable housing, citizenship, and income distribution. Even with a small federal role in education, the broader debates that shape the context for local school reform, vouchers, standards, and charter schools to name a few, have a significant national component.

The federated networks of the IAF do offer a promising organizational structure for building a nationwide effort that can strengthen civic participation locally while addressing issues that can only be solved nationally. The IAF itself, though, has yet to translate its strong local and growing regional foundation into a basis for national action. This failure is understandable in that the IAF has only recently expanded into enough parts of the country to make national action a viable possibility. But that is not the whole story. The IAF has retained a single-minded emphasis on the training of leaders locally, rather than on the pursuit of issues nationally. There are some good reasons for this choice. In particular, national action could drain limited resources away from the network's raison d'être, leadership development, and extend the network too quickly and too far beyond its base.

The relentless emphasis on local work, however, has left the IAF ill equipped to undertake national action now that it has the foundation to do so. The IAF has paid little attention to elaborating national level structures that could begin to facilitate such efforts. The IAF remains not a national network, but rather a collection of regions, each headed by a relatively autonomous supervisor.[30]

There is a degree of national-level coordination in the IAF. The IAF's cabinet of senior organizers meets nationally on a regular basis to share ideas and, mainly, to standardize the training of organizers and leaders. Organizers and leaders interact at national training sessions. They sometimes travel to visit and learn from each other's initiatives. The IAF has even sponsored national-level meetings of local leaders, but these have been infrequent.

Despite these activities, the network has no functioning national leadership body. The IAF's national director, Ed Chambers, stands alone as the only person with responsibility for the whole network.[31] Not surprisingly, then, the IAF has yet to translate its local organizing into a common national initiative in Congress or anywhere else. More troubling may be that the network as constituted in separate regions cannot even set national action as a goal towards which to build together.

Instead, IAF regional networks have begun to try to influence national policy on their own. The Southwest IAF lobbied the Clinton administration and testified before Congressional hearings to influence the reform of federal job-training programs and to increase federal support for improving conditions in border area *colonias*. In the fall of 1999 the East Coast IAF regional network brought 1,000 supporters to Washington to call on the presidential candidates to support a federal "living wage," which would require any entity benefiting from federal support to supply its workers with a minimum pay-and-benefits package of $25,000.[32]

The IAF will likely continue to follow this pattern, that is, regional networks will begin to take more national initiatives. Certainly, these experiments could lead to important gains. Yet, at some point, the IAF will have to tackle its lack of national integration. It will have to expand its federated network structure to the national level.

At the national level, however, there is no equivalent of Cortes in the sense of someone who has proven authority in all local organizations. The national director, Ed Chambers, is widely respected throughout the IAF, but he has not tried to lead the national IAF in the way Cortes has done in the Southwest region. Transforming itself into a national network will require the IAF to elaborate a set of institutional procedures entirely lacking at the moment. The network needs processes to build consensus among leaders from across the country and to develop authoritative leadership at the national level. Until it does, national initiatives will remain the province of the separate IAF regions.

Community Building and Political Renewal
beyond the Faith Context

Building a broad and national effort to renew American democracy will require strong alliances among the range of institutions that incorporate poor and working families. If and when the IAF forges a national network, it will still not encompass the full range of constituencies that need to be part of these collaborations. But the IAF's recent efforts to expand its organizing beyond faith institutions to engage schools, unions, and other community-based institutions hold an important key to how such alliances can be built. In its new approach, the IAF engages these groups not primarily in tactical coalitions around issues. Rather, the network attempts to incorporate them into long-term relationship building processes. The IAF seeks to connect faith and more secular institutions around values as well as interests. If these efforts prove successful, and can be expanded to the national level, they hold the promise of a significant transformation of American politics.

In the last ten years, the Southwest IAF has put a tremendous amount of resources into expanding its membership beyond congregations to incorporate schools, unions, and a variety of other associations, some that it has helped to build, like the immigrant family associations along the border of Texas and in Arizona. The Alliance Schools comprise the largest set of nonfaith institutions the Southwest IAF has tried to recruit. Over 100 schools are now involved in efforts by Texas IAF organizations to engage parents and school staff into collaborative reform efforts, and other IAF organizations in the Southwest have developed their own analogous initiatives. Like faith institutions, public schools represent stable institutions that are located in every American community. Being in the public realm, however, schools cannot become official, dues-paying members of IAF organizations. The program has brought many new leaders into the IAF, helping the network expand its organized base to parents and teachers it could not reach in congregations.

Unions, meanwhile, have begun to join IAF organizations in small, but significant numbers as well. Their contribution could potentially be great because many have significant financial resources and an organizing staff that can be committed to IAF efforts. Compared to schools, unions have a more independent capacity for political action. In Los Angeles, seven SEIU locals and the teacher's union are joining the reorganized Metro LA group, and funds for IAF organizing there have been supplied by the hotel and restaurant workers union and the local AFL-CIO.

As the prominence of prayer at the twenty-fifth anniversary convention suggests, school and union participation in the IAF occurs in a context infused with religious faith. One might think that less religious leaders from the secular institutions would find it difficult to work in this environment. The network's experience instead has demonstrated a respect for and interest in faith traditions as they inform democratic action. Even leaders with a strong critique of religious institutions, like those who object to the Catholic Church's positions on abortion rights or other social issues, appear interested in working with people of faith. Hard-nosed political animals among them recognize the potential power of organized religion. Perhaps the most averse to organized religion remain outside these efforts. But there appears to be widespread interest in the possibility of forging deeper alliances around shared values for families and communities across institutions.

Even as the IAF broadens its base, the network retains an historic reputation for fierce independence. Competition among faith-based community organizing networks and community development projects runs high. As perhaps the biggest and most prominent network, the IAF gets its share of criticism for sectarianism, although competitiveness is probably a more accurate description. Public officials who butt heads with IAF leaders come away bruised and complain loudly about the IAF's lack of civility. Advocacy groups, for their part, appreciate the political base and power of IAF organizations, constantly seek their support, and complain when the IAF declines in order to concentrate on its own agenda.

The IAF does jealously guard its independence and prides itself on its accomplishments. Competition is not entirely a bad thing. In fact, it can help spur organizers, as social capitalists, to redouble their efforts, resulting in greater organization for low-income communities. At the same time, competition needs to be tempered with collaboration for the good of all groups and communities. When the provisions of the federal Community Reinvestment Act were reduced in 1999, local community development groups and many IAF organizations lost out because those provisions are critical to their affordable housing programs. Yet they failed to act as a united front to defend the act in the face of strong opposition from financial institutions and conservative Republicans.[33]

Until recently, the kinds of alliances the IAF built were largely for the benefit of campaigns that it initiated. There was little sense within IAF organizations that they were part of a larger movement. Indeed, the IAF's famous dictum, "no permanent enemies, no permanent allies," reflects such thinking—that IAF organizations stand alone, entering tactical alliances from time to time. To be fair, Southwest IAF organizations have long sought to cultivate long-term allies where they organize, people and institutions with which they regularly seek to work. But, until recently, these other groups remained tactical allies for IAF initiatives.

Tactical alliances, however, are insufficient for national transformation. If all the IAF does is campaign for issues nationally, it may become just another issue advocacy group. Some IAF organizers realize this and that is part of the reason why they fear national-level action as a drain on the "real work" of base building and leadership development. Here is where the IAF's newer efforts to incorporate unions, schools, and other organizations become so important.

We can find a key to the possibility for a political revival for America's working families and low-income communities of color in the IAF's efforts to connect to the values as well as the interests of these more secular institutions. This study has stressed the central role of faith traditions to provide a set of values that expand democratic participation and ground our political discourse in the needs and aspirations of families and communities. While faith institutions may be critical, they are not the only organizations in American society and politics committed to values of economic and social justice.

A wide array of organizations work hard to engage Americans not just around issues, but around deeply held values as well. The broader community-building movement represents an important set of such initiatives. I have emphasized the relative accomplishments of the Southwest IAF in building participation, connecting interracially, and empowering people by building explicitly political organizations. Nevertheless, the breadth and diversity of the growing number of other community-building initiatives around the country, and their accomplishments, are quite impressive.[34] Some are development oriented, like the community development corporations (CDCs), which now build the majority of affordable housing in our nation's cities. Since their formation in response to the riots of the sixties, CDCs have grown steadily to number over 4,000 nationally. While focused on housing, and to a lesser extent economic development, many tap the community commitments of residents to work in a broad range of neighborhood improvement efforts, like neighborhood cleanups, neighborhood watches, and cultural celebrations. CDCs work in and through a variety of community institutions like churches and tenant associations.[35]

Other community-building efforts grow out of new approaches to social service delivery. Community organizing has become the watchword for new public health initiatives in many poor communities. Residents have become involved in the full array of activities formerly monopolized by professionals, including conducting community-relevant research, setting priorities, determining policy, and campaigning for broader support for public health interventions.[36] Health issues speak closely to the values Americans, especially women, express as caretakers of their families, both of their children and of their elderly relatives. Public health professionals and community activists have been struggling to develop new forms of partnerships and institutions that break the old paradigm of provider/client relations.

Local capacity building constitutes the heart of a new set of comprehensive community revitalization efforts. Premised upon the understanding that the needs of low-income families must be addressed in a holistic fashion, comprehensive community initiatives (CCIs) work to create neighborhood change through new forms of collaborations between residents, service providers, and private foundations.[37] CCIs engage the community attachments of residents to help determine and work for a variety of antipoverty efforts. To build the capacity for neighborhood change, CCIs place a strong priority on education and leadership development.

Community-based efforts to improve public education, like the IAF's Alliance Schools, also connect deeply to family and community values.

Schools historically have played an important role as centers for community life and public citizenship. Parental and community involvement in schools has a long tradition in America, although the connection between schools and communities has weakened significantly in the recent period. Despite much public attention to the need for successful schooling as a way for children to compete in the new economy, parental and community concern for education has always reflected an interest in the holistic development of children as future citizens and community leaders. School-based reform efforts draw from these kinds of value commitments to children, their families, and the community.[38]

The environmental movement has spawned an incredibly wide array of locally based efforts, many of which have deep participatory roots. Much attention goes to the national environmental organizations, which often follow a staff-driven advocacy model. But thousands of Americans have sustained their activity for many years now in local groups. In his study of local environmental efforts, Paul Lichterman shows that activists in a wide variety of campaigns draw upon shared values to make a long-term commitment to political action. According to Lichterman, low-income activists of color tap religious traditions to construct a communitarian basis for their environmental justice organizations, as do white working-class women. But even white middle-class activists, who emphasize personalized politics and individual agency, demonstrate commitment to a shared community and the common good. They are working to build a political community by constructing a new tradition out of various strains of democratic, feminist, and Green Party values.[39]

Women play a predominant role in almost all of the community-based activity across the country. They stand out in the IAF's faith-based organizing, in environmental efforts, and in school reform efforts. Women organize services for battered women, sustain public housing associations, and represent the core group in many recent union-organizing campaigns. Although women's or feminist activism is quite diverse, all forms appear to incorporate some definition and experience of community at their heart. A number of initiatives, like the IAF's, have found a way to connect to women's central role in caring for families and communities. Meanwhile, the transformative power of political action can challenge the limits of what is traditionally women's work, so that women can enter and transform the public sphere. In this way, what have been considered the private values of family and community can become the basis for public action.[40]

Our national political discourse has failed to appreciate the contribution that these kinds of community-based activities and grass-roots institutions can make to democratic renewal. We have yet to find a way to reconstruct a national political process that can engage the value commitments that lie at the heart of such locally rooted initiatives. In part, this failure derives from the domination of top-heavy advocacy groups and media-driven politics. But it also reflects a fear that unleashing such values will prove detrimental to broader democratic goals. Yet, to the extent that our political institutions ignore community-oriented values and institutions, many Americans will remain disconnected and alienated from politics, especially but not only those who lack other avenues for political participation. To the extent that our political discourse remains valueless, it will be impoverished.[41]

In fact, people from different backgrounds and value traditions are working out forms of collaboration at the ground level already. In many of the efforts just discussed, like the newer IAF organizations that incorporate unions and schools, people from different religious faiths are forging modes of political discourse with people motivated by more secular community values. The phenomenon is not limited to the IAF, or to faith-based community organizing. One of the largest and most successful community development corporations in the country is headed by a white Catholic priest, yet is located in the predominantly African American central ward of Newark. Reverend Bill Linder, black Protestants, and a variety of secular community builders have been working out ways to collaborate in the New Community Corporation since the riots destroyed much of central Newark in the late sixties.[42] The labor movement has taken some steps to overcome its historic separation from community-based organizations in poor communities of color, working together with them on a range of local initiatives, including living wage campaigns and organizing drives for low-wage workers.[43]

There is more common ground around broadly shared values for family integrity, healthy communities, social justice, and economic fairness than our political discourse has recognized. Americans have diverse value commitments and express them in many ways. There will be controversy. And sharp conflict around issues of race, in particular, might break out. But there is also the potential for cooperation. Rather than avoid the conflict, American democracy would do better to seek ways for its citizens to discuss their deeply held views within the context of an effort to establish the public good. Only in this way can the diverse efforts represented by the IAF's organizing, the broader community building and development field, a revitalized labor movement, environmental groups, and other associations come together to provide a national force for political renewal.

If these efforts are to transform our politics, they will have to address the bias in our political parties and Congress. As long as our national political institutions remain more beholden to large campaign contributors and more influenced by inner-circle lobbying than they are by organized constituencies, our politics will fail to effectively address many of the needs of families and communities. Democratic renewal will likely require reform in the operation of our political parties and our electoral system. The IAF has worked hard to walk the electoral tightrope, that is, to influence elections and elected officials without compromising its independence and nonpartisan status. The IAF attempts to hold public officials accountable to its organized constituency through accountability nights and other public actions. And institutional innovations like the QUEST board of directors offer some promising directions for how to establish cooperative arrangements between the business community, public officials, and community-based organizations. Eventually, these efforts will have to be greatly expanded in order to directly reform the main institutions of our political processes.[44]

We can learn two key lessons from the Southwest IAF for how to develop collaboration among diverse groups to reinvigorate our democracy. First, the foundation for any lasting gains in democratic politics must come through patient base building at the bottom. We have no shortage of efforts to build coalitions at the top around various issues. One of the lessons of the Southwest IAF is that the answer will not come from the top. The "missing middle" must be built up from the bottom. That does not deny a critical role for political elites and policy experts. But what is most absent from American politics today is that firm foundation of participation at local level, a base from which to establish productive multilevel collaborations.

The second lesson comes from the IAF's emphasis on relationship building. We will have to respect diverse traditions, and find a way for collaborations to allow people to express their views differently. One organization will not encompass the diversity of America. At the same time, narrow interest-based alliances will not do either. While negotiating and compromising over interests plays an important role in any cooperative effort, it is not sufficient. We need processes of political discourse where people learn about each other's values, share their stories, and foster understanding of their traditions. Such a process should not seek to instill uniformity. Instead, it can generate mutual respect for diversity and establish important areas of common ground as well. Success here will take real political leadership, not the pandering to narrow constituencies which has become so common in American politics.

Collaboration can also be a force for change. Faith-based and more secular political efforts each have important limitations. Yet their limitations are more likely to be overcome when diverse communities attempt to engage in public discourse and action together. Some of the richest moments in American history have come when people motivated by religious faith and democratic aspirations have joined forces in a common effort. Movements against economic and racial oppression have expanded American democracy and reformed moribund institutions. The union-organizing drives of the thirties and forties dramatically improved the lives of industrial workers and brought millions of them into political life. The civil rights movement ended hundreds of years of legalized racism and transformed and invigorated American politics.

The faith-based organizing efforts of the IAF and other community-based initiatives are still in their early stages of development. They face many challenges before they can emerge with the strength and influence of past initiatives. But the broader lessons of their activity have much to offer to a politics mired in cynicism and alienation. IAF organizations are already making significant improvements to the quality of life for poor and working families and their communities. They offer new models for multiracial understanding and collaboration in the effort to combat poverty and racial isolation. And they revitalize our democracy by infusing it with an active and empowered citizenry.

Notes

Preface

1. I use the terms Hispanic and Mexican American, rather than Latino and Chicano, because that is how most participants from this community who are active in the Texas IAF refer to themselves.

2. Robert D. Putnam, *Making Democracy Work: Civic Traditions in Modern Italy* (Princeton, N.J.: Princeton University Press, 1993). The definition of social capital comes from Robert D. Putnam, "Bowling Alone: America's Declining Social Capital," *Journal of Democracy* 6 (January 1995): 67.

Introduction
Dry Bones Rattling

1. The following account is based upon field notes taken by the author, May 29, 1994, San Antonio, Texas.

2. The IAF's political opponents express criticisms. But scholars and activists can also legitimately disagree about effective strategies for confronting poverty and racism. Criticisms of the IAF are discussed in various chapters of this book, and especially in the Conclusion.

3. Chandler Davidson carefully documents this history in *Race and Class in Texas Politics* (Princeton: Princeton University Press, 1990).

4. Paul R. Campbell, *Population Projections for States by Age, Sex, Race, and Hispanic Origin: 1995 to 2025* (Washington, D. C.: U. S. Bureau of the Census, October 1996).

5. A few of the sixty organizations under contract to the IAF were at an early "sponsoring committee" stage in 1999, and so were not fully functioning. The national IAF is led by its national cabinet, consisting of senior organizers who supervise organizing staffs in local affiliates across the country. As of 1999, the IAF's cabinet consisted of national director Edward Chambers, and senior organizers Ernesto Cortes (Southwest), James Drake (Northeast), Michael Gecan (Northeast), Arnold Graf (Mid-Atlantic), Gerald Taylor (South), Larry B. McNeil (Northwest Coast), Stephen Roberson (Chicago), and Christine Stephens (supervising Texas and Louisiana under Cortes). Frank Pierson is not on the national staff, but supervises Arizona and New Mexico under Cortes. The IAF's Board of Trustees, a largely advisory body, includes Edward Chambers, Marvin D. Wurth, Barry Menuez, Monsignor Jack Egan, Sidney Perlstadt, Episcopal Bishop John Adams, Reverend Hays Rockwell, Thomas Boodell, Jr., and Jean Bethke Elshtain.

6. Project QUEST and the Alliance Schools are discussed in later chapters of this book. On Alliance Schools, see also Dennis Shirley, *Community Organizing for Urban School Reform* (Austin: University of Texas Press, 1997). On EBC and Nehemiah Homes, see Timothy Ross, "The Impact of Industrial Areas Foundation Community Organizing on East Brooklyn: A Study of East Brooklyn Congre-

gations, 1978–1995" (Ph.D. dissertation, University of Maryland, College Park, 1996). On BUILD's living wage campaigns, see Marion Orr "Urban Regimes and Human Capital Policies: A Study of Baltimore," *Journal of Urban Affairs* 14 (1992): 173–87. Luis Uchitelle charts the spread of living wage campaigns across the U.S. in "Minimum Wages, City by City," *New York Times,* November 19, 1999, pp. C1, C19.

7. The three networks are the Pacific Institute for Community Organization (PICO), the Gamaliel Foundation, and the Direct Action Research and Training Institute (DART). Of the member congregations, about 35 percent are predominantly black, 21 percent Hispanic, 36 percent Anglo, and 6 percent mixed racially. Overall, about 450 professional organizers work with these groups. See Mark R. Warren and Richard L. Wood, *Faith Based Community Organizing: The State of the Field* (Jericho, NY: Interfaith Funders, 2001). Richard L. Wood has conducted an extensive study of PICO; see his forthcoming book *Faith in Action,* based on his Ph.D. dissertation. "Faith in Action: Religion, Race, and the Future of Democracy" (University of California, Berkeley, 1994); also "Social Capital and Political Culture: God Meets Politics in the Inner City" *American Behavioral Scientist* 40:5 (March/April 1997): 595–605.

8. An overview of community development corporations can be found in Avis C. Vidal, "CDCs as Agents of Neighborhood Change: The State of the Art," in W. Dennis Keating, Norman Krumholz and Philip Star, eds., *Revitalizing Urban Neighborhoods* (Lawrence: University Press of Kansas, 1996), pp. 149–63. For an overview of the efforts of African American churches in community development, see June Manning Thomas and Reynard N. Blake, Jr., "Faith-Based Development and African-American Neighborhoods," in Keating, Krumholz, and Star, eds., *Revitalizing Urban Neighborhoods,* pp. 131–43. On faith efforts to "save" inner-city youth, see Joe Klein, "In God They Trust," *The New Yorker* (June 16, 1997), pp. 40–48.

9. Steven Greenhouse, "In Biggest Drive Since 1937, Union Gains a Victory," *The New York Times,* February 26, 1999, pp. A1, A18. Donald C. Reitzes and Dietrich C. Reitzes trace the broader legacy and influence of Saul Alinsky and the IAF in *The Alinsky Legacy: Alive and Kicking* (Greenwich, CT: JAI Press, 1987).

10. Figures reported by the National Community Building Network, Oakland, CA, May 17, 2000. Carol B. Stack, *Call to Home: African Americans Reclaim the Rural South* (New York: Basic Books, 1996). Richard A. Couto, *Making Democracy Work Better: Mediating Structures, Social Capital, and the Democratic Prospect* (Chapel Hill: University of North Carolina Press, 1999).

11. Robert D. Putnam has done the most to chart the decline of social capital in America and prompt widespread scholarly discussion of the issue; see his "Bowling Alone: America's Declining Social Capital," *Journal of Democracy* 6 (January 1995): 65–78, and *Bowling Alone: The Collapse and Revival of American Community* (New York: Simon & Schuster, 2000).

12. IAF organizations have undertaken important state-level initiatives in places where there are several affiliates, like Maryland and California. More recently, IAF organizations in Arizona and Louisiana have begun state-level coordination. The PICO organizing network has operated at the state level in California for a number of years.; see Wood, *Faith in Action.*

13. Project QUEST is discussed in chapter 6 and the Alliance Schools in chapter 3 of this book. Shirley, *Community Organizing for Urban School Reform*, treats the Alliance Schools initiative in detail. The experiences and accomplishments of IAF organizations in other parts of the country have been documented in a variety of works. See, for example, Jim Rooney, *Organizing the South Bronx* (Albany: SUNY Press, 1995); and Harry C. Boyte, *Commonwealth: A Return to Citizen Politics* (New York: Free Press, 1989).

14. See Ernesto Cortes, Jr., "Reweaving the Fabric: The Iron Rule and the IAF Strategy for Power and Politics," in Henry G. Cisneros, ed., *Interwoven Destinies* (New York: W.W. Norton, 1993), pp. 294–319. I discuss the views of Cortes and other IAF organizers in chapter 2.

15. Although sociologists call what I did "participant observation," I was not literally a participant in IAF activities. I observed the activities of the IAF network and talked with those present before and after. Sociologists appreciate the fact that the presence and unavoidable interaction with an observer creates a type of participation, and so call this method "participant observation."

Chapter One
Community Building and Political Renewal

1. Robert D. Putnam, *Bowling Alone: The Collapse and Revival of American Community* (New York: Simon & Schuster, 2000). The definition of social capital comes from Robert D. Putnam, "Bowling Alone: America's Declining Social Capital," *Journal of Democracy* 6 (January 1995): 67.

2. For a discussion of party politics at the turn of the century, see Michael E. McGerr, *The Decline of Popular Politics: The American North, 1865–1928* (New York: Oxford University Press, 1986). Lizabeth Cohen shows how industrial workers expanded their political participation through union organizing in *Making a New Deal: Industrial Workers in Chicago, 1919–1939* (Cambridge: Cambridge University Press, 1990).

3. Martin P. Wattenberg discusses the rise of candidate-centered politics in *The Decline of American Political Parties 1952–1988* (Cambridge: Harvard University Press, 1990). Marshall Ganz discusses the fragmenting effect of campaign technology in "Voters in the Crosshairs: How Technology and the Market Are Destroying Politics," *American Prospect* 16 (Winter 1994): 100–109. He shows that, rather than engaging communities, the internal logic of contemporary electoral campaigning further fragments the electorate as it targets ever smaller constituencies.

4. Steven J. Rosenstone and John Mark Hansen, *Mobilization, Participation, and Democracy in America* (New York: Macmillan Publishing Company, 1993), explain the decline in many forms of political participation since the sixties as the result of a decline in strategic mobilization by political leaders. They conclude "political parties, campaign organizations, and social movements presented voters with fewer chances to take part in elections, fewer opportunities to share the burdens of political involvement, and fewer occasions to gain the rewards and satisfactions of political activity. . . . People participate in electoral politics in all of its forms when they are mobilized to do so. When political mobilization falls,

so does the propensity of people to take part" (p. 227). Social networks and organizations feature in this view as important structures out of which people can be mobilized. While true, this view offers a rather one-sided and utilitarian understanding of the contribution of social capital. Participatory patterns and the values embedded in community institutions can also shape political processes. In this study, I prefer the term engagement, rather than mobilization, because it suggests the interaction between social and political processes that occurs in IAF organizations. For a related discussion of how religious culture shapes political action in the PICO organizing network, see Richard L. Wood, "Religious Culture and Political Action," *Sociological Theory* 17 (November 1999): 307–32.

5. Theda Skocpol, "Unraveling from Above," *American Prospect* 25 (March–April 1996): 20–25. On the role of women's association, see Theda Skocpol, *Protecting Soldiers and Mothers: The Political Origins of Social Policy in the United States* (Cambridge: Harvard University Press, 1992).

6. See, for example, the report by The Harwood Group, *Citizens and Politics: A View from Main Street America* (Dayton: Kettering Foundation, 1991).

7. Alexis de Tocqueville, *Democracy in America*, ed. J. P. Mayer, trans. George Lawrence (Garden City, N.Y.: Anchor Books, 1969). It should be noted that Tocqueville's analysis applied fully only to enfranchised white men in the small towns he studied. Tocqueville was aware that democracy in America excluded slaves and native Americans. He apparently shared the prejudice that women should not be full citizens.

8. Putnam, *Bowling Alone*. See also, Robert D. Putnam, "Bowling Alone: America's Declining Social Capital," *Journal of Democracy* 6 (January 1995): 65–78; and Robert D. Putnam, "Tuning In, Tuning Out: The Strange Disappearance of Social Capital in America," *PS: Political Science & Politics* 28 (December 1995). Putnam demonstrates that the decline of social capital is to a significant extent a generational phenomenon. Younger generations of Americans are less civically engaged, and they do not become as participatory as their parents even as they age. Consequently, without a major social capital building effort, the country is likely to experience a continued decline in social capital as the more civically engaged older generation of Americans dies off.

9. For a critical view of Putnam's thesis that stresses the continued strength of volunteering and the rise of new forms of group life, see Everett Carll Ladd, *The Ladd Report* (New York: The Free Press, 1999). Pamela Paxton looks closely at the General Social Surveys and finds a decline in trust, but not in associational life; see "Is Social Capital Declining in the United States? A Multiple Indicator Assessment," *American Journal of Sociology* 105 (July 1999): 88–127. Theda Skocpol has disputed the idea that civic life "bubbles up" from below, showing the many ways the American government has historically promoted participation. See her "How Americans Became Civic," in Theda Skocpol and Morris P. Fiorina, eds., *Civic Engagement in American Democracy* (Washington, D.C.: Brookings Institution, 1999), pp. 27–80.

10. Robert Wuthnow, *Sharing the Journey: Support Groups and America's New Quest for Community* (New York: The Free Press, 1994), p. 45. Wuthnow argues that small groups do contribute to social capital in important ways in

Christianity and Civil Society: The Contemporary Debate (Valley Forge, PA: Trinity Press International, 1996), pp. 34–39.

11. Debra C. Minkoff, "Producing Social Capital: National Social Movements and Civil Society," *American Behavioral Scientist* 40 (March/April 1997): 606–19. On the lack of participation in these groups, see Jack L. Walker, Jr., *Mobilizing Interest Groups in America: Patrons, Professions, and Social Movements* (Ann Arbor: University of Michigan Press, 1992); John B. Judis, "The Pressure Elite: Inside the Narrow World of Advocacy Group Politics," *American Prospect* 9 (1992): 15–30; John D. McCarthy, "Pro-life and Pro-choice Mobilization: Infrastructure Deficits and New Technologies," in Mayer N. Zald and John D. McCarthy, eds., *Social Movements in an Organizational Society* (New Brunswick, N.J.: Transaction Books, 1987), pp. 49–66; Pam Oliver and Gerry Marwell, "Mobilizing Technologies for Collective Action," in Aldon D. Morris and Carol M. Mueller, eds., *Frontiers in Social Movement Theory* (New Haven, CT: Yale University Press, 1992), pp. 251–72. Putnam makes a similar argument to mine in *Bowling Alone*, ch. 9.

12. See Skocpol, "How Americans Became Civic."

13. A similar point is made in Mark R. Warren, J. Phillip Thompson, and Susan Saegert, "The Role of Social Capital in Combating Poverty," in Susan Saegert, J. Phillip Thompson, and Mark R. Warren, eds., *Social Capital and Poor Communities* (New York: Russell Sage Foundation Press, 2001).

14. For an early critique of the view that all forms of social capital are beneficial for society, see Alejandro Portes and Patricia Landolt, "The Downside of Social Capital," *American Prospect* 26 (May–June 1996): 18–21, 94.

15. Church attendance and membership figures come from polls conducted by the Gallup organization, published in George H. Gallup, *Religion in America 1996* (Princeton: Princeton Religion Research Center, 1996). Results of the National Congregations Survey are reported in Michael W. Foley, John D. McCarthy, and Mark Chaves, "Social Capital, Religious Institutions and Poor Communities," in Susan Saegert, J. Phillip Thompson, and Mark R. Warren, eds., *Social Capital and Poor Communities* (New York: Russell Sage Foundation Press, 2001). Robert Putnam first suggested to me that religion accounts for half of the country's stock of social capital.

16. The data on volunteering come from Andrew Greeley, "Coleman Revisited: Religious Structures as a Source of Social Capital," *American Behavioral Scientist* 40 (March/April 1997): 587–94, and Virginia A. Hodgkinson and Murray S. Weitzman, *Giving and Volunteering in the United States: Findings from a National Survey* (Washington, D.C.: Independent Sector, 1994).

17. For a thorough discussion of the role of African American religion both as an inspiration for action as well as an institutional base for mobilization, see Frederick C. Harris, *Something Within: Religion in African-American Political Activism* (New York: Oxford University Press, 1999).

18. Tocqueville also thought religion played a key role in supporting democracy in America, although most contemporary observers do not emphasize this part of his thought. Tocqueville visited America near the end of the Second Great Awakening, a period of intense religious revival and church building. Churches stood at the center of associational life, sponsoring many of the schools and civic

associations in the towns Tocqueville visited. Moreover, these associations were connected to political institutions like town meetings and the mass political parties that first emerged in the United States during this period. For Tocqueville, religion supplied the "mores," or cultural and value underpinnings, that supported democracy. In his native France, Catholicism was often antidemocratic. But Tocqueville noted (*Democracy in America*, pp. 289–92) that "there is not a single religious doctrine in the United States hostile to democratic and republican institutions. . . . There is an innumerable multitude of sects in the United States. They are all different in the worship they offer to the Creator, but all agree concerning the duties of men to one another. Each sect worships God in its own fashion, but all preach the same morality in the name of God." Tocqueville concluded that "religion, which never intervenes directly in the government of American society, should therefore be considered as the first of their political institutions, for although it did not give them the taste for liberty, it singularly facilitates their use thereof."

19. The literature on the Christian Right is voluminous. Clyde Wilcox uses the concept "mixed blessing" in *Onward Christian Soldiers? The Religious Right in American Politics*, 2d ed. (Boulder: Westview Press, 2000).

20. Amitai Etzioni, "Old Chestnuts and New Spurs," in Amitai Etzioni, ed., *New Communitarian Thinking: Persons, Virtues, Institutions, and Communities* (Charlottesville: University Press of Virginia, 1995), pp. 16, 18.

21. For a discussion of how macro-level studies of social capital mask local variation, see Michael W. Foley and Bob Edwards, "Is It Time to Disinvest in Social Capital?" *Journal of Public Policy* 19 (1999): 141–73.

22. For an analysis of African American urban life in Chicago in the thirties and forties, see St. Clair Drake and Horace R. Cayton. *Black Metropolis: a Study of Negro Life in a Northern City* (New York: Harcourt, Brace and Company, 1945). Alan Ehrenhalt, *The Lost City: Discovering the Forgotten Virtues of Community in the Chicago of the 1950s* (New York: Basic Books, 1995), reconstructs the vibrant life of a black neighborhood (Bronzeville) and a white ethnic neighborhood (St. Nick's parish) in Chicago in the fifties.

23. William J. Wilson shows how the decline of manufacturing jobs and an exodus of the middle class have radically undermined inner-city communities in *When Work Disappears: The World of the New Urban Poor* (New York: A. A. Knopf, 1996). On "old heads," see Elijah Anderson, *Streetwise: Race, Class, and Change in an Urban Community* (Chicago: University of Chicago Press, 1990). The argument made here about the decline in social capital in the inner city does not necessarily imply that the inner city suffers a particular deficit in social capital compared to more affluent suburban communities. Although that is a commonly held view, to my knowledge no one has published any research to support that claim. Robert Putnam, for his part, has been arguing that communities across America have suffered similar declines in social capital. In addition, my argument does not ignore the important forms of social capital, like churches that continue to exist in inner-city communities. I have presented a brief discussion of a complex phenomenon. For a fuller consideration of those issues, see Saegert, Thompson, and Warren, eds. *Social Capital and Poor Communities*.

24. For a discussion of the role of social networks in getting by versus getting ahead, see Xavier de Souza Briggs, "Brown Kids in White Suburbs: Housing Mo-

bility and the Many Faces of Social Capital," *Housing Policy Debate* 9 (1998): 177–221.

25. Sidney Verba, Kay Lehman Schlozman, and Henry E. Brady, *Voice and Equality: Civic Voluntarism in American Politics* (Cambridge: Harvard University Press, 1995).

26. Sheldon S. Wolin, *The Presence of the Past: Essays on the State and the Constitution* (Baltimore: Johns Hopkins University Press, 1989), pp. 139, 150. Social capital and politics defined as cooperation does not deny the existence of conflicts of interest, as I discuss below. But politics can be a process of discussion and negotiation over these differences, engendering deeper mutual understanding and action for common purposes.

27. On "strong" understandings of democratic participation, see Benjamin R. Barber, *Strong Democracy: Participatory Politics for a New Age* (Berkeley: University of California Press, 1984). Barber argues that "strong democratic theory posits the social nature of human beings in the world and the dialectical interdependence of man and his government. As a consequence, it places human self-realization through mutual transformation at the center of the democratic process" (p. 215). On the role of black women in sustaining community life, see Cheryl Townsend Gilkes, "Building in Many Places: Multiple Commitments and Ideologies in Black Women's Community Work," *Women and the Politics of Empowerment*, ed. Ann Bookman and Sandra Morgen (Philadelphia: Temple University Press, 1988). For discussions of relational skills and the empowerment of women, see the essays in Bookman and Morgen, *Women and the Politics of Empowerment*, and Kathleen McCourt, *Working Class Women and Grassroots Politics* (Bloomington: Indiana University Press, 1977).

28. Michael J. Sandel, *Democracy's Discontent: America in Search of a Public Philosophy* (Cambridge: Harvard University Press, 1996), p. 349.

29. The terms bonding and bridging social capital have been used by Robert Putnam and others. See, for example, Ross Gittell and Avis Vidal, *Community Organizing: Building Social Capital as a Development Strategy* (Thousand Oaks, CA: Sage Publications, 1998); and Warren, Thompson, and Saegert, "The Role of Social Capital in Combating Poverty."

30. On racial segregation, see Douglas S. Massey and Nancy A. Denton, *American Apartheid: Segregation and the Making of the Underclass* (Cambridge: Harvard University Press, 1993). On economic segregation, see Paul A. Jargowski, *Poverty and Place: Ghettos, Barrios and the American City* (New York: Russell Sage Foundation, 1997). On segregation in schools, see Gary Orfield, Susan E. Eaton, and Elaine R. Jones, *Dismantling Desegregation: The Quiet Reversal of Brown V. Board of Education* (New York: New Press, 1997).

31. John T. McGreevy, *Parish Boundaries: The Catholic Encounter with Race in the Twentieth Century* (Chicago: University of Chicago Press, 1996), p. 189. Thomas Sugrue also discusses the development of racial polarization in postwar northern cities in *The Origins of the Urban Crisis: Race and Inequality in Postwar Detroit* (Princeton: Princeton University Press, 1996). Massey and Denton, *American Apartheid*, offer a thorough discussion of how residential segregation was developed and maintained in the urban North.

32. For data on the growing multiracial character of the United States, see Roderick J. Harrison and Claudette E. Bennett, "Racial and Ethnic Diversity," in Reynolds Farley, ed., *State of the Union: America in the 1990s, Volume Two: Social Trends* (New York: Russell Sage Foundation, 1995), pp. 141–210. Roger Waldinger, "Black/Immigrant Competition Re-assessed: New Evidence from Los Angeles," *Sociological Perspectives* 40 (1997): 365–86, discusses competition between African Americans and Latinos for jobs in Los Angeles. After Harold Washington's election as mayor of Chicago in 1983, the cooperation between African Americans and Hispanics that proved crucial to his election collapsed when Hispanics charged that they were not getting their fair share of municipal jobs; see Barbara Ferman, *Challenging the Growth Machine: Neighborhood Politics in Chicago and Pittsburgh* (Lawrence: University Press of Kansas, 1996). On relations between African Americans and newer black immigrant groups, see Philip Kasinitz, *Caribbean New York: Black Immigrants and the Politics of Race* (Ithaca: Cornell University Press, 1992).

33. This research is summarized in David W. Johnson, Roger Johnson, and Geoffrey Maruyama, "Goal Interdependence and Interpersonal Attraction in Heterogeneous Classrooms: A Meta-Analysis," in Norman Miller and Marilynn B. Brewer, eds., *Groups in Contact: The Psychology of Desegregation* (Orlando: Academic Press, 1984), pp. 187–212.

34. Of course, American religion has also justified racism. For a contemporary assessment of the different roles of religion in social and political action in the world, see Christian Smith, ed., *Disruptive Religion: The Force of Faith in Social Movement Activism* (London: Routledge, 1996).

35. Michael W. Foley and Bob Edwards, "Escape From Politics? Social Theory and the Social Capital Debate," *American Behavioral Scientist* 40 (March/April 1997): 550–61.

36. For one elaboration of this perspective, see John H. Aldrich, *Why Parties? The Origin and Transformation of Political Parties in America* (Chicago: University of Chicago Press, 1995).

37. The Harwood Group, *Citizens and Politics: A View from Main Street America* (Charles F. Kettering Foundation, 1991). David Matthews, *Politics for People: Finding a Responsible Public Voice* (Urbana: University of Illinois Press, 1994), discusses the implications of the study's finding.

38. Avis C. Vidal documents the accomplishments of CDCs as well as the limited nature of citizen participation in them in *Rebuilding Communities: A National Study of Urban Community Development Corporations* (New York: Community Development Research Center, Graduate School of Management and Urban Policy, New School for Social Research, 1992). For a discussion of the failure of CDCs to empower communities, see Randy Stoecker, "The CDC Model of Urban Redevelopment: A Critique and an Alternative," *Journal of Urban Affairs* 19 (1997): 1–22.

39. I will follow that practice and use the term "leader" to refer to IAF participants. The different levels of participation and leadership within IAF organizations are discussed in chapter 8.

40. Richard L. Wood, "Faith in Action: Race, Religion and the Future of American Democracy" (Ph.D. dissertation, University of California, Berkeley, 1995)

develops a similar analysis in his study of PICO, another faith-based community organizing network. He argues that PICO organizing is not parasitic on religious congregations. Rather, religion and politics create what he calls a symbiosis through PICO organizing.

41. The extent to which organizations in the national IAF are multiracial varies. Some of the strongest, like East Brooklyn Congregations (EBC) in New York and BUILD in Baltimore, operate in predominantly African American areas and are largely black. However, in principle, IAF organizations are supposed to be broad based; none are organized exclusively along racial lines. More recently, the IAF has been bringing organizations together on a metropolitan-wide basis, so that EBC is now linked to IAF organizations in the South Bronx, East Harlem, and the Upper West Side, creating a more multiracial network. For further discussion of this issue, see Richard Wood, *Faith in Action*, who analyzes what he calls the bridging institutional structure of local organizations affiliated to PICO, another faith-based organizing network.

42. IAF organizations in Texas are incorporated as either 501(c)3 or 501(c)4 nonprofit organizations.

43. The figure of sixty organizers is current as of July 1, 1999. In this figure, I include lead organizers, staff organizers, and education coordinators. Foundation funds, to be discussed in greater detail in chapter 3, are specifically earmarked for organizer training (the seminars) and to hire education coordinators to conduct school-based organizing. The more successful education coordinators, however, go on to become IAF organizers.

44. For brief early accounts, see Harry C. Boyte, *The Backyard Revolution: Understanding the New Citizen Movement* (Philadelphia: Temple University Press, 1980); and *Community Is Possible: Repairing America's Roots* (New York: Harper & Row, 1984). In *Commonwealth: A Return to Citizen Politics* (New York: Free Press, 1989), Boyte treats the IAF extensively.

45. In this vein, see Mary Beth Rogers' insightful and moving account, *Cold Anger: A Story of Faith and Power Politics* (Denton: University of North Texas Press, 1990). Jim Rooney treats the IAF's work in New York in *Organizing the South Bronx* (Albany: State University of New York Press, 1995). For a brief, but perceptive, account of the IAF's work in Texas, see William Greider, *Who Will Tell the People? The Betrayal of American Democracy* (New York: Simon & Schuster, 1992), chapter 10.

46. Peter Skerry, *Mexican Americans: The Ambivalent Minority* (New York: Free Press, 1993), p. 170.

47. I explore this question in more detail in chapter 8. For a discussion of Americans' aversion to all forms of authority, see Ehrenhalt, *The Lost City*.

48. Larry McNeil, one of the IAF's regional supervisors, discusses this issue in "The Soft Arts of Organizing," *Social Policy* (Winter 1995).

49. Other observers have used the term "new 'old-style' politics" to describe community building activities in America. See, for example, remarks by Xavier de Souza Briggs at a conference on Social Capital and Poor Communities, Fordham University, New York City, March 13, 1999.

50. Peter Skerry, *Mexican Americans: The Ambivalent Minority*, pp. 142–44, also calls IAF organizations the functional equivalent of political machines, but offers a somewhat different analysis.

51. On urban machines, see Steven P. Erie, *Rainbow's End: Irish-Americans and the Dilemmas of Urban Machine Politics, 1840–1985* (Berkeley: University of California Press, 1988). For one of the first discussions of the rise of political consultants, see Larry J. Sabato, *The Rise of Political Consultants: New Ways of Winning Elections* (New York: Basic Books, 1981).

52. Theda Skocpol discusses the role of cross-class federations and their decline in "Advocates without Members: The Recent Transformation of American Civic Life," in Theda Skocpol and Morris P. Fiorina, eds., *Civic Engagement in American Democracy* (Washington, D.C.: Brookings Institution, 1999), pp. 461–509. On the influence of globalization on the changing role of elites, see Theda Skocpol, "Unraveling from Above," *The American Prospect* 25 (March–April 1996): 20–25; and Charles Heying, "Civic Elites and Corporate Delocalization: An Alternative Explanation for Declining Civic Engagement," *American Behavioral Scientist* 40 (March/April 1997): 657–68. On the class bias that results from a political process dominated by monetary contributions and advocacy oriented issue messages, see Sidney Verba, Kay Lehman Schlozman, and Henry E. Brady, "The Big Tilt: Participatory Inequality in America," *The American Prospect* 32 (May–June 1997): 74–80.

53. Marilyn Gittell charts the 1960s–1970s transition of community groups from action to service provision in *Limits to Citizen Participation: The Decline of Community Organizations* (Beverly Hills: Sage Publications, 1980). For a later discussion of the shift from community empowerment to community development, see Robert Fisher, *Let the People Decide: Neighborhood Organizing in America, Updated Edition* (New York: Twayne Publishers, 1994).

54. J. Craig Jenkins, "Channeling Social Protest: Foundation Patronage of Contemporary Social Movements," p. 215, as quoted in Christopher Koliba, "A Progress Report: United States Foundation Giving to Domestic Citizen Participation Programs and Projects (1988–1997)," Virginia Hodgkinson, ed., *Civil Society in the United States* (forthcoming). On the role of foundations as a critical force in shaping the advocacy group world, see Jack L. Walker, Jr., *Mobilizing Interest Groups in America: Patrons, Professions, and Social Movements* (Ann Arbor: University of Michigan Press, 1991).

55. On the influence of conservative foundations, see Sally Covington, "How Conservative Philanthropies and Think Tanks Transform U.S. Policy," *Covert Action Quarterly* 63 (Winter 1998).

56. John D. McCarthy and Jim Castelli, *Working for Justice: The Campaign for Human Development and Poor Empowerment Groups* (Washington, D.C.: Life Cycle Institute, Catholic University of America, 1994), report that in its first twenty-five years, the CCHD funded 3,000 projects with a total of about $190 million.

57. See chapter 3 for a discussion of this issue.

58. For a discussion of the recent interest of private foundations in funding participatory democratic initiatives, see Koliba, "A Progress Report."

Chapter Two
A Theology of Organizing: From Alinsky to the Modern IAF

1. The following account comes from the author's interview with George Ozuna, May 30, 1994, San Antonio, Texas. Mary Beth Rogers provides a more extensive narrative in *Cold Anger: A Story of Faith and Power Politics* (Denton, Texas: University of North Texas Press, 1990), pp. 113–16.

2. Cortes' remarks to the Farm Crisis Workers Conference were published in Ernesto Cortes, Jr., "Organizing the Community," *Texas Observer*, July 11, 1986, p. 13.

3. Quoted in Harry C. Boyte, *Community Is Possible: Repairing America's Roots* (New York: Harper and Row, 1984), pp. 139–40.

4. Author's interview with Tom Frost, Jr., July 22, 1993, San Antonio, Texas. Frost is referring to Saul D. Alinsky, *Reveille for Radicals* (New York: Vintage, 1969) and *Rules for Radicals* (New York: Random House, 1971).

5. Sanford D. Horwitt has written an excellent biography of Saul Alinsky, which covers the evolution of his thought and organizing work, entitled *Let Them Call Me Rebel* (New York: Alfred A. Knopf, 1989). The account of Alinsky in this chapter also draws from David P. Finks, *The Radical Vision of Saul Alinsky* (New York: Paulist Press, 1984); Robert Slayton, *Back of the Yards* (Chicago: University of Chicago Press, 1986); Robert J. Bailey, *Radicals in Urban Politics: The Alinsky Approach* (Chicago: University of Chicago Press, 1974); Donald C. Reitzes and Dietrich C. Reitzes, *The Alinsky Legacy: Alive and Kicking* (Greenwich, CT: JAI Press, 1987); Neil Betten and Michael J. Austin, "The Conflict Approach to Community Organizing: Saul Alinsky and the CIO," in Neil Betten and Michael J. Austin, eds., *The Roots of Community Organizing, 1917–1939* (Philadelphia: Temple University Press, 1990), pp. 152–61; and Robert Fisher, *Let the People Decide: Neighborhood Organizing in America* (Boston: Twayne Publishers, 1984).

6. For further discussion of the BYNC, see Reitzes and Reitzes, *The Alinsky Legacy*, pp. 66–73; Bailey, *Radicals in Urban Politics*; Slayton, *Back of the Yards*, pp. 188–229.

7. For a detailed discussion of the link between Alinsky and the CIO, see Betten and Austin, "The Conflict Approach to Community Organizing."

8. For a further discussion of these projects, see Reitzes and Reitzes, *The Alinsky Legacy*, and Finks, *The Radical Vision of Saul Alinsky*.

9. Charles E. Silberman's book about The Woodlawn Organization, *Crisis in Black and White* (New York: Random House, 1964), brought Alinsky broad public recognition. For a further discussion of The Woodlawn Organization, see Reitzes and Reitzes, *The Alinsky Legacy*; Finks, *The Radical Vision of Saul Alinsky*; and Horwitt, *Let Them Call Me Rebel*.

10. For a further discussion of FIGHT, see Finks, *The Radical Vision of Saul Alinsky*; Reitzes and Reitzes, *The Alinsky Legacy*; and Horwitt, *Let Them Call Me Rebel*.

11. Reitzes and Reitzes discuss this project in more detail in *The Alinsky Legacy*.

12. Reitzes and Reitzes discuss the variety of organizing efforts that drew upon Alinsky's methods in *The Alinsky Legacy*.

13. See Bailey's discussion of Alinsky's project in the Austin area of Chicago in *Radicals in Urban Politics*.

14. As reported from his interview with John Egan by Harry C. Boyte, *Commonwealth: A Return to Citizen Politics* (New York: Free Press, 1989), p. 61.

15. Quoted in "Playboy Interview: Saul Alinsky," *Playboy Magazine*, March 1972.

16. On the fate of TWO, see Reitzes and Reitzes, *The Alinsky Legacy*, p. 83.

17. On the history of FIGHT, see Finks, *The Radical Vision of Saul Alinsky*, pp. 176–228.

18. On the situation of the IAF at the time of Alinsky's death, see Reitzes and Reitzes, *The Alinsky Legacy*, p. 93.

19. For a further discussion of Chamber's role in the IAF, see Reitzes and Reitzes, *The Alinsky Legacy*, pp. 92–100.

20. Rogers refers to San Antonio's Hispanic community as a "sleeping giant" in *Cold Anger*. The essays in David R. Johnson, John A. Booth, and Richard J. Harris, eds., *The Politics of San Antonio* (Lincoln: University of Nebraska Press, 1983), provide a good overview of the history and structure of politics in that city in the seventies. For a discussion of the Good Government League, see the essay in that volume by John A. Booth and David R. Johnson, "Power and Progress in San Antonio Politics, 1836–1970." On services, see the essay by Robert Brischetto, Charles L. Cottrell, and R. Michael Stevens, "Conflict and Change in the Political Culture of San Antonio in the 1970s." On the Hispanic occupational structure, see the essay by Richard J. Harris, "Mexican American Occupational Attainments in San Antonio: Comparative Assessments."

21. Rogers discusses the election in detail in *Cold Anger*, chapter 10.

22. Budget information for COPS reported by Rogers, *Cold Anger*, p. 107.

23. For a broader discussion of the impact of Vatican II on the American church, see Gene Burns, *The Frontiers of Catholicism: The Politics of Ideology in a Liberal World* (Berkeley: University of California Press, 1992). John T. McGreevy explores the impact of Vatican II on the church's relationship with African Americans in the urban North in *Parish Boundaries: The Catholic Encounter with Race in the Twentieth Century* (Chicago: University of Chicago Press, 1996).

24. For a further discussion of Catholic social action traditions in San Antonio, see Joseph D. Sekul, "The C.O.P.S. Story: A Case Study of Successful Collective Action" (Ph.D. dissertation, University of Texas at Austin, 1984), pp. 157–61.

25. Author's interview with Reverend Al Jost, July 8, 1993, San Antonio, Texas.

26. Peter Skerry, *Mexican Americans: The Ambivalent Minority* (New York: Free Press, 1993).

27. The account of PADRES and the activities of Hispanic priests in San Antonio draws from the author's interview with Reverend David Garcia, July 15, 1993, San Antonio, Texas.

28. Quotations from Ernesto Cortes, Jr., come from Rogers, *Cold Anger*, pp. 108, 123.

29. The following account is based on the author's interview with Beatrice Cortez, July 12, 1993, San Antonio, Texas.

30. When her tenure as COPS President expired in 1983, Beatrice Cortez quit her job and began working for the diocese. She traveled to the western end of the diocese near the Mexican border to help build a parish among rural immigrants and to address the needs of impoverished border communities. That work laid the foundation for The Border Organization, an IAF organization formed later in the Eagle Pass area. Mrs. Cortez became national chairperson of the Catholic Campaign for Human Development in 1985.

31. The consequences of segregation for San Antonio Hispanics is explored more fully by Rudolfo Rosales, "The Rise of Chicano Middle Class Politics in San Antonio 1951–1985 (Ph.D. dissertation, University of Michigan at Ann Arbor, 1991).

32. For a fuller discussion of the demographic composition of San Antonio's Hispanic population, see the study conducted by the Urban Institute, *Growth Without Prosperity: San Antonio's Experience in the New Economy* (San Antonio: Partnership for Hope, 1993).

33. For a detailed discussion of the aquifer controversy, see Sidney Plotkin, "Democratic Change in the Urban Political Economy: San Antonio's Edwards Aquifer Controversy," in David R. Johnson, John A. Booth, and Richard J. Harris, eds., *The Politics of San Antonio* (Lincoln: University of Nebraska Press, 1983), pp. 157–74.

34. Author's interview with Charles Cottrell, May 30, 1994, San Antonio, Texas. See also Roddy Stinson, "COPS Tastes Victory; ABC Takes Medicine," *San Antonio Express*, January 17, 1977. Heywood T. Sanders provides details on the racial split in voting for the charter change in "Communities Organized for Public Service and Neighborhood Revitalization in San Antonio," in Robert H. Wilson, ed., *Public Policy and Community: Activism and Governance in Texas* (Austin: University of Texas Press, 1997), pp. 36–68.

35. Joseph D. Sekul, "Communities Organized for Public Service: Citizen Power and Public Policy in San Antonio," in David R. Johnson, John A. Booth, and Richard J. Harris, eds., *The Politics of San Antonio* (Lincoln: University of Nebraska Press, 1983), pp. 175–90.

36. Sanders, "Communities Organized for Public Service."

37. Sanders discusses bond elections in more detail in "Communities Organized for Public Service."

38. I discuss the EDF conflict in more detail in chapter 6.

39. For a detailed discussion of the Alamodome controversy, see Nancy Kates, *The Battle of the Alamodome: Henry Cisneros and the San Antonio Stadium*, Case Program, John F. Kennedy School of Government (Cambridge: Harvard University Press, 1989).

40. Mariachi bands play at its annual conventions; and COPS has a *corrido*, a traditional Mexican American song, to tell its history.

41. Author's interview with Virginia Ramirez, May 22, 1993, San Antonio, Texas.

42. "COPS Tenth Anniversary Program," November 10, 1983.

43. Reitzes and Reitzes trace the history of UNO in *The Alinsky Legacy*. For a comparison of UNO and COPS, see Skerry, *Mexican Americans*. In 1999 UNO was absorbed into a larger Metro LA organizing effort by the IAF.

44. Author's interview with Beatrice Cortez, July 12, 1993, San Antonio, Texas.

45. Rogers discusses Cortes' early study of theology in *Cold Anger*, pp. 73–74.

46. Quoted in Rogers, *Cold Anger*, pp. 131–32.

47. Quoted in Rogers, *Cold Anger*, p. 132.

48. Discussions of Pentecost and Sinai in UNO come from Rogers, *Cold Anger*, pp. 133–35.

49. Author's personal observation, IAF National Training, July 13, 1994, Los Angeles, CA. A full account of how Cortes uses the story of Moses can be found in Cortes, "Organizing the Community."

50. Author's interview with Maribeth Larkin, April 26, 1993, Dallas, Texas. Larkin returned to Los Angeles in 1999 to assist Cortes in reorganizing and reinvigorating the IAF's efforts there.

51. Edward Chambers, *Organizing for Family and Congregation* (Hyde Park, NY: Industrial Areas Foundation, 1978), p. 33.

52. See Skerry, *Mexican Americans*, for a fuller discussion of these differences.

53. Author's interview with Ernesto Cortes, Jr., March 20, 1997, New York City.

54. Author's interview with Ernesto Cortes, Jr., March 20, 1997, New York City.

55. Author's interview with Christine Stephens, June 3, 1993, Dallas, Texas. Stephens now supervises the IAF's organizers in Texas and Louisiana. For a fuller discussion of the origins of TMO, see Rogers, *Cold Anger*, chapter 13.

56. On the economic and political history of Houston, see Joe R. Feagin, *Free Enterprise City: Houston in Political-Economic Perspective* (New Brunswick, NJ: Rutgers University Press, 1988).

57. Author's interview with Reverend Robert McGee, June 10, 1993, Houston, Texas.

58. See the papal encyclicals *Rerum Novarum*, *Quadragesimo Anno* and *Gaudium et Spes*, as well as the *Charter on the Rights of the Family*, collected in Donal Dorr, *Option for the Poor: A Hundred Years of Vatican Social Teaching* (Maryknoll, NY: Orbis Books, 1983).

59. From an untitled document in the files of the Southwest Interfaith Education Fund, dated August 1980. The document quotes from Philip Murnion, "The Complex Tasks of the Parish," *Origins* 8 (December 28, 1978): 431, 435–41.

60. See Rogers, *Cold Anger*, pp. 149–150.

61. Author's interviews with Reverend Claude Black, July 21, 1993, San Antonio, Texas, and Reverend Archield, July 16, 1993, San Antonio, Texas. Reverend Black eventually did join with the IAF in 1996.

62. For example, Metro Alliance played a key role in establishing the San Antonio Education Partnership, a joint initiative of COPS and Metro Alliance that provided scholarships and job opportunities to high school graduates who maintained standards for attendance and grades.

63. Bernard Loomer, "Two Conceptions of Power," *Criterion* (Winter 1976): 12–29. The IAF stresses this distinction in all of its training. Ernesto Cortes, Jr., elaborates the IAF's understanding of power in "Reweaving the Fabric: The Iron Rule and the IAF Strategy for Power and Politics," in Henry G. Cisneros, ed., *Interwoven Destinies: Cities and the Nation* (New York: W. W. Norton, 1993), pp. 294–319.

64. Author's interview with Reverend Homer Bain, May 24, 1995, San Antonio, Texas.

65. Richard L. Wood, "Faith in Action: Religion, Race, and the Future of Democracy" (Ph.D. dissertation, University of California, Berkeley, 1995), p. 361. Wood's dissertation, soon to be published in book form, contains an excellent, close examination of the symbiosis between religious and political culture created by faith based community organizing. See also Richard L. Wood, "Social Capital and Political Culture: God Meets Politics in the Inner City," *American Behavioral Scientist* 40 (March/April 1997): 595–605. My discussion of the transformation of PICO comes from Wood's dissertation. Conversations with Frank Pierson have contributed greatly to my understanding of what I call the synergy between faith and politics.

66. Author's interview with George Ozuna, May 30, 1994, San Antonio, Texas.

67. Author's interview with Patricia Ozuna, July 20, 1993, San Antonio, Texas.

Chapter Three
Beyond Local Organizing: Statewide Power and a Regional Network

1. This account of the events in El Paso draws from the author's interview with Ernesto Cortes, Jr., and Sister Christine Stephens, May 22, 1996, Austin, Texas, and from Mary Beth Rogers, *Cold Anger: A Story of Faith and Power Politics* (Denton: University of North Texas Press, 1990), pp. 162–65.

2. Quoted in Rogers, *Cold Anger*, p. 165.

3. Author's interview with Ernesto Cortes, Jr., and Sister Christine Stephens, May 22, 1996, Austin, Texas.

4. For a discussion of the role of subsidiarity in Catholic social thought, and its relationship to questions of American civil society, see Jean Bethke Elshtain, "Catholic Social Thought, the City, and Liberal America," in R. Bruce Douglass and David Hollenbach, eds., *Catholicism and Liberalism: Contributions to American Public Philosophy* (Cambridge: Cambridge University Press, 1994), pp. 151–71. Although the concept is foreign to most political discourse in America, the European Community has adopted the principle of subsidiarity to regulate relationships between the Community's central authority and the autonomy of member states. Here, the principle has proved quite malleable, so that, although it offers a presumption of precedence of lower-level over higher-level governance, the central authorities of the Community have been able to attain a growing degree of power; see Wolfgang Streeck, "From Market Making to State Building? Reflections on the Political Economy of European Social Policy," in Stephan Leib-

fied and Paul Pierson, eds., *European Social Policy: Between Fragmentation and Integration* (Washington, D.C.: Brookings Institution, 1995), pp. 389–431.

5. For a fuller discussion of the state utility campaign from the IAF's point of view, see Texas IAF Network, *Vision-Values-Action* (Austin: Texas IAF, 1990).

6. In Texas, the Lieutenant Governor, as head of the legislature, holds a more powerful position than in most other states.

7. Richard Lavine, who has studied the reform effort closely, reports that many key players credit the IAF with providing crucial support for the bill's passage. For a detailed discussion of the school reform effort and the IAF's role, see Richard Lavine, "School Finance Reform in Texas, 1983–1995," in Robert H. Wilson, ed., *Public Policy and Community: Activism and Governance in Texas* (Austin: University of Texas Press, 1997), pp. 119–65.

8. *Texas Monthly*, September 1991, p. 166; see also Texas IAF Network, *Vision-Values-Action*.

9. Author's interview with Ernesto Cortes, Jr., and Sister Christine Stephens, May 22, 1996, Austin, Texas.

10. Pat Wong, "The Indigent Health Care Package," in Robert H. Wilson, ed., *Public Policy and Community: Activism and Governance in Texas* (Austin: University of Texas Press, 1997), pp. 95–118.

11. "Border Group to Fight for Colonias, Poor," *San Antonio Light*, April 24, 1989, p. A1.

12. "Colonias' Poor Living Conditions Described to Federal Committee," *San Antonio Express-News*, May 16, 1989, p. A11.

13. Robert H. Wilson and Peter Menzies, "The Colonias Water Bill: Communities Demanding Change," in Robert H. Wilson, ed., *Public Policy and Community: Activism and Governance in Texas* (Austin: University of Texas Press, 1997), pp. 229–74 (251). This account draws in part from their work.

14. Texas IAF Network, *Vision-Values-Action*.

15. The Progressive, September 1990, p. 36.

16. Wilson and Menzies, "The Colonias Water Bill," p. 266.

17. Sam Howe Verhovek, "Long Wait for Water Ending on Texas Border," *New York Times*, October 27, 1997, pp. A1, A16.

18. *San Antonio Light*, October 29, 1990. Despite the formal existence of a state steering committee, the body never met regularly. Instead, Cortes called ad hoc meetings of leaders from around the state for specific purposes. Author's interviews with Ernesto Cortes, Jr., July 10, 1993, San Antonio, Texas, and with Reverend David Semrad, July 7, 1993, San Antonio, Texas.

19. Author's interview with Virginia Ramirez, May 23, 1996, San Antonio, Texas.

20. *Fort Worth Star-Telegram*, December 3, 1988, p. 1A, and September 20, 1992, p. 1F.

21. For details of the increase in concentrated poverty and neighborhood distress in large Texas cities, see John D. Kasarda, "Cities as Places Where People Live and Work: Urban Change and Neighborhood Distress," in Henry G. Cisneros, ed., *Interwoven Destinies: Cities and the Nation* (New York: W. W. Norton, 1994), pp. 81–124.

22. Robert H. Wilson, Pat Wong, and Heywood T. Sanders, "The Place of Community in Public Policy," in *Public Policy and Community: Activism and Governance in Texas* (Austin: University of Texas Press, 1997), pp. 14–35.

23. Dennis Shirley offers a detailed discussion of the Alliance Schools in his book-length treatment, *Community Organizing for Urban School Reform* (Austin: University of Texas Press, 1997). My discussion draws, in part, from this work.

24. Texas Interfaith Education Fund (TIEF), *The Texas IAF Vision for Public Schools: Communities of Learners* (Austin: TIEF, 1990), p. 10.

25. Author's interview with Odessa Ravin, August 24, 1993, Fort Worth, Texas.

26. Author's interview with Leonora Friend, August 30, 1993, Fort Worth, Texas.

27. Shirley, *Community Organizing*, pp. 214–20.

28. See the unpublished 1998 Year End Report of the Education Initiative, by the Texas Interfaith Education Fund, Austin, Texas.

29. This list comes from data supplied by the Texas Interfaith Education Fund to the Ford Foundation.

30. Cortes has a core group of senior organizers that have been with him for over 10 years, some for 15–20 years, including Christine Stephens, Maribeth Larkin, Pearl Ceasar, Tom Holler, Perry Perkins, Mignonne Konecny, Tim McCluskey, Consuelo Tovar, Joe Higgs, and Elizabeth Valdez.

31. From information supplied by the Texas Interfaith Education Fund. Funds from private foundations support projects of the network, specifically school-based reform and organizer training and development. They do not directly pay the salaries of IAF organizers or fund the political activity of IAF organizations.

32. Quotations from the author's interview with Julia Lerma, July 22, 1993, San Antonio, Texas.

33. The number of organizers recruited out of the ranks of IAF leaders is difficult to determine with precision. Some leaders were hired as organizers almost from the moment of their contact with the network and so are difficult to categorize. The increasing numbers of African American organizers, and their influence on the Southwest network, is discussed in more detail in chapter 5. Chapter 8 examines the relationship between organizers and leaders.

34. Texas ranks well above the national average in the percentage of its population that attend church: 63.5 percent of Texas residents are adherents of Christian churches, compared to 52.7 percent of the U.S. population as a whole; see Martin B. Bradley et al, *Churches and Church Membership in the United States 1990* (Atlanta: Glenmary Research Center, 1992). The precision of these figures is open to question because they are based on the self-reporting of church denominations. But they do suggest the general picture quite clearly.

35. See Bradley et al, *Churches and Church Membership*, tables 3 and 4.

36. Texas bishops have consistently endorsed IAF organizing in their diocese. This support has come in part because of the IAF's ability to tap the strains of Catholic social teaching that orient the church to an expanded role in combating poverty and social injustice. But the Catholic Church in Texas shares a close mate-

rial interest with the IAF. The health of the church depends very much upon the vitality of its Mexican American members, both the material well-being of their communities as well as their continued adherence to Catholicism. In other parts of the country, the center of gravity of the Catholic diocese has remained with white ethnic Catholics, even as the Hispanic population has grown. Although the Church is concerned with the inroads that Protestant evangelicals have made among Hispanic Catholics across the country, these gains have not threatened the continued viability of the Church itself. However in Texas, the Church lives or dies with its Hispanic members.

37. David Mayhew has rated states on a scoring system for traditional party organization, ranging from a low of one to a high of five. The state of Texas achieved an overall score of two. Except for Houston, Texas cities scored a rock-bottom rating of one; see *Placing Parties in American Politics* (Princeton: Princeton University Press, 1986).

38. In New York, where political and community organizations are much more entrenched, the IAF had to start its organizing on the outskirts, in Queens and East Brooklyn. According to the IAF's supervisor there, Michael Gecan (author's interviews, February 2, 1998, and May 5, 1998, New York City), "if we had started in Harlem or the South Bronx, we wouldn't be here today." In East Brooklyn, the IAF required its leaders who were members of the local community board to quit those positions, in order to make a clean break from what it saw as the corrupt system of "politics as usual."

39. By contrast, the IAF in New York has faced well-entrenched and intransigent institutional failure in the public education system. The network there has identified 200 educational "dead zones," poor communities that lack even one effective school; see "Futures Denied: Concentrated Failure in the New York City Public School System," A Report of Parents Organized to Win Education Reform: Industrial Areas Foundation-Metro NY and Public Education Association, March, 1997. Rather than partnering with public institutions, the New York IAF has had to attempt to found entirely new schools, taking advantage of a charter schools-like program within the public system. On New York IAF schools organizing, see Jim Rooney, *Organizing the South Bronx* (Albany: SUNY Press, 1995).

40. Since elites were never that well organized at the state level, the network did not face open efforts to crush its work in Austin, even at the early stages.

41. For an overview of Arizona politics, see David R. Berman, *Arizona Politics and Government: The Quest for Autonomy, Democracy and Development* (Lincoln: University of Nebraska Press, 1998).

42. Author's interview with Frank Pierson, October 1, 1999, Austin, Texas.

43. See Norman Peckham, "Council Funds JobPath Program," *Tucson Citizen*, January 27, 1998, and Blake Morlock, "Jobs Programs Get Big Boost," *Tucson Citizen*, June 10, 1998.

44. Joe Burchell, "$8-an-hour Wage for City Contracts OK'd," The *Arizona Daily Star*, September 14, 1999, pp. 1A, 4A.

45. Beverly Medlyn, "Eye on State's Future: Thousands Join Forces for Better Arizona," *Arizona Republic*, April 3, 2000, pp. B1, B5.

46. See chapter 9 for a discussion of this convention.

47. Author's interview with Reverend Nehemiah Davis, March 6, 1997, Fort Worth, Texas.

48. Quoted in Rogers, *Cold Anger*, p. 42.

Chapter Four
Bridging Communities across Racial Lines

1. Author's interview with Reverend D. L. Ellison, August 30, 1993, Fort Worth, Texas. Reverend Ellison worked for a time as an organizer for the IAF in Fort Worth. He later became the pastor of a different church and eventually was no longer active in ACT.

2. Cornel West, *Race Matters* (Boston: Beacon Press, 1993), pp. 6 and 11.

3. For analyses of electoral coalitions, see the collection of articles in Rufus P. Browning, Dale Rogers Marshall, and David H. Tabb, eds., *Racial Politics in American Cities*, 2nd edition (New York: Longman, 1997).

4. Raphael J. Sonenshein stresses these factors in his analysis of electoral coalitions in municipal elections, "The Prospects for Multiracial Coalitions: Lessons from America's Three Largest Cities," in Browning, Rogers, and Tabb, *Racial Politics in American Cities*, pp. 261–76.

5. William Julius Wilson, *The Bridge Over the Racial Divide: Rising Inequality and Coalition Politics* (Berkeley: University of California Press, 1999).

6. *Statistical Abstract of the United States*, 1981 edition, table 24; 1994 edition, table 46.

7. Scores computed and reported by John D. Kasarda in "Cities as Places Where People Live and Work: Urban Change and Neighborhood Distress," in Henry G. Cisneros, ed., *Interwoven Destinies: Cities and the Nation* (New York: W.W. Norton, 1993), pp. 81–124.

8. U.S. Department of Commerce, Bureau of the Census, *Population and Housing Characteristics for Census Tracts and Block Numbering Areas*, 1993.

9. These neighborhoods represented fourteen census tracts; see Kasarda, "Cities as Places."

10. For a discussion of the history of Fort Worth politics, see Carl Abbot, *The New Urban America: Growth and Politics in Sunbelt Cities* (Chapel Hill: University of North Carolina Press, 1981); and Martin V. Melosi, "Dallas-Fort Worth: Marketing the Metroplex," in Richard M. Bernard and Bradley R. Rice, eds., *Sunbelt Cities: Politics and Growth Since WWII* (Austin: University of Texas Press, 1983), pp. 162–95.

11. Author's interview with Jeff Guinn, August 26, 1994, Fort Worth, Texas.

12. Joyce E. Williams, *Black Community Control: A Study of Transition in a Texas Ghetto* (New York: Praeger, 1973).

13. See Melosi, "Dallas-Fort Worth."

14. Author's interview with Perry Perkins, June 5, 1993, Dallas, Texas.

15. Author's interview with Reverend Terry Boggs, June 8, 1993, Fort Worth, Texas.

16. Author's interview with Reverend Nehemiah Davis, June 8, 1993, Fort Worth, Texas.

17. Author's interview with Reverend Terry Boggs, June 8, 1993, Fort Worth, Texas.

18. Author's interview with Reverend Nehemiah Davis, June 8, 1993, Fort Worth, Texas.

19. Author's interview with Reverend Nehemiah Davis, June 8, 1993, Fort Worth, Texas.

20. Author's interview with Homer Bain, May 21, 1993, San Antonio, Texas.

21. Author's interview with Raymond Rodriguez, August 25, 1993, Fort Worth, Texas.

22. The state utility campaign is discussed more fully in chapter 3.

23. Dennis Shirley discusses ACT's campaign at Morningside in detail in *Community Organizing for Urban School Reform* (Austin: University of Texas Press, 1997), chapter 3. This account draws in part from Shirley's study as well as the author's own research.

24. Author's interview with Odessa Ravin, August 24, 1993, Fort Worth, Texas.

25. Author's interview with Reverend Nehemiah Davis, June 8, 1993, Fort Worth, Texas.

26. Author's interview with Reverend Nehemiah Davis, June 8, 1993, Fort Worth, Texas.

27. *Fort Worth Star-Telegram*, December 3, 1988, p. 1A, and September 20, 1992, p. 1F.

28. Author's interview with Odessa Ravin, August 24, 1993, Fort Worth, Texas.

29. Author's interview with Leonora Friend, August 30, 1993, Fort Worth, Texas.

30. Author's interview with Odessa Ravin, August 24, 1993, Fort Worth, Texas.

31. Author's interview with Perry Perkins, June 5, 1993, Dallas, Texas.

32. Sustaining parental involvement in Morningside itself, meanwhile, presented a challenge to the organization. Since students pass through the school in three years, the community of parents is not nearly as stable as the church members with whom the IAF was used to working. According to the author's interview with Morningside PTA President Donnie Lee, March 6, 1997, Fort Worth, Texas, by the 1996–97 school year, parental involvement had declined precipitously, and ACT had to launch another round of parental organizing. Despite some turnover in staff, teachers continued to develop new initiatives. According to the author's interview with Morningside teacher Barbara Cabbil, March 6, 1997, Fort Worth, Texas, these initiatives included a "Turning Points" experimental after-school program where students have hands-on experience in visual arts, photography, theater, dance, and journalism.

33. For evidence and discussion, see Barbara Ferman, *Challenging the Growth Machine: Neighborhood Politics in Chicago and Pittsburgh* (Lawrence: University Press of Kansas, 1996).

34. Author's interview with Jeff Guinn, August 26, 1993, Fort Worth, Texas. Details of the campaign are drawn from the *Fort Worth Star-Telegram*, September 20, 1992, p. 1F, and the author's interview with Reverend Terry Boggs, June 8, 1993, Fort Worth, Texas.

35. Author's interview with Jeff Guinn, August 26, 1993, Fort Worth, Texas. This account of the 1990 bond election also draws upon the author's interviews with former mayor Bob Bolen, August 24, 1993, ACT organizer Perry Perkins, August 25, 1993, and former city councilor David Chappell, August 27, 1993, all in Forth Worth, Texas.

36. Author's interview with Reverend Terry Boggs, March 6, 1997, Fort Worth, Texas.

37. Author's interview with Reverend Terry Boggs, March 6, 1997, Fort Worth, Texas.

38. Sources for this data come from ACT Ad Book 1993; various interviews by the author, including ACT organizer Perry Perkins, August 28, 1993, Fort Worth, Texas; and the author's observations.

39. Author's interview with Rosemary Galdiano, August 30, 1993, Fort Worth, Texas.

40. Author's interview with Joyce Oliver, August 26, 1993, Fort Worth, Texas.

41. Author's interview with Juanita Cisneros, August 29, 1993, Fort Worth, Texas.

42. Author's interview with Juanita Cisneros, August 29, 1993, Fort Worth, Texas.

43. Author's interview with Reverend Terry Boggs, June 8, 1993, Fort Worth, Texas.

44. The IAF stresses that it taps traditions relevant to both Jewish and Christian faiths. Several Jewish synagogues are involved in Texas IAF organizations. But ACT itself, however, contains no synagogues, and the vast majority of its participants are Christians.

45. Author's interview with Maurice Simpson, August 28, 1993, Fort Worth, Texas. Simpson sees religious prejudice as stronger than race, but not so easily identified. He credits ACT with bridging denominational as well as racial divisions by appealing to shared religious values.

46. Author's interview with Reverend Terry Boggs, June 8, 1993, Fort Worth, Texas.

47. Compiled from comments made by ACT leaders in planning a November 1993 ecumenical service at the ACT Leaders Retreat, August 28, 1993, Fort Worth, Texas.

48. The following account, and the biblical quotations, come from Mary Beth Rogers, *Cold Anger: A Story of Faith and Power Politics* (Denton, Texas: University of North Texas Press, 1990), pp. 153–54.

49. *Fort Worth Star-Telegram*, August 26, 1993, p. 15A.

50. *New York Times*, March 25, 1993, p. A9(N). Brosky was later tried under Texas' organized crime law, convicted, and sentenced to forty years in prison.

51. Many ACT participants asked to speak off the record on the Brosky incident. The reasons discussed in the text are compiled from the author's interviews with Perry Perkins, August 28, 1993; Leonora Friend, August 30, 1993; Maurice

Simpson, August 28, 1993; Raymond Rodriguez, August 25, 1993; Monte Elliot, August 30, 1993; Claudia Camp, August 30, 1993; Reverend D. L. Ellison, August 30, 1993; Reverend C. M. Singleton, August 27, 1993; all conducted in Fort Worth, Texas.

52. Author's interview with Claudia Camp, March 6, 1997, Fort Worth, Texas.

53. Author's interview with Claudia Camp, March 6, 1997, Fort Worth, Texas.

54. Author's interview with Reverend Nehemiah Davis, March 6, 1997, Fort Worth, Texas.

55. This argument is based on interview material from a number of ACT leaders, many of whom wished their comments to remain confidential on this issue.

56. Author's interview with Reverend Nehemiah Davis, March 6, 1997, Fort Worth, Texas.

57. Author's interview by telephone with Perry Perkins, October 28, 1999.

58. Byrd took over as lead organizer in Fort Worth when Perry Perkins transferred to become the lead organizer of the Southwest IAF's new affiliate in New Orleans, the Jeremiah Group. The IAF has a practice of rotating lead organizers every five years in order to mitigate against their dominance in a local affiliate. This rotation policy, and the broader issue of the relationship between organizers and leaders, is discussed in greater detail in chapter 8.

59. With the new organizer, ACT started working with several new Alliance Schools, and rebuilt its initiative at Morningside Middle School. The organization also won funding for after-school programs from the city. Byrd (author's interview, March 3, 1997, Fort Worth, Texas) planned to extend ACT's work in schools by pioneering a cooperative relationship with the Fort Worth Parent Teacher Association. She also intended to expand the organization into the surrounding suburban areas in Tarrant County by addressing emerging issues like the lack of adequate public transportation. By 1999, however, Byrd's reorganizing efforts had not proved successful enough. She left to work with an organizing team expanding the IAF's work in Houston, and Willie Bennett, another black IAF organizer, took over in Fort Worth.

Chapter Five
Deepening Multiracial Collaboration

1. For a range of examples, see Robert L. Allen, *Reluctant Reformers: Racism and Social Reform Movements in the United States* (Washington, D.C.: Howard University Press, 1974).

2. Author's interview with Ernesto Cortes, Jr., March 20, 1997, New York, New York.

3. Author's interview with Reverend Claude Black, May 23, 1996, San Antonio, Texas.

4. Author's interview with Christine Stephens, June 3, 1993, Dallas, Texas.

5. Quotations from Bennett come from the author's interview with Willie Bennett, May 22, 1996, Austin, Texas.

6. Author's interview with Perry Perkins, September 21, 1995, San Antonio, Texas.

7. Author's interview with Reverend Claude Black, May 23, 1996, San Antonio, Texas. New young organizers like Sean Howe also pushed the network to discuss racism more openly; author's interview with Sean Howe, March 4, 1997, Dallas, Texas.

8. Author's interview with Maribeth Larkin, March 8, 1997, Austin, Texas. The list of guests is taken from data supplied by the Texas Interfaith Education Fund.

9. Quotations come from the author's interview with Bruce Fortner, March 7, 1997, Austin, Texas.

10. Author's interview with Reverend Gerald Britt, March 2, 1997, Dallas, Texas.

11. Author's interview with Maribeth Larkin, March 8, 1997, Austin, Texas.

12. Quotations come from the author's interview with Ernesto Cortes, Jr., March 20, 1997, New York, New York.

13. Author's interview with Ernesto Cortes, Jr., May 23, 1996, Austin, Texas.

14. Author's interview with Ernesto Cortes, Jr., March 20, 1997, New York, New York.

15. Author's interview with Christine Stephens, June 3, 1993, Dallas, Texas.

16. The following account draws from Darwin Payne, *Big D: Triumphs and Troubles of an American Supercity in the 20th Century* (Dallas: Three Forks Press, 1994).

17. Jim Schutze, *The Accommodation: The Politics of Race in an American City* (Secaucus, NJ: Citadel Press, 1986), p. 184.

18. Payne, *Big D*, p. 387.

19. Quoted in Robert Wilonsky, "A Kinder, Gentler Citizens Council?" Dallas *Observer*, December 24–December 30, 1992.

20. *Texas Catholic*, February 14, 1992.

21. *Dallas Morning News*, January 2, 1993. Cited in Payne, *Big D*, p. 395.

22. Data on black employment gains in the police and school department, and in city contracts, come from Payne, *Big D*, pp. 404, 410, and 414.

23. John D. Kasarda, "Cities as Places Where People Live and Work: Urban Change and Neighborhood Distress," in Henry G. Cisneros, ed., *Interwoven Destinies: Cities and the Nation* (New York: W.W. Norton, 1993), pp. 81–124. For these purposes, a poor neighborhood is defined as a census tract where more than 20 percent of the population lives below the federal poverty line.

24. Payne, *Big D*, p. 413.

25. By 1997 Hispanic children accounted for 45 percent of the students in the Dallas Independent School District, compared to 42 percent for blacks; see Dallas Independent School District February 15, 1997 Report Submitted to the Court on the Implementation of the Court Order Granting Unitary Status (Civil Action No. CA-3-4211-H).

26. From a leaflet in the possession of Reverend Gerald Britt.

27. See Schutze, *The Accommodation,* for a fuller discussion of the history of racism in Dallas and efforts by the black community to resist racial oppression.

28. Author's interview with William Farmer, March 5, 1997, Dallas, Texas.

29. The following account draws from Schutze, *The Accommodation*.

30. Author's interview with William Farmer, March 5, 1997, Dallas, Texas.

31. See Schutze, *The Accommodation*, chapter 30 for a further discussion of the civil rights movement in Dallas.

32. Quotations from the author's interview with Reverend Barry Jackson, March 4, 1997, Dallas, Texas.

33. Quotations come from the author's interview with Reverend Gerald Britt, March 2, 1997, Dallas, Texas.

34. Author's interview with Reverend Ignacio Cizur, June 4, 1993, Dallas, Texas.

35. The demoralization of some residents was evident from the author's observation of the "Fish Fry and Core Leaders Meeting" of Saint Cecilia's Catholic Church, June 4, 1993, Dallas, Texas.

36. Author's interview with Maribeth Larkin, March 8, 1997, Austin, Texas.

37. *Texas Catholic*, November 6, 1992.

38. Quotations come from the author's interview with Tony Fleo, March 2, 1997, Dallas, Texas.

39. Author's interview with Reverend Gordon Roesch, March 4, 1997, Dallas, Texas.

40. From comments made by Christine Stephens at an Organizer's Seminar of the Southwest IAF network, March 7, 1997, Austin, Texas, as recorded by the author.

41. Author's interview with Reverend Gordon Roesch, March 4, 1997, Dallas, Texas. "Cultural Critique Curriculum: A Proposal" by Gordon A. Roesch, May 1995.

42. Author's interview with Reverend Gordon Roesch, March 4, 1997, Dallas, Texas.

43. *Dallas Morning News*, March 21, 1994.

44. Dallas schools are widely seen to be performing poorly in educating the largely black and Hispanic student body. The district's scores on the Scholastic Assessment Test average in the lowest ten percent nationally.

45. Data on Roosevelt High School come from *Dallas Morning News*, September 14, 1992.

46. *Texas Catholic*, June 19, 1992.

47. Author's interview with Maryann Jenkins and Charmaine Bentley, March 4, 1997, Dallas, Texas.

48. Author's interview with Melvin Traylor, March 4, 1997, Dallas, Texas.

49. Quoted in the *Dallas Morning News*, September 14, 1992.

50. Author's interview with Maryann Jenkins and Charmaine Bentley, March 4, 1997, Dallas, Texas.

51. Author's interview with Melvin Traylor, March 4, 1997, Dallas, Texas.

52. Dennis Shirley provides some of these details in the brief discussion of Roosevelt High School he offers in his book-length treatment of Alliance Schools across Texas, *Community Organizing for Urban School Reform* (Austin: University of Texas Press, 1997), pp. 208–9, 217–18.

53. Author's interview with Maryann Jenkins and Charmaine Bentley, March 4, 1997, Dallas, Texas.

54. Quoted in Shirley, *Community Organizing*, p. 218.

55. Author's interview with Melvin Traylor, March 4, 1997, Dallas, Texas.

56. *Dallas Morning News*, July 21, 1994.

57. Shirley, *Community Organizing*, p. 209.

58. Author's interview with Melvin Traylor, March 4, 1997, Dallas, Texas.

59. Dallas Independent School District February 15, 1997 Report Submitted to the Court (No. CA-3–4211-H, Appendix A).

60. Author's interview with Maryann Jenkins and Charmaine Bentley, March 4, 1997, Dallas, Texas.

61. Author's interview with Maribeth Larkin, March 3, 1997, Dallas, Texas.

62. Quoted in Robert Wilonsky, "A Kinder, Gentler Citizens Council?" Dallas *Observer*, December 24–December 30, 1992.

63. From comments made by Steve Bartlett, as recorded by the author, June 8, 1993, Dallas, Texas.

64. Quoted in the *Dallas Morning News*, September 13, 1995.

65. Quoted in the *Dallas Morning News*, September 12, 1995.

66. Quoted in the *Dallas Morning News*, September 12, 1995.

67. Dallas *Observer*, n.d., 1996.

68. Quoted in Dallas *Observer*, n.d., 1996.

69. Author's interview with Jose Plata, March 5, 1997, Dallas, Texas.

70. Author's interview with Yvonne Ewell, March 2, 1997, Dallas, Texas.

71. Author's interview with Reverend Barry Jackson, March 4, 1997, Dallas, Texas.

72. Author's interview with Reverend Gordon Roesch, March 3, 1997, Dallas, Texas.

73. *Dallas Morning News*, August 24, 1996; December 12, 1996.

74. Author's interview with Maribeth Larkin, March 3, 1997, Dallas, Texas.

75. Author's interview with Reverend Gerald Britt, March 2, 1997, Dallas, Texas.

76. See, for example, Gary Delgado, *Beyond the Politics of Place: New Directions in Community Organizing in the 1990s* (Oakland, CA: Applied Research Center, n.d.); J. Phillip Thompson, "Universalism and Deconcentration: Why Race Still Matters in Poverty and Economic Development," *Politics & Society* 26 (June 1998): 181–219; and James Jennings, "The Politics of Black Empowerment in Urban America: Reflections on Race, Class, and Community," in Joseph M. Kling and Prudence S. Posner, eds., *Dilemmas of Activism* (Philadelphia: Temple University Press, 1990), pp. 113–33.

77. See, for example, Kwame Ture and Charles V. Hamilton, *Black Power: The Politics of Liberation* (New York: Vintage Books, 1992).

78. Cornel West, *Race Matters* (Boston, Beacon Press, 1993), p. 13.

79. Interview with Reverend Gerald Britt, March 2, 1997, Dallas, Texas.

80. Interview with Reverend Gerald Britt, March 2, 1997, Dallas, Texas.

Chapter Six
Effective Power: Campaigning for Community-Based Policy Initiatives

1. This account draws from the author's interview with Patricia Ozuna, July 20, 1993, San Antonio, Texas. See also, San Antonio *Light*, September 4, 1991.

2. See, for example, John B. Judis, "The Pressure Elite: Inside the Narrow World of Advocacy Group Politics," *American Prospect* 9 (1992): 15–30.

3. See, for example, Randy Stoecker, "The CDC Model of Urban Redevelopment: A Critique and an Alternative," *Journal of Urban Affairs* 19 (1997): 1–22.

4. On prospects and tensions in community participation in Comprehensive Community Initiatives, see *Voices from the Field* (Washington, D.C.: The Aspen Institute). On the importance of local knowledge, see James C. Scott, *Seeing Like a State* (New Haven: Yale University Press, 1998).

5. William Julius Wilson documents the economic decline of the inner city and its consequences in *When Work Disappears: The World of the New Urban Poor* (New York: A. A. Knopf, 1996) . For a discussion of the failure of public schools and its links to inner city decline, see Jean Anyon, *Ghetto Schooling: A Political Economy of Urban Educational Reform* (New York: Teachers College Press, 1997).

6. The Clinton administration placed a priority on increasing funding to job-training programs and reforming them, in part, by learning from community-based innovations like Project QUEST. See James Bennet, "Clinton to Seek $1 Billion for 'Skills Gap'," *New York Times*, January 29, 1999.

7. Paul Osterman and Brenda A. Lautsch, *Project QUEST: A Report to the Ford Foundation* (Cambridge, MA: M.I.T. Sloan School of Management, 1996). The report's findings are discussed in detail below.

8. San Antonio *Express-News*, April 1, 1996.

9. Author's interview with Reverend Will Wauters, May 2, 1993, San Antonio, Texas.

10. San Antonio *Light*, October 26, 1977; Southside *Sun*, January 19, 1978.

11. San Antonio *Express*, March 23, 1978.

12. "Joint Statement of San Antonio Communities Organized for Public Service and San Antonio Economic Development Foundation," May 30, 1978.

13. Nancy Kates, *The Battle of the Alamodome: Henry Cisneros and the San Antonio Stadium*, Case Program, John F. Kennedy School of Government (Cambridge: Harvard University Press, 1989).

14. Urban Institute, *Growth without Prosperity: San Antonio's Experience in the New Economy* (San Antonio: Partnership for Hope, 1993).

15. Author's interview with Steve Amberg, July 1, 1993, San Antonio, Texas.

16. Author's interview with Father Al Jost, July 8, 1993, San Antonio, Texas.

17. As recorded by the author from a talk given by Patricia Ozuna at a meeting of COPS on May 28, 1994, San Antonio, Texas.

18. Author's interview with Reverend Will Wauters, May 20, 1993, San Antonio, Texas.

19. Author's interview with Patricia Ozuna, July 20, 1993, San Antonio, Texas.

20. For a critique of federal Job Training Partnership Act programs, see Sar A. Levitan and Garth L. Mangum, *Federal Human Resource Policy: From Kennedy to Clinton* (Washington, D.C.: The George Washington University Center for Social Policy Studies, 1994), p. 38.

21. Author's interview with Patricia Ozuna, July 20, 1993, San Antonio, Texas.

22. Author's interview with Tom Frost, Jr., July 22, 1993, San Antonio, Texas.

23. Author's interview with Patricia Ozuna, July 20, 1993, San Antonio, Texas.

24. Author's interview with Patricia Ozuna, July 20, 1993, San Antonio, Texas. COPS preceded the city council meeting with visits to the editorial boards of the local newspapers to begin to lobby them for a positive attitude towards the job-training program. See, for example, San Antonio *Light*, January 31, 1991, p. B4.

25. San Antonio *Express-News*, March 11, 1991.

26. San Antonio *Express-News*, April 15, 1991, p. B1.

27. See, for example, the comments of Dallas officials in chapter 5.

28. A wide variety of public officials have corroborated this practice in interviews with the author, including city councilors Roger Perez (July 15, 1993, San Antonio, Texas) and Juan Solis (July 15, 1993, San Antonio, Texas).

29. For a city of its size, San Antonio ranks relatively low in per capita revenues and expenditures; see Urban Institute, *Growth without Prosperity*.

30. See, for example, San Antonio *Express-News*, March 19, 1991.

31. Candidate Van Archer refused to support the program. Candidate Jimmy Hasslocher declined to attend the session. San Antonio *Light*, April 15, 1991, p. B1; San Antonio *Express-News*, April 15, 1991.

32. San Antonio *Express-News*, May 14, 1991, p. F1.

33. San Antonio *Express-News*, July 9, 1991.

34. Author's interview with Tom Holler, July 10, 1993, San Antonio, Texas.

35. Patricia Ozuna (author's interview, July 20, 1993, San Antonio, Texas) described those efforts: "In negotiations with the governor, a couple of COPS people would go and sit with her and her staff. Once she said okay [to QUEST], it was a lot of work with her staff on the source of money, how much, the design of the program. The essence of our plan stayed."

36. San Antonio *Express-News*, November 18, 1991, p. 1A.

37. San Antonio *Light*, June 27, 1991.

38. San Antonio *Light*, September 4, 1991, p. D1. The final figure was $2 million.

39. Author's interview with Father Al Jost, July 8, 1993, San Antonio, Texas.

40. "Project QUEST Expenditure Report," March 31, 1993. Project QUEST, San Antonio, Texas.

41. According to city council member Roger Perez (author's interview July 15, 1993, San Antonio, Texas) who sat in on some of the meetings.

42. Author's interview with Patricia Ozuna, July 20, 1993, San Antonio, Texas.

43. San Antonio *Light*, September 1, 1991.

44. The six city councilors were Linda Billa Burke, Walter Martinez, Roger Perez, Frank Pierce, Bob Thompson, and Frank Wing. San Antonio *Light*, September 4, 1991. Author's interview with Patricia Ozuna, July 20, 1993, San Antonio, Texas.

45. San Antonio *Light*, September 13, 1991.

46. San Antonio *Express-News*, November 18, 1991, p. 1A.

47. Author's interview with Patricia Ozuna, July 20, 1993, San Antonio, Texas.

48. San Antonio *Light*, July 22, 1992.

49. Robert McPherson and Brian Deaton, *The Job Training Demonstration Project. Phase 1: The Conceptual Design* (Unpublished manuscript, 1992).

50. In some cases, they did agree to include one or two companies that promised rapid advancement to higher-paying jobs for trainees initially hired below the minimum pay level. Author's interview with QUEST board chairman Charles E. Cheever, Jr., July 21, 1993, San Antonio, Texas.

51. Sister Gabrielle Lohan (author's interview, July 7, 1993, San Antonio, Texas) said the IAF was quite clear on that point.

52. San Antonio *Express-News*, September 28, 1992.

53. Author's interview with Reverend Will Wauters, May 20, 1993, San Antonio, Texas.

54. Author's interview with Sister Gabrielle Lohan, July 7, 1993, San Antonio, Texas.

55. Author's interview with Genevieve Flores, May 21, 1993, San Antonio, Texas.

56. Author's interview with Mary and Pasquale Segovia, July 16, 1993, San Antonio, Texas.

57. Author's interview with Ruth Asher, July 8, 1993, San Antonio, Texas.

58. Statistics supplied by Project QUEST, Inc., San Antonio, Texas.

59. Author's interview with QUEST counselor Connie Zuniga, July 19, 1993, San Antonio, Texas.

60. Statistics supplied by Project QUEST, Inc., May 31, 1994. Of the participants 71.4% were Hispanic, 12% black, and 16.6% white; 61.4% were women compared to 38.6% men; 35.4% were single parents (mostly women). The average age was 29.4 years old.

61. Author's interview with Reverend Will Wauters, May 20, 1993, San Antonio, Texas.

62. From remarks recorded by the author at the COPS Twentieth Anniversary Convention, May 29, 1994, San Antonio, Texas.

63. Author's interview with Reverend Will Wauters, May 20, 1993, San Antonio, Texas.

64. "Council District Summary Report," Project QUEST, Inc., July 19, 1993.

65. QUEST Executive Director Jack Salvadore (author's interview, July 19, 1993, San Antonio, Texas) reported that there has been no "political heat" from areas outside of QUEST's concentration in the west, south, and east sides.

66. Author's interview with Genevieve Flores, May 21, 1993, San Antonio, Texas.

67. Author's interview with Ruth Asher, July 8, 1993, San Antonio, Texas.

68. Author's interview with Gabriela Guerra and Mary Rivas, July 20, 1993, San Antonio, Texas.

69. Osterman, *Project QUEST*, pp. 19–20.

70. San Antonio *Business Journal* V8, No. 15, April 29–May 5, 1994, p. 1. The identity of QUEST's opponents remains unclear.

71. As recorded by the author, May 29, 1994, San Antonio, Texas.

72. San Antonio *Light*, May 29, 1992.

73. Author's telephone interview with QUEST staff member Cliff Borofsky, March 30, 1995. By the time of the 1994 vote, the PIC board had once again been reorganized and given another new name, the Alamo Workforce Development Council.

74. Charlotte-Anne Lucas, "$525,000 Sweetens Project QUEST Purse," San Antonio *Express-News*, March 27, 1996, pp. 1D, 2D.

75. Author's interview with Charles E. Cheever, Jr., July 21, 1993, San Antonio, Texas.

76. See "Treading Water: The Stagnation of Family Incomes Since 1973," Austin, Texas: Texas Interfaith Education Fund, August 27, 1993; "Declining Middle: The Polarization of Job Quality," Austin, Texas: Texas Interfaith Education Fund, April 20, 1993; and "Every Step Seems Down: The Chaos of Labor Market Entry and Promotion," Austin, Texas: Texas Interfaith Education Fund, August 29, 1993.

77. The document underwent a series of revisions, none of which was ever declared final. The following quotations are drawn from the last draft version ever produced, entitled "Southwest IAF Vision for Work," Short Version 1.3 of February 7, 1994, Austin, Texas: Texas Interfaith Education Fund. Accounts of proceedings at meetings come from the author's personal observation of Southwest IAF "meetings on work," held on June 5, 1993, Dallas, Texas, and July 10, 1993, San Antonio, Texas.

78. The vision paper quotes from Arthur Okun, *Equality and Efficiency: The Big Tradeoff* (Washington, D.C.: Brookings Institution, 1975), p. 199.

79. Osterman and Lautsch, *Project QUEST*. In addition, Project QUEST reports that its trainees have very high retention rates in the community colleges that provide most of QUEST training. According to QUEST staff member Cliff Borofsky (author's telephone interview, March 30, 1995), their grades are above the average for community college students.

80. Data on 1998 come from Project QUEST, Inc., as reported in the Interfaith Education Fund's 1998 Annual Report for Re-organizing Work Projects.

81. The discussion of community colleges draws from Osterman and Lautsch, *Project QUEST*, as well as from the author's interviews.

82. See Osterman and Lautsch, *Project QUEST*, for a fuller discussion of the impact of the program on San Antonio's business community.

83. Data on program withdrawal and remediation reported in Osterman and Lautsch, *Project QUEST*.

84. From data reported by Osterman, *Project QUEST*, p. 44.

85. Untitled memo in the files of the Texas Interfaith Education Fund, dated June 2, 1993.

86. Details in the following discussion of new initiatives are drawn from the Interfaith Education Fund's 1998 Annual Report for Re-organizing Work Projects, Texas Interfaith Education Fund, Austin, Texas.

87. See the letter from Governor Ann Richards to President William Jefferson Clinton, dated January 25, 1993, reprinted in Brett Campbell, *Investing in People: The Story of Project QUEST* (San Antonio: Communities Organized for Public Service and Metro Alliance, 1994), p. 33.

88. San Antonio *Express-News*, April 1, 1996, p. 1A.

89. See, for example, Bennett Harrison, *Building Bridges: Community Development Corporations and the World of Employment Training*, A Report to the Ford Foundation, September 1994.

90. Harrison, *Building Bridges*, p. 53.

91. Author's interview with Father Rosendo Urrabazo, July 19, 1993, San Antonio, Texas.

Chapter Seven
Congregational Bases for Political Action

1. Richard L. Wood, "Social Capital and Political Culture: God Meets Politics in the Inner City," *American Behavioral Scientist* 40 (March/April 1997): 595–605, stresses a different contribution of faith traditions. He shows how shared symbolic meanings help congregants make sense of politics and thereby project power in the public arena.

2. Author's interview with Frank Pierson, October 1, 1999, Austin, Texas.

3. From data supplied by the Texas Interfaith Education Fund, Austin, Texas.

4. As recorded by the author, May 29, 1994, San Antonio, Texas.

5. Data on ACT come from the author's interview with lead organizer Perry Perkins, August 25, 1993, Fort Worth, Texas.

6. Exactly how to defend those rights has often been controversial, especially in Latin America, where the Pope opposed liberation theology. For a more thorough discussion of Catholic social thought, see Donal Dorr, *Option for the Poor: A Hundred Years of Vatican Social Teaching* (Maryknoll, NY: Orbis Books, 1983).

7. On liberation theology, see Daniel H. Levine, *Popular Voices in Latin American Catholicism* (Princeton: Princeton University Press, 1992). For a further discussion comparing the IAF to base communities, see Mary Beth Rogers, *Cold Anger: A Story of Faith and Power Politics* (Denton: University of North Texas Press, 1990), pp. 136–39.

8. *Gaudium et Spes: Pastoral Constitution of the Church in the Modern World, 1965*, reprinted in David J. O'Brien and Thomas A. Shannon, *Renewing the Earth: Catholic Documents on Peace, Justice and Liberation* (Garden City, NY: Image Books, 1977), p. 200.

9. Ernesto Cortes, Jr., "Reflections on the Catholic Tradition of Family Rights," in John A. Coleman, ed., *One Hundred Years of Catholic Social Thought* (Maryknoll, N.Y.: Orbis Books, 1991), pp. 155–71.

10. Author's interview with Reverend Mike Haney, July 19, 1993, San Antonio, Texas. A pastoral obligation to respond to the parish's social and economic needs was expressed in many interviews conducted with IAF-affiliated priests, including Father Al Jost, July 8, 1993; Father James Janish, May 27, 1994; Father Ed Pavlicek, July 9, 1993; Father Mike Haney, July 19, 1993; all in San Antonio, Texas; and Father Ignacio Cizur, June 4, 1993, Dallas, Texas.

11. For a broader discussion of the changing role of laity in the church, see William V. D' Antonio et al., *American Catholic Laity in a Changing Church* (Kansas City: Sheed & Ward, 1989). On the changing roles of men and women in the Catholic Church, see Mark Chaves, *Ordaining Women: Culture and Conflict in Religious Organizations* (Cambridge: Harvard University Press, 1997).

12. Peter Skerry, *Mexican Americans: The Ambivalent Minority* (New York: Free Press, 1993), pp. 166–73 offers a related, but somewhat different discussion of the organizational affinity between the IAF and the Catholic Church. He emphasizes, one-sidedly in my view, the hierarchical nature of the two organizations.

13. The encouragement and support of bishops was mentioned in many interviews with priests, for example, author's interview with Father James Janish, May 27, 1994, San Antonio, Texas.

14. Author's interview with Reverend Rosendo Urrabazo, July 19, 1993, San Antonio, Texas.

15. According to Skerry, *Mexican Americans*, p. 190, perhaps as much as 10 percent of San Antonio's Hispanic population was Protestant by the mid-eighties. See Rodolfo O. De la Garza and Robert Brischetto, *The Mexican American Electorate: A Demographic Profile*, Hispanic Population Studies Program, Occasional Paper No. 1 (San Antonio: Southwest Voters Registration Education Project; and Austin: Center for Mexican American Studies, University of Texas, 1982), p. 10. On the challenge posed by evangelism to the Catholic Church nationally, see Eleace King, *Proselytism and Evangelization: An Exploratory Study* (Washington, D.C.: Center for Applied Research in the Apostate, Georgetown University, 1991).

16. See chapter 2 for a further discussion of parish development.

17. See the discussion of Beatrice Cortez and St. Patrick's parish in chapter 2. A number of lay women leaders of COPS mentioned experiencing both cooperation and conflict with priests as they came to assert more leadership in the parish.

18. There are several sources for this conclusion: the author's personal observation; examination of active committee member lists of the organizations; and the author's interviews with several Catholic pastors, for example, Father James Janish, May 27, 1994, San Antonio, Texas.

19. Author's interview with Pauline Cabello, July 21, 1993, San Antonio, Texas. Emphasis made by Cabello.

20. Author's interview with Patricia Ozuna, July 20, 1993, San Antonio, Texas. The "banging heads" reference was mentioned at the end of chapter 2.

21. Author's interview with Beatrice Cortez, July 12, 1993, San Antonio, Texas.

22. See James H. Cone, *Black Theology and Black Power* (New York: Seabury, 1969); and Cornel West, *Prophesy Deliverance! An Afro-American Revolutionary Christianity* (Philadelphia: Westminster, 1982).

23. See C. Eric Lincoln and Lawrence H. Mamiya, *The Black Church in the African American Experience* (Durham, NC: Duke University Press, 1990); and Mary Pattillo-McCoy, "Church Culture as a Strategy of Action in the Black Community," *American Sociological Review* 63 (1998): 767–84.

24. Aldon Morris, *The Origins of the Civil Rights Movement: Black Communities Organizing for Change* (New York: Free Press, 1984).

25. Katherine Tate, *From Protest to Politics: The New Black Voters in American Elections* (New York: Russell Sage Foundation, 1991). For a thorough discussion of the role of African American religion in politics, see Frederick C. Harris, *Something Within: Religion in African-American Political Activism* (New York: Oxford University Press, 1999).

26. Two of the IAF's most successful and long-established organizations are predominantly black, East Brooklyn Congregations and BUILD in Baltimore.

27. Author's interview with Ernesto Cortes, Jr., May 23, 1996, Austin, Texas.

28. See the discussion of the views and experience of Reverend Claude Black and other black ministers in chapters 2 and 5.

29. Author's interview with Reverend Barry Jackson, March 4, 1997, Dallas, Texas.

30. For a treatment of the social and political activist traditions in COGIC, see Robert Michael Franklin, 'My Soul Says Yes': The Urban Ministry of the Church of God in Christ," in Clifford J. Green, ed., *Churches, Cities, and Human Community: Urban Ministry in the United States 1945–1985* (Grand Rapids, MI: Eerdmans Publishing, 1996). Omar M. McRoberts discusses the more recent entry of black Pentecostal churches into social and political action in Boston in "Understanding the 'New' Black Pentecostal Activism: Lessons from Ecumenical Urban Ministries in Boston," *Sociology of Religion* 60 (Spring 1999): 47–70.

31. Baptists represent the largest African American denomination and make up the vast majority of black churches in the Texas IAF. Some African Methodist Episcopal churches are also involved. Black Methodist congregations are not quite as fiercely independent as Baptist ones.

32. See the discussions in chapters 4 and 5.

33. Sidney Verba, Kay Lehman Scholzman, and Henry E. Brady, *Voice and Equality: Civic Voluntarism in American Politics* (Cambridge: Harvard University Press, 1995), chapter 11.

34. For an extensive discussion of these issues, see Harris, *Something Within.*

35. There are a couple of exceptions where the black minister is not involved in the IAF organization. But, in these cases, the church as a whole is currently inactive in the IAF, although officially still a member.

36. For a related discussion of African American Protestant participation in the IAF, see Skerry, *Mexican Americans*, pp. 166–68. Skerry argues that the entrepreneurial nature of black pastorship makes the minister fiercely independent and generally difficult to organize into any collective process.

37. Author's interview with Reverend Gerald Britt, March 2, 1997, Dallas, Texas.

38. Author's interview with Reverend Barry Jackson, March 4, 1997, Dallas, Texas.

39. Based upon the author's analysis of membership data supplied by COPS, Metro Alliance, and ACT.

40. Author's interview with Maurice Simpson, August 28, 1993, Fort Worth, Texas.

41. Author's interview with Reverend Barry Jackson, March 4, 1997, Dallas, Texas.

42. The absence of Southern Baptists is discussed in the concluding chapter of the book.

43. This conclusion is based on the analysis of turnout figures primarily for ACT in Fort Worth and Metro Alliance in San Antonio, presented at the beginning of this chapter, and is compatible with the author's observations of the actions of other network organizations.

44. On the support of mainline Protestants for the IAF in the sixties, see P. David Finks, *The Radical Vision of Saul Alinsky* (New York: Paulist Press, 1984).

45. Author's interview with Reverend Homer Bain, May 24, 1995, San Antonio, Texas. On the social gospel tradition, see, for example, Ronald C. White, Jr., and C. Howard Hopkins, *The Social Gospel: Religion and Reform in Changing America* (Philadelphia: Temple University Press, 1976). For a discussion of the changing political role of mainline Protestantism in the last half of the twentieth century, see Robert Wuthnow, *The Restructuring of American Religion: Society and Faith since World War II* (Princeton: Princeton University Press, 1988).

46. Author's interview with Reverend Bill Bruggeman, May 31, 1994, San Antonio, Texas.

47. Author's interview with Reverend Homer Bain, May 24, 1995, San Antonio, Texas.

48. For a discussion of different strands within the Jewish tradition and their orientations towards social justice, see Michael Lerner, *Jewish Renewal: A Path to Healing and Transformation* (New York: Harper, 1995).

49. Author's interview with Rabbi Ken Roseman, June 7, 1993, Dallas, Texas.

50. Author's interview with Jennifer Barrash, March 5, 1997, Dallas, Texas.

51. Robert D. Putnam, *Making Democracy Work: Civic Traditions in Modern Italy* (Princeton: Princeton University Press, 1993).

52. Verba et al., *Voice and Equality*, chapter 11.

53. Verba et al., *Voice and Equality*, chapter 11. Verba's study remains vitally important because he shows that religious institutions are key social capital sites for increasing political participation and because he is able to quantify the impact of social capital through the mechanism of skill acquisition. Accepting the current institutional arrangements of the American polity, he shows how religious communities can offset class and racial bias. But these current arrangements limit participation drastically so that, despite the equalizing role of churches, many Americans remain marginalized.

Chapter Eight
Leadership Development: Participation and Authority in Consensual Democracies

1. *IAF 50 Years: Organizing for Change* (New York: Industrial Areas Foundation, 1990), p. 18.

2. Alan Ehrenhalt, in *The Lost City: Discovering the Forgotten Virtues of Community in the Chicago of the 1950s* (New York: Basic Books, 1995), argues that an aversion to authority in favor of individualism has been central to the loss of community since the fifties. Although he acknowledges the costs of the less than fully inclusive or democratic authority of the past, Ehrenhalt calls for a return to a more communitarian life. This study, by contrast, is concerned with identifying new models of authoritative leadership that strive for participatory and democratic ends.

3. Jo Freeman, for example, finds that the women's movement in the seventies suffered from unaccountable domination by oligarchies and by ineffectiveness; see *The Politics of Women's Liberation* (New York: Longman, 1977).

4. Local affiliates contract with other faith-based organizing networks, like PICO, for leadership training services too. To that extent, the processes described in this chapter apply to the faith-based organizing field in general, although the specifics of their application may vary.

5. Edward T. Chambers, *Organizing for Family and Congregation* (New York: Industrial Areas Foundation, 1978), p. 20.

6. The following discussion reflects remarks made by IAF organizers at the IAF's National Training sessions, July 12–21, 1994, Los Angeles, California, attended by the author. It also draws upon the author's observation of a wide range of IAF activities during the course of this study.

7. Some IAF affiliates have steering committees, where more active secondary leaders meet monthly with members of the executive committee. Each IAF organization has its own constitution that defines specific organizational arrangements. There is some minor variation among organizations, but all follow the essentials of the summary given in the text.

8. This rule is regularly enunciated at all IAF training sessions, and can be found formally stated in an official publication of the IAF, entitled *IAF 50 Years: Organizing for Change* (New York: Industrial Areas Foundation, 1990), p. 31.

9. The transformation of activist community organizations to staff-dominated community development corporations is discussed in Randy Stoecker, "The CDC Model of Urban Redevelopment: A Critique and an Alternative," *Journal of Urban Affairs* 19 (1997): 1–22.

10. One of the reasons that the IAF's organization in Houston, TMO, languished in the early nineties could be that the lead organizer there fell into this trap.

11. These conclusions are based upon the author's study of the composition of the executive committees of IAF affiliates in Texas during the period 1993–1995. African American leaders report somewhat greater previous political experience, in electoral activity or in interest groups, than Hispanic or Anglo leaders.

12. The motivations of clergy to join the IAF are discussed in chapter 7. For most of these clergy, advancing in leadership is closely tied to developing an interest in personal growth as well. But decisions to join and remain relate closely to the role of these participants as formal institutional leaders. As such, various theological traditions, like Catholic social thought, and institutional responsibilities influence these decisions as well.

13. Author's interview with Rachel Salazar, July 8, 1993, San Antonio, Texas. Former COPS co-chair Mary Piccione (author's interview, May 21, 1993, San Antonio, Texas) joined originally to help get a drainage project for her neighborhood, so that the street in front of her house would no longer flood. Metro Alliance co-chair Genevieve Flores (author's interview, May 21, 1993, San Antonio, Texas) worked through the IAF affiliate to get Community Development Block Grant funds to renovate the community center at which she works. COPS leader Gabriela Guerra got involved in an effort to build a drainage project in her neighborhood because her house flooded every rainy season (author's interview, July 20, 1993, San Antonio, Texas).

14. Author's interview with Patricia Ozuna, July 20, 1993, San Antonio, Texas. See chapters 2 and 7. In chapter 7 I discuss how Hispanic Catholic parishes

create a situation where participants can fuse their self-interest with broader community caring.

15. Joseph D. Sekul also found personal development to be a key benefit to participation in his study of COPS conducted in the late seventies; see *The C.O.P.S. Story: A Case Study of Successful Collective Action* (Ph.D. dissertation, University of Texas, Austin, 1984).

16. The following quotations come from the author's interview with Virginia Ramirez, May 22, 1993, San Antonio, Texas.

17. Author's interview with Josie Duran, June 8, 1993, Fort Worth, Texas.

18. Author's interview with Pamela Walls, July 21, 1993, San Antonio, Texas.

19. Author's interview with Reverend D. L. Ellison, August 30, 1993, Fort Worth, Texas.

20. Author's interview with Claudia Camp, August 30, 1993, Fort Worth, Texas.

21. Author's interview with Joe Rubio, July 6, 1993, San Antonio, Texas. Rubio has since become the lead organizer for the IAF affiliate EPISO in El Paso.

22. Chambers, *Organizing for Family and Congregation*, p. 20.

23. From remarks made by Ernesto Cortes, Jr., at the IAF National Training sessions, July 16, 1994, Los Angeles, California.

24. Chambers, *Organizing for Family and Congregation*, pp. 22–23.

25. Ernesto Cortes, Jr., "Reweaving the Fabric: The Iron Rule and the IAF Strategy for Power and Politics," in Henry G. Cisneros, ed., *Interwoven Destinies: Cities and the Nation* (New York: W.W. Norton, 1993), pp. 294–319.

26. The description of individual meetings presented here draws from several sources: the training in how to conduct these meetings observed by the author at the IAF National Training sessions, July 12–21, 1994, in Los Angeles, California; the author's observation of several individual meetings conducted between lead organizer Perry Perkins and ACT leaders in Fort Worth, in August of 1993, the details of which are confidential; and the author's observation of interactions between organizers and leaders in a variety of settings over the course of the research conducted for the study.

27. Author's interview with Carmen Badillo, July 16, 1993, San Antonio, Texas.

28. Chambers, *Organizing for Family and Congregation*, p. 21.

29. More recently, the IAF has also experimented with shorter, regional training sessions.

30. The following analysis is based upon the program of the national training sessions attended by the author in Los Angeles, California, from July 12 to 21, 1994. Although individual trainers have some latitude in the way they teach the curriculum, the program is set nationally by the IAF.

31. For a fuller descriptions of the IAF's use of this role-playing, see Harry C. Boyte, *Commonwealth: A Return to Citizen Politics* (New York: Free Press, 1989), pp. 48–49, and Dennis Shirley, *Community Organizing for Urban School Reform* (Austin: University of Texas Press, 1998), pp. 87–88.

32. From remarks made by Ernesto Cortes, Jr., at the IAF National Training sessions, July 13, 1994, Los Angeles, California.

33. From remarks made by Ernesto Cortes, Jr., at the IAF National Training sessions, July 13, 1994, Los Angeles, California.

34. Story told in IAF National Training sessions, July 15, 1994, Los Angeles, California.

35. Story told in IAF National Training sessions, July 18, 1994, Los Angeles, California.

36. From remarks made at IAF National Training sessions, July 15, 1994, Los Angeles, California.

37. From remarks made at IAF National Training sessions, July 15, 1994, Los Angeles, California. In another incident at the same session, a white woman from Beaumont, Texas, told of her resentment against a black school superintendent who assigned her to an all-black school whose other teachers all were black as well.

38. At the national training sessions I attended, several participants confidentially expressed to me their feeling that IAF organizers were arrogant.

39. Author's interview with Joyce Oliver, August 26, 1993, Fort Worth, Texas.

40. Author's interview with Claudia Camp, August 30, 1993, Fort Worth, Texas.

41. Author's interview with Josie Duran, June 8, 1993, Fort Worth, Texas.

42. The following discussion is taken from Jane Mansbridge, *Beyond Adversary Democracy* (New York: Basic Books, 1980).

43. Because of the hegemony of adversary democracy, many citizens assume it is the only legitimate form. In fact, Mansbridge argues that different types of democracy are appropriate to different situations. According to Mansbridge, "any democratic group has to decide if its members have predominantly common or conflicting interests on matters about which the group must decide." In practice, no democracy is purely adversary or unitary, although in each case one type predominates. Western governments, for example, are essentially adversarial, but they allow for face-to-face interactions within representative bodies and the possible emergence of shared understandings of the common good.

44. In its relationships with other political actors, the IAF also rejects the idea of a permanent conflict of interests, articulated by its well-known slogan, "no permanent allies, no permanent enemies." Nevertheless, in external relations, the network emphasizes more the adversary side of Mansbridge's dichotomy, although it also seeks to build alliances as well.

45. From remarks made at IAF National Training sessions, July 14, 1994, Los Angeles, California. In further remarks at the training sessions, Stephens suggested that the distinction between public and private relationships is often ambiguous. IAF leaders build both types of relationships with most people.

46. IAF affiliates vary somewhat in exactly how leaders are selected. The constitutions of most affiliates require the election of co-chairs or executive committee members at conventions. Some have nominating committees select the slate. None, however, hold contested elections.

47. Author's interview with COPS' first president, Andres Sarabia, July 15, 1993, San Antonio, Texas.

48. George Ozuna, a member of the first set of co-chairs, explains it this way: "The transition from presidents to co-chairs was the best thing for us. Politicians

don't know how to deal with us. We do CDBG, housing, QUEST, HOME, water and sewer—all at the same time." Author's interview with George Ozuna, May 30, 1994, San Antonio, Texas.

49. From remarks made at IAF National Training sessions, July 20, 1994, Los Angeles, California.

50. How much opposition is sufficient to derail a course of action appears to vary depending on the circumstances. At IAF National Training (July 20, 1994, Los Angeles, California), Christine Stephens suggested that, in general, there should be no more than 10 or 20 percent of leaders opposed to any course of action taken. But, if all those opposed are Hispanic, while the supporters are white, the course of action should be abandoned despite a small amount of opposition.

51. Author's observation of ACT Leaders Retreat, August 28, 1993, Fort Worth, Texas.

52. Author's observation, May 29, 1994, San Antonio, Texas.

53. Author's interview with former Fort Worth city council member David Chappell, August 27, 1993, Fort Worth, Texas.

54. Author's interview with Carmen Badillo, July 16, 1993, San Antonio, Texas.

55. The IAF actually has two reasons for this policy. One is to ensure that leaders really "own" their own organization. The second reason for rotating lead organizers is so that they can develop their organizing ability by experiencing diverse situations and new challenges.

56. Author's interview with Rachel Salazar, July 8, 1993, San Antonio, Texas.

57. Author's interview with Virginia Ramirez, July 20, 1993, San Antonio, Texas.

58. Here again the IAF's consensual democracy differs significantly from what Jane Mansbridge calls unitary democracy. Mansbridge criticizes unitary democratic institutions for their frequent refusal to recognize when interests conflict and their lack of appropriate mechanisms to resolve such conflicts. For an extensive treatment of the limitations to unitary democracies, see *Beyond Adversary Democracy*, pp. 149–62.

59. Mansbridge discusses this issue in *Beyond Adversary Democracy*, p. 33.

60. The IAF itself presents a somewhat different list of its fundamentals in *IAF 50 Years: Organizing for Change*, pp. 29–31. The network's list includes accountability, action, broad-based organization, collective leadership, evaluation, ownership, power, professional organizers, public life, and self-determination.

61. Respondents requested anonymity in expressing these views to the author.

62. Mansbridge discusses this issue in *Beyond Adversary Democracy*, pp. 290–99.

63. Verba et al., *Voice and Equality*.

64. Mark E. Warren, one of the few political theorists to address the issue at all, has attempted to construct an argument for the role of democratically accountable authority in more deliberative forms of democracy. In his view, authority is essential to structure the participation of people so that they can allocate their time, energy, and knowledge to the issues most significant to them. In this way, Warren

identifies the importance of procedural leadership, but has little to say about its substance. We are still left with an individualistic model of decision making and action, where leaders help each citizen find the time to come to his or her own opinion and take action. See Mark E. Warren, "Deliberative Democracy and Authority," *American Political Science Review* 90 (March 1996), pp. 46–60.

65. Author's interview with Homer Bain, May 21, 1993, San Antonio, Texas.

Chapter Nine
Conclusion: Restoring Faith in Politics

1. This account of the twenty-fifth anniversary convention comes from the author's field notes, based on a videotape of the proceedings, as well as news reports, including Matt Flores, "COPS Celebrates Silver Anniversary," San Antonio *Express-News*, November 8, 1999, p. 1A.

2. Theda Skocpol, *The Missing Middle: Working Families and the Future of American Social Policy* (New York: W.W. Norton, 2000). Skocpol presents this analysis of the defeat of Clinton's health reform proposal, in greater and more nuanced detail, in *Boomerang: Clinton's Health Security Effort and the Turn against Government in U.S. Politics* (New York: W.W. Norton, 1996).

3. One study of systems of neighborhood participation suggests that COPS engages almost 15,000 people in community and political action on a fairly regular basis. However, the authors of that study, Jeffrey M. Berry, Kent E. Portney, and Ken Thomson, *The Rebirth of Urban Democracy* (Washington, D.C.: Brookings Institution, 1993), argue that COPS' involvement of 4.8 percent of the Hispanic residents of San Antonio with low socio-economic status compares unfavorably to the average of 16.6 percent of residents (of all races and economic groups) that citywide government-sponsored systems of neighborhood participation in places like Birmingham, Dayton, St. Paul, and Portland, Oregon, produce. Low-income Hispanic Americans (with high proportions of immigrants and non-English speakers), however, were some of the least represented by city-sponsored systems in the localities studied, where, by the way, Hispanics constituted a small percentage of the population. Moreover, although city-sponsored associations made government responsive to their neighborhood issues, the associations failed to expand their public influence beyond their own neighborhood, something which COPS has accomplished through the IAF network. Moreover, the figure of 15,000 actively involved in one locality (which I estimated from the study's findings) is quite large, if we compare to most advocacy groups today.

4. A national study of congregations shows that poor communities remain well represented by religious institutions, despite the decline they may have experienced in other social organizations; see Michael W. Foley, John D. McCarthy, and Mark Chaves, "Social Capital, Religious Institutions and Poor Communities," in Susan Saegert, J. Phillip Thompson, and Mark R. Warren, eds., *Social Capital and Poor Communities* (New York: Russell Sage Foundation Press, 2001). The accomplishments of the IAF in promoting political participation are the more significant because, according to Cathy J. Cohen and Michael C. Dawson, concentrated poverty communities are plagued by conditions that make social and political life difficult; see "Neighborhood Poverty and African American Politics,"

American Political Science Review 87 (1993): 286–302. Much of the work of the Southwest IAF centers in such concentrated poverty neighborhoods. According to John D. Kasarda, "Cities as Places Where People Live and Work: Urban Change and Neighborhood Distress," in Henry G. Cisneros, ed., *Interwoven Destinies* (New York: W. W. Norton, 1993), pp. 81–124, 150,000 San Antonio residents lived in concentrated poverty in 1990. For the most part, these residents fall within COPS' organizing territory. Some critics, nevertheless, have suggested that faith-based organizing fails to incorporate the poorest of the poor; see Gary Delgado, *Beyond the Politics of Place: New Directions in Community Organizing in the 1990s* (Oakland, CA: Applied Research Center, 1994).

5. Faith-based community organizing refers to the larger field of networks of which the IAF is the oldest and largest. Other networks include the Pacific Institute for Community Organization (PICO), the Gamaliel Foundation, and the Direct Action Research and Training Institute (DART). In general, all the networks root their organizing primarily in faith institutions and pursue nonpartisan political action.

6. Evangelical Protestantism is often used as an umbrella term for a diverse group of denominations and independent congregations, some of whom emphasize fundamentalism in theology while others have more charismatic worship styles. For a useful overview, see Nancy Tatom Ammerman, "North American Protestant Fundamentalism," in Martin E. Marty and R. Scott Appleby, eds., *Fundamentalism Observed* (Chicago: University of Chicago Press, 1991), pp. 1–65.

7. For a useful overview of the religious right, see Clyde Wilcox, *Onward Christian Soldiers? The Religious Right in American Politics*, 2nd edition (Boulder: Westview Press, 2000).

8. Comments by Richard L. Wood and Frank Pierson have helped me clarify the distinction between the IAF and the Christian Right. This particular formulation, however, is my own and I bear sole responsibility for its accuracy.

9. Richard John Neuhaus makes this point clearly in *The Naked Public Square: Religion and Democracy in America* (Grand Rapids: Eerdmans, 1984), pp. 36–37. Neuhaus calls these beliefs private, rather than particular. The term particular is more appropriate, however, because faith traditions are not restricted to the private sphere. For a related discussion, see José Casanova, *Public Religions in the Modern World* (Chicago: University of Chicago Press, 1994).

10. John Dewey called these shared values a common faith; see *A Common Faith* (New Haven: Yale University Press 1962 [1934]). Some scholars have argued that this democratic creed has deeply religious roots, in fact, that all American political discourse is fundamentally grounded in religiously based concepts. Over time, the religious connotations have been lost. But, nonetheless, religious conceptions remain more central to secular discourse than most Americans realize. See, for example, Rhys H. Williams, "Visions of the Good Society and the Religious Roots of American Political Culture," *Sociology of Religion* 60 (Spring 1999): 1–34, who argues that all significant visions of the public good in America have religious roots. Even the more contractual discourse, based upon classical liberal notions of justice and rights, draws from the Puritan covenant tradition.

11. The Christian Right as a movement does contain internal diversity. In fact, American evangelicalism is quite divided within itself. But the organizations built by this political movement are largely homogeneous and unified around a narrow moral agenda. For an overview, see Ammerman, "North American Protestant Fundamentalism."

12. Douglas Blackmon, "Racial Reconciliation Becomes a Priority for the Religious Right," *Wall Street Journal*, June 23, 1997, pp. A1, A6. Ralph E. Reed, the former executive director of the Christian Coalition, spoke out against racism in the history of white evangelicalism and called for broadening the movement in *Politically Incorrect: The Emerging Faith Factor in American Politics* (Dallas: Word Publishing, 1994).

13. For an early account, see Robert C. Liebman, "Mobilizing the Moral Majority," in Robert C. Liebman and Robert Wuthnow, eds., *The New Christian Right: Mobilization and Legitimation* (New York: Aldine, 1983).

14. For self-criticism in this regard, see Reed, *Politically Incorrect.*

15. For a discussion of the mobilization of Southern Baptists by the Christian Right, see Nancy Tatom Ammerman, *Baptist Battles: Social Change and Religious Conflict in the Southern Baptist Convention* (New Brunswick: Rutgers University Press, 1990).

16. For church membership figures, see Martin B. Bradley et al., *Churches and Church Membership in the United States 1990* (Atlanta: Glenmary Research Center, 1992).

17. See, for example, Robert C. Linthicum, *Empowering the Poor: Community Organizing among the City's "Rag, Tag and Bobtail"* (Monrovia, CA: MARC, 1991). White evangelical Christians committed to economic and social justice have also founded the magazine *Sojourners* and more recently initiated a network named Call to Renewal. For a statement from their perspective, see Jim Wallis, *The Soul of Politics: A Practical and Prophetic Vision for Change* (New York: The New Press and Orbis Books, 1994).

18. See, for example, Yvonne Yazbeck Haddad, ed., *The Muslims of America* (New York: Oxford University Press, 1991).

19. The IAF's sister network in the United Kingdom includes South Asian Sikhs, Hindus, and Muslims, along with white and Afro-Caribbean Catholics, Anglicans, and other Protestants. See Jay MacLeod, *Community Organising: A Practical and Theological Appraisal* (London: Christian Action, 1993); and Richard Farnell et al., *Broad-Based Organising: An Evaluation for the Church Urban Fund* (Coventry: Centre for Local Economic Development, Coventry University, 1994).

20. William Julius Wilson, *The Bridge of the Racial Divide: Rising Inequality and Coalition Politics* (Berkeley: University of California Press, 1999).

21. J. Phillip Thompson III, for example, argues that cross-racial policies to combat inner-city poverty are flawed because they ignore the continued salience of white racism as well as black nationalism. Thompson argues that African Americans need strong, independent civic and political organizations that, at the same time, are engaged in processes of dialogue with white America. See "Universalism and Deconcentration: Why Race Still Matters in Poverty and Economic Development," *Politics and Society* 26 (June 1998): 181–219.

22. Kwame Ture (Stokely Carmichael) and Charles V. Hamilton, *Black Power: The Politics of Liberation* (New York: Vintage Books, 1992 [1967]).

23. James Jennings, "The Politics of Black Empowerment in Urban America: Reflections on Race, Class, and Community," in Joseph M. Kling and Prudence S. Posner, eds., *Dilemmas of Activism* (Philadelphia: Temple University Press, 1990), p. 116.

24. Gary Delgado, *Beyond the Politics of Place: New Directions in Community Organizing in the 1990s* (Oakland, CA: Applied Research Center, 1994), p. 67.

25. According to Reverend John Heinemeier, a founding member of East Brooklyn Congregations (EBC), in essentially all-black IAF organizations like EBC, discussions of racism are quite common (author's interview, March 1995, Boston, MA). Nevertheless, even those organizations apparently do not address questions of racial justice per se.

26. For a related discussion of this issue, see James C. Scott, *Seeing Like a State: How Certain Schemes to Improve the Human Condition Have Failed* (New Haven: Yale University Press, 1998).

27. For example, in the East Coast region, IAF organizations have worked to coordinate living wage strategies. In Maryland, IAF organizations lobbied Governor Parris Glendening to devote a portion of the budget surplus to future social service needs.

28. Chapter 1 discusses the similarities between the IAF's structure and the old cross-class federations that characterized an earlier period of American civic and political life. Both types of federations were capable of lobbying government at many levels. For a discussion of the effective structure of the old federations, see Theda Skocpol, *Protecting Soldiers and Mothers: The Political Origins of Social Policy in the United States* (Cambridge: Harvard University Press, 1992), and "How Americans Became Civic," in Theda Skocpol and Morris P. Fiorina, eds., *Civic Engagement in American Democracy* (Washington, D.C.: Brookings Institution, 1999), pp. 27–80.

29. Chapter 3 discusses some of the tensions that have arisen between local and state level work. Chapter 8 considers the problems of relying upon Cortes' personal authority and informal methods of accountability at state and regional levels.

30. The East Coast region, unlike the others, is supervised by three directors, Arnold Graf, Mike Gecan, and Jim Drake.

31. More recently, the national IAF established an executive committee consisting of Ed Chambers, Ernesto Cortes, Mike Gecan, and Arnold Graf.

32. Michael A. Fletcher, "Religious Leaders Push 'Living Wage' as Issue in Election," *The Washington Post*, October 31, 1999, p. A10. See also, Mike Gecan, "A Living Wage for All American Workers—Nonprofit Workers Too?" *NFG Reports* 7 (Spring 2000): 6–8.

33. The CRA placed obligations upon banks across the country to invest in low-income communities. For discussions of the fragmentation of the community building and development movement, and the Community Reinvestment Act, see Peter Dreier, "Community Empowerment Strategies: The Limits and Potential of Community Organizing in Urban Neighborhoods," *Cityscape* 2 (May 1996):

121–59; and Karen Paget, "Citizen Organizing: Many Movements, No Majority," *American Prospect* (Summer 1990): 115–28.

34. For a useful overview, see Lisbeth B. Schorr, *Common Purpose: Strengthening Families and Neighborhoods to Rebuild America* (New York: Anchor Books, 1997).

35. For an overview of community development corporations, see Avis C. Vidal, *Rebuilding Communities: A National Study of Urban Community Development Corporations* (New York: Community Development Research Center, Graduate School of Management and Urban Policy, New School for Social Research, 1992).

36. See, for example, E. A. Parker, A. J. Schulz, B. A. Israel, and R. Hollis, "Detroit's East Side Village Health Worker Partnership: Community-based Lay Health Advisor Intervention in an Urban Area," *Health Education and Behavior* 25 (1998): 24–45, and Therese M. Blaine et al., "Creating Tobacco Control Policy at the Local Level: Implementation of a Direct Action Organizing Approach," *Health Education and Behavior* 24: 640–51.

37. See, for example, *Voices from the Field: Learning from the Early Work of Comprehensive Community Initiatives* (Washington, D.C.: The Aspen Institute, 1997).

38. On parental and community involvement in the recent wave of school reform efforts, see, for example, Anthony Bryk et al., *Charting Chicago School Reform: Democratic Localism as a Lever for Change* (Boulder, CO: Westview Press, 1998). On engaging youth in school reform, see Michelle Fine, ed., *Chartering Urban School Reform* (New York: Teachers College Press, 1994).

39. Paul Lichterman, *The Search for Political Community: American Activists Reinventing Commitment* (Cambridge: Cambridge University Press, 1996).

40. On the diversity and commonalities of women's activism, see the collection of articles, and the concluding chapter, "Women's Community Activism: Exploring the Dynamics of Politicization and Diversity," in Nancy A. Naples, ed., *Community Activism and Feminist Politics* (New York: Routledge, 1998). Naples emphasizes the development of feminist identities and oppositional consciousness through political activism, showing how these can vary by race and class. Although I am aware of these differences, and the fact that many women leaders of the Southwest IAF may not consider themselves feminists, I have stressed here the commonalities that we can find across different kinds of community-based action.

41. In a similar vein, Michael Sandel argues that our politics will be richer to the extent it engages civic virtues, rather than avoids them. See *Democracy's Discontent: America in Search of a Public Philosophy* (Cambridge: Harvard University Press, 1996), pp. 6–7.

42. On New Community Corporation, see Schorr, *Common Purpose*, pp. 348–52.

43. For a consideration of new initiatives for labor/community cooperation, see Margaret Levi, "Capitalizing on Labor's Social Capital," in Susan Saegert, J. Phillip Thompson, and Mark R. Warren, eds., *Social Capital and Poor Communities* (New York: Russell Sage Foundation Press, 2001). See also, Gregory Mantsios, ed., *A New Labor Movement for the New Century* (New York: Garland

Pub., 1998) and Jeremy Brecher and Tim Costello, eds., *Building Bridges: The Emerging Grassroots Coalition of Labor and Community* (New York: Monthly Review Press, 1990).

44. For a discussion of institutional reform and the need to link grassroots organizing to the Democratic Party, see Margaret Weir and Marshall Ganz, "Reconnecting People and Politics," in Stanley B. Greenberg and Theda Skocpol, eds., *The New Majority: Toward a Popular Progressive Politics* (New Haven: Yale University Press, 1997), pp. 149–71.

Index

PRINCETON STUDIES IN AMERICAN POLITICS:
HISTORICAL, INTERNATIONAL, AND COMPARATIVE PERSPECTIVES

SERIES EDITORS
IRA KATZNELSON, MARTIN SHEFTER, AND THEDA SKOCPOL

Dry Bones Rattling: Community Building to Revitalize American Democracy
by Mark R. Warren

The Forging of Bureaucratic Autonomy: Reputations, Networks,
and Policy Innovation in Executive Agencies, 1862–1928
by Daniel P. Carpenter

Disjointed Pluralism: Institutional Innovation and the Development of the U.S. Congress
by Eric Schickler

The Rise of the Agricultural Welfare State:
Institutions and Interest Group Power in the United States, France, and Japan
by Adam D. Sheingate

In the Shadow of the Garrison State: America's Anti-Statism and
Its Cold War Grand Strategy
by Aaron L. Friedberg

Stuck in Neutral: Business and the Politics of Human
Capital Investment Policy by Cathie Jo Martin

Uneasy Alliances: Race and Party Competition in America
by Paul Frymer

Faithful and Fearless: Moving Feminist Protest inside the Church and Military
by Mary Fainsod Katzenstein

Forged Consensus: Science, Technology, and Economic Policy in the
United States, 1921–1953 by David M. Hart

Parting at the Crossroads: The Emergence of Health Insurance
in the United States and Canada
by Antonia Maioni

Bold Relief: Institutional Politics and the Origins of
Modern American Social Policy
by Edwin Amenta

The Hidden Welfare State: Tax Expenditures and Social Policy in the
United States by Christopher Howard

Morning Glories: Municipal Reform in the Southwest
by Amy Bridges

Imperiled Innocents: Anthony Comstock and Family Reproduction in
Victorian America by Nicola Beisel

The Road to Nowhere: The Genesis of President Clinton's Plan for
Health Security by Jacob Hacker

The Origins of the Urban Crisis: Race and Inequality in Postwar Detroit
by Thomas J. Sugrue

Party Decline in America: Policy, Politics, and the Fiscal State
by John J. Coleman